DATE DUE

MAR 6 1980 DEPAUL		
FEB 18 1981		
MAR 1 9 1981 DiGRAZIA		
APR 6 1981		
		DEC 1 0 REC'D
DEC 1 9 1994		
GAYLORD		PRINTED IN U S A

Japan: The Paradox of Progress

Japan: The Paradox of Progress

Edited by Lewis Austin

with the assistance of
Adrienne Suddard and
Nancy Remington

New Haven and London   Yale University Press
1976

Designed by John O. C. McCrillis
and set in Baskerville type.
Printed in the United States of America by
The Murray Printing Co., Westford, Massachusetts.

Published in Great Britain, Europe, Africa, and Asia
(except Japan) by Yale University Press, Ltd., London.
Distributed in Latin America by Kaiman & Polon,
Inc., New York City; in Australia and New Zealand by
Book & Film Services, Artarmon, N.S.W., Australia; and in
Japan by Harper & Row, Publishers, Tokyo Office.

The Seminar on the Future of Japan gratefully
acknowledges financial assistance from the
Ford Foundation and the Japan Foundation.

Contents

Introduction

In the mid-seventies Japan faces more intensely and more urgently than perhaps most other nations the problems of a rapidly changing and unpredictable world. These problems are not unique to Japan. But its position—uneasily poised between modernity and tradition, affluence and austerity, underdevelopment and postindustrial over-development, between the liberal capitalist West, the state economies of the East, and the struggling new nations of the south—makes the range of choices wider, the tension between alternatives greater, and the pressure on policymakers more severe. The rewards for skilled management of uncertainty are greater and the penalties for error more dangerous.

As in 1868, when Japan was confronted with the challenge of the new world of the industrial and imperial revolutions, its position is paradigmatic. Japanese successes in dealing with the challenges of change will be models to be studied with admiration by those who must follow after; Japanese failures, object lessons in the pitfalls of progress.

In the contemporary world the levers of power and policy that affect social change are more than ever before at the disposal of governments, and the necessity for choice is correspondingly more vividly sensed. Power is greater, and, correspondingly, responsibility also. As our perception of the interlocking mesh of social, economic, and political relationships grows more sophisticated, and our vision of the chains of cause and effect grows more complex, choices become harder to make and are felt to be more consequential. But the quality of the people who make the choices and who suffer their consequences does not change. Their goals may change, but they become no more gifted at attaining them. This is a difficult situation.

It is ironic that it is Japan that faces the future in this paradigmatic position of eminent visibility. Traditional Japanese thought regarded change with disapprobation: what was unexpected (*angai*) was opprobrious. Ideally, reliance on custom and precedent should make choice almost unnecessary. Reluctance to choose and fear of the unknown are of course universal human characteristics. Nevertheless, that a nation whose traditional values enshrined the positive conservatism of which this fear and reluctance are the negative side must now, before most others and before all else, come to grips with the inevitability of dramatic social choice and change is ironic but not

inappropriate, for tradition itself in the world of the seventies is a
vital aspect of the problem of change. If not an enemy standing in the
way, it is at the least an ambivalent and inadequate guide to the paths
of the future.

Japan is presently at the cutting edge of a worldwide process of
social adaptation. It is rich in human potential but, in the midst of
unprecedented wealth, increasingly threatened by the specter of
material poverty. It is ruled by a government that has the levers of
change under its control but hesitates to use them. What is essential,
and what is lacking, is a widely shared vision of the proper direction
of change. The traditional paradigm of approximation to a static,
ideal image of social harmony is no longer helpful; the more recent
goal of catching up to and surpassing the West is increasingly outdated
by success and invalidated by serious doubt about the long-term viability of the course the West is on; a newer goal has not yet been
suggested. Japanese uncertainty in these circumstances mirrors the
uncertainty of the world in general about the direction of future
growth.

In this symposium we assume that dramatic change in Japanese
society will inevitably occur. We know that attempts will be made to
control the process of change, to maximize its benefits and minimize
its dangers. Our immediate concerns in this volume are with the
political process that will judge among competing values, with the
economic and material limits that will set bounds to freedom of choice,
and with the values themselves that will give content and direction
to the process of attempted control. Our ultimate concern is to point
to some of the interlocking consequences, direct and longer term, of
action and inaction within this framework of political, economic, and
sociocultural parameters.

We do not present any authoritative vision of the future of Japanese
society or of the goals that ought to guide its development. Our individual biases are apparent, however, from the chapters; they are,
by and large, liberal, humanist, and reformist. The reader is warned
to evaluate our conclusions accordingly.

The chapters in this volume approach the problem of identifying
and analyzing the elements likely to shape the future of Japan from
three different directions. The first section of the book deals with the
political variables that will affect the direction of change and the
political processes that will mediate and guide it. The chapters in this
section are Thayer's, on the politics of the right; MacDougall's, on
the politics of the left; and Cummings's on the politics of education—
the social subsector that is particularly responsible for shaping the
future.

The second section of the book deals with economic variables in the broadest sense: with land, labor, and capital and, beyond these, with the structures of trade, technology, and investment that determine the material subsistence of the nation. If politics allocates values authoritatively and provides an arena for the clash of ideas about value, economics creates values. This section, then, deals with the physical limits to growth and change. Patrick treats the Japanese economy as a part of the international system; Long reviews its technological self-sufficiency with an eye to military and security implications; and Cole and Azumi and McMillan deal with the most important and most imponderable element of the productive system: the people who make it work, the labor force.

If the first chapters deal with the process by which conflicts of value are decided, and the middle chapters deal with the creation and exchange of values, the chapters in the third section of the book deal with values themselves in a different sense: ideas of the good as guidelines to change. The focus of this section is the problem of people raised in the second section by Cole and Azumi and McMillan: who are the Japanese people and what do they want, what will they want, from their future? The section is sociocultural in its approach. Austin treats those ideas about interpersonal relations that have special relevance to political culture and attempts to measure across two generations the change in Japanese values that reflects increasing movement in the direction of the West. Frager and Rohlen examine the content of a traditional Japanese value system, the ideology of "spirit" (*seishin*), and consider its viability for the future. Kiefer, on the other hand, contemplates the culture and the personality structure likely to be created by that future—a future of radical urbanization— and finds values and personality likely to be considerably changed from their traditional patterns. Pharr, finally, looks at the status of women and at their goals. The group in Japanese society whose future holds the most dramatic change, it is also the group whose shift of values in the direction of modernization is likely to have the most turbulent effects on the overall structure of society.

Let us look more closely at the crucial factors singled out by the authors as those variables most likely to affect the development of the Japanese future.

Thayer's chapter on the politics of the conservative party considers the mesh of political style, structure, and technique. Thayer is concerned with the evolution of the mechanisms of government and with their planned change, with the recruitment of leaders, and with the styles of leadership that will be most effective in the future accumulation of power. On the basis of these considerations he lays out what he considers the most probable future scenarios for the politics of the ruling right-wing party.

MacDougall deals with the strategies of the left in the sector of political life in which they have shown the greatest strength, local politics. The crucial problems here are the dilemmas faced by the planners and policymakers of the progressive parties. As to goals: reformist or revolutionary? As to tactics: work from within government or criticize from without? As to arenas: local control and local innovation, or the top levels of the centralized bureaucratic hierarchy? As to image: clean hands, but empty ones, untainted by responsibility; or compromised hands that may yet hold the possibility of small and incremental improvement? As to fellow-progressives: party competition or party cooperation? The question MacDougall asks of the future is whether left successes at the local level can provide the basis for victory at the national level. He answers this question in a manner that is likely to disappoint both conservative and radical but that may comfort the voting citizen.

Cummings treats a more limited political arena, but one which has a particular significance for the future. He analyzes the politics of the Japanese educational system, that is to say, the politics that takes the form of a struggle for the power to shape the minds of the next generation of leaders and voters. Control of the educational system means the ability to answer the crucial question, How much money will be spent for what sort of learning? The debate about education has three main foci; dichotomized views about each create opposing camps whose struggle ultimately culminates in the creation of educational policy. These foci, the crucial variables in Cummings's study, have to do with control, content, and comprehensiveness. As to control: local autonomy or centralized guidelines? As to content: traditional values or pluralist-humanist-cognitive ideals? As to comprehensiveness: large-scale mass education for the populace at large or smaller-scale, more elitist education for the training of policymakers in particular? In the arena defined by this set of exaggerated dichotomies the struggle for control of the educational process and for the right to shape the thinking of the next generation plays itself out. Cummings sees victory going to an uneasy partnership of ideological opponents whose shaky but dominant coalition will be subjected to strains the severity of which will depend on extraeducational factors.

Economic variables are less slippery than political ones, but their interrelationships are no less complex. Patrick singles out for attention as a key variable the growth rate of the Japanese GNP with its two immediate consequences: the extent of change in living standards and the distribution of income within the population. He views trade and foreign exchange constraints as among the factors potentially most limiting to economic growth. This set of factors comprises the constraints of the international environment. One factor is the world's raw material supply problem, whether energy and food will be abundant or scant. Another is the prevailing mood of the world economic system, competitive or cooperative. On the other hand, another set of constraints limiting Japanese prosperity is not external but internal. These are the human problems, centering around the key variables of inflation, alienation, and productivity. This complex—inflation producing alienation producing a drop in productivity producing inflation—Patrick views as a more serious potential threat to Japanese social cohesion and economic well-being than either a beggar-thy-neighbor international environment or a world critically short of food and energy.

Long's analysis addresses two aspects of Patrick's economic overview in more detail: technology and military security and their linkages. Long sees military power as a direct function of economic growth and economic growth as largely dependent on education and technology. The key factors he considers include the role of the state as innovator and guide in the technological marketplace, the institutionalization of innovation, and the production of, and trade in, the specific high-technology products that are key elements in national power: computers, missiles, aircraft, and explosives.

Cole pursues to some disturbing conclusions Patrick's warning that internal factors, and specifically the problems of people, may be the most important limitations on Japanese growth and prosperity. His analysis focuses on the labor force, the most complex and unpredictable element in the formula for economic growth and national prosperity. Key variables include its size, rate of growth, composition, and age. Some secondary variables of importance that are contingent upon the nature of the labor force are the degree of labor shortage, the extent of economic dependency in the population, the pressure to innovate and rationalize in business firms, the durability of traditional Japanese hiring and salary practices based on the concepts of permanent employment and compensation in status and salary by seniority, and labor mobility. Finally, Cole considers the variables at a third level of consequence in terms of cause and effect and at the highest level in terms of national importance—the prospects for the survival of the traditional work ethic, the likelihood of a growth in alienation, and the potential among Japanese workers for sharply increased class war, generational conflict, industrial strife, and political activism.

Where Cole considers the Japanese worker's situation in global terms, Azumi and McMillan focus more sharply on morale or job satisfaction. They distinguish the variables that increase and decrease contentment and estimate the likely trend of on-the-job happiness among different groups in the coming years.

The mechanics and structures of the political process and the material givens of the economic-technological-military underpinning provide the parameters within which the development of Japanese society will take place over the years to come; but as the authors of the papers in these first two sections point out, the direction and the speed of change will depend on the people themselves: on their ideas of the suitable, their definitions of the attainable, their goals for themselves and for their society. The question of changing values is the final one addressed in these pages and perhaps the one most difficult to answer with any degree of certainty.

Austin views the changing Japanese tradition from the standpoint of political culture. He attempts to measure the extent of change in Japanese political and personal values, and the degree to which these values approach those of the United States. In this endeavor he takes into consideration the variables of personality (among them authoritarianism, trust, and autonomy), attitude (views regarding conflict and harmony), and value (rationalism, universalism, and secularism).

Frager and Rohlen delineate the theory and practice of seishin, a central element in the rich Japanese cultural tradition. Their treatment of the future of this tradition rests on an examination of the serviceability and adaptability of qualities of character: strength, fortitude, perseverance; singlemindedness, self-discipline; group spirit, loyalty, devotion to a master; and the development of "style." These qualities are viewed as they manifest themselves in the context of voluntary groupings that serve as seedbeds for tradition: clubs, youth groups, schools of the traditional arts, new religions.

Kiefer, too, is concerned with character and personality. But his list of variables is quite different: leisure, mobility, anonymity, atomization, standardization, regimentation, frustration, sense of loss, millenarian activism. He explores the development of a new lifestyle, with a new social ethic and a new set of motives for action, in all its implications. The seishin detailed by Frager and Rohlen and the danchi-zoku ethos described by Kiefer represent the two extreme possibilities between which the Japanese value structure of the future will take shape.

Pharr, finally, treats the struggle over values as it affects the less powerful but perhaps more crucial half of the population, the women. Her organizing concepts are types: "Neotraditionals," "New Women," and "Radical Egalitarians." What the women she interviews have to say about the reconciliation of opposing values in their lives and in a

society that, especially in their case, is not wholeheartedly cordial to
change exemplifies the painful quality of the struggle for the definition
of an identity that will determine most basically the Japanese capacity
to cope with the future.

We have titled this volume *The Paradox of Progress*.

At the heart of the problem of Japan's future development and at
the core of the analysis in each of the papers presented here is the
paradoxical relationship between tradition and modernity in the
process of social change. In Japan, as everywhere, tradition and
modernity are at odds in a violent conflict of custom, form, and value
that pits parents against children and men against women. This conflict is paradoxical because tradition sometimes fosters modernity,
and modernity sometimes preserves tradition. And at times these easy
labels lose their applicability and we find ourselves forced to confront
facts and to judge them on their own merits without the easy emotional
security that comes from tagging our opponents as decadent or reac-
tionary and ourselves as courageous progressive pioneers or staunch
defenders of the eternal truths. There is progress in human relations,
to be sure. But it is not inevitable nor does it always take the forms we
have decided that it should. Our conclusions about the future of Japan,
then, take final form as a set of paradoxes.

Thayer's Paradox: The sooner the conservative ruling Liberal
Democratic Party loses its parliamentary majority, the longer the
traditional Japanese political style of private factional bargaining
behind the scenes will endure; conversely, the continued dominance
of the conservatives in Japan will depend on a drastic overhaul and
modernization of their party machinery and leadership style and recruitment.

MacDougall's Paradox: The more successful the left at the local
level, the stronger the conservative dominance at the center; for left
innovation in the cities and the provinces provides the ruling establishment with new ideas and new initiatives it would not have developed on its own.

Cummings's Paradox: The violent student revolt of the sixties has
led to a reconciliation of left and right and the dominance of moderate
reformers in the seventies.

Patrick's Paradox: The single most crucial bottleneck in the Japanese economic system is the capacity to import essential food, raw
materials, and energy; but the severity of this limiting factor is most
likely to be affected not by the international economic environment,
threatening as it may appear, but by a set of circumstances wholly
internal to Japan—the attitudes of the labor force.

Long's Paradox: With all due respect to the Meiji reformers who coined the slogan, a "rich country" does not necessarily imply a "strong army."

Cole's Paradox: A more slowly growing economy and an aging labor force will create severe pressures for change in the traditional practices of lifetime employment and promotion by seniority. But the biggest and most modern firms will preserve these old ways the longest. Furthermore, if women should enter the labor force in large numbers after marriage, as the modernizing trend would imply, this will obviate the need for change in the traditional practices and thus tradition will be preserved by modernity.

Azumi and McMillan's Paradox: The Japanese worker is not the happily dedicated robot of comparative industrial folklore but is equally as alienated and dissatisfied as his European or American counterpart. But whereas unhappiness generally increases with work-place size, impersonality, and centralization, in Japan size increases happiness. In this case it may be that modernization induces satisfaction rather than discontent.

Austin's Paradox: Japanese values and attitudes are indeed changing and moving in the direction of "modernity." But because values elsewhere—as exemplified in the United States—are changing *faster*, the net result of the process of change over time is to widen the difference between Japan and the West.

Frager and Rohlen's Paradox: The more the pressures of change are felt in Japan the more traditional Japanese seishin will thrive; for the more rapid the change, the more traumatic its effects and the more in demand the qualities of endurance, strength, and perseverance that provide a stable set of values to grasp as an empirical aid in coping with a society that fosters insecurity.

Kiefer's Paradox: Urbanization, the development of mass society, and the spread of the danchi lifestyle will force people to become more autonomous, rootless, and mobile, less dependent and less anchored, and to take responsibility for voluntary sociability, diffuse gregariousness, and autonomous control of their sex lives. But the society that thus creates more individualistic and more conscious people will offer them fewer outlets for the energy of their conscious individualism. It will be more regimented and more bureaucratized, with power more centralized and less accessible. So the modernization of the individual psyche will lead to a growth of depression, neurosis, extremist politics, and millenarian social movements, as well as to a spread of irrationality in general.

Pharr's Paradox: The "New Women" will find victory in their struggle increasingly within their reach. But economic success and acceptance in the labor force will create new frustrations; a thriving and modernizing Japan will create new and radical discontents. Women, the most loyal bearers of traditional virtue and most long-suffering of those oppressed by tradition, will pose the most dramatic challenge for change that Japanese society and culture have yet faced.

Some of these paradoxes are peculiarly Japanese. Most are not. Japan, caught in the struggle between tradition and modernity, facing the future with the knowledge that change is inevitable and the certainty that no direction for change is without danger, presents us with an example for study that is relevant not because of its uniqueness but because of its typicality. *De nobis fabula narratur:* this story is about us, whether in affluent America and Europe or struggling Africa and Asia. There are no easy answers to the paradoxes of progress. Change is always gain for some and loss for others. But, as Polak has pointed out, we must at least try to be responsible for our own change: "The choice for modern man is no longer between this image of the future and that, but between images of his own choosing and images which are forced on him by outside pressures."[1]

---

1. Fred Polak, *The Image of the Future* (San Francisco, 1973), p. 302.

Elections, Coalitions, and Prime Ministers in Japan, 1976–1985

NATHANIEL B. THAYER

In this first chapter Nathaniel Thayer lays out the parameters that will govern the nature of conservative politics through the next decade. He predicts that the present ruling party will furnish the prime minister and the government through most of the eighties. The Liberal Democratic party (LDP) will probably win in 1979; it may be a minority party at some point in the elections of circa 1982, 1985, and 1988, but even so it is likely still to be in the governing coalition.

Liberal Democratic party dominance will be due to party discipline and skill in managing the complex electoral politics of the multimember constituency. An increase in Communist strength, which is to be expected, will hurt not conservatives but Socialists. Similarly Clean Government party (CGP) gains will be made more at the expense of the competing left than of the right. Party reforms designed to maximize member participation will also draw more voters to the LDP.

Coalition governments are probable, but the LDP will always be the most probable coalition candidate. The ideological distance between the parties will narrow because of the necessities of coalition government.

The sooner the LDP loses its parliamentary majority the more likely it is that the subsequent prime ministers will resemble past models: they will be in their sixties, longtime Dietmen, exministers of commerce, finance, or foreign affairs, holders of important party posts, leaders of large factions, and noncharismatic. Coalitions between parties, like those between factions, will reward this type of leadership. On the other hand, the longer the LDP stays in office, the more likely becomes new-style leadership and new-style organization, for only by means of new appeals to the voters will minority status and coalition be staved off.

Thayer predicts a paradoxical future in which more of the same—continued conservative dominance—will require radical changes in political style and institutions. But, on the other hand, a radical shift in power—away from the conservatives to a coalition of the center—will give new life to the politics of compromise and back-room maneuver that has been considered traditionally Japanese.—L.A.

In undertaking in this chapter to predict elections, coalitions, and prime ministers in Japan over the next decade, I assume that neither internal revolt nor external attack will forcibly change the formal institutions of government. No political group will become strong enough to force the revision of the constitution; the Diet will continue to be the highest organ of state; the party that controls the Diet will control the government; control over the Diet will be determined by national elections; and the rules for these elections will remain fundamentally as they are today.

My analysis is in two parts. The first, which deals with the elections to the House of Representatives, describes how the election system works, forecasts which elections the conservative Liberal Democratic party will win and by what margins, and predicts what may happen if the conservatives lose their majority after 1980. This first section outlines the rules for future coalitions and discusses the probability of six possible coalitions and a breakup of the present parties. It concludes that the present conservative party will furnish the prime minister throughout most of the next decade.

The second part deals with the conservative party, describing the elections in which party president and prime minister are determined and the conservative factions and their role in party elections. This section provides a political silhouette of prime ministers who have been chosen through these elections, describes the move toward and the possibility of reform of these elections, explains how reform will influence future prime ministers, and, finally, predicts what type of politician will lead the possible coalitions. It concludes that Japanese prime ministers will be predictable, at least in behavior, throughout most of the next decade.

ELECTIONS TO THE HOUSE OF REPRESENTATIVES

The highest organ of state power in Japan is the Diet. It is composed of two houses, namely, the House of Representatives and the House of Councillors. Of the two houses, the lower house, the House of Representatives, is the stronger, numbering among its powers that of choosing the prime minister.

Article 67 of the constitution states that the prime minister will be designated from among the members of the Diet by a resolution of the Diet. If the upper house and the lower house fail to agree on who this man shall be, then the decision of the lower house will be the decision of the Diet. Our first concern is, How do representatives get elected to the lower house?

The present electoral system for the lower house was created in 1927 when the nation was divided into 124 electoral districts that followed administrative divisions as closely as possible. Depending on the number of its residents, each district sends three, four, or five men to the Diet. These representatives are chosen by a single entry ballot. In a three-man district, for example, the three men receiving the greatest number of votes become its representatives.

The Japanese vote is stable. In each district there are a certain number of conservative votes and a certain number of, say, socialist votes. The result is that the conservatives fight among themselves to gain office and the socialists fight among themselves to gain office. Candidates from one party clash with each other more than they clash with candidates from another party.

Japan has held seventeen general elections under the present electoral system, twelve of these since World War II. With one exception, the conservatives have won every postwar election. Immediately after the war, better than sixteen conservative parties cluttered the political landscape. By 1953 these parties had reduced themselves to two—the Liberal party and the Democratic party—and in 1955 these two merged to form the Liberal Democratic party (LDP).

Opposition parties presently number four. The second largest party is the Japan Socialist party (JSP), a group of quite doctrinaire Marxists. The third largest is the Japan Communist party (JCP), which is not so doctrinaire. The fourth opposition party is the Clean Government party (CGP), a party that grew out of a religious movement. It denies being either Marxist or conservative but finds it hard to explain just what it does stand for. The weakest opposition party is the Democratic Socialist party (DSP), which is quite similar to the socialist parties of Western Europe.

The Japanese constitution specifies that elections must be held every four years though the prime minister can dissolve the lower house and thus call for elections whenever he wishes. In recent years, elections have been called, on the average, every three years. Nothing suggests that this trend will not continue. The last general election was held in December 1972. We will probably see two elections before 1980, the first in 1976 and the other in 1978 or 1979. Succeeding elections will be in 1982, 1985, and 1988.

Table 1.1 gives the percentages of the total vote that each party has received for lower house elections since 1958,[1] the first year in which the conservatives faced an election with a single party. The conserva-

---

1. Electoral statistics are from Jichishō Senkyo Kyoku [Self-government Agency, Electoral Bureau], *Shūgiin Giin Sōsenkyo, Saikō-Saibansho Saibankan Kokumin Shinsa: Kekka Shirabe* [Survey of results of the general elections of the House of Representatives and people's judgment of the legal officers of the Supreme Court] (Tokyo, 1953, 1955, 1958, 1960, 1963, 1967, 1969, 1972).

tives won quite handsomely. But in each election since that time the LDP percentage has gradually decreased. In 1967 the LDP lost a popular majority, a loss that continued into the 1969 and 1972 elections, though the percentage decrease lessened. In the election of December 1972, the LDP received 46.8 percent of the popular vote.

TABLE 1.1   Percentage of Total Vote Among Parties
in Lower House Elections, 1958–1972

Party	1958	1960	1963	1967	1969	1972
LDP	57.8	57.6	54.7	48.8	47.6	46.8
JSP	32.9	27.6	29.0	27.9	21.5	21.9
DSP	—	8.8	7.4	7.4	7.7	7.0
CGP	—	—	—	5.4	10.9	8.5
JCP	2.6	2.9	4.0	4.8	6.8	10.5
Regional	0.7	0.4	0.2	0.2	0.2	0.3

Our next question is, What percentage of the popular vote will the LDP receive in the 1976 and 1979 elections? A conservative method of making this projection is to calculate the percentage the LDP dropped in each election and then to take either the median or the average of these figures:

0.2	5.9
2.9	2.9
5.9	1.2
1.2	0.8
0.8	0.2
——	——
2.2	1.2 median

Subtracting these results from the 1972 electoral percentages, we get:

	1976	1979
average	44.6	42.2
median	45.6	44.4

Given the trend of the last three elections, I believe that the medians (45.6 and 44.4 percent) are the more accurate figures.

The popular vote, however, does not translate directly into seats. Table 1.2 gives the percentage of seats each party has won since the 1958 elections and shows the LDP still holding 55.2 percent in 1972. Table 1.3 presents a breakdown by party of the difference between the percentage of the popular vote and the percentage of seats (a plus indicating more seats than the party's popular vote warranted, a minus indicating less).[2]

TABLE 1.2   Percentage of Division of Seats Among Parties
in Lower House Elections, 1958–1972

Party	1958	1960	1963	1967	1969	1972
LDP	61.5	63.4	60.6	57.0	59.3	55.2
JSP	35.5	31.0	30.8	28.8	18.5	24.0
DSP	—	3.7	4.9	6.2	6.4	3.9
CGP	—	—	—	5.1	9.7	5.9
JCP	0.2	0.6	1.1	1.0	2.9	7.7
Regional	0.2	0.2	0.0	0.0	0.0	2.9
Unaligned	2.6	1.1	2.6	1.9	3.3	0.4

TABLE 1.3   Difference Between Percentage of Popular Vote and
Percentage of Seats in Lower House Elections, 1958–1972

Party	1958	1960	1963	1967	1969	1972
LDP	+3.7	+5.8	+5.9	+8.2	+11.7	+8.4
JSP	+2.6	+3.4	+1.8	+0.9	−3.0	+2.1
DSP	—	−5.1	−2.5	−1.2	−1.3	−3.1
CGP	—	—	—	−0.3	−1.2	−2.6
JCP	−2.4	−1.3	−2.9	−3.8	−3.9	−2.8
Regional	−0.5	−0.2	−0.2	−0.2	−0.2	+2.6
Unaligned	−3.4	−1.8	−2.2	−3.7	−2.0	−4.6

Over the years, the LDP has been able to get the most seats for its percentage of the vote. Our purpose now is to determine the distortion for the future elections in 1975 and 1979. Again we may list the percentages over the past six elections and strike both a median and an average:

3.7	3.7
5.8	5.8
5.9	5.9
8.2	8.2
11.7	8.4
8.4	11.7
7.3 average	7.0 median

2.   These statistics on party turnout are from Nishihira Shigeki, *Nihon no Senkyo* [Japan's elections] (Tokyo, 1972).

Though these calculations are mathematically correct, they are politically wrong. They are too low. The explanation, though not simple, should be made because it demonstrates some of the subtleties that must go into election politics and the changing nature of the LDP.

In a lower house election, the best way to get the greatest number of seats for the least number of votes is to limit the number of candidates. The 1972 election results for the first electoral district of Wakayama prefecture, a three-man district, were:

LDP	Bo	70,715	elected
CGP	Sakai	55,354	elected
JCP	Noma	52,399	elected
LDP	Kaibori	49,472	not elected
JSP	Kishi	46,622	not elected
LDP	Kanaya	27,267	not elected
Unaffiliated	Nakanishi	21,052	not elected

Wakayama 1 sends three men to the House of Representatives. The LDP endorsed three candidates. On first thought, that might seem like a sensible policy. But it cost them a seat. If Kanaya had not received the endorsement of the party, either he would have run as an independent or he would have dropped out of the race. And in either event his vote total would have dropped. Kaibori, the other LDP candidate, would have received many of the votes that went to Kanaya and probably would have replaced the Communist candidate Noma as the third successful candidate.

Look again at the LDP line in table 1.3. The percentage increases without a falter until 1972. With each election the conservatives have become more efficient at turning votes into seats. The LDP line in table 1.3 is a short history in the growth of discipline and coherence within the party.

When formed, the LDP was little more than an alliance of conservative politicians determined to prevent the Socialists and Communists from taking over the government. Its only other role was to serve as a façade behind which half a dozen conservative politicians, heading factions, fought for control of the prime minister's chair. Lower house elections were a shambles. The party was obliged to distribute party endorsements as the faction leaders demanded and to stand by while the conservative politicians of one faction fought the conservative politicians of the other factions for the limited number of conservative votes.

Now circumstances have changed. Over the past seventeen years power has gradually accrued to the party. The nature of the electoral system still means that conservative must fight conservative, but the party can, in many instances, limit these fights by limiting the number of candidates. Table 1.4 shows how the party has been able to decrease the number of endorsements over the years with a corresponding increase in the win rate.

TABLE 1.4   LDP Endorsements for Elections to Lower House, 1958–1972

Election	Number of endorsements	Number of winners	Win rate (in percentages)
1958	413	287	69.5
1960	399	296	74.2
1963	359	283	78.8
1967	342	277	81.0
1969	328	288	87.8
1972	339	271	79.9

There is a limit to how rigidly the party can restrict its endorsements, and I think that limit was reached in 1969. The 1972 elections showed a greater willingness to give the party endorsement in borderline cases, with the result that the win rate went down and the party did not get the most seats for its votes. This lesson will not be lost on the party. I would anticipate that it will attempt to tighten up again for the 1976 elections. I believe it safe to say that the party is strong enough to come up with an endorsement strategy that will maximize its votes greater than the 7.2 to 7.3 percent that we have calculated. A range from 8.2 to 11.7 percent would be more realistic.

Other considerations could be cranked into our forecast for the 1976 and 1979 elections. The number of registered voters will probably increase. The movement of the farmer to the city will also continue, though he probably will not move so fast. The average age of the population will increase. Living standards will continue to rise, though perhaps faster for one segment of the population than another. The work force will continue its migration from the primary and secondary sectors of the economy to the tertiary sector. All these changes may find reflection in the elections. It is possible, I suppose, to dig into the 1971 census statistics and make some guesses. I am reluctant, however, to pile a political prediction on top of a population projection. I take refuge in the belief that nothing more drastic could happen in Japan during the next decade than has happened in Japan in the past seventeen years. These years did not seem to stagger the stately pace of Japanese politics one whit.

Where will the LDP be after the 1976 election? A sanguine projection gives it 45 percent of the popular vote distorted by 11.7 percent to give it 57.3 percent of the seats. A pessimistic projection gives it 44.6 percent of the popular vote distorted 7.2 percent to give it 51.8 percent of the seats.

Where will the LDP be after the 1979 election? A sanguine projection gives it 44.4 percent of the voted distorted 11.7 percent to give it 56.1 percent of the seats. A pessimistic projection gives it 42.2 percent of the popular vote distorted 7.2 percent to give it 49.4 percent of the seats.

In conclusion, both sanguine and pessimistic projections show the LDP maintaining a majority of the seats in the 1976 elections. A sanguine projection for the 1979 election shows the LDP maintaining a majority of the seats; a pessimistic projection shows the party losing its majority, but by less than a percentage point.

Mathematical predictions of elections after 1979 distort rather than explain. For example, straight-line projections show the LDP to be a minority party, and I am not sure that will prove to be true. The LDP might well continue as the majority party, though it will maintain its majority only by the barest margin. Several reasons underlie my belief:

1.   Many citizens vote for the opposition parties because they wish to register a protest vote against the ruling LDP, not because they want the opposition parties in power. When their votes will force the LDP from power, the voters will either abstain from voting or vote for the LDP and find another way to register their protest.

2.   In the elections after 1976 the CGP plans to run candidates in all election districts. Heretofore it has run candidates only in those districts where it thought it had a chance of winning. Most CGP votes come from opposition supporters rather than LDP supporters. This new policy will spread the opposition votes among a greater number of opposition candidates. The LDP will benefit.

3.   The LDP is presently considering and may adopt a system whereby all party members may participate in the selection of the party president, who, so long as the LDP remains the majority party, will become the prime minister. (See my explanation below.) The opportunity to vote for the prime minister will attract new voters to the party, some of whom may vote for conservative candidates to the lower house.

Rather than use these scattered facts to build a prediction that the LDP will remain in power for elections after 1979, I find it safer to assume that the LDP will lose its majority and to project what will happen under those circumstances.

If the LDP were to lose its majority, would another party come forth as the majority party? The date in table 1.2 suggest that the answer is no. The JSP is the second most powerful party but it had been steadily losing both in seats and in popular votes until the 1972 election, when it was able to expand a 0.4 percent increase in the vote to a 2.1 percent increase in the number of seats. The JCP has been growing steadily, but it could not take over in the next decade. The supporters of the CGP are supporters of its parent religious organization; most observers believe the religious organization has reached its peak, thus the party will not grow much more. The DSP is already a declining party. If no party becomes the majority party, what happens? The answer: coalition government.

Since the enactment of the present constitution in May 1947, there has been only a short period of coalition government. In the April 1947 election the Socialists received 143 seats to become the largest party, though they occupied only one-third of the seats in the lower house. The politicians were able to agree on two matters: that they would first have to form a coalition of parties controlling more than half the seats in the lower house, and that the prime minister would have to be the leader of the largest party in the coalition. This leader was Katayama. Before nine months had passed the coalition proved unable to stick together. The politicians held two opinions on who should be the next prime minister, one being that the prime minister should be the leader of the largest party in opposition to the coalition, the other that he should be the leader of the second largest party in the coalition. The second opinion prevailed.

The prime minister chosen from the second largest party of the coalition was Ashida, who subsequently resigned following charges of corruption. The members of the coalition were unwilling to have the leader of the third largest party serve as prime minister since he only controlled a handful of seats. Consequently, they turned to the second most powerful man in the largest party in opposition to lead the coalition. His name was Yamazaki. While some of the members of this opposition party would have gone along with the selection of Yamazaki, the majority of the members of the party would not. They demanded that the leader of their party be selected as prime minister or they would not cooperate. That leader was named Yoshida. The coalition accepted this demand and stepped down. Yoshida was elected prime minister even though his party was a minority party. He called an election almost immediately and from that election emerged as the leader of a party with an absolute majority. The coalition period was over.

This coalition period existed too briefly to form solid precedent but long enough to suggest some of the Japanese rules for coalition building: (1) the candidates for prime minister will be the leaders of the various parties; (2) the coalition will have to contain an absolute majority of the seats in the lower house; (3) the first leader of the coalition will be the leader of the largest party in the coalition; (4) the counters in coalitions shall first be the parties, though resort may be made to factions within parties from time to time.

Current politics suggest some other political rules. In theory, any grouping of the five parties would be possible so long as that grouping was able to control over half the seats in the lower house. In actuality, political conditions preclude the parties from skipping around in their search for coalition partners. A party must first cooperate with the party closest to it in ideology. In table 1.5 the parties have been placed in their position on the political spectrum, with boxes indicating the possible coalitions.

TABLE 1.5   Possible Line Coalitions in Japan in 1980s

Option	Parties				
1	JCP	JSP	KMT	DSP	LDP
2	JCP	JSP	KMT	DSP	LDP
3	JCP	JSP	KMT	DSP	LDP
4	JCP	JSP	KMT	DSP	LDP
5	JCP	JSP	KMT	DSP	LDP
6	JCP	JSP	KMT	DSP	LDP

So long as the political parties are not reorganized, the LDP will continue to be the party controlling the largest number of seats. If electoral trends continue the same way they have over the past two decades, the difference between the LDP and the next largest party will be significant for the 1979, 1982, 1985, and 1988 elections. Thus, the next rule is: (5) the politicians will find it easier to form a coalition excluding the LDP.

The first three options depicted in table 1.5 are more possible than the last three.

General coalition theory supports the proposition that a majority coalition composed of the smallest number of parties should be the strongest coalition. In numbers, a two-party coalition should be a stronger coalition than a three-party coalition. Japanese coalitions may be different. Since the parties in a coalition are next to each other on the political spectrum, little differentiates them. In a two-party coalition, the larger party will tend to blot out the smaller party. In time the smaller party will lose its identity; at election time, the smaller party will lose its parliamentarians. Accordingly, the next rule is:

(6) stable coalitions must contain enough parties so that each party can maintain its identity.

Despite rule six, option one in table 1.5 is a strong possibility because that coalition is easily formed. Option two is not likely. When the CGP first came into existence it had no political views. In the fifteen or so years that it has been in national prominence, it has tried both leaning toward the ruling party and leaning toward the opposition parties. It has found that it does best leaning toward the opposition parties.

Option two will be even less possible in the early and mid-eighties after the option one coalition has failed. The DSP will be much smaller than it is now. A CGP-DSP-LDP coalition will not be a three-party coalition but rather a two-and-one-quarter party coalition. The CGP will have seen the DSP example and will realize that entry into the option two coalition exposes it to the same fate that the DSP suffered in the option one coalition. The CGP will refuse the option. The politicians will aim for an option three coalition.

General theory holds that grand coalitions—coalitions that occupy most of the political spectrum—tend to break down. That rule may have been true in Japan in the past, though the examples of a grand coalition are few. The Waihan coalition of 1898 lasted four months. The Save the Constitution coalition of 1924 lasted one year. Three grand coalitions existed during the war from 1940 to 1945, though these coalitions were not parliamentary but national coalitions urged by Japanese military officers, one of whose purposes was the dissolution of the political parties.

Option three is a grand coalition. Its formation is a distinct possibility if the DSP refuses to enter into an option one coalition or after the option one coalition has fallen apart.[3] The latter occurrence would be after the 1982 or the 1985 election. Once formed, the grand coalition might splinter at the ends, with factions of the right wing of the LDP and factions of the left wing of the JSP departing to form ideological parties. But the grand coalition would probably continue for some years. Leadership of the grand coalition would change. The first leader would come from the LDP, the largest party; political success would allow that leadership to continue.

Political failure would bring a period of instability. The LDP would try to put forward another party member, most probably a faction

---

3. The Democratic Socialists might ally with the Liberal Democrats for the election of the prime minister but refuse to enter the cabinet. This coalition might last longer than a coalition in which the Democratic Socialists enter the cabinet and become immediately identified with the Liberal Democrats. This coalition delays but does not resolve the problems inherent in an option one coalition.

leader, to take over the leadership of the grand coalition. It might
succeed in this gambit, but it would have great difficulty in persuading
the other parties that the coalition benefited them. More likely, the
LDP would have to surrender leadership to the second largest party in
the coalition, the JSP. That party would have the prime minister's
chair until it failed, when the chair would revert to the LDP.

Should leadership pass from the LDP to the JSP and then back to
the LDP, the CGP would find little reason to remain within the coalition. Its departure might split up the grand coalition, but by then the
grand coalition would have been in power long enough so that ideological distance between the parties would have narrowed. No longer
would coalitions have to be line coalitions; thus the parties would be
free to engage in searches for coalition partners. These new coalitions
are impossible to predict now.

Let us explore the likelihood of an opposition coalition. The LDP
politicians talk a lot about refusing to form a coalition if they lose their
majority. They would turn that task over to the opposition parties.
Either the opposition parties would be unable to form a coalition or
they would form an unstable coalition. In either case, the conservatives
believe that the opposition parties would make such a mess out of
government that the populace would give the LDP back its majority
at the next election. This scenario has precedent. It is approximately
what happened in 1947.

When the conservatives lose their majority, they will lose it by only
a few seats. The opposition parties will have to form an option four
coalition (see table 1.5). The JCP will prove the sticking point. The
CGP fights with it over voters and the DSP fights with it over policy.
This coalition will be highly unstable.

If the LDP declines in a straight line using most extreme percentages
and if the DSP can maintain present strength, the opposition parties
might try an option five or an option six coalition after the 1985 elections. But maintaining those coalitions would be difficult. An option
five coalition would have just a majority. An option six coalition would
founder easily on the structural animosities between the CGP and the
JCP. I conclude that the opposition parties may be in power—but
only briefly.

Finally, let me describe an option that does not appear in table 1.5.
That option involves the breakup of the present political parties. The
new ruling group would be composed of the opposition parties without
the JCP and the JSP far-left wing and of enough LDP parliamentarians
to constitute a majority in the lower house. How likely is breakup?
The politicians and the journalists talk intensely about the question.
No one has the answer.

The great imponderable is, How cohesive is the LDP? When formed in 1955, it was no more than an alliance of politicians who decided that they, not the socialists, would decide who would be prime minister. Some commentators argue that the only reason that the party has held together over two decades is that it has been able to hold on to this power. Other commentators—I have been among them[4]—have argued that the LDP has come to do more than just elect the prime minister. But I will agree that if the LDP splits: (1) it will split along factional lines, (2) one of the bolting faction leaders will become prime minister, and (3) the bolting factions will constitute a majority of the LDP Dietmen in the lower house.

All these options lead to one conclusion: an LDP prime minister either chosen from within the party or from bolting factions of the party will rule Japan over most of the next decade. How does the LDP select the prime minister? What is the nature of the LDP factions?

THE CONSERVATIVE PARTY

The LDP follows the tradition of earlier conservative parties and gives the prime minister's chair to its party president. How does the LDP select the party president? It has rejected the conservative tradition of informal consultation among party elders and has chosen instead to elect the party president.

The franchise for this election is given to each LDP Dietman and to one member from each of the prefectures. The conservative councillors usually number less than 150; the representatives number over 250; the prefectures number precisely 47. The total vote is about 450. This party presidential election is held once every three years. Anybody can run, but the signatures of ten Dietmen are necessary for nomination. If one candidate does not receive a majority of the vote on the first ballot, a runoff vote is held between the two highest candidates. This winner becomes the party president and, at the next meeting of the Diet, becomes the prime minister.

These rules were unique in Japanese political history. But the politicians who wanted to be prime minister quickly realized that the door to the prime minister's office would open to the candidate who best organized the vote. Since the voters were few, the office seekers could approach each voter individually. In return for each voter's support, the office seeker promised funds for servicing his constituency, support in elections, and assistance in securing posts in the cabinet, the ministries, the Diet, and the party.

---

4. Nathaniel B. Thayer, *How the Conservatives Rule Japan* (Princeton, 1974), pp. xvi–xvii, 14, 305–18.

By the early sixties an elaborate political structure had been built. The lower house was divided into eight or so factions. Since general elections were frequent and hardfought, since constituencies required elaborate and thus expensive care, since party and cabinet posts were shuffled each year, these factions were particularly fierce in their loyalties. The upper house was also divided into factions, though the factional discipline was weaker since upper house elections came only every six years, since electoral districts required less care, and since the councillors came to be offered only a limited number of posts. The upper house factions ostensibly had their own leaders but these leaders responded to the wishes of the faction leaders in the lower house. Since prefectural federation representatives are never chosen until just before a party presidential election, there was no way of organizing them into factions.

Factions have come and gone over the years, as faction leaders have either gained the prime ministership and moved off stage, or have become too old to compete for the prime ministership, or have died. The followers have also changed as each upper house and lower house election brought in new Dietmen and sent away others. At one time there were as many as eleven factions. Today there are nine. Conservative politics is the alliance and counteralliance of these nine factions as their leaders maneuver to put together a large enough bloc of votes to win the party presidential election.

The party presidential election not only determines who will be prime minister; it also determines what type of politician may become prime minister. The Japanese candidate for prime minister need not be a public man. He accrues clout not through rally speaking but through quiet consultation. He need not lead the masses. He need only maneuver skillfully among his peers. He need never bother to appear on television. He sees face-to-face the people who matter. Although a Dietman, he need not debate well, he need not sponsor legislation, he need not even have been active on a Diet committee. Finally, he need not be a big vote getter. All he needs is enough votes to keep himself in office.

Table 1.6 gives age data for prime ministers who have been elected under the present system of party presidential elections.[5] All were members of the lower house. Hatoyama and Ishibashi were in their seventies when elected, but the factional system was not fully developed. Kishi, Ikeda, and Sato were in their early or mid-sixties. Tanaka broke this trend by becoming prime minister while still in his fifties;

5. Biographical data is from Kikuoka Yaozō, ed., *Kokkai Binran* [Parliamentary handbook] (Tokyo, 1974).

many regarded him as too young. Miki was sixty-seven. Thus four of the seven LDP prime ministers have been in their sixties.

TABLE 1.6   Physical Age of Prime Ministers
on Assumption of Office

Name	Age	Number of times elected to lower house
Hatoyama	73	14
Ishibashi	72	4
Kishi	63	5
Ikeda	61	7
Sato	64	7
Tanaka	54	10
Miki	67	14

All had been elected to the Diet many times. Kishi, Hatoyama, and Miki were first elected to the Diet before World War II. Ishibashi and Tanaka were first elected in April 1947, Sato and Ikeda in January 1949. The average time between first election to the Diet and first election to the prime ministership is nineteen years (see table 1.7).

TABLE 1.7   Political Age of Prime Ministers
on Assumption of Office

Name	Date of first election to Diet	Date of first election to prime ministership	Years in Diet before prime ministership
Hatoyama	May 1934	April 1956	22
Ishibashi	January 1949	December 1956	7
Kishi	April 1947	January 1959	12
Ikeda	January 1949	July 1960	11
Sato	January 1949	December 1966	17
Tanaka	April 1947	July 1972	25
Miki	April 1937	December 1974	37

The prime ministers had served in the important posts in the cabinet, these being the commerce (MITI), finance, and foreign ministries. They had served in at least one of the top three party posts, these being the Executive Council chairmanship, the Policy Affairs Deliberation Council chairmanship, and the secretary generalship. Some served as cabinet secretary. None ever served on an important post in the Diet (see table 1.8).

TABLE 1.8   Party, Cabinet, and Diet Posts Occupied by
Prime Ministers Prior to Assumption of Office

Name	Party posts	Cabinet posts	Diet posts
Hatoyama	Secretary General Rikken Seiyu Kai President Minshuto, Jiyuto	Chief Cabinet Secretary Education	None
Ishibashi	Policy (Jiyuto)	Finance Commerce	None
Kishi	Secretary General (Minshuto) Secretary General (LDP)	Commerce Foreign	None
Ikeda	Secretary General Party Council Chairman	Finance (3) Commerce (2)	None
Sato	Party Council Chairman Secretary General Executive Council Chairman	Postal Construction Finance Hokkaido Development	None
Tanaka	Executive Council Party Discipline Secretary General (2)	Postal Finance (2) Commerce	None
Miki	Secretary General (4) Policy Council Chairman (Kyodoto) Chief Secretary Organizational Chairman	Commerce Foreign Environment Economic Planning Science Postal Transportation	None

These prime ministers were all faction leaders. In theory, they could
have been leaders of small factions, for skill in leadership resides in
putting together a winning coalition, not necessarily a large one. The
records show, however, that each prime minister had a large faction
at the time of his election. I have been able to acquire fairly reliable
figures for the lower house factions of the last five prime ministers just
before they assumed office: Kishi, 50; Ikeda, 52; Sato, 55; Tanaka, 48;
and Miki, 38. The normal size of a faction was thought to be from 25
to 30 members during the sixties. Table 1.9 gives the size of the factions
in the seventies.

TABLE 1.9   Factional Strength Before and After Lower House Election
of December 1972

Faction	Strength after election	Strength before election	Change
Fukuda	53 (7)[a]	65	− 12
Tanaka	48 (9)	44	+ 4
Ohira	45 (7)	43	+ 2
Nakasone	38 (9)	34	+ 4
Miki	36 (4)	38	− 2
Shiina	18 (3)	17	+ 1
Mizuta	13 (0)	16	− 3
Funada	9 (0)	10	− 1
Sakata (Ishii)[b]	9 (0)	12	− 3

[a] Number of new men brought into the faction.
[b] Sakata is only a nominal faction leader. The former faction leader, Ishii, retired. Sakata took his place because he had been elected to the Diet twelve times, a record equaled by only one other faction member.

Building a faction takes time, money, and political skill. The new faction leader inherits the nucleus of an old faction or the remains of an old conservative party. He attempts to woo members of other factions. Sometimes he will obtain a disaffected member from an active faction. More often, he will obtain a group of Dietmen when a faction starts to break up. His faction will accrue some new members through the general elections (the change in faction strength after the 1972 elections is given in table 1.9). Some faction leaders will do better by building their factions at the hustings, others by working over other factions within the party. Both types of faction leader will have full opportunity to demonstrate all their political talents.

The factions have long been the bad boy of Japanese politics; each prime minister has denounced them and promised to do away with them. But the factions remain. They have outlasted each prime minister because factions fulfill fundamental political needs. The constitution gives the power of choosing cabinet members to the prime minister. He has many people whom he wishes to reward; he could, indeed, fill the entire cabinet with them. The existence of the factions means that the prime minister must share his power with the faction leaders, who look out for their followers.

New conservative candidates want a party endorsement, which means about 25,000 votes and an 80 percent chance of winning. They stand no chance of getting this endorsement unless they have the backing of a faction leader. Real election fights are between conservative candidates. The party cannot favor one conservative candidate over another. The faction leader should not, but does. The party gives money to its Dietmen, to whom the funds are welcome but insufficient. Dietmen must go to their faction leader for the additional funds. Even if the party supplies sufficient funds to its Dietmen, equitably distributes party endorsements, stops fights among its election candidates, and finds an objective system of awarding high posts in party and government, the factions will continue to exist. They will do so because they have proved to be the best way of organizing the vote for the party presidential election. That election, then, is the key. If its rules change, then the nature of conservative politics changes.

Will the present system for party presidential elections continue? No conservative politician denies that the rules for the election of the party president are flawed. Two basic proposals have emerged from politicians' suggestions for change, one calling for a return to the conservative tradition of selecting the party president through consultation among party elders, the other for the broadening of the electorate by means of an American-style convention with several thousand delegates or an election in which all party members cast a ballot.

Miki Takeo, the incumbent prime minister, has been a strong proponent of party reform. He wants to broaden the franchise in party presidential elections and has proposed that all party members select candidates from whom the LDP parliamentarians would choose the party president.[6] The party likes to accept recommendations from its leader, but this time it is having trouble. First, though many people support LDP candidates, few people join the party. Second, the party local organizations are at best rudimentary and often nonexistent. The party central headquarters has not figured out how to hold a national party election. Nevertheless, if Miki stays in office, the party will find some way to satisfy, at least in part, his desire for reform.

Adoption of the Miki plan would be the first significant move toward popular participation in conservative politics. I think the Miki plan is poorly conceived, but I believe that it would prove successful.[7] The opportunity to participate in the election of the nation's leader should attract voters to the party. Once a voter voted for a LDP president, he might even vote for a LDP Dietman.

6. The Miki plan is three-staged: ten Dietmen nominate each presidential candidate; the party members vote on these candidates; the Dietmen select the prime minister from the two candidates with the greatest number of votes.

7. Dietmen end up voting against many party members' wishes, which is bad politics. If the Miki plan were stood on its head it might work better. The Dietmen would propose a slate of two from which the party members would select the party president. This proposal could be improved further by giving the franchise not only to party members but to all registered voters.

Adoption of a plan that gives at least several thousand voters the right ultimately to select the party president would weaken the factions since they would no longer be an effective means of organizing the vote for the party presidential elections. An expanded franchise would produce a new type of political leader with a strong public personality. He would have to appeal to mass audiences, that is, he would have to be photogenic, to speak persuasively, and to inspire public trust.

Unlike the faction leader, who must spend many years within the Diet and party developing and demonstrating his political talents, the new political leader could develop his abilities outside the political world (and quickly, too, if movie stars and television commentators are examples). Though it would be unlikely, a political neophyte could win a Diet seat and the party president's chair within a year. The point I wish to make is that time of entry into the political world and time of accession to the prime minister's post would be considerably foreshortened. Accordingly, the course and character of future leadership would be difficult to predict.

Adoption of the Miki reform might stave off further reform for a few years, but it will not resolve the conservative dilemma, which is: the more the party moves toward full participation in the selection of its party president, the more popular it will become; but the more it moves toward full participation, the less its parliamentarians will be able to control the choice of party president—and the LDP parliamentarians are not agreed that the most popular politician is the best politician.

What will happen over the next decade? The imperative of maintaining a majority will slowly win out over the desire of the parliamentarians to control the party presidential elections. How far will the LDP advance before it loses its majority? If it develops a plan for full participation quickly, it may stay in power indefinitely. If it is slow to develop a plan, it will lose its majority, and reform will then slow down or halt. The need for a party leader who can arouse popular enthusiasm will be supplanted by the need for a party leader who can build a coalition. Coalition building with opposition parties is not so different from coalition building within the party. The faction leader will return to preeminence. The factions will have a new lease on life.

Eight scenarios are possible. I organize them in three clusters.

The LDP retains its majority. (1) The LDP will make no changes, or at most inconsequential ones, in the party presidential elections. The party president will continue to be chosen from among the faction leaders. (2) The LDP will initiate partial reform. The party president will have to be responsible to both constituencies, general party voters and Dietmen, but probably will still be a faction leader. (3) The LDP will broaden the franchise of the party presidential elections to include most or many members of the party with the Dietmen treated no differently from any other party members. The party president will become a public personality, but it will be difficult to predict who he will be or what his policies will be.

The LDP forms coalitions with opposition parties. (4) The LDP president will lead either a DSP coalition (option one in table 1.5) or a grand coalition (option three in table 1.5). At least initially he will be a faction leader. (5) Should a LDP-led coalition fail, leadership will devolve upon the JSP, the second largest party. Present JSP leaders are faction leaders, quite similar to their LDP counterparts. Coalition leadership will be predictable. (6) Reform can take place within the parties independent of the grand coalition. Reform will probably first occur within the LDP. If the LDP decides on the public election of its party president, the other parties will also have to institute such an election. Can the new leaders with public personalities learn the manipulative skills of the traditional leader to maintain the grand coalition? Or will the new leaders be isolated to run the parties and a new method of selecting a traditional leader be invented to run the grand coalition? In either case traditional leadership will hold sway. (7) In skip-around coalitions, leadership will go to the most effective coalition builder—a traditional leader. He will probably come from the LDP or the DSP, since the leaders of the JCP and the CGP are not ameliorative or manipulative types.

Several LDP factions break off to form a ruling coalition with the opposition parties. (8) This possibility is extremely remote: benefits for bolting factions will be temporary; where will factions return when coalitions break up? Even to consider such a possibility, the bolting factions will have to be promised the prime minister's post. Bolting factions will then have to decide who will be prime minister. This decision will undoubtedly be made through consultations among the bolting faction leaders. If they can agree, they will choose one of their own kind. This leadership will be most traditional.

Of the eight scenarios, only one promises new leadership. I conclude my analysis with a paradox: The longer the LDP remains in office, the more likely a new leadership style will emerge. The sooner the LDP loses its majority and a coalition is formed, the more likely the present leadership style will remain.

2

Japanese Urban Local Politics:
Toward a Viable Progressive Political Opposition

TERRY EDWARD MACDOUGALL

*Terry MacDougall's outline of the struggle of the parties of the left, the "pro-
gressives," to provide a viable alternative to Japanese voters gives depth and body
to Thayer's view from the right. Together the chapters comprise a stereoscopic
view into the political future.*

*Traditionally the left has done much less well in the countryside and the
provinces than the right. But in the sixties this pattern began to change as
increasing industrialization transformed the country and created new concentrations of a new kind of population. Now, ironically, the left is more successful
at the local and provincial level than at the national level: two-thirds of the mayors
in cities with a population of more than 500,000 are progressives. This is
paradoxical for several reasons, among them that power in modern Japan has
always been concentrated at the center, and that national reform, rather than
amelioration of the small-scale problems of daily life in the pollution-plagued
cities, has been the left's traditional goal.*

*The multi-member districts for city elections offer the parties of the left,
with their relatively more sophisticated organizational structure, a chance to hold
the balance of power. And the new problems of the quality of life, "public
hazards," and pollution have offered party strategists and intellectuals a chance,
and an imperative, to think creatively about alternate models of development.
Finally, the left, lacking a direct pipeline to the center at Tokyo of the sort the
conservative candidates claim, has had to emphasize contact with the citizen by
such means as store-front offices, citizens' advisory committees, and opening up
the planning process. These innovations may have more impact in the long run
on Japanese political life than much that seems of greater import now.*

*MacDougall envisages three results of the progressive wave in the provinces
and the cities. First, a viable left-wing victory will be based more and more on
coalition. This will not only bring the parties of the left closer together but will
also exert a centrifugal force on the moderate factions of the Liberal Democratic
party (MacDougall is much more skeptical than Thayer about the ability of the
conservatives to resist fragmentation). Second, the left will increasingly find its
innovations copied by the right to the extent that they are seen to be attractive to*

voters. Thus progressive local victories may result in nationwide reforms—but not in nationwide progressive leadership. Finally, MacDougall points out that local governments, to be effective in dealing with the increasingly complex and intractable problems of the cities, will have to push for greater local autonomy. But this battle with the bureaucratic elite in Tokyo, jealous of its powers, can only be won in alliance with the conservatives. Therefore, the left's best path to effective reform and meaningful victory lies in cooperation with the adversary.

MacDougall and Thayer concur in predicting for Japan a politics of coalition that will make relations between the parties across the entire ideological spectrum more intimate, complex, and delicate.—L. A.

Politics in urban Japan has undergone a dramatic transformation since the late 1950s. Conservative electoral support in the country's major urban areas—Tokyo, Yokohama, Nagoya, Kyoto, Osaka, and Kobe—has plunged from the 50 and 60 percent ranges, respectively, in national and local elections around 1960 to a third or a quarter of the vote today.[1] This has not affected the ability of the Liberal Democratic party (LDP) to hold onto the reins of the national government; its absolute majority in the House of Representatives is based on nationwide support and an electoral system that greatly overrepresents the conservative countryside.[2] In urban local politics, however, the conservative decline has resulted in the recent emergence of progressive control over many major local governments. For example, the governor of Tokyo and the mayors of Nagoya and Kyoto are supported by the Japan Socialist party (JSP) and Japan Communist party (JCP). The mayor of Yokohama, a longtime JSP national leader, is endorsed by that party. In Osaka, the mayor is backed by the JSP, the Democratic Socialist party (DSP), and the Clean Government party (CGP), while in Kobe the mayor is backed by all four progressive opposition parties. Also, since the mid-1960s, the LDP and the conservative independents have lost their previously unbroken absolute majorities in the Tokyo Metropolitan Assembly (TMA) and in the assemblies of the "big five"

1.   The term *conservative* will be used to refer to the Liberal Democratic party (LDP) and to local independent candidates and persons of influence who share a similar political orientation if not affiliation. *Progressive* will be used to refer to all four of the opposition parties, labor unions that support them, and local independent candidates backed by them. A distinction will at times be made between the left progressives, the Japan Socialist party (JSP) and Japan Communist party (JCP), and the moderate or center progressives, the Democratic Socialist party (DSP), and Clean Government party (CGP), based on fundamental ideological differences.

2.   Gerald L. Curtis, "The 1969 General Election in Japan," *Asian Survey* 10, no. 10 (October 1970): 859–71; Robert E. Ward, "Recent Electoral Developments in Japan," *Asian Survey* 6, no. 10 (October 1966): 547–67.

designated cities.[3] Winning coalitions of progressive parties are, there-fore, at least theoretically possible in each of these assemblies.

In short, the perpetual "outs" of Japanese politics are now the "ins" along much of the Pacific industrial belt of Japan and in an increasing number of regional cities as well. Their ability to govern, at least at the local level, as well as to oppose is now subject to public scrutiny. This experience of local power by a wide spectrum of the former "outs" of Japanese politics is a crucial stage in the process of the development of an effective, responsible, and constitutional political opposition in Japan—a process by no means inevitable.

Political opposition can be considered *effective* when it has the capability of winning office, that is, when it has the institutional structure and public support that make credible its bid to be considered as an alternative government.[4] It is *responsible* when it offers a sober critique of governmental politics (and not simply tries to outbid the government's promises), attempts to formulate policies that it believes are capable of execution, and presents competent personnel who would be able to govern. Finally, it is *constitutional* when it and the government are bound by some sort of fundamental consensus concerning legitimate procedures for contesting public office and for freely expressing op-position.

In this paper I will be concerned with only a single aspect of this process, which I will term the development of a viable political op-position. My attention will focus on the effectiveness of Japan's pro-gressive opposition at the local level. I will document and attempt to account for its growing effectiveness in the country's major urban areas and to assess the possibility that this might be a permanent, and not a transient, phenomenon. In conclusion, I will also suggest some possible implications for the overall viability of progressive opposition at both the local and national levels.

PREFECTURAL AND MUNICIPAL ASSEMBLY ELECTIONS

Local politics in Japan has often been described as a "conservative's paradise." The aptness of this description is illustrated in figure 2.1

3. Designated cities *(shitei toshi)* are established by action of the national Diet in accordance with the provisions in Article 252, paragraphs 19–21 of the Local Autonomy Law. A city must have a population of at least 500,000 to be so designated. Once designated, cities form admin-istrative and electoral wards, carry out a number of welfare, planning, and other functions normally reserved for the prefectures, and receive similar treatment to that of the prefectures in the allocation of permission for local bonds. The "big five" designated cities refer to Yokohama, Nagoya, Kyoto, Osaka, and Kobe cities.

4. Richard Hofstadter, *The Idea of the Party System: The Rise of Legitimate Opposition in the United States, 1780–1840* (Berkeley, 1972), pp. 1–39.

and table 2.1. Although there has been a steady decline in the percentage of conservative vote in prefectural assembly elections, it has been so gradual that over 60 percent of the vote still goes to conservatives. Of 2,742 prefectural assembly seats, the LDP held 1,525 and conservative independents 264 as a result of the April 1971 elections. Independents predominate in city, town, and village assemblies; most of them are conservative in orientation, if not affiliation. The level of partisan representation is particularly low in the smaller cities and the towns and villages.

TABLE 2.1   The 1971 Unified Local Elections: Assembly Seats

	Prefectures[a]	Cities	Towns and villages	Designated cities[b]
LDP	1,525	1,576	285	129
Independents		7,259	23,083	10
Conservative	264			
Neutral	24			
Progressive	60			
Others	26	6	18	2
JSP	499	1,243	498	87
JCP	124	705	534	52
CGP	120	869	455	60
DSP	100	341	47	50
Total	2,742	11,999	24,920	390

[a] Tokyo and Ibaragi prefectural assembly elections are scheduled at different times from the rest. These figures include the results of the July 1969 Tokyo and December 1970 Ibaragi elections. Two vacant seats are excluded.
[b] Yokohama, Nagoya, Kyoto, Osaka, and Kobe only.

Sources: Asahi Shimbun, April 13, 1971, and Mainichi Shimbun, April 28, 1971.

Viewed in a national perspective, the persistence of conservative electoral success is extremely impressive at all levels of election. Even the rate of decline in conservative support has slowed to a point that should make anyone question predictions of the conservatives' imminent demise. If this is true at the national level, it is even more so at the prefectural level. Only five of the forty-seven prefectural assemblies are without working majorities made up of LDP members and conservative independents; these are Tokyo, Nagano, Kyoto, Osaka, and Fukuoka. Only in two others—Kanagawa and Hyogo—is it conceivable that conservatives might lose their absolute majorities before the 1979 elections. Almost all city, town, and village assemblies also have conservative majorities.

Figure 2.1
House of Representatives and Prefectural Assembly Elections

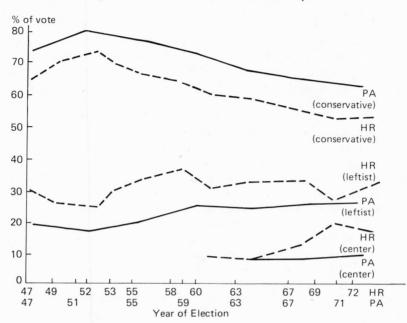

Note: "Conservative" includes the LDP, its pre-1955 predecessors, and independents; this slightly overestimates conservative strength, since a few progressive independents are included. "Leftist" refers to the JSP and JCP. "Center" refers to the DSP and CGP. PA means prefectural assembly, HR House of Representatives.

Sources: PA elections: *Asahi Shimbun* and *Mainichi Shimbun,* selected issues 1947–71. HR elections: Kōmei senkyo renmei [Fair Elections League], *Shūgiin giin senkyo no jisseki: dai ikkai dai sanjūkai* [The actual record of the election of representatives to the House of Representatives] (Tokyo, 1967); *Asahi Shimbun,* January 31, 1967; *Shimbun Geppō,* January 10, 1970; *Mainichi Shimbun,* December 12, 1972.

A number of important qualifications should be made to this picture of conservative dominance. First, independent conservatives usually form several assembly groups (*gikai dantai*), each of which constitutes a separate bargaining unit. Such a group can, and often does, become a major competitor with a mainstream LDP group. This opens up the possibility of its combining with JSP, labor, or other progressive assembly groups to form a conservative-progressive coalition. A number of progressive mayors—for example, those in Mishima and Tagawa cities—are supported by this type of coalition. Second, in addition to the prefectures named above, major exceptions to conservative assembly domination include the big five designated cities, an increasing number of suburban and satellite cities in the Tokyo and Osaka metropolitan areas, some medium-sized regional cities, and a few old coal-mining cities.

Among these "defections" from the conservatives' paradise are the most heavily populated and economically important areas of the country. Tokyo Metropolis and the cities of Yokohama, Nagoya, Kyoto, Osaka, and Kobe contained one out of every five Japanese in 1971; and fully 42 percent of the national population resided in the eight prefectures comprising the Tokyo, Nagoya, and Osaka metropolitan areas.[5] These areas contain even greater concentrations of the nation's financial, industrial, administrative, and cultural assets.[6] Tokyo, the national capital, is especially important as a pacesetter in everything from administrative practices to clothing styles. The significance of the loss of conservative majorities in the TMA and the assemblies of the big five cities has been magnified by the election of a progressive governor in the former and progressive mayors in each of the latter. The intrinsic importance of these areas justifies a closer examination of political trends within them.

Three characteristics of local assembly elections in Tokyo and the big five cities are of particular concern to us: (1) conservatives have traditionally been far stronger in local politics than in national politics in these areas—the opposite being true for progressives; (2) support for conservative candidates in urban local assembly elections has dropped dramatically since 1959 and has converged with the level of support conservatives receive in House of Representatives elections in the same area; (3) both the moderate progressive parties—especially the CGP— and the JCP have grown more rapidly than, and sometimes at the expense of, the JSP.

A gap has traditionally existed between the levels of conservative support in local and national elections, with higher rates of support appearing in the former. This continues to be the case today when prefectural assembly and House of Representatives elections are compared, as illustrated in figure 2.1. Rates of conservative support in Tokyo and the big cities have shown a similar difference according to level of election. For example, the combined LDP and independent share of the TMA vote was 66.3 percent, while it was only 47.3 percent in the 1960 House of Representatives election—a differential of 19.0

---

5. Asahi Shimbunsha, *Minryoku '72* [National strength 1972] (Tokyo, 1972), p. 50.

6. The eight prefectures that make up these three metropolitan areas account for 50.9 percent of personal income (1967), 59.4 percent of shipment of goods (1968), 65.6 percent of sales (1967–68, excluding Chiba and Saitama), 58.7 percent of private savings (1970), and 77.2 percent of corporate holdings (1970, excluding Chiba and Saitama). Yano tsuneta kinekai [Yano tsuneta memorial], *Nihon kokusei zue* [Japan national government] (Tokyo, 1971), pp. 84–86.

TABLE 2.2   Distribution of Seats in Urban Assemblies (1971)

	LDP	Indepen-dents	Others	DSP	CGP	JSP	JCP	Total
Tokyo[a]	51	2	0	2	26	20	24	125
Yokohama	26	2	2	12	12	21	5	80
Nagoya	28	2	0	9	9	22	6	76
Kyoto	24	1	0	8	9	12	18	72
Osaka	27	3	0	14	18	19	13	94
Kobe	24	2	0	7	12	13	10	68
Total	180	12	2	52	86	107	76	515

[a] 1973 Tokyo Metropolitan Assembly election results.

Source: Kyōto shikai jimukyoku chōsakai [Kyoto city assembly secretariat survey group], Shisei yoran: Shōwa 40-nendoban [A survey of city government: Showa 40 issue] (Kyoto, 1966).

TABLE 2.3   JSP and JCP Support in Big City Assemblies
(Percentage of Vote and Number of Seats)

	JSP				JCP			
	1963		1971		1963		1971	
	Vote	Seats	Vote	Seats	Vote	Seats	Vote	Seats
Tokyo[a]	27.8	32	20.5	20	4.5	2	20.2	24
Yokohama	19.1	16	26.1	21	3.3	0	9.2	5
Nagoya	24.6	22	26.2	22	3.9	0	10.8	6
Kyoto	19.1	13	19.1	12	12.5	8	23.6	18
Osaka	16.7	12	16.7	19	8.5	5	16.8	13
Kobe	21.8	16	18.2	13	4.2	1	13.4	10

[a] The last Tokyo election was held in 1973, not 1971.

Sources: Kyōto shikai jimukyoku chōsakai [Kyoto city assembly secretariat survey group], Shisei yoran: Shōwa 40-nendoban [A survey of city government: Showa 40 issue] (Kyoto, 1966). Asahi Shimbun and Mainichi Shimbun, selected issues 1965–73.

percent (see table 2.2, figure 2.2).[7] Similarly, in the big five cities the LDP and independent vote was consistently greater in city assembly elections than in those for the House of Representatives: 63.2 percent to 44.6 percent, respectively, in Yokohama; 65.5 percent to 44.8 percent in Nagoya; 62.1 percent to 44.1 percent in Kyoto; 59.9 percent to 43.1 percent in Osaka; 67.3 percent to 45.7 percent in Kobe (see tables 2.2, 2.3, figures 2.2, 2.3). Rates of support for the opposition parties showed similar differentials in the opposite direction.

7.   A small percentage of the independent vote in local elections includes progressives, but the distortion is not great.

Figure 2.2
Urban Local Assembly Elections: 1947–1973

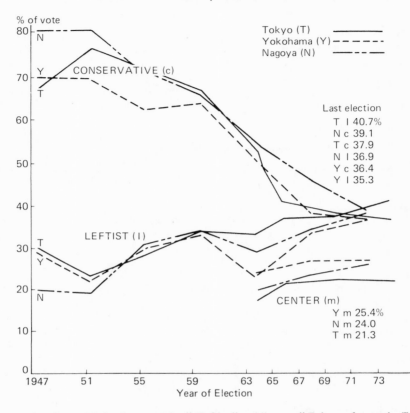

Note: See figure 2.1 for "conservative," "leftist," and "center." Tokyo refers to the Tokyo
Metropolitan Assembly, which represents the whole prefecture.

Sources: Kyōto shikai jimukyoku chōsakai [Kyoto city assembly secretariat survey group],
Shisei yoran: Shōwa 40-nendoban [A survey of city government: Showa 40 issue] (Kyoto,
1966). *Asahi Shimbun* and *Mainichi Shimbun,* selected issues 1965–73.

Support for conservative candidates has dropped sharply in urban
local assembly elections, to 37.9 percent in Tokyo in 1973, and to
36.4 percent in Yokohama, 39.1 percent in Nagoya, 37.1 percent in
Kyoto, 34.7 percent in Osaka, and 40.8 percent in Kobe in 1971 (see
figures 2.2, 2.3). The greatest decline in conservative support occurred
between 1959 and 1963 with the appearance of Sokagakkai-backed
candidates (formally CGP from 1964) and the separation of the DSP
from the JSP. These moderate progressive parties also cut into the

Figure 2.3
Urban Local Assembly Elections: 1947–1971

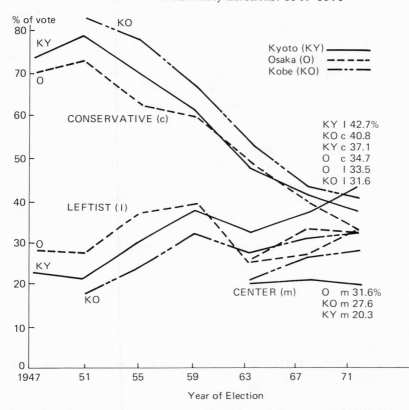

Note: See figure 2.1 for "conservative," "leftist," and "center." No data could be located for the 1947 Kobe City Assembly election.

Sources: Kyōto shikai jimukyoku chōsakai [Kyoto city assembly secretariat survey group], *Shisei yoran: Showa 40-nendoban* [A survey of city government: Showa 40 issue] (Kyoto, 1966). *Asahi Shimbun* and *Mainichi Shimbun,* selected issues 1965–73.

leftist (JSP and JCP) vote in 1963, but, whereas the left resumed its upward momentum in subsequent elections, the conservatives continued to decline. Conservative support in House of Representatives elections in these areas also dropped sharply between 1960 and 1972. The smallest drop was in Tokyo, from 44.6 percent to 26.0 percent, while the greatest was in Nagoya, from 44.8 percent to 21.8 percent (see figures 2.2, 2.3). The rate of decline, however, has been even greater in urban assembly elections, resulting in a narrowing of the differential between levels of conservative support in the two types of elections.

Figures 2.2 and 2.3 and tables 2.2 and 2.3 illustrate the point that both the moderate progressive parties and the JCP have become significant factors in urban assembly elections. In each of these assemblies the moderate progressive parties hold a sufficient number of seats to swing the vote in a conservative, leftist, or (perhaps) moderate direction as is the case with the CGP. In addition, table 2.3 indicates that a major shift in leftist support from the JSP to the JCP has developed since 1963. (A similar shift has occurred in prefectural assembly and national elections.) In the TMA and Kyoto City Assembly, JCP representation has surpassed that of the JSP. Figure 2.4 suggests two patterns in the distribution of leftist support: a "Yokohama pattern," in which the JSP retains a relatively strong position as leader of the leftist opposition; and a "Kyoto pattern," in which the JCP passes the JSP and assumes a greater leadership role. I will return to these points in a later discussion.

GUBERNATORIAL AND MAYORAL ELECTIONS

Gubernatorial and mayoral elections have been no less a conservative's paradise than local assembly elections. Today 6 of the 47 prefectural governors and 135 of the 625 city mayors are progressives.[8] These figures represent the highest numbers and highest percentages of executive posts ever held by progressives. Clearly, conservative or neutral candidates have dominated gubernatorial and mayoral posts, including almost all of those on the town and village level.

Progressive governors and city mayors have been elected in small numbers ever since the first postwar local elections in 1947. In that year four JSP governors, nine JSP city mayors, and sixteen independent progressive mayors were elected. Seven prefectures have had a progressive governor for at least two terms—Hokkaido (three), Tokyo (two), Nagano (three), Kyoto (seven), Fukuoka (four), Oita (four), and Okinawa (two). Early progressive governors often ran as JSP-endorsed candidates, but most of the present ones—in Saitama, Tokyo, Kyoto, Osaka, Okayama, and Okinawa—ran as JSP-JCP-backed candidates.[9]

The emergence of progressive city mayors can be divided, roughly, into three periods: 1947–54, 1955–62, and 1963–today. During the

8.   The figure of 135 progressive mayors refers to the membership of the National Association of Progressive Mayors (NAPM), an organization ostensibly independent from all political parties but in fact having a strong JSP coloration.

9.   After the July 1974 cutoff date for the data in this article, a seventh progressive governor was elected in Kagawa prefecture.

Figure 2.4
JSP and JCP Support Levels in Yokohama and Kyoto HR and City
Assembly Elections

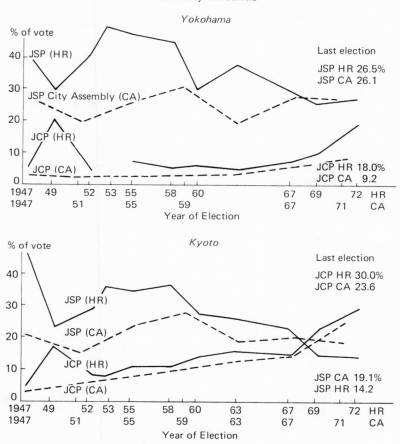

Note: Labor-Farmer party and left- and right-wing Socialist parties are included in the pre-1959 JSP. The DSP is excluded. Kyoto HR means District One in Kyoto Prefecture, or Kyoto City except for Ukyo and Fushimi Wards.

Sources: Kyōto shikai jimukyoku chōsakai [Kyoto city assembly secretariat survey group], *Shisei yoran: Shōwa 40-nendoban* [A survey of city government: Showa 40 issue] (Kyoto, 1966). *Asahi Shimbun* and *Mainichi Shimbun,* selected issues 1965–73.

first period, progressive mayors were elected in each of the big five cities and in a small number of coal-mining cities or prewar strongholds in Hokkaido and Fukuoka prefectures. Although progressives have held onto these posts in many of the coal-mining areas, they eventually lost all of the big city ones. During the second period, a large number of progressive mayors were elected in the Tokyo and Osaka metropolitan areas, Hokkaido, and the Tohoku region. Most of these have remained in office until today or have been followed by second or third "generations" of progressive mayors. In the most recent period, progressives have once again been elected to the mayoral posts in each of the big five cities. While their numbers have continued to increase most rapidly in the Tokyo and Osaka metropolitan areas, progressive mayors have been elected in considerable numbers throughout the country (see figure 2.5).

Progressives are currently governors or mayors in many of the country's most important urban areas. Among these are Tokyo, Kyoto, and Osaka prefectures and six of nine designated cities, including all of the big five cities. In addition, progressives hold the mayoral posts in sixteen of forty-six prefectural capitals: Aomori, Sendai, Yamagata, Yokohama, Toyama, Kanazawa, Kofu, Nagoya, Otsu, Kyoto, Osaka, Kobe, Takamatsu, Kochi, Kagoshima, and Naha. City size is an important factor in accounting for the distribution of progressive mayors: 57.1 percent of the large cities (500,000 or more population), 32.9 percent of the medium-sized ones (100,000–499,999), and only 17.1 percent of the small ones (99,999 or less) have progressive mayors.[10] Thus although the bulk of the gubernatorial and mayoral posts are still held by conservative or neutral politicians, 41.3 percent of the Japanese population lived in prefectures or cities having progressive executives in mid-1974—26.8 percent of the prefectural population and 38.2 percent of that of the cities. When judged in terms of the importance of the posts they occupy, progressives have clearly achieved a high degree of electoral effectiveness.

In trying to account for the increased effectiveness of progressives in urban assembly and executive elections, I will consider three questions: (1) What are some of the causes of the early weakness of progressives in local politics? (2) Why has conservative electoral support in urban areas declined so sharply since the late 1950s? (3) What other conditions have contributed to the increased appeal of progressive candidates in urban elections?

EARLY WEAKNESS OF THE LEFT IN LOCAL POLITICS

At least three factors have contributed to the progressives' poorer performance in local than in national politics: (1) a prewar legacy that

---

10.   A statistically significant chi square of 26.779 was obtained for this relationship between city size and progressive as opposed to conservative or neutral mayors.

Figure 2.5
Map of Japan

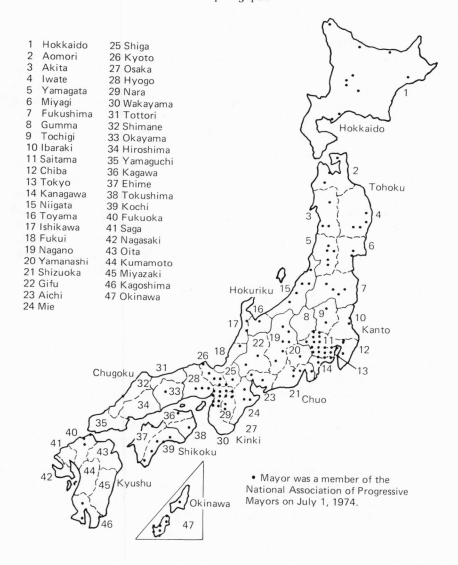

1 Hokkaido	25 Shiga
2 Aomori	26 Kyoto
3 Akita	27 Osaka
4 Iwate	28 Hyogo
5 Yamagata	29 Nara
6 Miyagi	30 Wakayama
7 Fukushima	31 Tottori
8 Gumma	32 Shimane
9 Tochigi	33 Okayama
10 Ibaraki	34 Hiroshima
11 Saitama	35 Yamaguchi
12 Chiba	36 Kagawa
13 Tokyo	37 Ehime
14 Kanagawa	38 Tokushima
15 Niigata	39 Kochi
16 Toyama	40 Fukuoka
17 Ishikawa	41 Saga
18 Fukui	42 Nagasaki
19 Nagano	43 Oita
20 Yamanashi	44 Kumamoto
21 Shizuoka	45 Miyazaki
22 Gifu	46 Kagoshima
23 Aichi	47 Okinawa
24 Mie	

• Mayor was a member of the National Association of Progressive Mayors on July 1, 1974.

impeded grassroots organization, (2) the principle of nonpartisanship in local politics, and (3) the electoral system for city, town, and village assemblies.

Prewar development of labor and socialist movements was retarded for a number of reasons.[11] The urban male labor force with stable industrial employment was small in size and scattered among numerous small-scale industries; these circumstances made unionization difficult. An appeal to class consciousness conflicted with strong local loyalties and the dominant value of social harmony. Police surveillance of the labor and socialist movements was constant, and strong state oppression of the former relatively enhanced the role of intellectuals in the latter, limiting the extent of its grassroots base. At the same time, the dominant prewar conservative political parties were competing rigorously with each other in building up contacts with local assemblymen and other local influentials; such linkages proved mutually beneficial for purposes of voter mobilization and patronage distribution.

Despite the rapid organization of labor unions in the immediate postwar years, the JSP failed to bring large numbers of workers and others into a party organization. Throughout the postwar period the JSP has seldom had as many as 50,000 members, and only a fraction of those have been committed activists. Unions could be mobilized, but this was easier in national politics, which labor identified as the most relevant site for its political activities. Even questions of local autonomy tended to call for national political struggles rather than local ones, since the perceived threat came more from the moves of the conservative national government to recentralize police, education, and other functions than from local abuses of them. Possibly the strongest appeal of the JSP was in terms of its defense of the new democratic political system; this could elicit support in national politics. Without strong local organization, however, the JSP tended to be removed from the concerns of local politics, which have traditionally centered on tangible benefits—a new school, road, bridge, or the like— for the community. In effect, local politics was abandoned to the conservatives who had long been entrenched in positions of community leadership and had the additional advantage of close contacts with the party in power nationally.

A principle of nonpartisanship has pervaded local politics in most areas of the country. In part, this reflects the kind of center-periphery gap in speed and level of politicization found in Western European countries that was, perhaps, aggravated in the Japanese case because of the skeletal nature of local party organization.[12] In addition, tight community organization and a value system that supports group

11. George O. Totten, *The Social Democratic Movement in Prewar Japan* (New Haven, 1966), pp. 3–15.

12. Stein Rokkan, "Electoral Mobilization, Party Competition and National Development," in *Political Parties and Political Development*, ed. Joseph LaPalombara and Myron Weiner (Princeton, 1966), pp. 241–65.

conformity provide positive incentives for communities to seek local political representation without regard to partisan differences that might divide members in national politics. Areal representation, in which a candidate runs with the explicit backing of one or more communities (hamlet or neighborhood) on the understanding that he will uphold their interests in the local assembly, has, therefore, had a strong appeal.[13] Although it is far more complex today than in the prewar period, voter mobilization based on an appeal to areal representation still functions either through official recommendation of a candidate by community associations—which are ubiquitous—or through his close association with community interests. In a 1971 Fair Election League national survey, 44.9 percent of town and village residents, 36.9 percent of residents of small- and medium-sized cities, and 35.6 percent of residents of large cities indicated that their community association recommends candidates for the local assembly.[14]

A major alternative or supplement to areal representation— necessitated by the amalgamations of towns and villages and increasing diversity among residents of the more urban areas—is the individual candidate support group.[15] People are drawn into such a group on the basis of areal, family, business, educational, and other particularistic ties with the candidate or someone close to him. Members benefit from the group by vicarious participation in the candidate's career, by the concern of the candidate—expressed through cards and gifts—for the members' well-being, the fellowship of group activities, and the areal groups, and by having an assembly representative to watch out for their interests.

Conservative local politicians have been very successful in using these means of mobilizing electoral support without resort to the LDP label. Their strength as local politicians does not depend on the LDP but on the trust that they can inspire in the voters and the impression that they will work for community benefits. Persons well known through community association, fire squad, PTA, and other leadership roles are particularly strong as assembly candidates; and those who occupy these positions are far more likely to be conservative than progressive in political orientation. Such candidates need not appeal to partisan slogans or causes, although some may imply that their

13.   Richard H. Beardsley, John W. Hall, and Robert E. Ward, *Village Japan* (Chicago, 1959), pp. 349–97.

14.   Komei senkyo renmei, *Dai-7 kai tōitsu chihō senkyo to yūkensha II* [The seventh unified local elections and the electorate II] (Tokyo, 1972), pp. 182–89.

15.   Gerald L. Curtis, *Political Campaigning Japanese Style* (New York, 1971); Bradley Richardson, "Japanese Local Politics: Support Mobilization and Leadership Styles," *Asian Survey* 7, no. 12 (December 1967): 860–75.

political compatibility with higher level authorities would be an asset to the community. In short, the dominant modes of local political representation and voter mobilization, built on the nonpartisan principle, militate against a strong progressive presence in most local assemblies.

The electoral system for city, town, and village assembly elections helps perpetuate the type of particularistic and nonpartisan local politics detailed above. In all these elections, with the exception of those in the designated cities, assembly candidates run on an at-large basis rather than from specific districts. All candidates must compete with each other, since there are no lists and each voter has only a single vote. This system would clearly attenuate the solidarity and effectiveness of all but the most highly disciplined party organization, because a strong candidate might draw support away from a weaker candidate of his own party, causing him to be defeated. Independent candidates running with the backing of specific communities or their own support groups, of course, do not face these difficulties. Where these mechanisms are effective for electing conservative candidates, it is generally not necessary (or economical) for the LDP to endorse them. Since far fewer progressive candidates have the advantage of community recommendations or their own support groups, they are more likely to run with party endorsements and are thus vulnerable to the bias of the system.

Only a small number of votes is needed for election to a local assembly with this type of system. For example, in Hachioji, a medium-sized city of 200,000 people, a candidate was elected to the thirty-eight-member city assembly in 1967 with only 1,542 votes. In most cities even fewer votes would have been necessary. Areal representation and individual candidate support groups depend on intense and particularistic contacts between a candidate and his backers. The at-large type of electoral system facilitates these modes of voter mobilization, since under it a candidate can physically and financially maintain close personal contact with enough persons to virtually guarantee his election.

In contrast, assembly elections in the designated cities are based on multimember districts—still with no lists and only one vote per person. All of these assemblies have become highly politicized with relatively poor performances by conservatives. A relatively large number of votes is needed for election. For example, in the eleven-member Tsurumi Ward district, which numbers approximately 200,000 people, a candidate needed at least 6,054 votes to be elected to the Yokohama City Assembly in 1967, four times the number needed in the case of Hachioji. Particularistic and nonpartisan politics, which favor the conservatives, may be more difficult to maintain when so many votes are necessary for election. This may provide a partial explanation as to why progressive candidates have done so much better in assembly elections in the designated cities than elsewhere. In sum, a prewar legacy that impeded grassroots organization, nonpartisanship in local politics, and the electoral system for city, town, and village assemblies all contributed to the early weakness of the left in local politics.

CONSERVATIVE ELECTORAL DECLINE IN URBAN LOCAL POLITICS

The rapid economic growth that has transformed urban areas since the late 1950s is intrinsically related to conservative electoral decline in urban Japan in both local and national politics. Suggestions that industrialization and urbanization contribute to increased political competition and possibly the rise of radical oppositions are borne out by the Japanese experience.[16] Elsewhere I have shown that greater degrees of industrialization, community instability, and population concentration—socioeconomic changes characteristic of economic growth—in Japanese cities and wards (of Tokyo and the designated cities) are negatively correlated with LDP vote and positively correlated with vote for the opposition parties as a whole.[17] These relationships held even when each of the variables was controlled for the others. Rapid economic growth has contributed to the erosion of a crucial basis of conservative support in the Japanese social system— the solidarity of the local residential community. I have just indicated that because of the intervening effect of the electoral system, the local residential community is less likely to shape the political orientations of voters in the designated cities than elsewhere. Even more important (and not limited to the designated cities) is the fact that rapid economic growth has created new problems for the cities, ones that the LDP has been slow in addressing and that cannot be adequately met through the particularistic type of representation offered by most conservatives. That is to say, rapid economic growth has contributed to the decline of conservatives in urban local politics by creating new issues of great salience that cannot be handled through the traditional conservative formula of dividing the benefits.

Table 2.4 indicates the change in public policy concerns of Tokyo residents between 1958 and 1972. The problems of road improvement, unemployment, and provision of educational facilities have been

16. Erik Allardt, "A Theory on Solidarity and Legitimacy Conflicts," in *Cleavages, Ideologies and Party Systems*, ed. Erik Allardt and Yrjo Littunen (Helsinki, 1964), pp. 78–96.

17. Terry E. MacDougall, "Political Opposition and Local Government in Japan: The Significance of Emerging Progressive Local Leadership," (Ph.D. diss., Yale University, 1975). See chapter 4.

TABLE 2.4   Public Policy Issues of Concern to Tokyo Residents

	1958	*1965*	*1972*
Road improvement	35	15	7 ₐ
Unemployment	21	1	
Educational facilities	18	2	—
Housing	17	25	16
Sewer construction	13	9	8
Traffic policy	—*b*	11	12
Consumer policy	—	11	12
Social welfare	12	2	13
Public hazards (pollution)	—	1	15
Others	73	40	17
Total	189	118	100

a Data were available for only the top seven issues.
b This item was not listed in 1958.

Note: Only the top five named issues in either of the years are included in this table; their frequency of citation for the other two years is also given. In 1958 respondents were asked to name two issues, in 1965 one or two, and in 1972 two.
Sources: Tōkyōto [Tokyo Metropolitan Government], *Tosei seiron chōsa* [Public opinion survey on Tokyo metropolitan government] (Tokyo, 1958–69). Tokyo Metropolitan Government, *Tokyo Municipal News* 23 (April 1973): 3.

ameliorated or eliminated; those of housing and sewer construction remain. Traffic, consumer, and pollution problems have newly emerged—or have become more salient—and social welfare concerns have reemerged. Most of the problems that have diminished in importance are ones that are amenable to solution through the particularistic type of representation characteristic of the conservatives' style in local politics—bringing special benefits like roads or schools to a community. Those that have become more prominent are structural problems in the society and economy and cannot be solved simply by enlarging and dividing the pie. Their solution requires the application of a different schedule of values and priorities from that which has provided so admirable (if one-sided) a formula for economic recovery and growth. The new concerns of urban residents may be instrumental in lifting their political consciousness from the position of seeking particularistic benefits through local politics to seeking broader policy changes. If this is the case (we could certainly use more survey data on the question) then a cornerstone of conservative dominance in local government may be beginning to crumble.

The weakening of the social bases of conservative support and the emergence of new public policy issues have offset some of the early advantages of conservatives in local politics. I can do no more than indicate here some of the important factors enabling progressives to take advantage of these changes to improve their electoral effectiveness. Of particular importance are (1) the mass organizations of the CGP and JCP, (2) the proliferation of citizens' groups seeking action by local governments on outstanding problems, and (3) the strategic position of the mayor or governor as an avenue of possible change.

INCREASED ELECTORAL EFFECTIVENESS OF PROGRESSIVES IN URBAN LOCAL POLITICS

Organization has been a crucial variable in accounting for the significant advances made by the CGP and JCP in urban local politics (see tables 2.2, 2.3). Sokagakkai, the lay association of Nichiren Shoshu Buddhism, grew phenomenally in the urban areas in the 1950s and 1960s—to over six million households—by appealing to those who were relatively left out in Japan's rush toward prosperity, especially to new migrants to the cities and older residents employed in smaller enterprises.[18] The CGP, as an outgrowth of the political action arm of Sokagakkai, therefore, has both a strong grassroots organization in Sokagakkai and a natural concern for the problems of the cities. By the late 1960s the JCP also emerged as a significant force in urban politics. It enhanced its acceptability at that time by its moves toward independence from both the Soviet Union and China, criticism of student violence, professions of a desire to work within the parliamentary system, and scrupulous attention to such problems as day care centers and welfare facilities. These two parties have adopted similar electoral strategies: when weak, avoid intraparty competition by placing only a single candidate, divide the district or city territorially among the party candidates and have each candidate restrict his or her campaigning to an assigned area—for example, by placing posters and operating a sound truck only within the allotted territory.[19] Since CGP votes come in large measure from Sokagakkai members, the latter's meetings and other activities offer additional opportunities for members to learn which candidate to support. In addition, the party's mass base in Sokagakkai and daily contact with the electorate through numerous party complaint and consultation centers give it the necessary grassroots contact to make an accurate assessment of its level and distribution of support. For the JCP, similar functions are performed through the daily activities of its 300,000-member party organization, other more loosely related groups, and the mass circulation newspaper *Red Flag*

18. James W. White, *The Sokagakkai and Mass Society* (Stanford, 1970), pp. 69–70.

19. These points are based on the writer's analysis of the placement of party candidates in postwar local elections in Tokyo Metropolis and on personal observations in the same area during the spring 1971 local elections.

(*Akahata*). Communist electoral cooperation with the JSP in jointly backing a growing number of independent progressive mayoral and gubernatorial candidates has offered another vehicle for furthering its legitimacy and developing grassroots contacts that can be turned to its advantage in local assembly and national Diet elections. In sum, the increased strength of the CGP and JCP in urban local politics rests in large part on their powerful organizations and their close attention to the problems of the cities.

Pollution, urban and regional development plans, and other urban problems have stirred widespread protests in recent years. The scope and intensity of these problems should not be underestimated. Many Japanese cities are literally "pollution department stores" (*kōgai depāto*), with every new variety of nuisance and serious threat to the living environment well represented. Most Japanese cities face these new problems before they have had the time, or the inclination, to deal with the old urban problems by creating adequate sanitation, health, home water, sewerage, park, and other facilities. Even the people's new wealth complicates the problems: the purchase of automobiles, for example, adds to air pollution and creates traffic accidents and congestion.

It is not surprising, therefore, that many Japanese have sought a reordering of priorities away from emphasis on economic growth and toward protection of the living environment. Local governments, which have long cooperated with national efforts at industrial expansion, have become the major target of protest.[20] These protests have escalated in recent years as citizens have increasingly organized themselves into residents' groups and citizens' movements.[21] The mass media have given great prominence to both the environmental and urban problems and the protests against them, thereby contributing to a sense of urgency. The protests have gone beyond the usual practices of petitioning for change to more activist demands for a larger citizen voice in decisions affecting the living environment. In many areas, citizens' movements have entered the arena of electoral politics, usually to the disadvantage of conservatives.

Protests against environmental and urban problems contribute to the electoral effectiveness of progressives in local politics in a number of ways. They increase the salience of issues on which the conservatives, who have been reluctant to abandon their emphasis on industrial expansion and their preference for central control of local authorities,

---

20.   Matsubara Haruo, *Nihon no shakai kaihatsu* [Japanese social development] (Tokyo, 1968).

21.   Matsushita Keiichi, *Shimin sanka* [Citizenship participation] (Tokyo, 1971); Miyamoto Kenichi, *Kōgai to jūmin undō* [Public hazards and resident's movements] (Tokyo, 1970).

have been relatively vulnerable. They help to legitimize the previously half-subversive concept that local governments may, on occasion, have to oppose national authorities if they are to carry out their putative function of protecting the welfare of their residents. And, finally, they provide a core area of agreement on issues of relevance to local politics that can serve as a basis for cooperation among the opposition parties in supporting independent progressive mayoral and gubernatorial candidates.

Mayors and governors are in strategic positions to initiate (or block) changes in local governmental policy. The tradition of executive dominance in Japanese politics survived attempts by the Allied Occupation to strengthen the legislature.[22] Not only does the mayor or governor present the budget, which is difficult for the assembly to change, but he presents most other bills as well. In 1967, for example, governors presented an average of 142.5 bills (46.1 of which were for ordinances), while assembly member bills averaged only 21.9 (1.2 for ordinances) per assembly. Most of the latter were simply opinions or resolutions. During that year in Tokyo, all but one of the 211 gubernatorial bills were passed. A similar situation pertains at the city level.[23] As administrative head of the local government, a mayor or governor has significant jurisdiction in appointments to posts in the local bureaucracy and various executive committees and in approving construction, applications for licenses, and a wide range of other activities. In negotiations with higher authorities and in communications with local residents, he is the chief representative of the local government. Leadership in Japanese local politics tends to emanate from the executive, headed by the mayor or governor.

Each city is headed by a mayor and each prefecture by a governor who is elected directly by the people for a four-year term. The singularity of the office is an incentive for the progressive parties to unite behind the same candidate. With few exceptions, it is only by such electoral cooperation that a progressive can be elected to a mayoral or gubernatorial post. Although ideological and policy differences among the progressive parties and disagreements among their respective support groups make agreement on a single candidate difficult, the frequency and variety of examples of joint support have increased in recent years. Of 103 progressive mayors for whom data, current as of July 1973, could be located, 32 had been backed by the JSP and JCP in their last election; 19 by the JSP alone; 10 by the JSP, JCP, CGP,

22. Kurt Steiner, *Local Government in Japan* (Stanford, 1965).
23. Tokyo togikai [Tokyo city council], *Shuchō shugi to chihō gikai* [Executivism and local assemblies] (Tokyo, 1971), p. 88.

and DSP; 9 by the JSP, JCP, and CGP; 6 by the JSP, CGP, and DSP; and 27 by other combinations of parties.[24] Electoral coalition making of this sort is usually accompanied by the parties and the candidate signing a policy agreement (*seisaku kyotei*), which is supposed to be a basis for ongoing support of the progressive mayor after election. These agreements tend to emphasize the new priorities of pollution control, expansion of social services, combating of urban problems, and greater citizen participation in local decision making.[25] In short, to reiterate a point made above, the new prominence of these issues provides the occasion for increased cooperation among the progressive parties.

Election of a mayor or governor who would be responsive to the environmental and other policy concerns of citizens' movements has become a major goal of the latter. The singularity of the executive post may be a crucial factor in channeling protest activities in this direction: it is easier to effect policy change by the replacement of a single powerful executive than that of a large number of assembly members with more restricted jurisdiction. Despite their nonpartisan character, citizens' movements often gravitate toward support for an independent progressive executive candidate, attracted by his policy priorities and advocacy of broader citizen participation in local government.

Progressive executive candidates in the metropolitan areas have at least two other advantages: first, mass media coverage is generally favorable to the progressives and an asset in helping to offset whatever advantage conservatives enjoy through their greater campaign expenditures; second, progressive organizations—party, union, and other—are heavily concentrated in these areas, whereas conservative organizations are relatively underdeveloped or fragmented. It is not surprising, therefore, that progressive electoral coalitions in the metropolitan areas tend to include the JCP, whose membership is heavily concentrated there. The latter advantage of the progressives can be illustrated by reference to the election of JSP-JCP-backed Motoyama Masao as mayor of Nagoya in 1973. It is estimated that the progressives could deliver leaflets to each household in the city three times a day, while the conservatives lacked the workers to do this more than once a week.[26]

In sum, then, progressive organizations (particularly the CGP and

24. Kokumin jichi nenkan henshū iinkai [People's local self-government education committee], *Kokumin jichi nenkan 1974 nenpan* [The people's local self-government annual 1974] (Tokyo, 1974), pp. 303–06.

25. Chihō jichi sentā [Local self-government center], "Saikin no shichō senkyo ni okeru senkyo kyōtei seisaku kyōtei no jissai" [The state of electoral agreements and policy agreements in recent mayoral elections] (Tokyo, n.d.).

26. *Ekonomisuto* [The economist] (8 May 1973), p. 25.

JCP), the more activist orientations of citizens discontented with environmental and urban problems, and the singularity of the mayoral or gubernatorial post have combined to increase the effectiveness of progressives in urban local politics.

SIGNIFICANCE FOR VIABLE PROGRESSIVE OPPOSITION

Progressive electoral effectiveness in urban local politics is conceivably only a transient phenomenon, the result of a protest movement that cannot be maintained. The evidence presented in this paper suggests the contrary: it is rooted in basic socioeconomic changes that have weakened the bases of conservative dominance, altered the political orientations of city dwellers, and provided the opportunity for progressives to build more enduring structures for political mobilization. Let us consider some of the possible implications of what has been presented here for the development of effective, responsible, and constitutional progressive opposition in Japanese local and national politics.

Electoral effectiveness of progressives in local politics has clearly increased. Progressive mayors continue to increase in number each year and are concentrated in large and important cities. Progressive governors are few in number, but they too are increasing and are concentrated in the more urban prefectures. To examine the effectiveness of progressive mayors in terms of reelection, I compared the December 1970 and July 1974 membership lists of the National Association of Progressive Mayors (NAPM). Total membership increased from 99 to 135; 48 of the new members were from cities not represented on the 1970 list.[27] Of the 99 cities on the 1970 list, 79 had mayoral elections by July 1974. Of these, 12 no longer had mayors in the NAPM by the latter date—3 progressive incumbents and 5 "next generation" progressives had lost, 2 others were reelected but dropped out of the NAPM, and the fate of 2 others could not be determined. Of the 67 cities represented on both lists, 57 had incumbent progressives reelected, and 10 had new-generation progressive mayors. How this 85 percent rate of success in reelection—by incumbent or new generation progressives—over a four-year period compares with that of conservative mayors I am uncertain; but, clearly, progressive mayors are not easily dislodged from office. The strengths of incumbency in Japanese local politics adhere to progressives as well as to conservatives.

A number of limitations on progressive effectiveness in local politics

27. Chihō jichi sentā, *Zenkoku kakushin shichō meibo* [Register of the national association of progressive mayors] (Tokyo, 1970 and 1974).

should be noted. First, conservatives still hold the bulk of mayoral, gubernatorial, and assembly posts. Progressive inroads have been mainly in the larger cities and the more urbanized prefectures. The conservatives' paradise remains relatively undisturbed in large areas of the country. Second, conservative assembly domination extends to many cities and prefectures that have progressive executives—this includes almost one-half of 110 cities with progressive mayors surveyed in July 1973. Even where this is not the case, majority coalitions that support the progressive mayor are not always present. Under these circumstances, progressive mayors have to rely more on an "administrative route" than a "legislative route" to effect change. Third, coalitions backing independent progressive mayoral or gubernatorial candidates are ad hoc ones; they do not in themselves imply a stronger institutional structure for progressive support or policy cooperation beyond the election. These things can be achieved only through ongoing and intensive consultation. Policy agreements and organizational agreements signed during mayoral or gubernatorial elections offer a possible basis on which such cooperation can be built.

A fourth limitation stems from the possibility of a conservative counteroffensive. Three such strategies are already apparent: (1) strengthening conservative local organization; (2) concentrating money and manpower on important elections—like the Tokyo governorship—or where a progressive incumbent is vulnerable; (3) coopting progressive policies or formulating bold new conservative ones. The difficulties faced by the LDP in pursuing the first strategy have been documented elsewhere.[28] The LDP has the financial resources to launch major media campaigns and to hire campaign workers. Bringing these assets to bear in small- and medium-sized cities where progressive organization is underdeveloped can be extremely effective, as was demonstrated in Akita City in 1971.[29] In the metropolitan areas these assets will be of dubious value, as the 1971 Tokyo gubernatorial election proved,[30] unless the LDP backs an executive candidate with strong credentials and public appeal. Co-optation of progressive policies has already begun. Conservative mayors have shown a remarkable capacity for adopting innovations made by progressives in other cities, among them increasing public hearing and public relations mechanisms, granting free medical care to the aged, and

28.   Fukui Haruhiro, *Party in Power: The Japanese Liberal Democrats and Policy Making* (Berkeley, n.d.).

29.   *Asahi Shimbun*, 16 August 1971. Large-scale conservative spending was an important factor in the defeat of an incumbent progressive mayor.

30.   Progressive Governor Minobe was easily reelected despite a far greater expenditure by his conservative opponent. See, for example, *Mainichi Shimbun*, 12 April 1971.

implementing various pollution control measures. The extent to which they can continue to pursue this strategy and still support the LDP in national politics is open to question. Miyazaki Tatsuo, mayor of Kobe, for one, found this impossible. Bold new policies originating with the national party have been few. Ex-prime minister Tanaka Kakuei's plan for remodeling the Japanese archipelago raised serious questions of expanded environmental pollution and ran counter to the growing demand for greater local jurisdiction and input into decisions affecting the living environment.[31]

Have the progressives acted responsibly and constitutionally in their positions as local leaders?[32] A minimal answer would note that no progressive mayor or governor, to my knowledge, has been removed from office by higher authorities or recalled by the people for malfeasance, although the law makes provisions for both. Likewise, immobilism has not plagued assemblies in which the conservatives have lost their absolute majorities; deliberations may be longer, but they are also less perfunctory. Electoral effectiveness has provided the progressives with the opportunity to further develop skills—in bargaining, coalition formation, planning, and the like—necessary for governance. At the same time, they now have the responsibility to formulate appropriate policies to meet concrete problems on a day-to-day basis and not simply in the abstract. Progressive executives appear to have met these challenges with a high degree of success. They have learned how to move the machinery of government—including the national bureaucracy—in order to carry out the normal functions of local government and to bring about policy innovations in certain areas. This should not be surprising when we consider that most of them are not amateurs but have had long experience in local, prefectural, or national administration or politics. In these minimal terms, at least, electoral effectiveness has been accompanied by responsible and constitutional behavior on the part of progressives.

Will progressive local government contribute to the development of a viable progressive opposition in national politics as well? One

31. For a critique of Tanaka's plan by the opposition parties, see Yomiuri Shimbunsha, ed., *Nihon kaizō ron hihan* [Criticism of the plan for remodeling Japanese archipelago] (Tokyo, 1972). For a collection of polls documenting the increased activist orientations of urban residents, see Tōkyō tosei chōsa kai [Tokyo city government research society], *Ryūdōka saru no seijiishiki* [The changing political consciousness of Tokyo citizens] (Tokyo, 1972).

32. This question is dealt with in greater detail in my dissertation cited above. Among the other useful works related to this question are the following: Asukata Ichio, ed., *Jichitai kaikaku no rironteki tenbō* [A theoretical perspective on reform of local government] (Tokyo, 1965); Asukata Ichio, ed., *Jichitai kaikaku no jissenteki tenbō* [A practical view on the reform of local government] (Tokyo, 1971); Narumi Masayasu, *Toshi kaikaku no shisō to hōhō* [The thought and practice of urban reform] (Tokyo, 1972).

possibility is that it will further progressive effectiveness in national politics through the development of local "machines" capable of delivering votes in all types of elections. To what extent this has been done remains to be shown; intensive studies of Kyoto, Yokohama, and other such areas are necessary. Effectiveness of progressives in national politics would clearly be enhanced by electoral cooperation at that level. Current experimentation in coalition formation at the local level, under the careful guidance of national party leaders, may contribute to a greater willingness to cooperate in national politics as well. An image of progressive responsibility in local government may also enhance the progressives' national appeal—this is the hope of the JSP. Accumulation of experience in formulating concrete policies and development of skills in dealing with the national bureaucracy and various interest groups—including business—may help provide a basis for responsible progressive opposition in national politics. Co-operation with conservatives at the local level, a necessity for most progressive executives and assembly members, may help bridge the gap of mutual suspicions that often separates conservatives and progressives in national politics, thereby contributing to constitutional opposition. These speculations should be balanced with a few notes of caution. Insofar as progressive local government provides a basis for strengthening the leadership role of the JCP within the progressive camp, a basic dilemma arises because the JCP is also the party that raises the greatest doubts concerning its commitment to the constitutional system. In addition, the initial successes of progressive local government might be followed by setbacks that could lead to disillusionment with efforts at gradual and piecemeal change.

At this point, however, the experience of progressive local government can be viewed as a positive force for bringing about viable progressive political opposition. At the minimum, progressives in local government have achieved two things: they, together with citizens' movements, have forced the JSP and other parties to put a higher priority on local politics and the type of concerns that have been expressed at that level of government. In addition, they have made out of their positions in local government a base for challenging and forcing changes in conservative policies at both the local and national levels. Innovations in such areas as pollution control, free medical care for the aged, childhood allowances, and planning for achieving at least a minimal standard for urban facilities began with progressive local authorities and later were adopted by conservative local governments and, in some cases, by the national government as well. In other words, the electoral effectiveness of progressives in local politics and their behavior in office have led to a policy competition between progressives and conservatives, which is at the heart of viable opposition.

3

The Problems and Prospects
for Japanese Higher Education

WILLIAM K. CUMMINGS

The politics of compromise envisioned by Thayer and MacDougall finds an apt illustrative case in William Cummings's analysis of the politics of Japanese higher education. Cummings predicts that this area will also experience a new consensus in the coming years.

Throughout the early postwar period Japan had no coherent educational policy because the educational establishment was torn between the left and the right. The lack of a clear policy and the consequent ineffectiveness of reform efforts were significant causes of the student revolt of the late sixties.

The Japanese university now faces three cumulative and overlapping crises: one, the young segment of the population that owes its existence to the baby boom of 1946–48 is now marrying and begetting, creating a second baby-boom wave; two, the shift in the values held by youth (treated also by Cole in his paper) means a new curriculum must be developed that takes into account the new attitudes of the student population; three, the nation's changing industrial structure creates the need for a new kind of occupational training.

The effort to deal with these overlapping crises is complicated by a three-way split among educators. Government-control hawks are pitted against local-control doves; traditional protagonists of a character-building curriculum (for the values of "spirit" [seishin] the paper by Frager and Rohlen should be consulted) are pitted against modernists, who want a curriculum built around pluralistic values and cognitive skills; and a debate over the scale of education has the education ministry pushing a large-scale mass-oriented system, while the finance ministry prefers a less expensive, more cost-effective, small-scale, elitist, and hierarchical system.

Conservatives and modernists, hawks and doves, big-education and little-education forces oppose various reforms for a variety of reasons. Neither side can fully force its views on the other, for those who pay for education are not always those who implement its policy.

Cummings sees an end to stalemate through the formation of a delicate alliance between moderates of the left and right, willing to compromise on issues that can be compromised and to ignore those that cannot. For the next decade he predicts sharply increased educational expenditures as a part of the national budget; a renewed liaison between business and education, with mutually beneficial links being formed for research and training; and the death of university radicalism because of exhaustion, public disaffection for extremes, and the rise of Communist (that is to say, relatively moderate) influence.

The politics of education in the late seventies and eighties, predicts Cummings, will be a politics of detente dominated by a coalition of moderates from left and right who recognize the legitimacy of each other's interests; revolution will have led to reform, and confrontation given place to compromise. Cummings's picture of the political future of education is a specification in detail of some of the implications of the broader-scale canvases painted by Thayer and MacDougall.—L.A.

In June 1971, following four years of investigation, Japan's Central Council for Education submitted to the minister of education the *Basic Guidelines for the Reform of Education*, which is intended to be the master plan for Japanese educational reform over the coming decades.[1] Although the council had been appointed by the minister of education and depended on government staff for research, representatives of various interest groups including the Japan Teachers' Union, labor, and the progressive parties were also consulted and, to a degree, accommodated. Thus, as recommended by the *Guidelines*, the rationalization of educational administration must not be at the expense of academic freedom, for example, nor the upgrading of educational and research quality at the expense of expansion of educational opportunities. Only two other times since the establishment of the modern educational system—during the mid-Taisho period and following World War II—has the Japanese government asked an official council to conduct such a sweeping reexamination of education, and each time there ensued major reforms.[2] The 1971 guidelines are the harbinger of Japan's "Third Educational Revolution," and I will pay careful attention to them as I outline the problems and prospects for Japanese higher education.

The focus will be on higher education because it is the weakest component of the Japanese educational system. Enrollment through the middle school level is compulsory, and by 1970 over 80 percent of middle school graduates of both sexes went on to complete high

1. The council's final report in 1971 was titled *Kongo ni okeru gakko kyōiku no sogo-teki no kakuju seibi no tame no kihon-teki shisaku ni tsuite* [Basic guidelines for the mutual expansion of facilities of education in the future], and was published in English in 1972 by the Ministry of Education as *Basic Guidelines for the Reform of Education* (Tokyo, 1972). See the July 1973 issue of *Minerva* (vol. 11, no. 3) for an abridged version of the report pertaining to higher education.

2. For a discussion of the Japanese reform pattern, see Kazuyuki Kitamura and William K. Cummings, "The 'Big Bang' Theory and Japanese University Reform," *Comparative Educational Review* 16, no. 2 (June 1972): 303—24.

school. According to recent tests coordinated by the International Educational Association, Japanese schools through the high school level provide an exceptionally high standard of education, at least in math and the sciences.[3] Approximately one-third of the well-trained high school graduates go on to an institution of higher education. However, in comparison with the success of the schools, Japanese universities are ineffective—whether in furthering the intellectual development of students, enriching character, or even fulfilling the traditional ivory tower mission of fostering significant scholarship. By the late 1960s public concern for the quality of higher education had come to a head. It is, therefore, not surprising that over half of the council's *Guidelines* is focused on the upper tier of Japan's educational system, the sector clearly destined to experience the most pressure for change over the next decade.

It is impossible accurately to forecast the future for an institutional sector as subordinate to broader economic and political forces as higher education. Following World War II, the American Occupation proposed a massive program of educational reforms only to see many of these reforms rejected for reasons of the changing political atmosphere and competing claims on public revenues. Appended to the council's *Guidelines* was an estimate of the proportion of total government revenues the proposed reforms would consume through 1980 based on assumptions of a 10.5 percent rate of sustained economic growth and an average annual inflation rate of 6 percent. These estimates were intentionally on the high side and, even so, implied only a modest increase in education's share of the national government's projected revenues (from 11 to 13 percent between 1971 and 1980) and an increase in the proportion of national income going to public educational expenditures (from 4.8 percent to 6.3 percent by 1980—compared with 6.4 percent in the United Kingdom and 6.2 percent in the United States in 1968).[4]

Presentation of the report coincided with the most euphoric stage of Japan's miraculous postwar growth experience, and the availability of revenues did not appear to be a problem. Indeed, through fiscal year 1973 the Ministry of Education was able to obtain government funds for several reforms, including a massive subsidy for private universities and seed money for the establishment of several new national universities. Rather, the major effort of the council and

3. See Thornstein Husen, ed., *International Study in Mathematics: A Comparison of Twelve Countries*, vols. 1–2 (New York, 1967); and L. C. Comber and John P. Keeves, *Science Education in Nineteen Countries* (New York, 1973).

4. *Guidelines*, p. 72; and Ministry of Education, *Educational Standards in Japan, 1971* (Tokyo, 1972), p. 140.

subsequently of the government was to develop political support for selected proposals of the *Guidelines*. My discussion will consider the context and events that affected this effort through 1974, with some reflections on the future.

Of course, in 1971 few could have anticipated the difficulties that the Japanese economy and the world economy would experience only three years later resulting from the oil crisis and rampant international inflation. Once again, the availability of resources to support institutional reform has become a critical concern. Reforms that require large amounts of public resources will be difficult to launch. For example, reforms of the primary and secondary school systems are especially costly as they have to be implemented across the nation in several thousand institutions; I expect the government will be forced to slow its reform pace at these levels. In contrast, the higher educational system is smaller in scale and has been receiving top priority in policy discussions over the last several years. A group of influential members of the conservative party recently indicated they would oppose the establishment of any additional national universities for some time, but these men remain supportive of other changes. Many of the reforms outlined in the *Guidelines* are primarily matters of reorganization and do not require large amounts of money for realization; hence they are unlikely to be abandoned even with the new economic situation. In this connection, it is useful to recall that one of the most dynamic periods of institutional reform in Japanese history was during the final years of World War II—a period of economic stagnation not unlike the present. Also, despite the widespread unemployment of intellectuals in the early 1930s in Japan, enrollments at higher educational institutions continued to increase.[5] My view is that political rather than economic conditions will continue to be the primary determinant of the prospect for change in Japanese higher education.

THE ISSUES FOR RESOLUTION

On the eve of Japan's modernization, the new Meiji leaders had expressed their firm commitment to the development of an integrated national educational system, and through World War II the central government played a dominant role in education, exercising virtually monolithic authority over educational programs, standards, resource allocation, and even personnel.

During the Occupation (1945–52) American authorities, regarding the centralized system as incompatible with the democratic ideals

5.   Walter M. Kotschnig, *Unemployment in the Learned Professions* (London, 1937).

being promoted, introduced reforms of the constitution and basic educational laws aimed at decentralizing educational control.[6]

From the beginning there was a gap between the intent of the American reforms and the reality. Initially this gap was narrowest at the primary and secondary levels: schools were made responsible to local elected boards of education—which selected texts, decided on personnel, and planned budgets—and finance came largely from local sources. However, the conservative government placed a high priority on the upgrading of the school system, with the result that the national Ministry of Education gradually increased its support to local school systems and came to exert a considerable influence in curriculum design, the selection of texts, and other areas. Furthermore, in 1956 national legislation was enacted replacing elected school boards with boards appointed by the prefectural governors. It should be noted that the influence of the Ministry of Education has been subject to constant surveillance by the Japan Teachers' Union and other groups, so despite these formal changes in the operation of local schools, the system has not returned to the prewar level of centralization.[7]

In contrast, at the level of higher education the Occupation was unable to legislate many of its intended reforms—especially in the area of control. The Occupation had intended to strip the Ministry of Education of its authority over most public higher educational institutions by making them responsible to prefectural governments or to a university committee similar to England's University Grants Committee. However, the legislation failed to achieve its purpose and the central government continued to maintain responsibility for some seventy-three universities together with a handful of other institutions, while local governments had by 1952 assumed responsibility for only thirty-two universities. The Occupation had also hoped to establish boards of trustees or some other fiduciary body as the ultimate authority in public institutions to mediate public need to the professoriate, but once again legislation failed. Thus public institutions developed a system of government with de facto academic authority vested in a president chosen by university personnel, with the governments providing financial support and staff to administer expenditures. For various reasons the governments have not liked this arrangement and therefore have tended to underfinance public institutions while

6. An informative account of the Occupation period is Kazuo Kawai, *Japan's American Interlude* (Chicago, 1960).

7. For accounts of the conflict at the school level, see Benjamin C. Duke, *Japan's Militant Teachers: A History of the Left-Wing Teachers Movement* (Honolulu, 1973); and Donald R. Thurston, *The Japan Teachers' Union: A Radical Interest Group* (Princeton, 1973).

allowing these institutions considerable autonomy to administer their affairs. On several occasions the central government has expressed its dissatisfaction with the control and performance of public higher educational institutions; by the late 1960s it was drafting reforms.

The Occupation did manage to legislate a private school law, and by 1952 some 116 private universities and 167 private junior colleges had gained official recognition. Within a few years the central government, having decided it would no longer aid private institutions, began to minimize its role in the supervision of their standards, although it has been dismayed by the rapid expansion of this sector and the low quality of education at many private institutions.[8] As will become apparent, the central government's potential influence, based on its command of financial resources and its authority over chartering and standards, is substantial.

The Occupation's unfinished educational revolution left many issues unresolved, and new ones have since emerged. As a background for subsequent analysis, let us briefly list these issues.

Goals. A basic issue is the purpose of higher education—whether it should be oriented to producing a small elite through the university and an army of clerks and technicians trained at lesser institutions or whether it should be more concerned with the development of character and knowledge appropriate to citizenship in a pluralistic society. Somewhat distinct from these goals is the problem of the proper degree of emphasis to be placed on the creation of knowledge and basic research.

Control. Related to purpose is the mechanism for control—should the government and the representatives of various interest groups have a direct role in the government of institutions of higher education or should the professors of universities be entrusted with exclusive authority? This question is particularly acute in the public sector where the governments provide support but have little influence, direct or indirect, in university planning or academic affairs. Also, the governments want professional managers to have more influence so that institutions can be run more efficiently. In contrast with the public sector, the government has for some time denied any interest in influencing private institutions, leaving their control to largely lay boards of trustees. But the excesses accompanying rapid expansion of the private sector have once again revived the concern of government officials and national leaders. Recognizing that private institutions

8. Two discussions of the private sector are William K. Cummings, "The Japanese Private University," *Minerva* 11, no. 3 (July 1973): 348–71; and T. J. Pempel, "The Politics of Enrollment Expansion in Japanese Universities," *Journal of Asian Studies* 33, no. 1 (November 1973): 67–86.

perform public services, educators are now asking how the efforts of the diverse private institutions can be monitored and coordinated.

Scale. Derivative from the purpose is the appropriate scale of higher education and the relative size of the public and private sectors. Insofar as the purpose is to train an elite, the government can restrict its role to the support of a few high quality institutions. If the purpose of educating citizens becomes more widely recognized, the government becomes responsible for providing mass higher education, either by expanding the public sector or subsidizing private institutions.

Quality and Diversification. Similarly, issues of educational standards, the types of fields to be emphasized, and the desirability of recognized specialized institutions follow from the definition of purpose. As legitimate purposes multiply can they all be achieved in a single type of institution? What should be the relative weight between fields that develop technical skills intimately related to economic growth and other fields that foster critical faculties vital for citizenship?

THE STRUCTURE OF THE JAPANESE EDUCATIONAL POLITY

The highest organ in Japan for the discussion of these issues is the national Diet composed of the upper and lower houses.[9] For all but a short interlude, the conservative political parties have held a majority in both houses during the postwar period and hence have had the votes to legislate any bill they proposed.

The principal support bases of the conservative party are rural areas, which have little need for higher education, and the business world, which until recently considered the labor force overeducated. Moreover, business leaders have tended to downplay the significance of university research. Responding especially to the concerns of business, the party's main public goal has been to achieve rapid economic growth, and educational reforms have not been vital in achieving this goal. In the rural areas, the conservatives have concentrated on promoting more equal educational facilities through the secondary level. As a party, therefore, the conservatives have felt little pressure to introduce legislation relating to higher education.

Those within the party who are involved in education can be divided into traditionalists and modernists. The traditionalists were disturbed by the democratizing reforms of the Occupation and now argue for the restoration of moral education and greater supervision of teachers. The modernists approved by and large of the goals of the Occupation's reforms but feel that the administration of educational institutions needs to be rationalized and that various new types of institutions

9. For an informative account of Diet behavior, see Hans H. Baerwald, *Japan's Parliament: An Introduction* (New York, 1974).

should be created. In the early sixties the modernists promoted the establishment of higher technical colleges—the only major post-Occupation innovation in Japanese higher education before 1970. The traditionalists, preponderantly from the rural areas and relatively numerous (especially in prefectural assemblies), hold few important national party positions; the modernists tend to be former government officials who were elected to public office after retirement and now occupy influential party positions. A somewhat different basis of intra-party conflict has arisen in response to student disorders. One group called hawks, which includes many influential party members, has been very critical of the permissive response of university administrators and the Ministry of Education to unruly students and has advocated much sterner measures—through legislation, if necessary. Opposing the hawks has been a small but articulate group of doves who stress the importance of university autonomy and maintain that student protest is a response to more fundamental societal problems; the doves believe that repression by itself is an insufficient response.[10]

Until recently, few university professors have had an open affiliation with the conservative party, although many have expressed support for one or the other of the opposition parties and even assisted in their campaigns. Labor unions, including the Japan Teachers' Union, are affiliated with the progressive parties. Encouraged by the intellectuals, the opposition parties have taken strong stands on the issue of control, insisting on the preservation of university autonomy from government interference. The opposition parties also fought the government's plan in 1958 to establish higher technical colleges, arguing that these schools were designed exclusively for the needs of industry and would make their students into robots. However, there has been surprisingly little reaction from this quarter to other higher educational issues. Despite their leftist ideologies, the opposition parties have not taken stands on the scale of higher education or on questions of cost that affect equality of opportunity. Nor have they expressed much concern with educational standards. Though sympathetic to the liberal goals of many private institutions, the progressives did not advocate government aid until the late 1960s.[11]

The Ministry of Education is the administrative branch of the government responsible for implementing educational policy and,

10.   I know of no systematic analysis of these differences in print. The source for the general-izations in the text is interviews with several politicians and political observers during the summer of 1972 and the fall of 1973. One account of differences within the bureaucratic world is Matsumoto Seiichi, *Gendai kanryoron* [The contemporary bureaucracy] (Tokyo, 1963).

11.   T.J. Pempel outlines the opposition parties' position on higher educational policies in "The Politics of Higher Education in Postwar Japan" (Ph.D. diss., Columbia University, 1973).

for much of this work, relies exclusively on ministerial authority. But there are a few areas where the limits of bureaucratic authority are vague. For example, the constitution "guarantees academic freedom" in institutions of higher education and the Special Law on Public Teachers limits the role of the ministry in personnel decisions. Partly for this reason, the minister of education appoints several regulative and advisory councils to assist him in the implementation of national laws. The University Establishment Council, composed of educators appointed by the minister, makes the principal decisions on recognizing new universities, and the Central Council for Education is occasionally asked to make recommendations on educational policy. As with other ministries, Education's officials through the rank of vice-minister are career public servants, but Education employs a larger proportion of professional staff with experience in educational institutions, and among the line officers are several individuals who once taught in a school or university. Many of the ministry officials are exceptionally able men trained at Japan's leading universities and possessing considerable expertise. Due to the long tenure of the conservative party, the higher officials of Education tend to be on intimate terms with leading conservative politicians. And the conservative party has tended to rely increasingly on the ministry to propose the bills for matters that require legislation. In the past, following retirement, top Education officials have obtained the support of the conservative party and run successfully for elective office.

Responsive to the priorities set by the conservative party, Education has tended in the postwar period to place most of its emphasis on the school system, despite an awareness of mounting problems in the higher educational sector. Indeed, several Education officers have been active in introducing minor pieces of legislation to the conservative party—for example, measures to increase aid to private institutions, to add chairs and faculties in national universities, and to provide more student aid. Until recently, those concerned with higher education have occupied a relatively weak position within the ministry and thus have not been able to mobilize much momentum for their proposals. On the issue of control, many of the officials responsible for higher education have been doves, but their views have often been disputed by officials in other sections of Education and by hawks in the conservative party.

While Education is the principal national bureau for higher education, other bureaus share responsibility in specific areas. The Ministry of Health and Welfare advises the Ministry of Education on training programs and manpower needs in the health sciences and on the operation of university hospitals. A longstanding dispute has been Health's opposition to Education's insistence on the need to expand medical education; only in 1971 did the conservative party rule in favor of Education. Similarly, the ministries of agriculture and justice maintain contact with respect to the activities of agriculture and law faculties respectively, and the foreign ministry supervises certain programs of cultural exchange. The Ministry of International Trade and Industry supports a considerable volume of applied research, as does the independent Science and Technology Agency. Needless to say, the activities of these and other government agencies sometimes overlap and even compete with those under the jurisdiction of Education, generating deeply-felt rivalries.

Standing in a different relation to Education is the prestigious Ministry of Finance, which determines the annual budget for all central government bureaus and agencies. While Finance is apt to be uncritical of ongoing programs, it carefully examines all new budgetary requests in the light of its own criteria, thereby exercising a critical influence on all reforms considered by the central government.[12] Officials in Finance are the elite of the Japanese civil service; invariably top graduates of the University of Tokyo, they see little value in much that goes on in higher education and are firmly opposed to public support for private institutions. Hence, Education officials promoting reforms of higher education find it necessary to mobilize powerful external support when they introduce these reforms as budgetary items to Finance.

A number of other organizations have been formed in an effort to influence policy on higher education. Several, such as the Association of National Universities, the Association of Public Universities, and the Association of Private Universities, came into existence during the Occupation. Since then, others have been established, and the Association of Private Universities has divided into two rival groups— one representing new small colleges and one older established institutions. University presidents and managers are the major participants in these associations, and they have become increasingly skillful in developing practical platforms for political lobbying. Moreover, individual private institutions have invited several conservative politicians to join their boards of trustees. Despite advances in lobbying strategy, a persistent handicap has been the incompatibility of the interests of the respective associations—for example, more public funds for one group means a smaller cut for another.

---

12. John Campbell presents an excellent analysis of the budgetary process in "Japanese Balanced Budgeting" (Paper presented at the Research Conference on Japanese Organization and Decision Making, Maui, Hawaii, January 1973).

Students also became organized in the immediate postwar period, first at individual universities and then in a national coalition called Zengakuren.[13] During the 1960s this national coalition splintered into several rival factions, and it is unlikely that a new coalition will form in the near future. Nevertheless, several of the splinter factions have a sizable membership and continue to mount public demonstrations on university and broader social issues.

In the immediate postwar period the faculty and staff of many universities formed unions, but for a long period the unions were relatively inactive.[14] Then in the late 1960s, as the financial conditions of private universities deteriorated, the unionization movement gained new momentum. The economic crisis of the mid-1970s will provide an additional stimulus for university unions; apart from their impact on intrauniversity decision making, the unions can be expected to begin to assert themselves at the national level for improved salaries and working conditions. Academic staff also belong to numerous societies, but these societies rarely assume a political role.

Outside the university are several other groups with an interest in higher educational affairs. The Japan Teachers' Union has shown increasing interest in higher education. The governors and assemblies of several prefectures have developed educational plans with implications for higher education. And whereas in the 1950s and early 1960s most business leaders avoided university problems, the business community has become increasingly outspoken. Indeed, several groups have released substantial and influential reports that I will note below.

GOVERNMENT POLICY AND CUMULATING STRAINS

While these various actors have some role in determining educational policy, the principal arena for major changes is the national Diet. In the Diet the conservative party has on several occasions considered legislative changes in the system for controlling higher educational institutions, but through the mid-1960s these attempts were successfully resisted by the opposition. Partly because of these failures, the conservative party has not introduced legislation relating to other issues.

13. Donald F. Wheeler provides a penetrating analysis of the organization of the Japanese student movement in "The Japanese Student Movement: Value Politics, Student Politics and the Tokyo University Struggle" (Ph.D. diss., Columbia University, 1974).

14. A helpful account of these developments is Hiroshige Tetsu, *Sengo nihon no kagaku undō* [The scientists' movement in postwar Japan] (Tokyo, 1960). See also Tesuya Kobayashi, "General Education for Scientists and Engineers in the United States of America and Japan" (Ph.D. diss., University of Michigan, 1965), especially the section beginning on p. 116.

Nevertheless, in the postwar period Japanese society experienced dramatic changes in several important areas: the nation expanded its contact with foreign nations; the occupational and industrial structures radically shifted from a late agrarian to a postindustrial composition; the national standard of living increased to a European level; the values of youths became more frivolous; and as a result of the postwar baby boom the age structure of the population became younger.[15] Increasing numbers of youths sought advanced education, and between 1950 and 1970 the proportion of the age cohort attending high schools increased from 30 percent to 80 percent.

The large number of students passing through high schools has resulted in a growing demand for university places, and beginning in the early 1960s, as the high schools began to release the baby-boom generation, this demand accelerated.[16] Between 1952 and 1972 the public sector roughly doubled its capacity for training students; much of this expansion was in engineering, as requested by big business; but it was far from sufficient to satisfy the growing popular demand for higher education.

In contrast with the public sector, private institutions vigorously responded to the demand: as many as 20 private universities and 40 junior colleges were established in some years. By 1970 there were 274 private universities and 426 junior colleges, providing places for 80 percent of all students seeking higher education (in 1952 the private sector's share had been only 62 percent).[17]

Private universities' expansion served to accommodate some of the growing demand, but it was accompanied by many severe problems. The war and the immediate postwar inflation exhausted the endowments of the established private institutions. Because the government refused aid, private institutions were reduced to depending on tuition and other fees for their revenues. Initially these institutions set their tuitions at a level that they deemed sufficient for maintenance. But they had not anticipated several related developments: continuing rapid inflation led to automatic raises in the salaries of staff at national universities, which in turn led to severe pressure from the academic

15. A useful summary of postwar trends is Hiroshi Akutō et al., *Hendōki no nibon shakai* [Changing Japanese Society] (Tokyo, 1972).

16. In 1952 the central government supported 71 universities, and various local governments supported an additional 33. In 1970 the respective numbers were 75 and 34, and governments also supported 53 technical colleges and 65 junior colleges.

17. The principal source for the statistics in this section is Ken Ogata, "Jikenhi hojo no imi suru mono (1) shiritsu daigaku no keiei to kokko hojo" [The importance of personnel expenses (1) Private universities and governmental aid], *Keizai Shirin* 39, no. 3 (July 1971): 1–32; ibid., no. 4 (October 1971): 1–75.

and staff unions of individual private institutions for salary increases. The private universities were forced to respond to these demands for salary raises as well as to pay rising sums for other services such as office supplies and building materials. The unanticipated expenses forced the private universities to seek additional income through combining four different strategies: seeking gifts, obtaining bank loans, raising tuition, and increasing the number of tuition payers relative to fixed facilities. Different institutions placed different weights on the respective strategies, but few developed a winning combination. Despite tuition hikes at roughly twice the rate of inflation, despite expanded enrollments and an increase in the average student-teacher ratio from 35.6 in 1960 to 40.4 in 1969, the debt level of virtually all private institutions increased severely. Several junior colleges went bankrupt and many universities approached this condition. The private sector was simply unable to bear the soaring costs of higher education in an inflationary economy.

In January 1965 the administration of Keio University, one of the leading private institutions, announced an increase in tuition and other fees that would have amounted for entering students to an increase of 230 percent over the previous year. A group of Keio students decided that these staggering increases were unjustified and began a strike that gained widespread support from the student body and continued for fourteen days. Strikes against the tuition hike continued at Keio University for several months until university authorities finally made concessions.[18]

This was the first of a large number of similar incidents at private universities over the next five years. At first there was a high frequency of incidents related to tuition fees; these were followed by complaints about curriculum. In 1967 and early 1968 many complaints were directed against exploitation in the internship system common to the medical training of both public and private institutions. Simultaneously, there was an increase in the number of incidents arising from the students' efforts to gain control over student residences and student unions. By this time the national universities were also having much difficulty with their students. Dissent moved generally from rather immediate practical issues to broader nonacademic and political issues; student disruptions began to focus on the role of government

18. This section is taken from an unpublished paper of mine summarizing material received from the Ministry of Education. On the incidence of revolt and the patterns, also see Ishida Tsuyoshi "Gakusei undō no shakai-teki bunseki" [A sociological analysis of the student movement], *Kyōiku shakaigaku kenkyu* 26 (October 1971): 53–67. In English see "University and Society," *Journal of Social and Political Ideas in Japan* 5, nos. 2–3 (December 1967), entire issue.

and business interests in the activities of universities and on military research, which the student leaders contended was aiding the Americans in Vietnam. As the agitation became more political, violence among students increased and the relations between students and academic and government authorities deteriorated.

THE GOVERNMENT'S RESPONSE

Opinions within the conservative party and the government were divided concerning the best measures to cope with student protest, the hawks favoring use of a repressive approach, doves favoring a restitutive approach respecting the autonomy of universities. When it appeared, initially, that these differences could not be resolved, the conservative regime adopted the stance that the student protest should be left to pursue its natural course. To act would precipitate the usual strong opposition from universities. And any serious approach to the problems might force the government into uncomfortable commitments. Through 1967 the government made few efforts to admonish university authorities and the National Riot Police treated the unruly students with remarkable restraint, but thereafter, in the face of rising public concern, the government began to take a more active role. One of the conservatives' first steps was to ask the ministry's Central Council for Education to examine in depth "fundamental policies and measures for the overall expansion and development of school education in the future."

As the student protest mounted, the general public began to show a surprising degree of sympathy for students. Many blamed the government for the revolt because of its negligence in postwar higher educational policy. Politically this was a dangerous development and, unless delicately handled, could have led to a rapid erosion of conservative support. It is apparent that from mid-1968 the government sought to counteract public sympathy for students and university authorities by allowing them to engage in increasingly irresponsible acts, and by the end of the year public opinion had turned against the students. In June 1968 the minister of education asked the Central Council for Education to suspend other work in order to develop a proposal for the "normalization of university life"; by the following spring the council had prepared its recommendations.

A reshuffling of the cabinet in November 1968 brought the appointment of an exceptionally able politician, Michita Sakata, as the new minister of education, an appointment that was to have important bearing on the conservatives' policies over the next years. Sakata had served in the Diet for over twenty years and had already been minister of welfare. Furthermore, he was relatively young and energetic and took great pains to inform himself on educational affairs. One example of his interest was the party conference he opened in mid-1968 on the university problem, the first such conference opened by a political party in nearly twenty years.[19]

Within the conservative camp Sakata was a dove and a modernist. During the two years of his leadership, steps were taken to insure that these policy orientations would survive, at least concerning higher education. Those in the Ministry of Education unsympathetic to his approach were gradually removed from the ministry's higher education and science division.[20] The result was a young and forward-looking division—at least by normal government standards—that was anxious to implement reforms. A key theme of the moderates was the development of new universities with innovative structures and curriculums appropriate to the new postindustrial and mass higher education era. As early as 1967, reports began appearing in the various education media on the new universities that were being established in England, West Germany, California, and elsewhere. Japanese educators began making tours of the campuses of these universities, and in October 1969 Sakata himself made a brief tour. In July 1969, following a cabinet meeting, Sakata announced that the government would establish twenty new universities over the next fifteen years. A related theme was the invitation to individual universities to develop and carry through their own programs of self-reform.

Several months after Sakata's appointment, the Central Council for Education presented its suggestions on measures to normalize universities as requested by Sakata's predecessor. Sakata and the moderates within the ministry were not anxious to promote a bill that would provoke strong opposition from the progressives and this inclination

19. The conference is published as Jiyū Minshutō Bunkyo Seido Chōsakai, *kokumin no tame no daigaku* [Universities for the Japanese nation] (Tokyo, 1969).

20. In a somewhat unusual development for a Japanese bureaucracy, the Sakata line has persisted even after his departure. Sakata's vice-minister throughout his tenure was Amagi Isao and his head of the Division for Higher Education and Science was Maruyama Matsuo through 1970 and then Kida Hiroshi. When Sato Eisaku resigned as prime minister, Sakata had to resign as minister of education and, according to bureaucratic custom, it was also time for Amagi to resign from public service. However, Amagi was given the customary privilege of suggesting a successor; passing over the most likely candidate, who reportedly had hawkish views, Amagi recommended Maruyama. Maruyama and his successor as vice-minister have kept Kida as head of the Division for Higher Education and Science. This has given Kida the opportunity to implant the moderate philosophy in his division. After Tsukuba, we can expect personnel changes, but no matter what these are the moderate position will remain in the division for several years, Since Sakata there has been a rapid succession of ministers of education, including Inaba Osamu and Okuno Seisuke, who were both reputed hawks. However, their higher educational policy statements have been remarkably temperate, reflecting the council of the moderate bureaucracy.

was reflected in their draft of the Bill of Provisional Measures Concerning University Government presented to the Diet in May 1969.[21] This bill expressed respect for university autonomy and placed the major responsibility for solving disputes in the hands of university administrators.

The next several months involved extraordinarily complex political maneuvering with respect to the bill. When it was presented, the opposition parties (excepting the Democratic Socialist party) indicated their intent to defeat it, but tempering their determination was the subdued conduct of many spokesmen at national universities. Moreover, the presidents of several leading private universities reportedly lobbied in favor of the bill, after having reached an understanding with Sakata that their institutions would be rewarded by government financial aid. Further, public opinion had shifted to deplore the violence employed by activist students. When in August the conservatives forced the bill through the Diet, strikes and other incidents erupted on 140 campuses. However, soon afterward the student rebellions subsided, and the minister of education never found it necessary "to give advice" to the universities or to invoke any of the sterner measures provided for in the law.[22]

Another significant reform was the government's decision to provide subsidies for the operating expenses of private universities. Sakata's skillful lobbying within the conservative party in consort with Shojiro Kawashima, a top party official and also the trustee of a private university, was critical in the success of this legislation. The political leaders of the country were finally convinced that a major cause of the student disturbances lay in the excessive tuitions and low quality of the private sector; they hoped government would alleviate these conditions. In 1970 the Private School Promotion Foundation, governed by appointees of the minister of education, was established for this purpose and beginning in the spring of that year awarded five percent of the cost of academic salaries to most private institutions. If plans proceed according to schedule (as they have through 1974), by the mid-seventies the foundation will be paying nearly half the salaries

21.   The text of the law and many criticisms are found in Suekawa Hiroshi, *daigaku rippō hihan* [Criticism of the University Law] (Kyoto, 1969). Ray Moore's translation of the law was published in *Minerva* 8, no. 4 (October 1970): 581–93.

22.   This account is based on my own review of the material available in newspapers as well as interviews with several of the principals including Sakata. For a different account, see Pempel, "Politics." On the Sakata promise to private university presidents, see Nogami Shuji, "Nihon Shigaku Shinko Zaidanhōō no Mondaiten" [Problems with the Private School Foundation Law], in *Shigaku no kyōikuken to kōhi jōsei* [The Right to Educate of Private Schools and Public Aid], ed. Ozawa Masaru and Nagai Kenichi (Tokyo, 1973), pp. 154–88.

of teachers at private universities in good standing as well as a sizable proportion of the salaries of other staff. The system of tying the foundation to personnel expenses serves as a partial buffer against inflation. Already the overall financial situation at private institutions is improving.[23] In the years to come the foundation will develop new programs of financial aid and supervision in order to improve the standards of the private sector.

THE CENTRAL COUNCIL FOR EDUCATION AND ITS REPORT

The two laws concerning university government and subsidies contributed considerably to the defusing of student protest. In that these laws reflected the philosophy of moderates in the conservative party and the Ministry of Education, they served to elevate the credibility of this group. In June 1971 the Central Council for Education released the *Basic Guidelines for the Reform of Education* as its final report to the minister of education.

The Council's report ranged over a wide array of problems, and while its tone was moderate in keeping with the new Sakata line, the overall thrust predictably supported the interests of the conservative party. The report was sharply criticized by the mass media and progressive intellectuals.[24] Even within the government the Ministry of Finance publicly expressed reservations with respect to the report's extravagant fiscal implications. Nevertheless, the moderates within the Ministry of Education have been working to achieve its realization and have already announced such concrete plans as internal reform of the ministry's organization, the establishment of several new universities, the reform of the entrance exam system, and the liberalization of university curriculums. Success in achieving these reforms will elevate the status of the Ministry of Education in the bureaucratic hierarchy. Moreover, those ministry officials who can demonstrate skill in promoting reforms will benefit in terms of public recognition and chances for postbureaucratic careers.

THE CONSERVATIVE PARTY'S CHANGING SITUATION

Within the framework of continuing conservative rule for at least another decade important changes are occurring in both the conservative and progressive camps that are favorable to the moderate reform

23. Some evidence on the improvements is presented in Ken Ogata, "shiritsu daigaku kyoshokuin no nenkin Jotai: 1972 nendo zemi Chōsa Kara" [The annual incomes of private university staff: Based on a survey by a seminar], *Keizai Shirin* 41, no. 2 (April 1973): 1–36.

24. One survey of these criticisms is found in Yokohama Kokuritsu Daigaku Gendai Kyōiku Kenkyusho, *Chukyōshin to kyōiku kaikaku* [The Central Council for Education and educational reform] (Tokyo, 1971).

plan. During much of the postwar period, business leaders have taken
an essentially apathetic orientation to public education, arguing that
it overeducated youths that should be working. Since the mid-sixties,
however, they have begun to think of a new economic structure specializ-
ing in knowledge-intensive industries and engaging more extensively
in international trade and capital investment—changes symbolized
by the catch phrases "information society" and "internationalism."
To accomplish both of these changes business recognizes that it will
need better qualified university graduates as well as more original
research. Business also recognizes that these are expensive needs:
whereas through the sixties business-supported laboratories were able
to adapt foreign technology for their purposes, step-level increases in
expenditures will be needed to support the basic research required for
new innovations. In the past, business firms were willing to hire inade-
quately trained university graduates and provide them with advanced
education at company expense, feeling that the investment would
yield returns over the employee's career. The recent increased turnover rate among employees with rare technical skills has forced business
leaders to question the wisdom of their heavy investments in in-service
training. Thus many business leaders have begun to take a more positive attitude toward educational reform by the public sector, and
several business groups have outlined their views in lengthy reports.[25]

Perhaps the most widely circulated statement from the business
world is *Human Development in the New Industrial Society*, released in
1972 by the Japan Economic Research Council.[26] The presidents of
major corporations joined with scholars and government officials in
the committees producing this statement, which advocates a shift
from the conformity of the past to a new respect for the diversity of
human values, the encouragement of creativity rather than uniformity
in the schools, the development of a more "international" consciousness and of the various capacities required by the "information society."
Because many of these themes had been promoted by progressive
educators since early in the postwar period, this statement can be
viewed as a conciliatory move on the part of big business.

During the fifties business firms developed a large number of their
own research laboratories, and following this the government began
to level off its support of university research (excepting that conducted
in university-affiliated research institutes). Furthermore, beginning

25. Kitamura Kazuyuki provides a summary of these reform reports in "Daigaku kaikaku
no dōkō ni kan-suru yobi chōsa: 1968–70" [Analytical survey of reform plans in Japanese
higher education: 1968–70], *Referensu* 245 (June 1971): 85–121. See also Michiya Shimbori
and Kazuyuki Kitamura, *Higher Education and the Student Problem in Japan* (Tokyo, 1972).

26. Nihon Keizai Chōsakai Kyogikai, *Atarashii sangyō shakai ni okeru ningen keisei* [Human
development in the new industrial society] (Tokyo, 1972).

in the mid-sixties student radicals sharply escalated their criticism of university-industry cooperation, making it increasingly difficult for university professors to engage in joint research efforts. These developments led some to speculate that Japan would intentionally shift the locus of higher research from the universities to government and industrial laboratories.

Many university leaders regretted these developments and campaigned for research funds to universities, insisting that universities can make major contributions to the nation's basic research effort. Interestingly, a recent poll suggests that over three-fourths of the presidents of major universities feel that universities and business should cooperate in research.[27]

The government's tendency to neglect university research was not criticized by business groups, but a recent survey suggests that business leaders have a much more positive attitude toward university research than is commonly assumed—even the government was surprised by the survey's results.[28] This national survey of 697 corporations conducted by the Tokyo Chamber of Commerce in 1972 indicates that the majority of large corporations, especially those in manufacturing, have some cooperative relation with a university group and that they find these relations fruitful and intend to maintain and even expand them. From the report, it is apparent that business's development of its own research facilities has resulted, if anything, in an increased demand for cooperation with university groups.

THE POLITICAL PRESSURE FOR MODERATION

Members of the conservative party are aware of the changed perspective of their major support group. At the same time, many of the younger conservatives are aware of a potential crisis for their party unless they can expand their support base. Three trends in voting behavior have been particularly disturbing: the declining number of voters in the traditional rural strongholds, the increasing frequency of success of progressive candidates in urban elections, and the decreasing defection of youths from politics in general. These trends, if not coped with, might result in the conservative party's fall from power (or force it into a coalition government) by 1980.

In 1972 Eisaku Sato retired as prime minister, and following a vigorously contested party election the young and innovative Tanaka Kakuei was chosen over Sato's preferred successor, Takeo Fukuda,

---

27. Tokyo Shoko Kaigisho, "Sangaku kyōdo" [University industry cooperation], serialized in issues 82, 83, and 84 of *Daigaku kōhō*, a newspaper concerning university affairs. The survey of university presidents is reported in issue 84, 21 June 1973, pp. 5–6.

28. Ibid., issues 82–83.

to lead the party and head the government. The choice of Tanaka signaled the party's desire for changes that would improve its public image and counter the depressing election trends.

Almost as soon as he became prime minister, Tanaka was beset by a series of debilitating economic problems, and it became doubtful that he could provide the needed new image. Despite vigorous campaigns, the conservatives were barely able to hold their own in the general elections of that year. In late 1974 Tanaka was charged with misusing his office for private gain and chose to resign. Several faction leaders vied for selection as his replacement, but finally, in a surprising move, the Liberal Democrats chose Miki Takeo, perhaps the most moderate of the contenders. Immediately Miki initiated several bold steps designed to appeal to the general public, including the appointment of two nonpoliticians to his cabinet. One of these, Nagai Michio, became the new minister of education, an action which earned the approval of the Japan Teachers' Union. It is likely that the conservative party will attempt to retain a moderate image.

Changes in the social concerns and the voting patterns of the general public are contributing to pressure for moderation in parliamentary behavior. At a general level, the public is becoming disaffected from the extremist politics of both the right and the left. Centrist issues of social welfare, leisure, prices, and pollution have been rising in importance. Neither of the political camps has had the foresight really to plan for these shifts in public concern, and thus both have been placed on the defensive. Seemingly the conservatives would be most affected in that their past policies of rapid economic growth have given rise to inflation, pollution, and other of these vanguard issues. However, within the opposition, the socialists' unimaginative campaigns emphasizing such abstract issues of modest public concern as Okinawa and relations with China have cost them votes, particularly among the young.

Thus in the national elections of the late sixties and early seventies, both major parties lost votes to the new Clean Government party (CGP) and to the resurgent Japanese Communist party (JCP), though it is the Japanese Socialist party (JSP) that has suffered the most. The left faction of the JSP has been responsible for campaign strategy in these recent elections. Taking into account the rise of the moderate CGP and the "new" JCP, which has campaigned much like a moderate left-of-center European democratic socialist party, it can be maintained that the center of gravity of the progressive camp has shifted toward the center.[29] In 1972 the progressive parties formed a coalition for

29.   For a clever account of the rise of the Communists, see Asahi Shinbunsha, ed., *Nihon kyōsantō* [The Japanese Communist Party] (Tokyo, 1973).

the purpose of coordinating election and Diet strategies to overthrow the conservative regime. Whereas several independent progressive parties tended to aid the conservatives in the elections, the new coalition poses a serious threat. The likelihood of a conservative demise is small. But the increasing possibility of a near defeat or the necessity to enter into a coalition with a progressive party has forced the conservatives to pay more attention to opposition views, including those on education.

MODERATION IN THE EDUCATIONAL WORLD

The collapse of the student revolt triggered a shift toward moderation in the educational world. Within universities there was a definite tendency to choose presidents with leftist political convictions in the late sixties, but since then many universities have tended to choose men with conservative reputations for their top offices, the most notable example being the University of Tokyo's choice of Kentaro Hayashi for president in 1973. The pressure of the student revolt had led to the selection of leftists, and the relief of the pressure induced a reverse trend. Given the past history of cycles in the momentum of the student movement, we can predict that universities will be free of substantial radical student pressure for the foreseeable future.

The general public's respect for the university's righteous defense of university autonomy declined as the student revolt became more violent, and yet university authorities lacked the strength to respond. The universities felt increasing pressure to invite police onto their campuses, especially after the passage of the University Normalization Law. Private universities facing bankruptcy were forced virtually to beg for government aid. The police's restrained handling of the campus interventions and the government's granting of aid to private institutions was appreciated by many university educators, especially those in administrative positions. These people have since that time shown a new willingness to participate in dialogue with the government. For example, in 1972 the heads of all the major university, junior college, and high school associations joined with government officials and business leaders in a Higher Education Round Table Conference sponsored by the Ministry of Education. This conference produced a joint report with concrete proposals concerning the future size of Japanese higher education. A second conference was begun in 1973. Another important example of the government-university detente was the willingness of three well-known leftist intellectuals to participate as members of the recent Central Council for Education.

It is possible that these conciliatory actions by educational leaders do not reflect real shifts in the attitudes of the publics they represent, at least at the university level. One's view on this issue depends on his interpretation of several recent trends in university politics: the tendency of *Minsei* (pro-Communist party) to regain control of most of the self-government associations at national universities, the increase in support for the Communist party by university intellectuals at the expense of both Democratic Socialists and the left wing of the Socialist party, and the resurgence of unionism at many private institutions. Using the early sixties as a baseline, these trends suggest a shift toward campus radicalism, but using 1968 as a base they mark a drift toward moderation.

At another level, in 1970 the minister of education invited the head of the Japan Teachers' Union to consult on educational problems for the first time in nearly ten years, and they have since held meetings at least once a year.[30] The ministry has begun a new campaign within the government substantially to raise teachers' salaries and made headway in 1973. In addition, the government promised in August 1973 to reconsider its position of denying teachers and other public employees the right to strike.

As for higher education, two examples of moderation at the national level are the legislative processes leading to the approval of Tsukuba University and the handling of the University Normalization Law.[31] The Tsukuba University story goes back over ten years to the time that Tokyo Education University expressed an interest in moving to a new campus. During the late sixties a faction within the university gained control of the university senate and proposed a new plan for university government that would substantially enhance the Ministry of Education's influence on academic affairs. The ministry expressed great enthusiasm for the new plan and began to work with the faction leaders in realizing it. However, both the ministry and the university intentionally ignored the opposition of a sizable minority of professors at the university. Subsequently this minority mobilized the support of many progressive intellectuals and the progressive parties in opposition to the Tsukuba vision. Such opposition did not deter the government from enacting a law establishing Tsukuba University, though the government did make numerous concessions to the opposition in the course of passing the law.

In mid-1974 the Law of Provisional Measures Concerning University Government, legislated in 1969, was due to expire, and the government considered several alternatives: to introduce a stronger

30. Thurston, *Japan Teachers' Union*, p. 56 and following, argues that the Japan Teachers' Union has consistently moderated its approach to the government since Sadamitsu Miyanohara became president.

31. For a detailed account of the Tsukuba University affair, see my article "The Conservatives Reform Higher Education," *Japan Interpreter*, Winter 1974, pp. 421–31.

law that would stand permanently, to renew the old law, or simply to drop it. The hawks preferred the first course whereas the progressive parties advised the government to abandon the legislation. Ultimately the government followed the middle course.

THE FUTURE OF JAPANESE HIGHER EDUCATION

Over the past several years the conservatives have passed three major bills that increase government influence in universities: the Law of Provisional Measures Concerning University Government, the Private School Promotion Foundation Law, and the Tsukuba University Law. These legislative successes have encouraged the conservatives, and they will attempt additional reforms in the near future, some through legislation and others through administrative measures and persuasion.

There will be reactions and efforts by educators of both the right and left. Progressive educators, at least in public, will be critical of government reform plans, but in comparison with past negativism the progressives will propose alternatives. The Japan Teachers' Union has published a four-volume statement of its views on educational reform and each of the opposition parties now includes a detailed statement on educational change in policy statements.[32] Also, more leftists are agreeing to participate in government committees.

Private universities have gained new prominence in the educational system with the government's establishment of the Private School Promotion Foundation, and we can expect the private institutions to exert continuing pressure for favorable treatment. They will oppose measures that threaten the viability of existing private institutions. While many private institutions still have serious financial problems, others are beginning to enjoy renewed fiscal strength and are talking more boldly of innovation. Within the limits of their financial capacity the private institutions will be seeking ways to expand their services.

Given the detente in the politics of education and the concerns that are uppermost in the minds of both educators and the government, it seems possible to make several broad predictions about the future of Japanese higher education.

The purpose of higher education. Possibly the most significant development of the past decade has been the establishment of a normative climate that approves multiple goals for higher educational institutions.

32. These were published by Keiso Shobo in 1972 with the following titles: (1) *Nihon no kyōiku dō aru beki ka?* [What should be done with Japanese education?]; (2) *Kyōiku kaikaku no genri o kangaeru* [Thinking about the fundamental principles of education]; (3) *Nihon no kyōiku o dō aratameru beki ka?* [What should be changed in Japanese education?]; and (4) *Hoiku ikkenka no Genri* [Integrating the process of child development].

Prior to the student revolt, it was possible for politicians and powerful bureaucrats to argue for an elitist university combined with vocational colleges and to downgrade all other institutional types. Today the same people would be hesitant to defend this narrow vision. Virtually all the major reports on higher education, whether written by business groups or radical educators, recognize the need for higher educational institutions that provide the knowledge essential for the education of thoughtful citizens. Additionally, these reports endorse higher education as a setting for the development of individuality and an understanding of culture. Included in these new concepts is the acceptance of lifelong or recurrent education. The shift toward a pluralistic purpose for higher education is irreversible and is having subtle effects on various concrete reforms.

The control of higher education. The most controversial issue of the future, as of the past, will be the control of higher education. The recent laws passed by the Diet enhance the capacity for government influence. The government on the basis of its new relations with private schools has exerted influence to upgrade standards. The Private Universities Council, for example, decided in 1972 to extend its period of review for new university applications from one to two years and has officially expressed its reluctance to recognize additional private medical universities. As government aid to private schools increases, its influence on this sector will correspondingly grow.

The Tsukuba University Law, in recognizing an advisory council to the university composed of minister of education appointees, provides the government with a direct route for influencing this university; moreover, with the changes in the university establishment laws the government can now add advisory councils to other national universities. The government has said it will not add advisory councils to existing national universities, but it will most probably attempt to install them in any new university it establishes.

The inclusion of students in university government has been one of the most disputed issues over the years. During the heat of the student revolt, the ministry opposed student participation and thus did not acknowledge the choices for president of several universities where students played a role in elections. Since the revolt, the government's position has apparently relaxed. Kobe University's choice of a president, made with student participation in the first ballot, was approved by the ministry. And the ministry has not objected to a system of bicameral government developed at Miyagi Education University even though students participate in preliminary decision making on most university matters.

Enrollment in higher education. In 1969 some 500,000 high school youths plus a possible 200,000 *rōnin* (literally, "masterless samurai"; here, would-be scholar who failed the examination the first time around) competed for 320,000 openings in institutions of higher education. The youths who succeeded in this competition were approximately one-fourth of this cohort and roughly one-half of that part of the cohort who were interested in higher education. Taking account of the number of future graduates from high school (roughly stable at 1.4 million annually over the seventies) and the proportion who are likely to be interested in higher education, various groups have estimated the demand for higher education in 1980 as ranging from 484,000 to 778,000 or from 35 percent to 56 percent of the 1980 class of high school graduates. In that by 1980 high schools will accommodate nearly 95 percent of the age cohort, these proportions essentially stand for the age cohorts. Higher education will not expand to accommodate all of these aspirants to higher education, but it may go a good part of the distance. Several estimates, including a recent one by the Higher Education Round Table Conference, predict that roughly 40 to 50 percent of high school graduates will attend some higher educational institution in 1980.[33] This would mean approximately 700,000 entering students in 1980 and a total enrollment of 2.3 million. Of the various levels of students, there is likely to be the highest rate of growth for graduate students, especially in the master's course. By 1980 an estimated 10 percent of all undergraduates will be going on for some graduate training.[34]

Distribution by fields. Tsukuba University and the University of the Air are the first of several new universities that the government has been planning for some time. The government is interested in increasing the proportion of all higher educational students studying practical subjects such as engineering, science, medicine, and nursing. To achieve expansion in the first two subjects, the government will have to rely to a considerable degree on incentives to private institutions because national universities are already heavily weighted with these disciplines. At the same time the government has already decided to establish one new science-engineering university to provide an opportunity for further training to graduates of higher technical colleges and to technicians who have been working in organizations and want refresher courses or advanced training.

33. For one summary of various estimates, see Amano Ikuo, "Kongo no daigaku shingaku-shasu no doko" [The trend in university entrance], *Nihon rikurūto sentā kyōiku kikan kohobo* [Reports of education from the Japan Recruit Center], June 1972.

34. For evidence on the trend, see Tomoda Yasumasa, "Tokei-teki ni mita daigakuin no mondai" [A statistical review of graduate education], *I.D.E.*, no 151 (September 1974), pp. 20–26.

In the case of medicine, several recent scandals at newly established private medical universities have led the government virtually to forbid any expansion of the private effort. One exception is Jichi Ika Daigaku, a "private" university established with funds from some ten prefectural governments and a government grant to train physicians for the participating prefectures.[35] Beyond this, the government has committed itself to establish several new national medical faculties and universities over the next few years and by 1980 there will be a nationally supported medical faculty in nearly every prefecture.

The expansion of teacher training is a policy of high priority for the government, but efforts in this area will meet with strong resistance. The government wishes to create teacher-training schools under its more immediate control in an effort to weed out radical educators; in addition, the government wishes to upgrade the qualifications of those who teach mainly at the primary level and those who administer schools. At present, most teacher's certificates are awarded to graduates of the ordinary faculties of four-year colleges; for many private universities their ability to "train" teachers is one of their few attractions. To the extent that the government raises the standards for teaching or creates new teacher-training schools, these private schools will suffer. In 1973 the Ministry of Education announced its intent to establish a new physical education teacher training university. But, given the strengths of the private sector and the current economic situation, it is doubtful that the government will be able to establish additional teacher-training schools for some time.

The diversification of higher educational institutions. A high priority reform of the Central Council for Education's *Guidelines* was the formal diversification of higher educational institutions.[36] In fact there is already considerable formal diversification with junior colleges, higher technical schools, universities, and graduate schools; and within each of these types there is much informal diversity. The council's proposal intended to institutionalize this informal diversity by establishing curricular and other requirements, as was done in the prewar period. One effect of diversification would be to make it more difficult for a poorly equipped institution to establish a graduate school. Diversification might induce some of the weaker institutions to open up adult education programs and cater to the supposedly growing demand for lifelong education.

The intent of the government's diversification proposal has been

35. A discussion of this university can be found in Kawakami Takeshi, *Gendai no iryō mondai* [Contemporary problems of medical care] (Tokyo, 1972), especially pp. 238–41.

36. See Tetsuya Kobayashi, "Changing Policies in Higher Education—The Japanese Case," *World Yearbook of Education 1971–72* (London, 1971).

vague, and many private institutions object to it. Four-year institutions see it as a potential threat to their right to train teachers. Junior colleges worry that they may begin to experience competition from existing four-year colleges if these start awarding three-year bachelor's degrees. On the other hand, the leading private universities have little to lose. In 1974 the government took the first step toward diversification in announcing its draft of new laws for university standards. The proposed standards are not a major departure from the present laws.

Distribution in public and private institutions. In 1970 institutions of higher education were accommodating 1.65 million youths. The higher educational system will only have to expand 35 percent over the next decade to meet the 1980 target of 2.3 million, yet over the sixties it expanded 136 percent or at an average annual rate in excess of 14 percent. Many private institutions are still counting on a program of expansion in order to solve their fiscal problems. Given that public institutions will also be expanding and charging less tuition (in 1980 probably one-third of the average tuition at private institutions, though possibly the government will raise public university tuitions to about one-half), many private institutions are going to experience difficulty in recruiting the students to fill their new buildings. The relative ability of public and private institutions to survive in an inflationary slow-growth economy is a topic deserving careful research; it is possible that public institutions may suffer restricted revenues due to legislative curbs on public expenditures, while good private institutions may be able continually to raise fees in pace with inflation. Yet enrollments at lesser private institutions will most probably slacken, and I expect that several private institutions may go bankrupt. Given the perilous future of private higher education, leaders of this sector will be exerting strong pressure to restrain expansion of the public sector, and at most it will increase from the current 20 percent to 30 percent of all student places in higher education in 1980.

Dispersion of higher education. Another priority item will be to increase the number of institutions and students in the provinces. In mid-1973 the Ministry of Education established a second Higher Education Round Table Conference to discuss this problem. No one has a strong basis for opposing dispersion, as long as he is not the one to be dispersed. But with few new institutions being established, it will be difficult to reduce the present high concentration of institutions in urban areas.

Traditionally the peripheral areas have not been attractive for scholars, but improved transportation and the broader trends of regional equalization will reduce the disadvantages of the periphery. The Central Council for Education proposed that the universities in each of Japan's major regions reorganize themselves into university networks sharing facilities and exchanging scholars and students. Some progress may be made along these lines, especially in Kyushu or Hokkaido where rivalries between universities are not so strong.

Internationalization. The concept of internationalization is getting much lip service, but is extremely difficult to define and develop operational programs around it. There will be extensions of such existing programs as sending Japanese students and teachers overseas and providing improved scholarships for foreign students. Also, major government subsidies will be made to language research centers and for the construction of language laboratories on university campuses. But these reforms will not lead overnight to a more cosmopolitan Japanese citizenry.

Entrance exams. Important progress toward reform of the entrance exam system has already been made, and the National Universities Association is now working on a unified entrance exam that it plans to initiate on a trial basis in 1976. Initially this exam will supplement the exams given by individual universities, though eventually some of the national universities will rely almost wholly on the results from this exam and high school records in deciding admissions. Many private institutions have already begun to admit students based on criteria other than their entrance exam performance.[37]

Scholarships. A considerable expansion of the scholarship program for graduate students will occur, but there may be little change in the amount of government funds available for undergraduates. On the other hand, the guaranteed loan program through banks will expand.

Research organization. The academic chair and academic cliques were the target of many reform reports of the sixties. To some degree, cliques are naturally breaking down as the system expands and competition increases.[38] The academic chair will continue as a formal unit in most existing national universities, but increasingly formal organization will be based on research interests of those employed at these universities. Those who hold academic chairs will lose many of their prerogatives. New universities established by the Ministry of Education are unlikely to have chairs but will imitate the research committee and project principles introduced by the Tsukuba University Law.

Research funds. In the early sixties it appeared that the government

37. For a summary of some of these developments, see Ulrich Teichler, "Some Aspects of Higher Education in Japan," *Kokusai Bunka Shinkokai Bulletin on Japanese Culture,* no. 114 (June–July 1972): 1–20.

38. A discussion of the chair's transformation is found in William K. Cummings, "The Changing Academic Marketplace and University Reform in Japan" (Ph.D. diss., Harvard University, 1972), published in Japanese as *Nihon no daigaku kyōju* [The Japanese university professor] (Tokyo, 1972).

was developing separate policies for higher education and for higher research. The former was to be conducted by the universities whereas the latter was to occur largely in government and business research laboratories. Indeed, since the mid-sixties there have been only marginal increases in the research funds distributed to university faculties (though university-affiliated research laboratories have received substantial increases) and in general the government has tightened its control over the process of distribution. However, many of the major corporations still look to the universities for guidance in their research efforts. While the government does not feel that the organization of existing universities is conducive to outstanding research, it is enthusiastic about new proposals for organization such as those embodied in the Tsukuba University vision. As new experiments in research organization prove themselves, the government may substantially increase its support of university research.

Japan entered the postwar period offering higher education to most, though not all, of its citizens, whereas many Western nations still based their higher education on the principle of elitism. In the quarter century since then, the higher educational systems of all advanced societies have rapidly expanded. However, although in the West most of this expansion was in public institutions or promoted by public funds, in Japan it was achieved by private effort.

One reason for the rapid expansion of the private sector was simply that there was a demand for higher education that the government was not prepared to satisfy. For much of the postwar period, the government's educational funds have been tied up in constructing and upgrading secondary education. The government's major interest in higher education apart from the institutions it already supported was to expand science and engineering faculties to facilitate rapid economic growth. To expand in other fields risked the possibility of providing salaries for progressive intellectuals who would indoctrinate youths against the government. The system as inherited from the prewar period was sufficiently large to perform its traditional function of selecting an elite. While all of these reasons lay behind the government's tendency to neglect higher education, it should also be noted that some within the conservative camp criticized this policy.

Despite government neglect, private institutions might not have exerted such vigorous efforts to expand under different economic conditions. But due to wartime damage and the inflationary economy that raised educational costs beyond the darkest expectations, private universities found that expansion at the expense of educational standards was one of their few hopes for survival. Japan is one of the first nations to experience the pressure of unions of college professors and to discover that these unions are prepared to bankrupt their employers in the quest for a "fair income."

This style of expansion was the major precipitant of the student revolt of the late sixties. As the revolt escalated, it took up many issues totally unrelated to educational conditions and the financing of higher education. But in the opinion of Michio Nagai, a shrewd observer of university affairs, university disorganization was the most significant factor in the Japanese student revolt whereas in the United States and elsewhere international problems and the broad conditions of societal alienation were more significant.[39] The student revolt stimulated a remarkable educational reform fever in Japan. At the same time, it played a not insignificant role in promoting a moderation of the relations between the various actors in the educational world. The politics of Japanese education was by no means neutralized, but at least behind the public confrontation the conservatives and progressives began to recognize each other's interests. Furthermore, within the conservative camp a relatively stable coalition of moderate politicians and bureaucrats developed that began promoting a reform program, and this moderate coalition has received the support of many educators. The most recent expression of this trend was the appointment of Michio Nagai as minister of education.

Two immediate outcomes of this new situation were the Law of Provisional Measures for University Control and the Private School Foundation Law. Since the passage of these laws, the government reform coalition has promoted several new universities including the University of the Air and, most recently, Tsukuba University. I can only guess at the future of Japanese higher education. In making my guesses I have attempted to take account of the respective attitudes and interests of the principal participants. Over the coming years Japanese higher education is unlikely to experience drastic changes, but it will see many innovations. For this reason Japanese higher education is likely to be one of the more interesting systems to watch. The broad contours will not be altered, but desirable modifications in detail may well be effected.

My optimism is predicated on an essentially stable political and economic future. The recent shocks to the Japanese economy related to the inflation of oil prices have led some to predict major economic and political difficulties for Japan over the next several years, but Japan's leaders are exerting vigorous efforts to buffer the impact of world economic instability. In the measure that their effort is successful,

39.   Michio Nagai, *Higher Education in Japan* (Tokyo, 1971).

my predictions are meaningful. If that effort fails—and I doubt this prospect—it will be difficult to make any predictions for Japan. The most interesting prospect relating to future developments is for progressive forces to increase their influence in policy making; to the extent that they succeed, Japanese higher education will accelerate its movement toward becoming a large pluralistic educational system.

4

Japanese Growth in Alternative
1980 World Economic Environments

HUGH PATRICK

The second section of our overview of the trends shaping the future of Japanese society deals with economic factors. Hugh Patrick's paper traces the general framework of the possibilities through a consideration of the economic growth rate and its relationship to the international environment.

Patrick forecasts a Japanese growth rate over the next decade averaging between 6 and 9 percent per annum: less than in the past, but more still than the growth rate of the European Community or the United States. This lowered rate of growth will be due to five principal factors. First, a new emphasis on social welfare and on "quality of life" goals will mean that industry will have less capital to invest as government has more, and capital output ratios on the average will be higher. Second, productivity will decrease, as investment moves increasingly into housing and out of manufacturing into the service sector of the economy, as the pool of new technology for exploitation dries up, and as the share of investment in GNP declines, providing less capital per worker. Third, inflation will become increasingly threatening as government is tempted to try to increase expenditures without raising taxes, as workers try to maintain wage raises in the face of sluggish productivity, and as world shortages of energy and food drive up the costs of imports faster than the rise in the costs of Japanese exports. As inflation rises, growth will have to be slowed to keep it within bounds. Fourth, the rate of personal and corporate savings will decline as the growth of incomes is slowed, as social benefits increase, as the threat of inflation increases and the implications of a negative rate of real return on savings are seen more clearly, and as profit margins are squeezed; with the drop in savings the investment rate will drop also. Fifth, increasing dissatisfaction in the labor force, with a decline in motivation and an increase in alienation and strife, will slow productivity increases and thus the economic growth rate.

This revision of the paper presented in February 1973 to the Yale Research Seminar "Japan in 1980" focuses on the international environment. The portion of the initial draft dealing with alternative scenarios of domestic factors affecting Japan's growth performance has been eliminated. The oil scenario is fundamentally as it appeared in the original presentation; the oil crisis and subsequent events have required some updating but no change in the main thrust of the argument. My thanks for suggestions go to participants in the seminar, particularly Larry Meissner.

A slower Japanese growth rate, however, will not be a cloud lacking a silver lining. Slower rates of growth will mean less economic friction between Japan and the rest of the world. This relationship is considered in the form of three scenarios for the international environment: cooperation, conflict, and/or competition for scarce resources.

The first scenario, cooperation, is overwhelmingly the most desirable for Japan because of the nation's economic goals: world liquidity, diversified markets and sources of supply, adequate supplies of energy and food, and free trade. This is also the best possibility for world consumers in general. Patrick's prediction is cautiously optimistic. He reckons that technological innovation and diplomatic good sense will make cooperation more probable and competition and conflict less probable. But he warns that, while the external threats to a healthy Japanese economy can be dealt with, the internal problem may be more difficult to solve. His analysis points forward to and sets the scene for Long's chapter on technology and security in the external environment and Cole's and Azumi and McMillan's papers on the labor force as the key factor in the internal environment.—L.A.

My purpose here is to consider the implications of alternative world economic environments for the economic growth performance of Japan in 1980 and for Japan's economic relations with the rest of the world. Three such environments—cooperation, conflict, and resource-short—have been chosen for discussion and are described below. The year 1980, proxy for the period of the early 1980s, is assumed to be an economically "normal" year of average growth and average change in other major economic variables.

The importance of the rest of the world for Japan's economy is so obvious as to be a truism, one that should never be allowed to recede in any economic analysis. This derives from three basic facts: poorly endowed by nature, Japan must import virtually all major natural resources in order to maintain and increase industrial production; as a densely populated nation Japan has only one route to high standards of living, through industrialization; Japan like other major industrial nations increases labor productivity by significant importation of foreign technology and know-how in addition to reliance on domestic research and development (R & D) efforts. Yet despite these facts, Japan's imports and exports each have comprised a relatively low proportion (about 10 percent) of GNP—higher than the United States but less than Western countries. The main impetus to growth is domestic.

The Recent Past

Japan benefited during the 1950s and 1960s from an increasingly liberal world economic environment in which trade and capital flows expanded vigorously due both to general liberalization of trade and foreign capital restrictions and to rapid world growth. Initially Japan's interactive impact on the world economic environment was insignificant, but by the late 1960s Japan's GNP and foreign trade were large enough to have substantial effects, not just on certain smaller countries, but on the world as a whole. In many ways Japan's surge to the forefront of economically advanced nations was both a partial cause of and a catalyst for fundamental changes in the world economic system. The early 1970s marked the end of an era both for the world economy and for Japan's situation in it.

The changes in world environment are symbolized by the Nixon "economic shock" of August 1971 and the October 1973 Israeli-Arab conflict and attendant Arab-nation restrictions on oil production. The Bretton Woods fixed exchange system ended, to be replaced by controlled but nonetheless floating exchange rates among major currencies. Fissures opened in the liberal trade stance of the United States, a traditional leader of efforts toward freer trade and capital flows. The longer-run implications and consequences of high prices and possible production restrictions for petroleum are not yet clear, but a host of new problems and new power relations have emerged. And in 1974 the industrial world was bedeviled by the twin plagues of inflation and recession.

Japan has been a major actor, if not protagonist, in these changing world circumstances. Not only was the balance of payments by the late 1960s no longer a constraint on growth, as it had been overwhelmingly until then, but under the fixed exchange rate system Japan ran up a huge surplus in trade and capital flows. Foreign exchange reserves (official plus those "hidden" in other governmental foreign assets) increased dramatically from $2 billion in 1968 to about $25 billion in 1972. The government was politically unable to adjust economic policy rapidly enough to prevent a substantial exacerbation of its economic relations with others. If belatedly, nonetheless it did take a variety of major measures to change these trends and reduce foreign exchange reserves—extensive import liberalization of manufactures, removal of remaining export subsidies, replacement of restriction with encouragement of business investment abroad, exchange rate revaluation, and tolerance of some heightened rate of domestic inflation (thereby making exports less competitive and imports more attractive). The yen appreciated almost 35 percent vis-à-vis the dollar by early 1973, at that time the largest of the major currency adjustments after August 1971.

The subsequent turnaround in Japan's foreign exchange reserve position in the spring and summer of 1973 was initially gratifying, but it proceeded much more rapidly and further than expected. The decline was sharpened by intolerably heightened inflation in Japan, a general run-up in world raw material import prices, and then the dramatic jump in oil prices after October 1973. The perceived effects of the oil crisis were particularly strong. The yen suddenly looked weak, and the economy weak, and the yen was devalued some 13 percent in January 1974 (almost back to its level a year earlier). While some of the inflation was "imported," its basic cause lay in the excessively expansive monetary policy of 1972 and early 1973; the fears of the monetary authorities about the adverse impact of revaluation had proved groundless. The antiinflation recession of 1974 was the most severe in the postwar period; for the first time GNP on an annual basis declined absolutely.

The gyrations in Japan's balance of payments, foreign exchange reserves, yen exchange rate, prices, and real GNP were so large, so sudden, and so unanticipated that it will take some time for the lessons of the experience to be learned. What is clear from these events is that the world is in major respects economically highly interdependent. For Japan this is particularly true: Japan is now a sufficiently major economic force that its leaders, and those elsewhere, must assume that whatever Japan does in international economic activities will result in reactions elsewhere that will feed back into the Japanese economy.

Some Basic Assumptions

In the following projection of possible interactions of Japan with the world economy, the approach is on the whole speculative, qualitative, and intuitive, reflecting my best present judgments. I take this approach because the real world is too complex to model fully. It is certainly preferable not to make a single projection. Inter-relationships among variables are multifaceted, involving not only economic but political, social, and security dimensions. Moreover, it is too simple to visualize Japan either as participating in a homogeneous world or as competing against that world; countries cooperate in some aspects under some circumstances, compete in others, and are neutral or uninvolved in still others. I use a scenario approach since scenarios provide a means of identifying the major variables, non-economic as well as economic, and of weaving them into a (presumably) consistent framework for analysis. I focus mainly on the implications for Japanese economic growth of different world environments, together with Japan's probable reactions and policies in these various contexts. Because the variables are so numerous, and because a priori limits on their range of values are difficult, many different scenarios are possible. I therefore develop "reasonable extremes," with my best-guess estimate falling somewhere within the area so bounded.

The discussion is at a high level of aggregation, using the balance of payments as the standard measure of the nature and extent of Japan's economic relationship with the rest of the world. I remind readers that the current account of the balance of payments records the flows of all physical goods and services: exports and imports of commodities; services such as transportation; tourism; dividend, royalty, and licensing payments; and government and private gifts, including gifts of aid. The capital account measures all financial transactions, including short-term and long-term private borrowing, government loans and credits (including most aid), foreign direct investment by businesses, and changes in official foreign exchange reserves. There are several definitions of surplus in the balance of payments; we may regard it here as including the net balance on current account plus the balance of almost all private direct investment and long-term borrowing plus government aid.

Underlying my analysis is a set of basic assumptions about the future into the 1980s, domestic and international, that applies to all scenarios:

1. The Japanese government will continue to be ruled by the conservatives or perhaps a centrist coalition, moderate in its policies. In other words the Liberal Democratic party will remain in power, alone or in coalition with another middle-of-the-road party. There will be no major shift or drift in domestic economic policy from a market to an essentially planned economy, or a shift to alliance with the Communist bloc in international relations. This does not preclude substantially increased trade and other relations with Russia and/or China.

2. There will not be nuclear war among any of the major powers.

3. The United States and the USSR will remain militarily far ahead of all other nations, and their military supremacy will not be challenged by Japan, China, or any other nation.

4. Communist nations will remain a separate bloc or two blocs, though there may be substantially greater economic interchange between planned and market economies.

5. The relative decline in world economic power of the United States will continue, while relatively both Western Europe and Japan will rise. Essentially this means the GNP growth rate in the United States will be lower than that of the European Community (EC) or Japan.

6. The less developed countries (LDCs) other than the major oil-producing nations will not become a major force in the world economy or polity. While the LDCs may have continued substantial

GNP growth, they will also have very serious domestic economic problems, especially unemployment, related to inability to absorb the rapidly growing labor force resulting from high population growth rates beginning in the early 1950s. The balance of payments constraint on growth will remain severe for most LDCs (excluding those with large oil, and perhaps other mineral, deposits). Concessionary aid from economically advanced countries is not likely to grow rapidly in aggregate. Many LDCs will have severe difficulties in borrowing as they reach high levels of foreign debt servicing requirements relative to their exports. Thus the LDCs will be forced to place greater emphasis on exports, both of labor-intensive manufactured goods and of primary materials, particularly natural (depletable mineral) resources. To achieve sufficient exports to pay for the imports needed for growth, many LDCs will feel the need to accept some degree of foreign participation in any natural resource development and in production for exports of manufactured goods.

7. The major oil-producing LDCs are a special case. Oil probably is also a special case among depletable natural resources because of its broad range of uses, the relatively high cost of substitute sources, and its high degree of geographic concentration in the Middle East. Most natural resources are more dispersed geographically, in countries of differing needs and goals, with lesser though by no means nonexistent chances of producer (country or international company) cartels. The problem of oil is discussed as the third scenario in this paper. Oil-producing countries can be divided into two categories: those with sufficiently large populations, economic development potentialities, and/or military expenditure goals that most foreign exchange earnings from oil exports will be used to import goods and services; and those whose potential revenues far exceed potential imports, thus leading to the buildup of large amounts of foreign exchange reserves and other short-term and long-term foreign assets. Numerically most oil producers—Iran, Iraq, Indonesia, Nigeria, Algeria, Venezuela—are in the former category. But the latter category includes countries with some of the largest low-cost oil reserves—Saudi Arabia, Kuwait, Abu Dhabi, and Libya, all in the Middle East and all Arab. A very large-scale increase in their foreign assets appears inevitable, and is so assumed here, though the amount and rate of speed may vary considerably. This constitutes a major new and potentially destabilizing force for the international financial system, as is recognized in the scenarios.

JAPAN's DOMESTIC ECONOMIC PERFORMANCE

Japan's rate of growth through the 1970s and the 1980s will be determined by a variety of factors, domestic and foreign. The pendulum of projections of Japanese growth swung from great optimism to excessive pessimism within a few months in 1973. The late-1973 projections of zero growth in 1974 due to the oil crisis produced a wave of hysteria that is belied by any reasonable approach, particularly in the longer run. This first point is that those zero-growth projections were contingent on the extent to which oil imports were reduced by supply constraints. It is highly unlikely Japan or other nations will be subject to physical rationing of oil over long periods of time, as is discussed later. The probability zero or very slow growth will be imposed on Japan in this manner for any sustained period of time appears to be very low. In fact Japan's 1974 negative growth record was due primarily to the extremely restrictive fiscal-monetary policy to combat inflation. Indeed, by mid-1974 Japan was awash in oil, having more than it needed and able to buy even more if it wished.

I anticipate that the Japanese growth rate will recede in coming years due to domestic factors from the 11 to 12 percent rates of the late 1960s but will continue to be more rapid than the economic growth rates of Western Europe or the United States. A reasonable range for the GNP growth rate, based on domestic conditions, is 6 to 9 percent.[1] It could be further reduced by an unfortunate world economic environment—the issue this paper explores. It should be noted that the less rapid the Japanese growth rate, the less disruptive Japan's impact will be on the world economy, other things equal.

Major Possible Constraints on Growth

Three main factors, together with several minor ones, will tend to slow the GNP growth rate to within the 6 to 9 percent range. It is difficult to project how much each will change, or even to appraise relatively how important each is, because the relationship between each factor and GNP growth is not known with certainty.

The first main factor is a shift in the relative importance among various economic goals, with lesser emphasis on maximum economic growth and greater emphasis on quality of life goals that require government expenditures. I anticipate an increase relative to GNP in government investment as well as current expenditures on social welfare. Even if such government expenditures substitute equally for private investment and consumption expenditures so that the

---

1. Japanese growth rates are in constant yen, that is, adjusted for changes in price levels. Growth rates in current yen or dollars will be substantially higher due to rises in prices in Japan and the United States and probable further changes in the yen per dollar exchange rate.

aggregate investment/GNP ratio remains unchanged, the increased share of government investment, with its relatively low outputs in measured GNP, will result in higher capital-output ratios even though welfare will be greater. Specifically, I visualize increased governmental and private investment expenditures on transportation, housing, pollution control, sewerage and water systems, and the like.

Despite all the rhetoric in Japan, it remains unclear as to how rapidly and to what extent such changes will occur. Will the government be able to mobilize the resources through increased taxation or slower rates of tax reductions than in the past? Will it be able to impose serious constraints on private business, such as pollution controls? What will be the disruptive or beneficial effects of geographical dispersion of industrial activity? How seriously and rapidly will this occur? Perhaps most important of all, will the government deliberately restrain the flow of investable resources to private business in a boom, even at the cost of ending the boom and slowing growth? Or will the government do as it has in the past: allow the private sector first claim on resources and keep government expenditures relatively small?

These questions—more political in nature than economic—suggest how difficult it is to predict the impact of this factor. Moreover, the quantitative effect on the growth rate is difficult to assess. One extreme assumption is that GNP growth is produced solely by private business gross fixed investment, while government investment contributes nothing. If the incremental capital-output ratio for the period 1966–70 of 1.92 rises to 2.0 by 1980, then a reduction in private business fixed investment of 4 percentage points of GNP (from 20 to 16 percent of GNP) in order to increase government investment by an equal amount would reduce the growth rate of GNP by 2 percentage points.[2] While simplistic, this method of calculation does provide an order-of-magnitude estimate for the effect of what would be a substantial reallocation of investment from the business sector to the government.

The second major factor reducing GNP growth is a slowdown in the rate of productivity increase, measured either by total factor productivity (that increase in output after increases in both capital and labor inputs are taken into account) or by labor productivity (the increase in output per worker). One cause of such a slowdown is shifts in the composition of investment. One such shift will be toward

2. The capital-output ratio is estimated by dividing private gross domestic fixed investment, excluding dwellings, in constant prices by the increase in real GNP for the period fiscal 1966–70, using data from Economic Planning Agency, *Annual Report on National Income Statistics, 1972*, pp. 28–31.

housing, which in Japan as elsewhere has high capital-output ratios.[3] The shift in investment from manufacturing to the tertiary sector also affects productivity, but with results less obvious than appear on the surface. For example, the use of computers in banking or commerce could substantially increase labor and, perhaps, total factor productivity in those sectors.

A second cause of a slowdown in productivity growth is a less rapid rate of absorption and diffusion of new technology than has characterized the past fifteen years. The gap between Japanese practices and foreign best practices in production technology has narrowed substantially, disappearing in some fields (in a few, Japan is preeminent, as in the production of giant ships). Putting it simply, the cream of foreign technology has been skimmed; what remains will make a much less rich contribution to future growth. This is important in an economy where, although measurements of the input of labor and capital are significant, so too are the unmeasured causes, including technological change.[4] Japan's domestic R & D efforts will increase substantially but probably will not completely offset the declining benefits from importing technology. It is possible also that there will be reductions in productivity growth due either to decreases in the rate of growth of capital per worker (the share of net investment in GNP) or to labor alienation, as discussed below among relatively less important factors.

The third major factor to cause a slowdown in the growth rate is inflation. Until 1973 rapid growth brought with it an increase in the consumer price index of 5 to 6 percent annually, which the government and most people apparently accepted as a tolerable upper limit. The government's five-year plans set goals of slowing consumer price increases to 3 to 4 percent a year, but the government in practice was unwilling to pursue the required fiscal, monetary, or other policies because the cost in terms of slower growth was deemed too high. Indeed, during the 1950s and 1960s the main concern about inflation was that it would reduce export competitiveness, essential in a system where the exchange rate was fixed and the balance of payments the main constraint on growth. Consumer price rises of 5 to 6 percent were consistent with export price stability as labor became less abundant, wage differentials narrowed, and prices of agricultural and

3.   The examples of housing and government investment suggest the difficulties in using measured GNP as an indicator of social welfare, given our intuitions and value judgments.

4.   See Watanabe and Egaitsu, "Rōdōryoku no tachi to keizai seichō" [Labor force quality and economic growth], *Riron keizai gaku* [Journal of economic theory], March 1968; and T. Watanabe, "Labor Force Quality and Economic Growth," *Economic Development and Cultural Change*, October 1972, pp. 33–53.

small-scale manufacturing products and services rose relative to large-scale manufactured exports.

The sudden surge of inflation to intolerable rates in 1973 and 1974—with almost all price indexes increasing more than 20 percent— had many special causes and features. It remains difficult to assess how rapidly it will be curbed, whether it will generate real strife in labor relations in the process, and what the longer-run implications will be. Moreover, it is not clear where that experience fits into the complex relationship between inflation and real economic growth. It may well be that the negative-growth recession of 1974 was so disruptive an experience that it will be extremely difficult for the economy to resume the previous path of very rapid growth.

From the late 1950s to the early 1970s an accelerating rate of real growth was accompanied by an unchanging rate of consumer price increase. In the future the relationship may well move in the opposite direction: continuance of a certain real growth rate will generate a more rapid rate of inflation; put conversely, a socially tolerable maximum rate of consumer price increases of 5 to 6 percent annually will be consistent with a lower (6 to 9 percent) growth rate than was previously the case. If so, the government will have to pay greater attention to inflation in its policy mix, slowing down economic growth to keep inflation at acceptable levels. Such an increase in inflationary pressures could result: from new demand-pull pressures as the government increases its expenditures in competition with private sector demand without increasing taxes sufficiently; from cost-push pressures as unions and other workers press to maintain the present high rates of increases in money wages while productivity increases slow; or from rises in import prices as world prices of natural resources and agricultural products increase more than Japan's export prices, so that exchange rate changes do not compensate fully and Japan's terms of trade worsen. Moreover, as the phrase cost-push inflation implies, inflation could be the consequence of a slowing of growth as well as a cause of it. The main way in which inflation slows growth, in this approach, is not particularly through adverse effects on resource allocation, savings, and incentives (though these could occur) but in the government policy reaction to excessive rates of inflation.

Other Factors

There are numerous other factors that probably will contribute to some slowing of Japan's economic growth rate. I believe on the whole they will not be of major importance, though several merit consideration. First, the investment rate might decline, due either to reduced private demand for investment or to a decreased savings rate. I do not visualize Japan's economy within the coming decade as suffering from deficient aggregate demand, or even deficient investment demand. Concomitant with the evolving pattern of demand and production will be decreases in investment in certain industries. However, these will be compensated for by investment increases in other sectors—more sophisticated machinery, pollution-control equipment, services, government, housing.

The more likely cause of a decline in investment rates would come from a decrease in the domestic savings rate. The personal savings rate is high in Japan, approximately 20 percent of disposable income. While the personal sector is a heterogeneous mixture of wage earners, professionals, unincorporated businessmen, and farmers, nonetheless Japanese wage earners save a substantially higher proportion of their disposable income than do those in other countries. If growth rates of income slow, if housing credit becomes more readily and cheaply available, if government and private retirement and other social benefits increase, then present incentives to save may weaken substantially. However, personal savings constitutes only one-third of gross domestic savings, so even a 15 percent decline in the personal savings rate would reduce the aggregate gross savings rate by only 5 percent. The savings (retained earnings) rate of corporations might decline somewhat, either because they pay out a higher proportion of profits as dividends (in reaction to institutional changes permitting issue of stock at market price, greater liquidity, etc.) or because the profit share in GNP will be squeezed as growth slows. However, corporate retained earnings are a relatively small component, from one-sixth to one-eighth, of gross domestic savings. A more substantial decline may come from reduction in depreciation as a percentage of GNP. This is likely if the private business fixed investment does slow down, together with the using up of the accelerated depreciation provisions that make depreciation rates so high in periods of high investment activity. On the other hand, the government savings rate is likely to rise somewhat as the government finances at least part of its additional investment activities from tax revenues. In summary, I do not anticipate declines in domestic savings or investment sufficient to pull down the GNP growth rate substantially.

Another potential retardant to sustained rapid growth is the labor force—its supply, its training, and its motivation. Cole's paper in this volume provides important data and a substantial analysis of these issues. My view is that overall labor supply—in quantity, quality, and motivation—will not be a major retardant to growth of GNP. This is not to deny specific problems and shortages; the educational and on-the-job training systems may not produce enough highly qualified scientists, engineers, and technicians to meet the staff requirements generated by new R & D programs, the rapidly growing use of computers, and the like. Nonetheless, thus far labor input, though significant, does not seem to be a major explainer of Japan's postwar rapid growth; moreover, there still remain substantial reservoirs of labor in low productivity use. Labor problems appear more institutional than economic. Japanese labor market institutions and behavior appear to be changing rather rapidly and more flexibly than many stereotypic images, as Cole ably delineates. Motivation, labor alienation, and labor strife do appear potential future problems. Cole notes the lag between the rate of increase in wages and the changes in rates of productivity growth: wage growth appears to have lagged behind the increase in labor productivity in the 1950s, caught up with productivity increases sometime in the 1960s, and in the early 1970s exceeded productivity increases. These statements are somewhat hazardous because the aggregate data tend to be poor and because there are great differences in productivity increases by different firms and sectors, as well as differences in rates of wage increase. If the growth rate does begin to slow—as we anticipate—will labor be willing to accept some reduction in the rate of increase in real wages, and will the adjustment occur fairly rapidly and without great strife? Labor strife will probably increase in the late 1970s. The question is how serious it will become. Only about one-third of the wage-earning labor force is unionized. The enterprise nature of union structure, coupled with low interfirm mobility for most blue-collar workers in unionized firms, makes industry-wide bargaining difficult and enterprise strikes unrewarding. Japanese workers in the future may indeed be somewhat alienated and less happy in their work environment but it is not clear they will be able to do much about it.

Regardless of the rate of Japan's GNP growth through the early 1980s and hence the level of GNP in those years, the high likelihood that very considerable growth will occur enables us to know broadly the nature, if not the degree, of the evolution of the structure of production. The relative share of agriculture, forestry, and fishing in total production—in 1971 only 6.6 percent—will continue to diminish. How rapidly this occurs depends not only on the rate of GNP growth but on the rapidity of the import liberalization for agricultural products as well as the politicoeconomic effects of whatever geographic decentralization of industrial activity occurs. Decentralization could retard the reduction in the number of farm households and help perpetuate the existence of miniscule, fragmented farms worked by old people, many retired from industry. The relative share of the manufacturing sector in GNP will rise slightly. More important, the composition of manufacturing production will continue to evolve toward more complex, skill-intensive, resource-saving commodities. In aggregate, the tertiary (service sector) share in GNP will rise. The tertiary sector is a particularly heterogeneous aggregation, ranging from labor-intensive personal services (prices of which will continue to rise rapidly) to transportation, retail and wholesale trade, banking and finance, and the government. It is such heterogeneity that makes it difficult to generalize about possibilities for technological change and substitution of capital for labor so as to increase labor productivity. The continuing evolution of the structure of production will be caused predominantly by the changing composition of domestic demand as incomes rise in Japan, reflecting also a new emphasis on improvements in the quality of life as well as Japan's changing comparative advantage in international trade as capital per worker, productivity, and wages increase.

This evolving structure of production has substantial long-run implications for the rate of growth and composition of Japan's foreign trade. Amounts imported of agricultural commodities, of labor-intensive manufactured goods, of certain types of specialized machinery will increase relatively more rapidly, while the rate of growth will be somewhat decelerated by the shift in production toward services and relatively away from what are frequently referred to as heavy and chemical industries. Export growth may be accelerated by the increased diversification of manufactured goods competitive in export markets, particularly of more sophisticated machinery. Within the services component of the current account, a notable increase will take place in Japanese net expenditures on tourism abroad.

JAPAN'S FOREIGN ECONOMIC POLICY GOALS

Any consideration of Japanese foreign economic policy must be within the context of general foreign policy goals. Clearly the paramount duty of any nation is to ensure its security against external threat. One point so obvious as to be trite, though it has dominated the past policy of Japan and of other nations, is that Japan will have negligible territorial ambitions—the northern islands in dispute with Russia and the Senkaku Islands in dispute with China.

In the interrelated set of security, economic, and political objectives, I expect Japanese policymakers will continue to give highest priority to economic goals, although perhaps somewhat less overwhelmingly than in the past twenty-five years. Many of Japan's difficulties with other nations will emanate primarily from economic problems, thereby becoming political issues, and perhaps degenerating ultimately into security issues. In some important circumstances, however, the source of difficulties will be political or security. For example, the Arab restrictions on oil exports to Japan in late 1973 were politically motivated; they had potentially strong adverse effects on the Japanese economy; this economic lever, at the extreme an issue even of Japan's security, was used to bludgeon Japan into political acts friendly to the Arab position. Such political pressures are not uncommon in international relations; obvious examples are seen in bilateral foreign aid relationships and in past U.S. pressure on other industrial nations for trade restrictions against Communist countries.

Who will define what is in Japan's national interest? Economic policies that benefit some interest groups in Japan harm others. I anticipate that Japanese policymakers and the pluralist political system, as in other advanced democratic societies, will continue to place more emphasis on benefits to Japanese producers than to consumers. This differs from the norm of most economists who accept the primacy of consumer sovereignty, both globally and nationally.[5]

The fundamental goal of Japanese foreign economic policy is to import those goods and services essential to keep the economy producing at full employment levels of its human capital resources. The most immediate and obvious import requirement is for natural resources (oil and minerals), given their almost total lack within Japan's territorial limits; agricultural products follow closely behind since about one-half of Japan's direct and indirect caloric intake is imported. The import problem can be divided into two categories: physical interruptions of selected, essential import supplies and the ability to generate the foreign exchange through exports to pay for these imports. Export earnings may potentially be insufficient either because of restrictions in foreign markets on imports from Japan or because the prices of imports into Japan rise substantially more than exports. Such terms of trade adversity can be met in the longer run by resource reallocation, with fewer of the benefits of growth remaining in Japan, and slower growth.

A second major goal of Japan, subject to the caveats mentioned below, is to participate as a first-class partner in a world system of free, unrestricted trade.[6] The principles are globalism and nondiscrimination, in opposition to national or regional protectionism. Japan has now reached a level of industrial development and per

    5. Andrew Shonfield, *Modern Capitalism: The Changing Balance of Public and Private Power* (Oxford, 1965).

    6. For an interesting if quite vague MITI foreign policy statement see the spring 1972 report of its Industrial Structure Council, appearing in English as *Japan in World Economy: Japan's Foreign Economic Policy for the 1970s* (Tokyo, 1972). The more recent report of the council, *Sangyō kōzō no chōki bijon* [Long-term vision of the industrial structure], November 1974, reaffirms this position.

capita income such that it benefits greatly from a free trade environment even if that means that Japan, too, has to allow imports freely. In principle Japan aims for a trade system of no tariffs, no quotas, and no other nontariff barriers to the movement of goods and services. Japanese exports in particular benefit from such a world trade environment. On the import side, Japanese bureaucrats increasingly accept that a free trade policy benefits consumers and increases the efficiency of domestic resource allocation. At the same time it is recognized that a free trade policy cannot be achieved overnight because of the adjustment problems in moving resources out of now inefficient but still large industries or in making those industries efficient. Japanese policymakers accept the principle that time should be allowed for such adjustments but also feel governments should undertake positive actions to ease and accelerate the adjustment process so any restrictions on free trade are only temporary. This goal of free trade is more pragmatic—in terms of broadly perceived national interest—than ideological.

Yet Japan like other countries wants to have its cake and eat it too: to have its own special exceptions to the free trade principle while minimizing those of others. This brings Japan into conflict with other major protagonists in the world economy and makes negotiation and compromise essential if cooperation is to prevail.

There are three main areas of Japanese exception to the free trade principle: national security, agriculture, and new high-technology industries. National security goals dominate the free trade principle. In the future this might apply not only to trade in weapons and nuclear materials but to petroleum and other essential raw materials.

The degree to which Japan will apply the free trade principle to agricultural products is unclear. How the European Community resolves the conflict between its present protectionist agricultural policy and pressures from the United States to liberalize agricultural trade will be one factor, though it most probably depends on direct pressures from the United States and other agricultural exporters. Japanese agriculture, like European agriculture, has special problems in the old age of its labor force (making difficult its absorption into nonfarm activities), a much less rapid decline in the number of farm households than in the number of farm workers, and the great political power of farmers (relatively greater in Japan because of inequalities in voting district population). In the long run these are transitory phenomena that will be resolved once the present generation of farmers dies off. However, this certainly will not occur by the early 1980s. Moreover, industrial decentralization and programs to improve transportation networks may perpetuate the number of farm households. Urban workers might commute from their farm homes and retire to farm work when they become old. Japan's fragmented, inefficient agriculture would continue—and constitute a potent vested interest group against trade liberalization.

A separate issue is the definition of the degree of agricultural self-sufficiency required for national security. There is clearly a trade-off between efficiency in production and the guarantee of domestic food supply, since import supplies are subject to interruption by external factors. The U.S. imposition of an embargo on soybeans in the summer of 1973 made Japanese well aware of this problem. Conflict between efficiency by specialization and minimization of the risks of uncertainty by inefficient production is by no means limited to agriculture, since interruptions of the supply of petroleum and other industrial raw materials could also bring the Japanese economy to an effective halt. Japanese policymakers have not yet resolved the problem of the optimum degree of agricultural self-sufficiency.

A highly restrictive agricultural import policy would put Japan on a collision course in trade negotiations with the United States as well as with Canada, Australia, and many less developed countries. However, agricultural production is so inefficient in Japan relative to alternative uses of labor and capital, and the job opportunities for young people will remain so strong, that domestic production will not be able to grow as rapidly as demand, and imports will continue to grow. Under such circumstances Japanese policymakers may reduce the minimum self-sufficiency criterion to perhaps the British level, on the order of 40 percent of consumption domestically produced. This may be overly optimistic, however; Japan may not be able to resolve its conflicts among domestic vested interest groups in a way that enables it to adopt a relatively liberal trade stance. At the least rice imports will continue to be regulated and restricted in 1980 despite some continued gradual liberalization of other agricultural commodities, and self-sufficiency may well be defined in terms of rice alone. Beef will be the real test of trade policy in agriculture.

A third, important area in which it appears that Japan will continue to make an exception to the free trade principle is in new (infant), high technology, high income elasticity industries. Ministry of International Trade and Industry (MITI) officials believe Japan should be in the vanguard of such industries, both because of some vague definition of national security and because of the sense that this is where Japan's economic prospects lie. MITI strategy will continue to be to protect such industries, though the means may have to be domestic subsidies rather than trade restrictions. One important illustration is the computer industry, in which Japan is the only nation (except the Soviet Union, which apparently has a very inefficient industry) still trying to mount a full-scale challenge to American technological supremacy in hardware and software. It is uncertain whether the Japanese computer industry will be competitive in its home markets, much less in international markets, by 1980. Japanese computer firms may well become efficient in certain product lines without being competitive over the full range. Another example is MITI's desire to develop large commercial aircraft. Whether the Japanese can challenge American supremacy in large subsonic aircraft or European supremacy in supersonic aircraft is moot. Surely Japanese policymakers will identify other areas as key future growth industries to be protected if they have already developed elsewhere. Japan may develop some industries first—certain types of pollution control, use of ocean resources, etc. Again, Japan may be on a collision course with the United States if it defines "high technology infant industry" widely and protects accordingly.

The free trade principle does not apply to all nations in the world. First, Communist nations use state trading organizations and try to achieve trade balance with each bilateral partner. Typically, both sides rely upon world prices determined by trade among the market economies in negotiating deals. Second, Japan, like other economically advanced nations, accepts or at least tolerates the practices by less developed countries to restrict their imports for maintenance of a balance of payments equilibrium and for protection of import-competing domestic (presumably infant) industries. Will Japan and other economically advanced countries maintain the free trade principle for the exports of the LDCs? Japan's principles of freedom and nondiscrimination apply to imports of agricultural and manufactured goods from less developed countries; indeed present policies give preferences, though quantitatively limited, to such imports. Import restrictions of economically advanced countries are not aimed directly at less developed countries but in fact hit particularly their areas of comparative advantage, including certain agricultural products and such labor-intensive manufactured goods as textiles or electronic consumer goods, which in advanced economies are the areas of comparative disadvantage and hence declining industries. How this problem is resolved underlies the first two scenarios of the next section.

Japan realizes that a prerequisite for a world free-trade environment is an international monetary system in which countries can restore balance of payments equilibrium in the face of disequilibrating forces fairly readily and without great pressure upon the international monetary system itself. Japanese policymakers are actively involved in the negotiations to create a more flexible international monetary system. The government still appears in principle to favor fixed exchange rates that are adjusted fairly often as need arises, without protectionist regional currency blocs and without the burden of exchange rate adjustment falling solely on either the surplus or deficit nations,[7] and increases in world liquidity in the form of supplementary drawing rights (SDRs) rather than dollars emanating from a deficit in the U.S. balance of payments.

In addition to these comprehensive goals of world relatively-free trade and a relatively flexible international monetary system making balance of payments adjustments easier, Japan has other foreign economic objectives. One will be geographical and commodity diversification of exports, in feedback response to the pressures from countries where Japanese exports have "disrupted" and "caused severe injury to" certain domestic industries. Japan will also attempt to diversify the sources of its raw materials (agricultural and natural resources) by nation, region, and multinational company. These policies emanate from well-founded fears, as exemplified by the oil crisis, that Japanese imports would be interrupted due to changes in the international environment beyond Japan's control or that Japan might be charged excessive prices by a dominant supplier or group of suppliers. This problem is discussed at some length in the third scenario.

Japan's goals regarding international capital movements in 1980 are more difficult to specify. It seems unlikely Japan will have accepted the present American principle, which may change, of free capital movements. Government regulation of short-term capital movements will continue, both to prevent speculative pressure on the yen and for reasons of domestic monetary-fiscal policy. Nor is long-term portfolio capital movement likely to be free, since this, too, interferes with domestic monetary policy and balance of payments objectives. Also, some controls and guidelines on the outflow of capital are probable because of perceived effects upon and reactions by recipient countries. At the same time, the government anticipates a vigorous outflow of

7.   The burdens of exchange rate revaluation or devaluation are frequently political; they affect certain interest groups particularly strongly. The circumstances in which an exchange rate adjustment is required usually mean the adjustment is more beneficial to consumers than alternative solutions, but it does hurt particular interest groups. Since those hurt are likely to complain more vociferously, while those who benefit are viewed as receiving windfalls, it is not surprising that governments in pluralistic democratic societies oppose exchange rate readjustment in either direction. In Japan, fear of the effects of revaluation were initially great, based upon the twenty-two-year postwar experience of rate stability and ignorance of the actual effects of changes. As Japan has more experience with adjustments, presumably people will be better informed about the impact and become more acquiescent about further changes. Even so, those hurt by exchange rate changes can be expected to put much pressure on the government not to carry them out.

business direct investment, especially in foreign natural resource development and primary processing. Large-scale outflows, combined with the need to pay for high-priced oil imports, will require Japan either to borrow more from abroad or to increase exports. The alternative of further yen devaluation is strongly resisted by the United States, which fears renewal of bilateral and global trade imbalance if Japan thus promotes exports and makes manufactured imports less competitive.

There are trade-offs among the various foreign economic goals and among alternative means of achieving these goals. Even though Japanese consumers, and most businessmen to the extent that they avoid a revaluation, benefit from unilateral tariff reductions, it seems unlikely Japan will eliminate all import tariffs without demanding quid pro quo's from other major trading nations. This will also be true of reductions or eliminations of quotas and other nontariff barriers. Given the prevailing perception until late 1973 that Japan would tend toward persistent excessive surplus in its balance of payments, followed by the uncertainties engendered by the oil crisis, Japan will oppose the development of an international monetary system in which special punitive restrictions are imposed upon either surplus or deficit nations. In many of these areas Japanese policy on the relative importance of the trade-offs has not been formulated, so projection is particularly difficult.

SCENARIOS OF THE WORLD ECONOMIC ENVIRONMENT

It is not my purpose here to analyze comprehensively a wide range of alternative scenarios of the 1980 world environment in which Japan's economy will participate, or even to incorporate a sophisticated analysis of successive interactions within each scenario. A major difference that will figure in Japan's future economic relationships with the rest of the world, as compared with those of the past twenty-five years, is that Japan is perceived by *all* nations (not just small Southeast Asian ones) as a major economic power, in the league of the United States, USSR, and European Community—and it is in fact a major economic power. Whatever Japan does in foreign markets has significant impact there. No longer is Japan a relatively small, price-taking competitor; rather, both as an importer and as an exporter, it affects world prices by the sheer volume of transactions. These can mean substantial feedback interactions between Japan and other countries, in which each must take into account how the other will react to its own actions. Thus while Japan may be more powerful in international economic relationships it is also more interdependent and constrained because of these new feedback reactions. These have to be considered in tracing through possible Japanese policy reactions to the several different world environments.

The main protagonists directly influencing the world economic environment are the United States, the European Community, Japan, and the OPEC (Organization of Petroleum Exporting Countries) nations. The USSR, China, and the non-oil LDCs are less likely to be important initiators of major changes in the world economic system, either through active intervention or the amassing of effective power in international economic transactions, so they do not play major independent roles in the following scenarios. This is consistent with the expectation that trade with Communist nations will increase, that there may be considerable American, Japanese, and/or European capital and technological participation in large-scale projects in the USSR, and that trade may have significant influence on specific commodity markets (U.S. wheat to the USSR, Japanese chemical fertilizer to China).

The nature of the world economic environment—defined in terms of the trade, payments, and capital flow systems—will be determined primarily by the behavior of the United States, the European Community, and Japan (the Big Three). However, what OPEC tries to do, and the extent to which it succeeds, concerning the supply availabilities and price of crude oil constitute a major problem in determining the nature of the world economic environment. Will the Big Three respond by coming closer together or by going their individual ways? How will the holding of large foreign assets be made attractive to Saudi Arabia et al. and their disruptive impact on the world financial system minimized? These constitute sufficiently important issues to justify treatment in a special scenario.

The basic issue in determining the world economic environment is whether cooperation or conflict will predominate. In a world of cooperation the major nations through discussion and negotiation agree to general rules of economic behavior and establish supporting institutions; these rules encourage and enhance trade and capital flows, typically through reliance on the market mechanism. With increased gains from trade goes increased interdependence, but cooperation reduces the risks involved in specialization and reliance on others. In a world of cooperation there certainly is competition, and even conflict, but it is primarily between companies and industries, within an internationally determined framework. A world of conflict occurs when major nations do not succeed in negotiating a mutual set of general rules of behavior and revert instead to nationalistic competitive practices, at the worst beggar-thy-neighbor. This might well be described as a world in which regional blocs predominate, with discriminatory trade and/or currency arrangements favoring bloc members. Typically, major countries would be protectionist, perhaps neoisolationist, certainly inward-looking. Trade and finance are clearly interrelated; it is unlikely a cooperative world environment could exist for one and a bloc environment for the other.

In crude extremes, the United States may evolve into an import protectionist and neoisolationist nation (in a series of ad hoc actions or perhaps by deliberate policy as embodied in legislation such as the Burke-Hartke Bill). Or it may reaffirm and continue its policy of the last forty years to create a cooperative, nondiscriminatory, world free-trade environment.

The extremes are only slightly more complex for the European Community. We can pose two questions. First, to what degree will the EC become economically and politically integrated? Severe problems remain in the achievement of full economic integration, even after internal trade and investment flows are free. Will exchange rates among the currencies of members be rigidly fixed? Correspondingly, will the EC achieve a common monetary-fiscal policy and a common monetary unit, or will members retain high degrees of national economic sovereignty? The more integrated the EC becomes, the more powerful and active it can be in international negotiations. Second, to what degree will the European Community be inward-looking (regional and protectionist) or outward-looking (internationalist)?

For Japan the same choices between outward and inward stances exist, though to a lesser degree. Japan cannot be as autarkic as the United States or the EC because of its small raw materials base. Nonetheless, it was able to pursue a quite protectionist policy until the late 1960s. It can no longer do so without retaliation from the United States and the EC; it simply is too large. Moreover, as already discussed, Japan now stands to benefit more from a cooperative, free trade world, with itself behaving the same way, than from a world of blocs.

The most pressing economic issue in international relations is how to deal with the energy crisis, more narrowly the oil crisis, still more narrowly Saudi Arabia and the others with the potential to build up large foreign assets. Because of the importance of this crisis, and its newness, a special scenario is devoted to a world of competition for natural resources, for which oil is taken as the most extreme case. How the Big Three and the Middle Eastern nations work out matters will be significant in determining the nature of the world economic system (the world environment) in the 1980s.

There are a number of other international economic problems that will similarly be important. Probably the most fundamental is the development of an acceptable new international monetary system to resolve the problems of creation of international liquidity and flexible balance of payments adjustment. The major outlines of a new, if de facto, system are fairly clear, though the specific features remain to be negotiated. A second issue is the remaining general trade restrictions on manufactured goods—tariffs and particularly nontariff barriers. Presumably Japan, the EC, and the United States will be taking initiatives to reduce these general trade restrictions.

Third, "special industry problems" are an issue in economically advanced countries—those still large, labor-intensive industries that are no longer internationally competitive and hence face severe import competition. How are the social costs of such import competition to be met? One route is protectionism—import restrictions by whatever means. These include unilateral imposition of specific tariffs or quotas by the importing country, internationally agreed-upon quotas as in the Cotton Textile Agreement, or the forcing of so-called voluntary export quotas upon the newly competitive exporting nations. Will such "safeguard" protection be permanent or can ways be found to limit its duration while domestic adjustment occurs and is accelerated by government action?

A fourth problem area is agriculture. The nature of the problem depends vitally upon whether there will be a tendency for world marketable food supplies to be greater or less than demand at reasonable prices. The United States has a comparative advantage in many agricultural products, the European Community and Japan comparative disadvantages. In order to expand production the United States will want access to foreign markets and a sharing by others of the burden of reserve stockpiling. Japan and the EC will want unrestricted access to American supplies while continuing to protect their own agrarian interests. Famine-ridden LDCs represent a further complication of great importance in a humanitarian world. The crosscurrents of difference in interests and perspectives will put considerable pressure on efforts at cooperation among the Big Three.

Trade of the EC, the United States, and Japan with less developed countries is a further concern, though probably of lesser economic importance, particularly in terms of the effects on the relationships of the Big Three with each other. There is a host of problems involving the LDCs, including their exports of labor-intensive manufactured goods (the "special industry" problem for the economically advanced countries), natural resource development, food, and the evolution of historical trade patterns.

Definition of a new set of common rules for trade with the Communist nations also remains, though it is a less pressing matter. Issues include the revision of goods embargoed, most-favored-nation treatment, credit terms, and arrangements for development of natural resources for export to the Big Three. A partially related set of issues involves the role of multinational firms in the world economy. Will multinational firms dominate the world economy? To what degree can they be controlled by individual nations? What new rules of the game will be formulated to control their behavior?

I consider three alternative scenarios of the world environment: a scenario of cooperation, one of conflict, and a scenario of competition for resources.

A SCENARIO OF COOPERATION

In this scenario all goes well; it is an optimistic projection of the pre-1973 world economic environment. The Big Three pursue international economic policies cooperatively. They succeed in reforming the international monetary system so that current problems are reasonably well resolved. Countries are able to handle balance of payments difficulties relatively quickly, smoothly, and without severe domestic or foreign disruptions. Trade becomes more free. Oil flows freely, though at higher prices and with substantially higher revenues for oil-producing nations. However, these revenues are absorbed into the system either as increased imports or as capital outflows into stable investments in the rest of the world. Adjustment mechanisms work sufficiently well and the distribution of these trade and capital flows is such that balance of payments of individual major nations are not seriously disequilibrated. China and Russia are drawn increasingly into world trade and pursue nonconfrontation foreign policies. The LDCs grow rather rapidly, pursue more trade-oriented policies, and are able to increase their exports, including manufactured goods, to the Big Three. International agreements on national adjustment policies are worked out so that noncompetitive segments of industries in the Big Three are gradually phased out with minimum social cost. Other problems—security, political, or economic—are not of sufficient force to break up or even erode seriously the international economic system. Essentially it is the best of worlds for world consumers, for the national interests of the United States, Japan, and the EC, and probably for the OPEC nations. The achievement of this scenario is Japan's present foreign economic policy aim, embodies the goals to which liberal economists aim, and is consistent with the past goals and policies of U.S. foreign policy. Its achievement depends importantly upon the behavior of the United States and the European Community, as determined both by internal factors and by the performance of Japan.

This scenario certainly does not imply that no economic problems will remain for Japan in its relations with other nations or that there will be no problems among other nations. Let us assume that Japan's excessive balance of payments surplus of 1971–73, eliminated by inflation, oil crisis, trade liberalization, and exchange rate adjustments, does not reappear. Japan and the EC may have to resolve the overhang of the dollar glut, together with any surplus foreign exchange reserves. Perhaps by the 1980s the present levels of dollars will simply be absorbed by the growth in world trade and by active international capital flows. In this area what Saudi Arabia does may be more important than what Japan does. The degree and speed of agriculture import liberalization will be a particularly thorny issue for the Liberal Democratic party and the Japanese government bureaucracy. The Japanese definition of future key industries suitable for protection, and the means of protecting them, will pose issues in which the United States and EC will be involved. All such issues will be negotiable in this scenario and will be handled relatively well in a continuing process of negotiations. Japan by the 1980s will have become generally accepted as an equal partner in the Big Three and will be an important leader in determining the world environment; it will be for Japan the best of all possible worlds. The economic strife of the early and mid-1970s will then be regarded as only transitional frictions inherent in the processes of Japan adapting its trade behavior to the international free trade rules, all countries developing means of adjustment to strong competition, and the EC and the United States learning to accept Japan as an important and equal partner.

A Scenario of Conflict

In this scenario international economic cooperation among the Big Three breaks down, to be replaced by reactive nationalism and international economic conflict, though not war. The United States by the 1980s is protectionist in import policy because of the serious competition a number of relatively inefficient large domestic industries face from Japan and other countries, mainly LDCs. The United States might evolve into this protectionist stance along any of several paths— a deliberate policy decision forced by organized labor in manufacturing and import-competing business; the cumulation of a series of ad hoc case-by-case decisions to restrict imports; inability to resolve the U.S. balance of payments deficit by monetary reform; or the failure of domestic antiinflation and antirecession policy diverted to a search for foreign (import) scapegoats. In this scenario the United States is likely to be politically more inward-looking as well, reducing substantially its role as international leader.

Similarly, the European Community is trade-protectionist and inward-looking. The problems of internal economic and political integration absorb the energies of Europe's leaders; they remain basically uninterested in Japan and in a global outlook and role; they feel their main role is as a counterfoil to the United States. The international monetary system will probably have degenerated into competing regional currency and trading blocs, with the United States and perhaps Latin American countries comprising one bloc, the EC and perhaps most African countries a second bloc, the Communist countries a third bloc, and Japan, Southeast Asia, Australia-New Zealand and any other countries with which Japan has large trading ties a fourth bloc. The various currency blocs might cooperate at some times and compete at other times, but basically there would be a narrow rather than a global view of self-interest.

How might this world environment come about? The domestic economic and political pressures within both the United States and European Community that encourage increasingly protectionist and neoisolationist stances on the part of each are very real. Moreover, the Big Three may not succeed in resolving cooperatively the economic issues that currently plague them. The strains on cooperation in the fields of trade and international finance were substantial even prior to the 1973 Middle East conflict, and problems of oil supplies and prices and dealing with the Arabs (and Israelis) have further exacerbated the strains. Each of the Big Three might well go its way, in conflict with the others, in its oil and energy policies. Tensions could spill over into other international economic arenas. Agreement in detail may not be reached on either the balance of payments adjustment mechanism or on the role of the dollar; global monetary reform fails. Competition in relatively labor-intensive sectors in the European Community, the United States, and Japan from imports will become more severe. While much of this competition will emanate from less developed countries, some will involve commodities traded among Japan, the United States, and the EC. The Big Three governments may find it easier to respond by restricting imports than by going through the budgetarily expensive and perhaps politically expensive adjustment process of shifting resources out of their inefficient industries. The political and social pressure on behalf of farmers in the European Community and Japan might prevent those governments from liberalizing trade in agricultural products sufficiently rapidly for the United States not to retaliate with import restrictions on manufactures. The continuing exacerbation of a series of economic frictions could well create sufficient frustration and irritation among the leaders of the Big Three that they find themselves on a path of increasing antagonism toward each other.

Some of the international political pressures tending to bring the

Big Three together will continue to decline, so that envisaging the
world as a series of regional economic blocs does not appear as dangerous as it did in the past. For example, detente and increasing economic
exchange with Russia and China would reduce Big Three fears of a
security threat from the Communist powers. The cessation of American
involvement in Vietnam and Indochina generally might result in U.S.
rejection of its role as "leader of the free world" in order to "contain
Communism." Similarly, in the United States a feeling that aid programs have failed to achieve successful economic and political development in the less developed countries, combined with increasing trade
pressure in labor-intensive manufactured goods from those countries
and balance of payments difficulties in paying for oil imports, might
well lead the United States to abandon its commitments to the LDCs.
The European Community would perhaps react less strongly, but
would view its relationships with LDCs within rather narrow confines,
typified by the economic and political relationships between France
and its former colonies in Africa today.

Relationships among the Big Three in this scenario would be complex
and probably changing, since there are some areas of cooperation and
other areas of competition for each bilateral pairing. The United States
has the kingpin role since it is the largest and has extensive relationships
with both Japan and the EC, while the direct relationship between
Japan and the EC remains small. The United States and Japan might
well join in opposing internal discriminatory European Community
trade preferences, in formulating a different role from the EC position
on gold vis-à-vis the dollar, and perhaps on issues of exchange rate
adjustment. The exchange rate between the yen and the dollar might
well be more stable—a political as well as economic decision to peg—
than between either of those currencies and a European Community
currency (either a unified currency unit or whatever *numéraire* is appropriate). However, it is also conceivable that Japan and the European
Community might join against the United States over the role of the
dollar in the international monetary system and in reaction against
American pressures for them to liberalize agricultural imports; they
might even peg their exchange rates with each other in reaction to
threats either of an overvalued or an undervalued dollar.

The United States and Europe might well join against Japan because of its relative balance of payments surplus, Western perceptions
of continuing de facto Japanese trade and investment restrictions, the
aggressiveness of Japanese direct investment abroad, and, particularly,
continuing Japanese market penetration in certain commodities in EC
and U.S. markets. Arguments that somehow the government-business
relationship in Japan, together with other Japanese economic institu-

tions and practices, constitute a sufficiently different economic system that special trade rules should be devised for trade with Japan might well provide an ideological basis for an anti-Japan position. Joint U.S.-EC cooperation against Japan is a frightening specter for the Japanese.

How is Japan likely to react in this pessimistic scenario of conflict? Certainly such a world environment would greatly heighten Japan's existing psychological sense of isolation, now due to physical distance from Europe and America; perceptions of Western racism; cultural, racial, and language differences from the West, together with Japan's own homogeneity; a sense of hierarchy in international relationships; realistic fear of being made a scapegoat for either noneconomic or economic reasons; and desire for equality.[8] One can imagine at the extreme a strong reactive nationalism emerging in a Japan determined not to let the rest of the world impinge upon its own domestic and foreign goals. Cole suggests some of the ramifications of this for labor and economic performance in his paper in this volume. Reactive nationalism would probably generate improved economic performance by Japan's domestic economy. This is one of the few scenarios in which it might seem reasonable to Japan to develop nuclear military power. I cannot envisage a single plausible situation in which Japan would have the capability and the will to exert military power to resolve problems and frustrations in foreign relations. Any decision to have nuclear weapons would be justified along the lines that all major nations have nuclear weapons, so it is quite natural, and to be accepted as a major power one must have military power: it is capability, more than will, that counts in the reckoning of others. No one should regard a nuclear Japan as a threat, even in the highly uncertain world of conflict in this scenario.

However, it is both possible and much more likely that Japan would exist and even continue to thrive reasonably well within a world environment of conflict without going to the extreme of nuclear armament or military confrontation with anyone. Much depends on what the concrete alternatives will be for Japan. This in turn depends substantially on U.S. goals and policies, particularly U.S. expectations in its total relationship with Japan, as well as Japan's own perceptions of self-interest. In this scenario the geographic pattern of Japan's international economic relationships would change substantially. Certainly its trade with the European Community and the United States would

8. For an interesting discussion see Hiroshi Kitamura, *Psychological Dimensions of U.S.-Japanese Relations*, Harvard University Center for International Affairs Occasional Paper, no. 28 (Cambridge, Mass., August 1971).

not disappear altogether; their protectionist movements would not be
so severe as that. But the absolute increase in Japan's exports to the
European Community and the United States would be too slow to
generate sufficient foreign exchange earnings to pay for the imports
needed to support a relatively high rate of economic growth.

A likely Japanese reaction would be to become the friend and cham-
pion of the less developed countries, especially natural resource producers, both economically and politically. Japan would drastically
shift the locus of its trade growth, with exporters looking to the LDCs
for markets as American and EC markets became restricted. The
Japanese government would retaliate against the United States and
the EC by competitively shifting imports to LDCs. Japan more than
the European Community and the United States is prepared to purchase the actual and potential exports of less developed countries. It
needs their agricultural products and natural resources. Japan more
than other economically advanced countries will be prepared to buy
LDC labor-intensive manufactured exports while pursuing active
policies to accelerate the shift of resources out of declining domestic
industries. Japanese industry will produce increasingly the machinery and other manufactured goods the LDCs want to import.
All this interaction will be enhanced by vigorous economic aid whereby
Japanese firms help develop agricultural and natural resources in the
LDCs for export to Japan and engage in production of their labor-
intensive manufactured goods for shipment to Japan and elsewhere.
Various trade and payments preferences, subsidies, and the like would
be used both in regional bloc contexts and in competition in LDC
markets in other blocs.

The economics, and probably the politics, suggest that this alternative (Japan as friend of the LDCs) will be more attractive and viable
for Japan than the alternative of sharply increasing the proportion of
its trade with the Communist bloc. Russia and China will not be
willing or able to engage in a sufficient total amount of trade, either in
directing such a high share of their trade to Japan or in promoting the
degree of specialization in production implied, to be large enough
economic partners to meet Japan's needs.

In terms of Japan's relationships with the other two of the Big Three,
the major change would be with the United States. Japan's economic
and political relationship with the European Community is more
limited; Japan's trade with the United States in 1972 was more than
double that with the EC. The many areas of economic and political
cooperation between Japan and the United States could be expected
to deteriorate to noncooperation or competition.

The reaction of the less developed countries to this increasing leadership role by Japan and to fears of economic invasion by Japan would by no means be homogeneous or simple. (The following discussion applies also to the cooperation scenario, but not to the same degree.) The present antagonisms in Southeast Asia, in part a legacy of World War II, in part fears of new economic domination by Japan, will intensify, since Japan's share of their total trade and Japanese investment in their countries can only increase. However, the economic benefits of increasing their trade with and obtaining investment from Japan will be very great. Since there may well be no viable alternatives for the leaders of Southeast Asian countries—unless they want to go the Burma route—they may have to accept, if reluctantly and with various displays of hostility, this increasing economic dependence. In this situation Japan will be wise to take a low profile, as the government has so far attempted to do. Yet Japanese attitudes and behavior in these countries probably will not ameliorate the tensions inherent in such an economic relationship.

In other parts of the Third World the situations will be rather different. The Middle East and North African nations will continue to be major sellers of petroleum to the world, particularly to Japan. Japan is presently in a very weak bargaining position with them, and while it will become more nearly equal (see the next scenario) nonetheless perhaps the best Japan can hope for is a close relationship of mutual interdependence of relatively equal powers. It seems likely Latin Americans would actively welcome an increasing economic relationship with Japan, to speed their own growth and to serve as a countervailing force to their sense of excessive North American domination, particularly in a regional bloc context. Moreover, to the extent Latin American countries develop competitive manufactured exports and U.S. markets are protected, Japan could well appear a natural alternative trading partner. The trade relationship between Latin America and Japan is now relatively small. That, together with the lack of any great historical relationship, suggests tensions between Japanese and Latin Americans would not become great. Both would cooperate against the North Americans. Africa is more complicated. Presumably the European Community would enhance its ties to keep Africa within its regional bloc. On the other hand, Japan would be a good market for African exports and a good supplier of the commodities African nations import. The trade relationship would not be sufficient to shift African allegiance from Europe to Japan, but Africa could well become an area of considerable conflict between Europeans and Japanese.

This discussion suggests Japan would react vigorously and pragmatically in its domestic and foreign economic policy to the deterioration of the world environment envisaged in this scenario. There would be considerable trauma for Japan in feeling rejected by the United States. Nevertheless, I do not expect the economic repercussions of this pessimistic environment would be so great that Japan would no longer be able to import as much as it needed to sustain whatever growth rate it could achieve domestically. One way or another Japanese exports would be sufficient to pay for the needed imports. If necessary, Japan would revert to export promotion activities sufficient to guarantee this, and to competitive exchange rate changes. In this scenario of world conflict we might expect substantial competitive governmental policies by the Big Three nations to secure external markets. Japan's past history of success in such environments suggests it would be able to play that game well in the future, too.

A COMPETITION-FOR-RESOURCES SCENARIO

In this scenario the competition for natural (mineral) resources among major industrial nations of the world—including, importantly, Japan—becomes so severe as to provoke serious political and security as well as economic problems. It becomes a strained competition between countries, not simply the normal economic competition between companies. This scenario has been implicit in the rather confused, occasionally hysterical, public discussion in the United States, Japan, and perhaps elsewhere on the natural resource problem, and particularly on the oil or energy crisis. The situation in winter 1973–74 appeared severe enough, but it was also a harbinger of the way the future may be. While the shortages of natural resources were artificial, some fear they will become all too real, leading to an energy crisis by the early 1980s and comparable crises in other natural resources soon thereafter.

The discussion and analysis of potential competition for natural resources has many dimensions: a time dimension, focusing on the future from 5 to 100 years hence; national or regional problems versus global problems; the issue of physical interruptions of supplies due to a variety of noneconomic factors (wars, blockades, strikes, etc.); engineering·problems of locating and developing natural resources; the economic costs of exploration and development; the possibilities of substitution among various natural resources; the price changes of natural resources relative to prices of manufactured goods; and the roles of multinational mineral corporations, of the governments of major national producers, and of consumers.

In its simplest, starkest, long-run form the natural resource supply problem is a variant of Malthusian logic: the demand for mineral resources increases exponentially as world GNP and GNP per capita grow exponentially, while the global supply of natural resources is fixed by the physical characteristics of this planet. At some point, in this simplistic approach, all resources will be used up. Data on the number of years of reserves of major minerals combined with moderate rates of growth of their consumption suggest that with even a substantial increase (fivefold) in known reserves many major natural resources will be fully depleted within the next 50 to 75 years.[9] A pollution variant of this Malthusian argument is that in the process of producing higher per capita incomes for the growing world population the byproducts of production will so pollute the environment as to kill off most of the population even before the world's mineral resources are used up. These limits-to-growth arguments assume, unrealistically, that technology will be unable either to develop sufficient sources of materials and energy or to solve the pollution problems of ever higher global per capita incomes. More important here, these arguments relate to a time horizon of 50 to 100 years, whereas our concern is the next 5 to 10 years. One might argue that by 1980 world leaders will be trying to develop offsetting policies. This requires a high degree of cooperation and would thereby perhaps make that scenario more likely.

An essential ingredient of most discussions of the natural resource problem, and of this scenario, is that most known deposits and production of natural resources are located in countries different from the major users. Use is dictated by a country's per capita income and population size. The greatest consumers of natural resources are the United States, USSR, Japan, and West Germany, followed by the other main West European nations. Among major users, the USSR is closest to self-sufficiency. While having large reserves of some natural resources, even the United States imports virtually all (over 85 percent) of its bauxite, chromium, manganese, nickel, and platinum, as well as 50 to 60 percent of its tungsten and zinc. The paucity of Japan's natural resource base is so well known that details are not necessary: virtually all (about 90 percent) must be imported. Since 1967 Japan has ranked as the world's largest importer of natural resources, one of the few number one positions it could do without. Because of this geographic imbalance between demand and supply, analyses of the natural resource problem can be treated in three interrelated categories: insurance of stable supplies of natural resources; their prices; and the trade (balance of payments) effects on supplying and using nations. Within each of these categories we can consider short-run (six months to two years), intermediate (1980), and long (ten to twenty years) time dimensions.

While in some respects the natural resource problem is similar for

9. Donella Meadows et al., *Limits to Growth* (New York, 1972), table 4, pp. 64–65, citing U.S. Bureau of Mines, *Mineral Facts and Problems* (Washington, D.C., 1970).

a number of minerals, I consider only a single commodity—crude oil.
Not only does it illustrate the issues well but it is the most immediate
and probably by far potentially the most serious within our time frame.
It is the most important mineral in world production and trade. More
important, petroleum is now the predominant primary energy source
throughout the world, in the United States, and particularly in Japan,
having supplanted coal during the past forty years. It is anticipated
that petroleum will continue to be the predominant source of energy at
least until the 1990s.[10] It is particularly in this interim period that
world and national demand for petroleum will continue to grow
rapidly. Not surprisingly, especially given the oil crisis of 1973–74,
most policymakers are focusing on oil as the commodity for which the
competition for resources will be most severe. In part this is because of
the projections of rapidly growing imports by the United States, as
discussed below. There is an intensity to the discussions that makes
perceptions about oil qualitatively as well as quantitatively different
from those about other natural resources. Moreover, the likelihood of
cartels or supply interruptions in other minerals appears far lower, in
substantial part because of the high degree of substitutability among
them.[11]

Basic Facts about Petroleum

Let us review some salient facts about petroleum.[12] First, approximately 56 percent of the world's proved reserves are in the Middle East
(or, in order of size, Saudi Arabia, Kuwait, Iran, Iraq, Abu Dhabi, and
the Neutral Zone), another 7 percent in North Africa (Libya and
Algeria), about 8.5 percent each in the USSR and the United States,
and 5 percent in Venezuela.[13] Proved reserves are highly conservative
estimates, particularly for the Middle East. In addition, major new

10.   An excellent study of the very long-run changes among energy sources and their efficient
allocation and pricing among different uses is William D. Nordhaus, "The Allocation of Energy
Resources," Brookings Institute Papers on Economic Activity 3 (Washington, D.C., 1973),
pp. 529–76.

11.   U.S. Government, Council on International Economic Policy, *Special Report on Critical
Imported Materials* (Washington, D.C., December 1974).

12.   The following are excellent basic sources: James C. Burrows and Thomas A. Domencich,
An Analysis of the United States Oil Import Quota (Lexington, Mass., 1970); Morris A. Adelman, *The
World Petroleum Market* (Baltimore, 1972); Joel Darmstadter et al., *Energy in the World Economy*
(Baltimore, 1971); and Sam H. Schurr and Paul T. Homan, *Middle Eastern Oil and the Western
World* (New York, 1971). The first is a study sponsored by Charles River Associates, the others by
Resources for the Future. There are a number of more recent, unpublished manuscripts that up-
date but do not fundamentally change the main thrust of the following discussion, including some
prepared for the Atlantic Institute-Keidanren conference "The Energy Policies in the Industrialized World: Cooperation or Rivalry?" held in Tokyo, in October 1973.

13.   Burrows and Domencich, *United States Oil Import Quota*, pp. 88–89, for 1967. Darmstadter,
Energy, provides similar estimates for 1968, though with less detail, on p. 48.

finds ("each a Libya or larger") in the North Alaskan Slope, the Canadian Arctic, and the North Sea off Europe add to known reserves. Probable additional reserves especially important to Japan are in the areas of Indonesia, the China Sea, and Siberia.

Second, the geographic distribution of production is quite different from reserves, so the proved reserves to production (R/P) ratio varies considerably. In 1972 the Middle East produced about 34 percent of the world's oil, North Africa 6, the United States 18, USSR 15, and Venezuela 7. While the global R/P ratio is over 30, it is less than 11 for the United States, about 25 for the USSR, and over 70 for the Middle East.

Third, there is a high degree of substitutability in most energy uses (except for land vehicles and aircraft) among the primary energy sources—petroleum, natural gas, coal, hydroelectric power, and nuclear power. One reason is that most uses can be met by electricity, and all sources can be converted into electricity. Moreover, the technology exists or is in development to extract oil from oil sands and oil shale and to produce gas and synthetic oil from coal. The main factors for substitution among fossil fuels are relative prices and time lags of three to ten years in developing major new or alternative supplies, with simple know-how a less important constraint. Countries have differing dependence on the alternative energy sources depending upon their specific natural resource endowments; the main trade-off is between coal and petroleum.

Fourth, international trade in oil is very important by economic, political, and security criteria. It constituted about 10 percent of world trade, even in the pre-1973 period, and in terms of pre-1973 prices. Two of the four major consumers—Japan and the EC—must import essentially all their oil. The United States imports about one-quarter of domestic consumption. Only the USSR is self-sufficient in oil; indeed it is a small oil exporter, to Western Europe. Most world imports of oil come from the Middle East and North Africa; both Japan and the EC obtain 85-plus percent of their imports from there, a great economic dependence. U.S. imports to date have been mainly from Venezuela and Canada. However, the total energy situation is much less severe, since countries have substitutes, mainly of domestic origin. Thus the United States only imports 10 percent of total energy consumption; West Germany and the United Kingdom, also with substantial coal mining, import 45 percent; France is higher at 70 percent; and Japan has gone the farthest among major industrial nations, relying the most on oil (75 percent of total energy), so that when imported coking coal is included, about 85 percent of Japan's energy is imported.

Fifth, there are immense differences in the marginal costs of produc-

ing oil from different fields, and an immense gap between the lowest cost
sources of production and the world market price. Middle East and
North African oil, in ample supply, is extremely cheap to produce—15
to 30 cents per barrel in terms of 1970 prices, perhaps double that in
1974. Costs of production are considerably higher in the rest of the
world and probably highest in the United States (excluding the USSR,
for which cost data are not available).[14] The world market price of
crude oil (Persian Gulf) in August 1973 was about $2.50 per barrel;
low-sulphur crudes had a premium on the order of $1.25, reflecting
environmental restrictions and costs of removing sulphur from ordinary
crude. The Arab oil production cuts in late 1973 were combined with
dramatically increased posted prices for relatively small amounts
available for quick delivery. Throughout 1974 the world price of oil
averaged about $10 per barrel. These increases were sustainable in the
short run of a year or two because of the time it takes to develop
substitutes—new petroleum fields, alternative energy sources.

Sixth, the continual existence of high prices for oil relative to costs
of production has been, in substantial part at least, a consequence of
an oligopolistic market structure in the world oil market. There are
two sets of actors on the production side: international oil companies
and host governments of oil-producing and exporting nations. Most
exploration, production, transportation, refining, and marketing of ex-
ported oil has been done by seven major international oil companies that
are involved in slightly over 60 percent of non-Communist world oil
output. Five (Exxon, Texaco, Gulf, Standard Oil of California, Mobil)
are American owned and controlled, one (British Petroleum) is British,
and one (Shell) is joint Dutch-British. There are strong government-
sponsored national companies for refining and distribution in Italy and
France. While earlier the international companies had considerable
control over production and pricing, this has been eroded, first, by the
increasing importance of a number of independent oil companies and,
then, by the producing-country governments, especially since the
formation of their cartel, OPEC. OPEC includes all the important
oil-exporting nations; they are a diverse group geographically,

14.   The high marginal cost in the United States is mainly because the U.S. price has been
high, and production pushed to the margin. U.S. long-run supply elasticity is estimated at about
1: a change in price of 10 percent would change supply by an equal percentage (see Burrows and
Domencich, *United States Oil Import Quota*, p. 72). However, this estimate probably does not apply
directly to ranges of price increases seen in late 1973. As of summer 1973 the U.S. cost of crude oil
was about $3 per barrel; during the 1960s the U.S. price was considerably higher than the world
price because imports were restricted by quotas. The cost to consumers in 1968 alone of import
quotas is estimated at between $5.6 and $6.2 billion, and the cost to the country (which ignores
transfers from consumers to producers) at between $3.3 and $4.6 billion. The transfer to U.S. oil
producers was about $3.9 billion and to refiners $500 million (see Burrows and Domencich, p. 158).

economically, politically, and in goals. The main objectives of OPEC have been economic: to increase revenues derived from oil exports. OAPEC (Organization of Arab Petroleum Exporting Countries) is a separate organization of exclusively Arab membership; its goals are more political. OPEC now sets world oil prices, in conjunction with the major international oil companies. Most of the bargaining between the governments of oil-producing countries and the international oil companies is over the division of the large difference (monopoly rent) between costs of production and world market price. Adelman has characterized the companies as tax collectors for OPEC, though he notes they also apparently obtain a share of any price increases.[15] The international oil companies maintain considerable power nonetheless because of superior knowledge and skills (technological, organization, marketing), immense amounts of capital, and integrated operations (transport, refining, and distribution), as well as connections with the United States and other major governments.

The Winter 1973-74 Oil Crisis

Prior to the October 1973 Arab-Israeli conflict, the main concern among policymakers in the United States, the EC, and Japan apparently was that there would develop within a relatively few years secular world shortages of oil and energy supplies relative to growing demand. I return to this issue below. The subsequent winter 1973-74 oil crisis of production cuts and partial embargoes brought to the forefront a number of issues also relevant for a 1980 resources scenario. As is now known, the winter 1973-74 supply interruption was limited in amount and duration. At the same time, however, it produced great uncertainty, anxiety, and pessimism. The actual situation was not at all clear. It was impossible to know very well at the time how much oil was being produced in the world, where it was being shipped, and at what price. Only the Arab oil nations (excluding Iraq) actually reduced production, though to what extent was uncertain; other producers (Iran and Indonesia for example) increased production. In early 1974 shortages appeared to be potential rather than actual, based on fears that inventories might be reduced to critical levels as the embargo persisted. In fact, the cutback was never serious and did not last long. By late summer, consuming countries had all the oil they wanted and stockpiles were overflowing. It was higher prices and the world recession, not supply constraints, that held down demand.

Nonetheless, the embargo emphasized the tremendous importance

15. Morris Adelman, "Is the Oil Shortage Real?—Oil Companies as OPEC Tax-Collectors," *Foreign Policy*, no. 9 (Winter 1972-73), pp. 69-107.

both of petroleum in all industrial economies and of the accommodating facilities to transport, refine, and distribute petroleum products. It also demonstrated the capability of producers to push up prices dramatically through unified action. These high prices have had strong impacts on the balance of payments and terms of trade of importing (and exporting) countries. How can importers earn the added foreign exchange needed for high-price oil imports? How will the selling countries spend these gains for goods, services, and foreign assets?

The nature as well as degree of the winter 1973–74 problem and the alternatives differed by country. For the United States the real problem was not just the oil embargo but the emerging shortage of refining capacity and, to a lesser extent, port facilities; even if oil could be imported freely it would be several years before adequate domestic refining capacity could be built. In the interim the United States must continue to rely on European refineries. On the other hand, a much higher proportion of energy use in the United States than elsewhere goes into nonindustrial, final consumption uses, especially automobile gasoline. For Japan, and to a lesser degree the EC, the problem is the high reliance upon imported petroleum for industrial activity; refining capacity is not the problem. However, the only way to adjust in the short run to oil shortages is to cut industrial production, especially of high-energy-using and petrochemical industries.

It is very unlikely such supply interruptions can be continued for long, or even created very often, as was evidenced by Arab easing and lifting of production and embargo restrictions. A prolonged or severe embargo or reduction in production is intolerable to the Big Three, much less smaller nations, and all kinds of pressures would mount on nations seriously restricting oil exports; Kissinger's remarks in January 1975 were merely explicit expression of the obvious. For this and other reasons Arab leaders recognize that it is not in their interest to resort to such drastic action for long. More in their interest is to keep supply (production) in line with growth of demand at a high price, but this strategy is limited over time by the supply price of alternative energy substitutes as is discussed below.

The scenario of competition for (oil) resources will be influenced by changes that occur between now and the 1980 target period. First, the global demand for energy and for oil will probably increase at about 4 to 6 percent per year, depending upon GNP growth rates, changes in structure of production and transportation, reactions to higher prices, and energy conservation measures. Second, in the absence of a major autarkic effort, U.S. oil imports will increase dramatically as demand increases outstrip domestic supply increases. Pre-October 1973 projections were that by the early 1980s the United States might import up to

11 million barrels a day, almost half domestic consumption; higher prices alone will stimulate U.S. domestic production and reduce demand so as to cut back on imports. Most of the imported oil would, in peaceful and stable circumstances, come from the Middle East and North Africa. Third, the demand for imported oil by Japan and the EC will increase at rates approximately equal to GNP growth. Fourth, Saudi Arabia et al. will have accumulated large amounts of foreign exchange and other foreign assets. The main area of competition for oil among the Big Three, in these circumstances, would be in the Middle East.

Any discussion of the economic aspects of a competition-for-resources scenario boils down to two related issues: availabilities of supplies and the price charged. Traditionally, bureaucrats and policymakers, concerned about national security, have focused on problems of lack of physical supplies; the recent quadrupling of oil prices has also made them acutely aware of the implications of high prices. A competition-for-oil scenario incorporates both supply quantity and price effects; I will consider the physical supply issue first.

Energy Supplies

Either lack of long-run supply availabilities or short-run interruptions of supply can produce a hostile world environment of competition for oil. Virtually all sensible projections indicate no global physical shortage of oil supply relative to world demand by even the late 1980s. Put simply, there are immense reserves of oil in the Middle East. These will be supplemented by development of other known reserves—in the North Sea, Indonesia, the North Alaskan Slope, and Canadian Arctic—and by the high probability of substantial new discoveries in the coming decade. The spurt of private exploration since 1974 as a consequence of high prices virtually guarantees substantially increased, and more diversified, global oil supplies.

More important in the longer run is the opportunity for substitution of other energy sources. Substantial substitution could occur by the 1980s—and will if petroleum prices remain high or if national policies so dictate. There apparently is at least three times as much oil in oil shale, sands, and tars as in both proved and unproved-but-projected world reserves of petroleum pools, and seven times as much coal in terms of common energy units. Of the crudely estimated world reserves of recoverable fossil fuels, petroleum is only about 8 percent, coal 61, shale oil 25, and natural gas 6.[16] There are ample supplies for energy

16. Nordhaus, "Allocation of Energy Resources," table 2, p. 542. See also Schurr and Homan, *Middle Eastern Oil*, pp. 53–66.

demand projections for the rest of this century. Which energy resources are developed when will depend on the differing costs of production and the degree to which the economically low cost of petroleum is offset by continued monopoly pricing.

In the even longer run, during the twenty-first century, nuclear energy will replace fossil fuels as the dominant source of energy, and it will provide the dominant portion of the increase in energy demand long before that. In effect, in the next fifty years under anticipated technologies the world will be making a transition from now relatively low cost but increasingly scarce fossil fuels to higher cost nuclear energy with virtually infinite supplies of raw materials, based first on breeder reactors and later on nuclear fusion. (The supply of U-238 alone is estimated to yield two thousand times the energy of all recoverable fossil resources.) The costs, in amounts of capital and labor needed to extract and prepare energy raw materials for commercial use, differ substantially by type of energy resource. As a particular resource become scarce, lower-grade, less accessible deposits are then developed, but at higher cost. The capital requirements for nuclear energy are particularly large. Given knowledge about the long-run supply curves of the different fossil fuels, the costs of nuclear energy, future demands, and relevant technological change, it is in principle possible to calculate an efficient transition path from fossil to nuclear fuels. An example of such a path, estimated at a high level of aggregation, has been computed in an excellent analysis by Nordhaus.[17] It is possible new technologies will develop other, superior energy sources—solar, geothermal, magnetic field. But such assumptions are not necessary to infer that even in the very long run mankind is not doomed to lack of energy supplies at reasonable costs, even taking into account the costs of environmental protection. The nuclear energy substitution will not occur soon enough, however, to have a significant impact by the early 1980s. The gestation period on most nuclear energy projects is seven to ten years, and light water reactors, currently in use, are technically much less efficient than breeder reactors in energy conversion.

The relevant supply constraints making a competition-for-resources scenario possible are either short-run interruptions of oil supplies or production restraints to maintain a high price. Most projections of interruptions are based on noneconomic factors. In the late 1960s, long before the recent crisis, the U.S. Department of Defense considered four alternative scenarios of interruption of free-world oil supply.[18] The first was that of major nuclear war. In this scenario oil production

17.   The results are given in Nordhaus, "Allocation of Energy Resources," table 5, p. 552.
18.   Burrows and Domencich, *United States Oil Import Quota*, p. 177 and after.

and transportation facilities are far less likely to be destroyed than the consumption activities of the major industrial nations, and the war is not likely to last long, so the problem of lack of oil is minor relative to other problems. It is also considered highly unlikely. The second scenario posited conventional hostilities between two or more major powers, a likelihood also considered very small. A brief war would probably not cause serious problems, but a more protracted (two to three years) conventional war involving the United States, the EC, and/or Japan could have serious effects upon their domestic economies due to possible inability to import sufficient supplies of oil. The third possibility was protracted limited war in certain parts of the world not involving directly the United States or Japan but involving directly or indirectly major oil producers, particularly those in the Middle East. The fourth scenario involved serious interruptions of supply for certain countries due to strikes and the like. Such interruptions are likely to be relatively limited, however, in their impact in either time or location.

The third scenario has of course occurred. Apparently contingency planning did not lead to any actions by the U.S. government to minimize the impact of this event. It now seems quite possible, though I think not likely, that in the 1980s political difficulties in the Middle East could interrupt the flow of oil. It might emanate from a new flare-up of hostilities between Israel and the Arab nations, or a conflict between the low population, oil abundant countries (Saudi Arabia, Kuwait, the Trucial States) and any of their more densely populated neighbors (Egypt, Jordan, Syria, Iraq, Iran), or internal subversion (including actions by discontented Palestinians). Under such circumstances the present effects on the Big Three economies could be repeated unless, as is highly likely, each takes alternative steps between now and the 1980s.

The Price of Oil

What is clear is that the OPEC nations will continue to attempt through cartel decisions to obtain a high price for their oil, so the most probable competition-for-oil scenario is one of artificially high prices rather than lack of supplies at any price. There is, however, a substantial difference between intent and capability. Will OPEC be able to keep prices high in 1980? High price is an elusive concept that requires some elaboration. First, prices are relative; what concerns OPEC nations is not simply the absolute dollar (or other foreign currency) price but what those dollars will buy in the form of imports or foreign assets. If those prices rise as much as oil export prices (strictly speaking, the revenues derived by the producing countries' net of the take of the international companies), then the OPEC nations derive no real benefit—only world inflation results. Second, a price is high to the extent it reflects the exercise of oligopoly (monopoly) power by the sellers, namely, the difference between the actual price and the price that would prevail in competitive markets.

This is shown diagrammatically in figure 4.1. The competitive equilibrium price is P_0; Nordhaus estimates it was about $1.20 per barrel for 1970.[19] The actual free market price (P_1) in 1970 was $2.38, about double. This higher price predominantly reflects the combined market power of oil-producing countries and the international oil companies, and the relatively higher costs of production of substitute energy sources.[20] If the oil producers can succeed in restricting production in the short run, price rises sharply to P_2, as occurred in late 1973. This heuristic diagram excludes three important dynamic components: over time the demand for oil grows (the demand curve shifts to the right); the longer-run supply curves may also shift to the right in response; and energy substitutes for oil are developed if price remains high.

While energy substitutes are physically available, the important question is: at what price? Price is in relative terms—petroleum relative to other energy sources. However, the issue of prices has been further complicated by the general inflation in the prices of virtually

Figure 4.1
Short-run Supply and Demand Curves for Oil

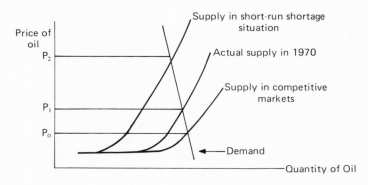
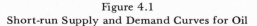

19.   Nordhaus, "Allocation of Energy Resources," table 8, p. 556.

20.   Two points should be made. First, the difference between the actual price in 1970 and the efficiency competitive price calculated by Nordhaus may be in deficiencies in the data; the market may have worked well and price may have been quite competitively determined. This does not vitiate the point that monopoly profits accrued to the OPEC cartel from late 1973. Second, to the extent that monopoly market power exists, supply curves are not independent of demand curves; technically it is preferable to think of the curves giving the P_1 and P_2 solutions as offer curves.

all goods since 1970, and also by the substantial and continuing shifts among relative prices of oil, other fossil energy resources, other minerals, foodstuffs, and manufactured goods. Thus, using 100 as the base in 1970, the export price indexes in April–June 1974 were, for fuels and combustibles 519, foodstuffs 213, and manufactures 156.[21] Since the Middle East imports about eleven times as much manufactured goods as foodstuffs, to maintain parity in relative price terms oil would have risen in mid-1974 by 62 percent, to $3.86 per barrel in 1974 prices. In fact, the price was almost three times that high, implying a favorable tripling in the relative prices for OPEC nations.

In terms of 1970 constant prices, coal is highly price competitive with oil at $3 to $4 per barrel, nuclear energy in the $4 to $5 range, and shale oil at $5.50 to $6.00. These are conservative estimates; extensive substitution may occur at even lower relative prices. (Natural gas has been underpriced; as its price is made more free and rises to levels comparable with petroleum, supplies may be expected to increase substantially also.) These prices of substitutes are sufficiently low that they set an upper limit to the longer-run price of petroleum. The high degree of substitutability among energy sources in the longer run, say five years, when alternative supplies can be developed, means the price of oil, coal, or any other specific energy source is highly constrained by the prices of other energy sources; there are high cross-price elasticities of demand. This is quite consistent with the fact that the demand for energy in aggregate is quite price-inelastic and rather income-elastic, on the order of 1 to 1.5.

I predict that the 1980 free-world market price of petroleum will not be greater than $5.00 per barrel in terms of 1970 dollar purchasing power; in terms of mid-1974 dollar purchasing power this would imply a price of about $8.10. This is still double the 1970 price, and about three times the efficient competitive equilibrium price of $1.70 (in 1970 dollars) estimated by Nordhaus for 1980. Thus the actual market price could well be considerably lower than my prediction if the OPEC nations are not able to maintain their price cartel. This prediction implies that considerable development of energy sources alternative to Middle Eastern oil will take place, thereby forcing the oil price down from high current levels and keeping it down.

Policy Alternatives

What are the policy alternatives for Japan to obtain adequate supplies of oil at reasonable prices in the 1980s? Perhaps oil more than

21. Calculated from United Nations, Department of Economic and Social Affairs, *Monthly Bulletin of Statistics*, (December 1974), pp. xviii–xix.

anything else indicates the economic interdependence of nations and the effects of the actions of each of the major nations on the alternatives of the others. For Japan the oil environment will be determined greatly by U.S. and EC policies between now and the early 1980s. For all nations the risk of short-term interruptions of imported energy (oil) supply can be covered by domestic stockpiling programs. The risk, or cost, of oligopolistically determined high prices can be offset by diversification of energy sources of supply, which also reduces the impact of short-run interruptions of oil supplies, and by conservation, which by reducing demand puts pressure on price.

The United States, with its abundance of various energy sources as well as capital and high technology skills, has the greatest range of options among the Big Three. Its growing demand for energy and, especially, potential demand for imported oil make it a major new force in world energy markets. The alternatives for the United States are to rely on a relatively free and competitive world petroleum market importing large amounts of oil, particularly from the Middle East and North Africa, or to rely mainly on domestic (and other Western Hemisphere) petroleum and other primary energy fuels. These may be defined in the extreme as free trade versus autarky.

In Nordhaus's discussion of efficient energy resource allocation in a competitive world market equilibrium with free trade, without oligo-poly oil pricing or supply interruptions, the United States would be a major oil importer in 1980 (about 7 million barrels) and for the next thirty years, thereafter becoming a major exporter of energy in the forms of coal and shale oil. Nordhaus estimates for 1970 this solution would be only two-thirds as expensive economically for the United States as autarky. The risk of supply interruption could readily be covered by the stockpiling of oil; it would be cheaper to store the equivalent of several years' imports than to bear the higher costs of an autarkic approach.

An American autarkic policy of energy self-sufficiency would require restriction of domestic demand through higher prices, conservation measures, and perhaps rationing and expansion of domestic supplies. The latter would necessitate major development of Alaskan North Slope oil, offshore oil, and probably tar sands, oil shale, and coal hydrogenation. To make this development possible the U.S. govern-ment would have to provide substantial incentives to private business: tax benefits, relaxation of environmental constraints, and particularly the de facto guarantee of sufficiently high domestic energy prices. The fixed capital costs of such new projects will be very large; profitability is threatened by the possibility the Middle East producers might reduce prices to summer 1973 relative levels. Thus a U.S. self-sufficiency approach would require policies to restrict once again the imports of low-cost oil to residual levels consistent with U.S. supplies, through quotas or import taxes.

The presumed threats to national security and welfare and the U.S. balance of payments make it very likely the United States will go far along the autarkic path, as was indicated in President Nixon's statements on energy policy and more recently in President Ford's "project independence." This projection goes against the economics of the matter; it would be more efficient (cheaper) to meet security needs by stockpiling and to effect balance of payments constraint by making it attractive to reallocate resources (capital, labor, and land) to export production. But I anticipate U.S. policymakers will be more willing to put up with the economic inefficiencies of greater reliance on domestic energy sources in order to feel American power is more secure. The main beneficiaries of an autarkic approach will be the owners of domestic energy resources, including importantly the major U.S.-based international oil companies. The main loser will be the American consumer who, directly and indirectly, will pay higher prices for energy. Of course, one might interpret American government adoption of a self-sufficiency policy as simply a tactic to force OPEC to reduce the oil price, whereupon the policy will be dramatically eased. This would be an excellent approach, but it would seem that the current policy is being used for strategic rather than tactical purposes.

The options available to the European Community are narrower. The reliance on imported oil from the Middle East and North Africa is already substantially greater. Existing estimates indicate in 1980 Western Europe will import 69 percent of its energy supply compared with 63 percent in 1970, mainly (64 percent of total energy) in the form of oil from North Africa and the Middle East. However, Odell argues that if Western European governments and the oil and gas companies move rapidly in developing the North Sea (hence indigenous) oil and natural gas deposits, reliance on imports will decline sharply. In his estimates for 1980 only 40 percent of West European energy is imported, with 44 percent coming from domestic oil and natural gas. Oil imports, 33 percent of total energy, are absolutely smaller than in 1970.[22] The capital costs of North Sea oil and natural gas development are high, but Odell's estimates suggest operations would be profitable at a world price (net of transport costs) of $3 per barrel in 1970 prices. An even somewhat higher cost nonetheless puts great pressure on a high oil-price policy by the OPEC nations. At the same time the internal

22. P. R. Odell, "Europe's Oil," *National Westminster Bank Quarterly Review*, August 1972, pp. 6–21. See also his book *Oil and World Power: A Geographical Interpretation* (New York, 1970).

strains on the European Community will become increasingly severe; the energy have-not nations—France and Italy in particular—may have fundamentally different interests from the United Kingdom and perhaps West Germany, preferring, as France has, to make special bilateral deals with individual OPEC nations. This too could undermine OPEC, as well as the EC.

Energy for Japan

Between now and the 1980s Japan too will attempt even more than before to diversify supply sources—by country, region, political system, type of supplying company—to prepare against the possibility of a resource-competitive world environment. The alternative of reliance on domestic energy resources, even at high prices, does not really exist for Japan. We can expect an enhancement of present government policies to promote Japanese private foreign investment, aided by government loans and subsidies, in natural resource (including oil) development in a variety of ways.[23] Japan will thus be undertaking vigorous steps to diversify geographically its sources of petroleum imports and to increase the proportion of imports that are under some degree of Japanese control to a target of 30 percent—also a target in the early 1960s that was never reached.

Throughout this period, and particularly in the next few years, Japan will have to do whatever it can to appease, or at least not to alienate, the Arab oil-producing (OAPEC) nations. It is important that Japan be deemed among the friendly nations, like England and France. Arrangements for diversification will vary from joint ventures with international oil companies (as in Indonesia) to joint ventures with government companies in oil-producing nations to financing exploration and development through loans (Russia, China). Oil and natural gas from Siberia will have high costs of production, but Japan may be willing to pay the price for the sake of geographic and political diversification. Even so, it is projected that at the maximum only 20 percent of Japan's natural gas and 10 percent of oil imports would come from Russia. The discovery of large deposits of oil under the China Sea could also have profound implications for Japan's relations with China. Though unlikely, it is not impossible by the mid-1980s to have as much as 20 percent of Japan's oil coming from China Sea wells owned by

23.   For a more detailed analysis see the 1971 natural resources white paper in MITI, Coal and Mining Bureau, *Shigen mondai no tenbō* [A view of natural resource problems] (25 November 1971), summarized in English as "Prospect of Natural Resource Problems in Japan," in Japan External Trade Organization (JETRO), *Trade and Industry of Japan: Economic Reports* 21, no.1 (no.167) (1972): pp. 34–60; and MITI, *Sangyō kōzo no choki bijon* [Long-term vision of the industrial structure] November, 1964.

China but explored and developed by Japanese firms, financing (in addition to developmental costs) substantial Chinese imports from Japan. Another possibility is that Japan will invest heavily in extraction of oil from shale in Venezuela, from sands in Canada, or from whatever such new, safe sources may be discovered. As with the United States, development of all these high-priced sources involves the risk of losses from possible low prices for Middle Eastern oil. In Japan's case the government will directly share in the investment risks and probably take other policies (such as forced prorating of expensive oil to all domestic refineries and users) to ensure that private Japanese business will undertake the desired international development of energy resources.

Several general points must be stressed, nonetheless. First, it is highly improbable that Japan by the 1980s can diversify in developing alternative sources of energy sufficiently to reduce overwhelming reliance on Middle Eastern oil. At the least, 50 percent of its oil will be imported from the Middle East in 1980, compared with slightly over 80 percent in 1973; probably the proportion will be much higher. Second, Japan now relies heavily on Iran, by far its largest supplier with almost two-fifths of Japan's market. Iran is a major oil producer, with large reserves it is anxious to sell to earn foreign exchange to finance ambitious economic development and military programs. Iran is the only non-Arab Middle Eastern or North African oil nation; it responded to the OAPEC oil production cuts and temporary world shortages by raising production as well as prices, and it has been one of the OPEC leaders. Japan's reliance on and relationship with Iran is likely to intensify as Japan becomes ever more heavily involved in providing the capital goods and technology for the Iranian development effort. Third, Japan's oil import reliance is double-pronged: on both Middle Eastern producing nations and international oil companies. Six internationals sell Japan 62 percent of its oil, and other internationals another 12 percent; the direct deals of Japanese producing and trading companies provide only some 26 percent of Japan's oil. Japan has to deal with the oligopolistic practices of both the international oil companies and the OPEC nations. Moreover, in periods of short-run supply interruptions, Japan cannot prevent diversions of oil deliveries by the international oil companies away from Japan. This occurred to a limited extent in the 1973–74 oil crisis, though at the time estimates suggested it was substantial. The Japanese government will probably intensify its efforts to reduce reliance on imports through the major international companies as an integral component of its general policy of diversification.

In a real sense, in energy American security interests and Japanese economic interests converge. For Japan the best of all possible 1980 world oil environments is one in which the United States has moved quickly and strongly toward energy self-sufficiency and the EC has rapidly developed the North Sea energy resources. These steps would both substantially increase the world supply of energy, including oil, and greatly reduce the U.S. and EC demand for Middle Eastern and North African oil, leaving Japan in a strong bargaining position as the world's largest oil importer. The OPEC cartel would find it very difficult to maintain oil prices in a world of rapidly developing and increasingly abundant alternative energy sources. Individual producing countries might well violate agreements by cutting prices slightly in efforts to sell much more and by using new national companies to take markets away from the major international companies by price competition. While prices may not drop to competitive levels, nonetheless price declines could be substantial. One school of thought, led by Morris Adelman, regards this as a likely prospect.[24] I regard a scenario of ample supplies and moderate prices for oil for Japan through the 1980s as considerably more likely than a scenario of shortages, high prices, and tense competition with other major powers. Indeed, the Arab oil cutbacks associated with the 1973–74 Arab-Israeli conflict, by hurting the United States, the EC, and Japan in the short run, hurt OPEC economic interests in the long run by accentuating or altering government policies in the Big Three to develop new energy sources.

Despite this judgment, we should explicitly consider the implication of possible competition-for-oil scenarios. There will be no long-run physical (or economic) shortage of oil or energy, so a scenario cannot be built upon that assumption. Temporary or sporadic short-run supply interruptions are possible. They could have strong adverse short-run effects on the Japanese economy. The best solution is stockpiling of crude oil inventories. Until 1973 Japan's stockpiling policy entailed a 45-day supply, to be increased within a few years to 60 days, and eventually more; these inventories were substantially less than the EC 60-day ones and the Organization for Economic Cooperation and Development (OECD) Oil Committee recommendation of 90 days. Cost estimates of storing oil, mainly interest on the funds used to build storage facilities and to buy the oil itself, are in the range of 60 to 90 cents per barrel per year in 1970 prices. A six-month stockpile would add no more than 15 percent, probably considerably less, to the price per

24. See Adelman, *World Petroleum Market* and "Is the Oil Shortage Real?" For a similar view see Schurr and Homan, *Middle Eastern Oil*, chapter 11. The alternative position—dangers of politically motivated supply interruptions, production restrictions, and the likelihood of high prices—is effectively presented by James E. Akins, "The Oil Crisis: This Time the Wolf Is Here," *Foreign Affairs*, April 1973, pp. 462–90.

barrel of crude oil consumed. This is an inexpensive insurance premium relative to the expense of developing high-cost alternative energy sources. Moreover, the very existence of large inventories in Japan and elsewhere reduces the likelihood that short-run supply interruptions would be used as an instrument of policy by a cartel of oil producers; it becomes a less creditable threat. I anticipate that Japan, the EC, and others will move in the next few years to substantially greater stock-piling.

A potentially more serious set of problems emerges from a scenario of continued high world prices for oil. Oil-importing nations will have balance of payments difficulties in generating enough exports to pay for oil; the terms of trade will remain adverse, meaning the oil pro-ducers obtain a greater share of the gains from trade and growth of oil-consuming nations; Saudi Arabia, Abu Dhabi, and Libya will have large current account surpluses that will have to be absorbed as foreign exchange reserves and foreign assets. All these factors could put tremendous strain on the international trading and financial system, on the international rules of the game (and who determines them), and on cooperation among the United States, the EC, and Japan in the world economic environment.

A high-oil-price scenario is likely if alternative energy sources (both new oil reserves and substitutes for petroleum) are not developed rapidly enough, that is, if supply increases do not keep pace with demand growth. Much depends on the time period within which alternative supplies are developed and on government policies in the United States, the EC, Japan, and elsewhere. It also depends on the policies of the major oil-producing nations, particularly Saudi Arabia. Most other major producers such as Iran, Iraq, and Indonesia can be expected to increase production; they need the foreign exchange in order to finance developmental and military imports.

Saudi Arabia, however, has both the greatest potential for expansion in the production of low-cost oil and the least likelihood of spending all export earnings on imports of goods and services. Saudi Arabia could take the lead in maintaining high prices by allowing others to produce as much oil as they wished but restricting its own (increases in) production. This has the attraction to Saudi Arabia of high prices, high income, maintenance of large oil reserves, and avoidance (de-pending upon price elasticities or demand) of large foreign exchange earnings that have to be invested abroad in one form or another.

How might Saudi Arabia, Kuwait, and others in similar circum-stances be persuaded that such a policy would be less successful than the alternative of higher production and somewhat lower world prices? The most important point is that the long-run great availability of

energy substitutes price-competitive with oil at $4 to $6 per barrel in
1970 prices, and perhaps at lower prices as research and development
proceed, places an upper limit on the long-run relative price of oil. If
the current price is at or above that level, then the yield on holding oil
in the ground is zero or negative; and the opportunity cost of interest
and profits foregone on the foreign investments into which the petroleum could be transformed is substantial.

At the same time the world monetary and investment climate has to
become attractive to Arabian investment. Big Three leaders fear that
oil countries with immense foreign assets might disrupt the international monetary system by large-scale foreign exchange reserve
accumulation or destabilizing short-term capital movements and
might obtain control over import sectors by direct investments in their
productive activities. These fears appear exaggerated, since Saudi
Arabia also would bear substantial losses in the value of foreign assets
as well as the danger of expropriation or blockage in times of crisis.
Recognition of these potential difficulties could do much to encourage
cooperation among the Big Three and between them and the Arabs.
Moreover, it suggests that Japan (and the EC and the United States)
would be wise to encourage Arabian investment in short-term and long-
term Japanese assets—yen, bank deposits, bonds, shares, directly in
companies—while trying to minimize the amount of foreign control.
This would provide Japan with Arabian hostages and make hostile
acts against Japan much less attractive. In addition, Saudi Arabia and
Kuwait will be under tremendous pressure to provide financial resources to those LDCs needing foreign assistance for their own development. Such funds will flow through Arab financial institutions to
other Arab nations, and through the World Bank and International
Monetary Fund to other LDCs. The basic point remains that the
large foreign assets of Saudi Arabia, Kuwait, and other oil producers
will give them power the Big Three will have to accommodate.

A high price for oil has quite different direct and indirect balance of
payments implications for each of the Big Three. I regard these as the
major sources of strain on cooperation among the Big Three and hence
the main factor potentially leading to a world of conflict. Japan would
have to export much more and/or restrict other imports to earn the
foreign exchange to pay for oil, especially if it has difficulty in directly
or indirectly borrowing petrodollars. This could lead to new export
promotion and import restriction programs that the United States
and EC would find intolerable since, from their point of view, Japan
would be foisting on them the burden of adjustment to high oil prices.
The temptation would be great on all to make special, preferential,
bilateral, barter-type deals with the oil producers to obtain markets
as well as oil. The United States would have to pay more for energy

imports until domestic substitutes become available. However, the need to generate more exports to pay for oil imports would be greater for the United States in a low price, free-trade oil context in which much less domestic substitution occurs. The United States then might well engage in export promotion measures that Japan and the EC in turn find intolerable. The EC appears intermediate in the effects; perhaps its expenditures on Middle Eastern and North African oil will not be overwhelmingly different under either high or low price situations, with the adjustment factor being the speed with which the North Sea deposits are developed.

I believe that over time Japan will be able to resolve the balance of payments problems of a substantially increased oil import bill due to higher prices without having the balance of payments constrain domestic economic growth to a lower rate. Japan has had long and successful experience with the problem of earning foreign exchange to pay for essential raw material imports. Only for the United States is this a new problem, which is why it may be frightening to some.

The more severe problem of high oil prices for Japanese domestic economic performance lies in the adverse movement of the terms of trade. Japan would have to sell much more exports to buy a barrel of oil imports. Relatively more of the benefits of Japanese growth would go to foreign oil producers than to Japanese. The causal chain from changes in terms of trade to effects on Japanese GNP growth and welfare is complex, involving interactions among a number of variables including savings and investment. While no direct empirical studies are available to me, I doubt that a doubling of the relative price of oil alone would reduce the long-run potential growth rate of the Japanese economy substantially. It simply would be one of a number of factors causing some slowdown from the very rapid rates of the late 1960s.

While a competition-for-oil scenario does not seem likely for the 1980s, nonetheless there are elements in the issue that put considerable strains on general economic cooperation among the Big Three and make going-it-alone tempting for each. This makes it less likely that a world of mutual understanding, high cooperation, and negotiated compromise of differences will be achieved. The 1973–74 crisis brought these strains to the fore. Extensive cooperation among the United States, the EC, and Japan, particularly in organized opposition to the OPEC nations, is unlikely in the short run. On the other hand, it seems even more unlikely the present crisis will deepen sufficiently to put the Big Three onto a collision course of open economic conflict. How the Big Three resolve current differences on oil will influence their abilities and willingness to cooperate on other trade and finance issues as well in the longer run.

I can imagine quite different world economic environments in which Japan might find itself in the early 1980s. Each would engender quite different responses on the part of Japan: cooperation and harmony with the European Community and the United States in one scenario; competition with them in a scenario of conflict and regional blocs; and competition with them, or at least with the United States, in an oil scenario. However, it appears that in all three world environments Japan would have sufficient economic power and capabilities of international economic policy to be able to adjust without severe reductions in its capacities to import. And it is the capacity to import that will continue to be the dominant potential external constraint upon Japanese domestic growth. In most relevant world scenarios the Japanese economy should be able to prosper. The real constraints on future growth are more domestic than foreign. However, what sort of economy, polity, and society Japan becomes depends considerably upon the international environment. If the international environment should be perceived by Japan as hostile and threatening, a high degree of reactive nationalism might well emerge. While this might affect the economy's performance in some ways, its major importance clearly will be in other areas of Japanese society. One specific point: Japanese military armament (nuclear weapons systems) will do very little if anything to provide Japan with oil or other natural resources; gunboat diplomacy no longer works, and Japanese are well aware of that.

The world economic system forged after World War II of multi-lateral, nondiscriminatory, increasingly free trade and capital flows in a system of fixed exchange rates under rules set by negotiation and cooperation found itself unable to adapt to the rise in economic power of the European nations and Japan and the relative decline of the economic power of the United States. The international monetary system did not provide an adequate mechanism for balance of payments adjustment by surplus and deficit nations or a mutually satisfactory means of creating international liquidity. These exacerbated problems of decreasingly competitive but politically and economically important domestic sectors in all major industrial countries; labor and capital have not been transferred out of inefficient, low productivity, labor-intensive manufacturing and agriculture as rapidly as the increasing competitiveness of imported goods would warrant. To these strains on economic relationships has been added the oil crisis, first in embargoes and more importantly in terms of prices. Fortunately, many of these economic tensions have been relieved by the abandonment of the Bretton Woods fixed exchange rate system, the subsequent exchange rate adjustments, and the substantially greater flexibility among exchange rates.

It would be optimistic to predict that a new world environment of cooperation and harmony will prevail. Yet deterioration into a go-it-alone world of economic conflict with regional blocs, trade, capital, and natural resource (oil) preferences seems unlikely. It is difficult to conceive of competition for oil leading to such a world of conflict. The basic economics of very low cost oil in a number of OPEC nations and of quite abundant alternative energy sources at reasonable prices makes such a scenario unlikely; the cartel will find it very difficult if not impossible to maintain such a high price. Moreover, all major consuming nations are likely to overreact: to overestimate risks and dangers, to be very conservative in trying to cover those perceived risks, and hence to develop alternative energy sources at costs beyond those dictated by economic alternatives or bargaining needs. The United States appears particularly likely to behave in this manner, since it has alternative domestic energy resources to develop, places high priority on national security, and can bear the costs of such inefficiency without undue strain.

Japan is also likely to overreact by investing in excessively high-cost energy resource development abroad and perhaps by signing long-term purchase contracts at prices that will turn out to be above subsequent world market prices. That investment in natural resources abroad provides control over production and supply is a chimera; increasingly this power will reside in the host-country government. As in the past, history has dealt Japan's hand a quarter-century too late. The main benefit of Japan's investment in foreign natural resources is as a bargaining tool with supplying countries and with international companies. It provides a lever to prevent diversion in times of shortage, to bargain on price in oligopolistic markets, and hence to increase the assurance of more stable supply. However, the overall price of such imports will be lower only if the high-cost, and hence high-price, imports from Japanese-controlled sources are more than offset by lower prices of these imports from elsewhere, with prices being lowered as a consequence both of increased Japanese bargaining power and increased world supply due to Japanese investment.

My best-guess estimate of the international economic environment of the early 1980s is not much different from the present: some strain will persist in areas of disagreement, but generally cooperation will prevail. The specter of highly competitive, discriminatory regional blocs will be too frightening. A fully articulated, well-defined new economic system will not have been worked out; it is as likely to evolve through customary acceptance of sensible practices on a de facto basis as through formal negotiations and international agreements. Exchange rates will change more often, but in an environment of friendliness rather than beggar-thy-neighbor. Rules on trade and adjustment for declining manufacturing industries will have become accepted, though perhaps not for agriculture. The problems with relation to natural resources will not be (and will not be seen as) physical shortages or extremely high prices but will consist in the amassing of large amounts of capital and high technology. Private and governmental financial intermediaries will effectively recycle Arabian foreign exchange earnings, again perhaps with some general rules developed among the Big Three and the Arabs. Both Europe and Japan will act more independently of the United States but will still deem it essential to have the United States as a friend. Cooperation among the Big Three may not be as great as in the past, but perhaps the needs for cooperation will not be as great in a more flexible world economic environment.

5

Technology and Power:
Japan Catches Up

T. DIXON LONG

Whether the economic growth rate is relatively fast or slow Japan will indisputably remain one of the great world centers of mercantile power. But this power is not automatically translated into military security. T. Dixon Long examines the roots of military power in industry, technology, and innovation, as well as the special technologies crucial to national security: aircraft, missiles, computers, and nuclear energy.

Education and technology account for up to half of long-term economic growth, it has been argued, and are thus intimately related to military security as well. Historically the state has been a leader and innovator in Japan's effort to catch up to and surpass the West in these fields. But the results of the state effort are mixed.

The balance of payments in technology is still relatively unfavorable to Japan, but this deficit in exchange means a very high growth rate as imported technology is translated into capital investment in new facilities. Long places less emphasis than Patrick on the drying up of this source of the energy for growth. But in spite of the efforts of the state to stimulate technological innovation at home, Long does not yet see a profound domestic capacity for sustained achievement in basic research.

Japan's military-economic situation in terms of technology is ambiguous: independence in missiles, dependence in warheads; independence in airframes, dependence in engines; high computer utilization, but heavy reliance on foreign joint-venture manufacturers. Long's conclusion is that Japan has the missile technology to deliver a nuclear weapon it does not have, does not want, and could not get in present circumstances.

But this ambiguous power position may be a key to the future not only of Japan but of many of the technologically advanced nations that are not great powers. Long suggests that successful innovation and competition, coupled with a basic international dependence in the area of certain raw materials and certain technologies, may be a pattern that will become more widespread, and that Japan's development in this sphere as in others may provide a model.—L. A.

Technology has long been acknowledged to have a modest influence on the power positions of nation-states, but until the twentieth century its effects were gradual and cumulative. Such influence is illustrated in White's analysis of the impact on European warfare of the stirrup, which, by providing a secure base for the mounted lancer, in time led to the ensconcement of the cavalry as the elite of the military profession.[1]

Analysts of international politics have observed the growing importance of the technological factor. It was particularly noticeable in the armories and strategies of late nineteenth- and early twentieth-century Europe, where iron and steel technology and the rapidly growing chemical industry became recognized as the sinews of power in peace as in war.[2] The clear lesson of two world wars has been that technology destabilizes the established ranking of nations, providing opportunities for (or examples of) movement up and down the ranks of the international pecking order.[3]

Japan has been a somewhat curious case, having introduced and then abandoned in the sixteenth century the key element of conventional military power, the gun. The Shogun Yoshimune's nationwide search and seizure of swords in the early seventeenth century left Japan doubly disarmed. The record of Western "opening" beginning in the 1850s is unequivocal with respect to technology: in the military and industrial spheres, Japan was essentially without national power or the technological foundations on which it could be built.

Although the record of the past century is well known, its lessons are perhaps not so widely appreciated. Japan steadily improved its position in the ranks of nation-states through the application of Western science and technology in the military and industrial spheres. A nation essentially outside the rankings in the closing years of the nineteenth century was, by the time of the Washington Conference in 1930, acknowledged to have the fifth or sixth most powerful navy in the world—the battleship then being like the nuclear-tipped missile now, the ultimate symbol of national power and prestige.

Power in the nuclear age apparently is a more complex phenomenon, comprising an element of nuclear deterrence whose ultimate significance is its nonuse. The ambivalence thus injected into international power relations has tended to reinforce the importance of diverse, technologically sophisticated conventional armaments. It has also

1.   Lynn T. White, Jr., *Medieval Technology and Social Change* (Oxford, 1962).

2.   Victor Basiuk, *Technology and World Power*, Foreign Policy Association, Headline Series, no. 20 (New York, 1970).

3.   Quincy Wright, *The Study of International Relations* (New York, 1955), pp. 369–89; and Warner Schilling, "Technology and International Relations," *International Encyclopedia of the Social Sciences*, vol. 15 (New York, 1968), pp. 1325–35.

served to underline the importance of the weapons of economic competition. Japan's emergence in the 1960s as the third industrial power in the world—after the United States and the Soviet Union—puts a kind of punctuation mark at the end of what has been termed "Japan's modern century."[4]

The real and important issue is: what kind of punctuation mark, and what shall follow it? The pursuit of military and industrial advance led through world war and a fierce economic offensive, a drive to expand exports that was characterized by the warlike phrase "landing in the face of the enemy."[5] It is not possible to peer very far into the future, or to derive much satisfaction from the mere extrapolation of trend lines, but there may be some utility in addressing the character and the limits of the advance of Japan's power through the application of modern technology. The question is not where is it going but what are the constraints—both internal and external—on where it might go. In the last analysis, this will lead to a consideration of whether the Japanese are themselves content with the "place in the world"[6] that has been gained and that may be secured largely through technology.

MILITARY POWER

In Japan's first modern wars, with China in 1894–95 and with Russia in 1904–05, the country's technological advantage was its efficient absorption and utilization of existing Western military technology. Russia's army was ill-organized and badly led; Russian ships were literally rotten. China had not yet learned one lesson of imperialism: that the West could be defeated with its own weapons. Japan's involvement in World War I was no real test of its military capability, though the Allies' desire to associate Japan with their cause testified to their respect for Japan's record and potential.

Japanese leaders entered World War II aware that their resources were limited. This situation was counterbalanced, however, by two factors of major significance. First, the nation was better disciplined and more homogeneous in social attitudes and organization than its potential opponents, as manifested in the pride Japan's leaders took in the amorphous but very real "spirit of the nation." The second factor was Japan's navy, the classic instrument of nineteenth-century imperial expansion. Built and organized with the best of Western know-how,

4.   A widely used text of Japanese history bears this title; Hugh Borton, *Japan's Modern Century* (New York, 1955).

5.   This phrase and its connotation was brought to my attention by Professor Otis Carey, Director of Amherst House, Doshisha University, Kyoto, Japan.

6.   The idea of place in the world is examined by Ronald Dore, "Japan's Place in the World," *World Today*, July 1966, pp. 293–306.

it was to be the means for achieving rapid expansion and ensuring the future defense of an empire nine-tenths ocean.[7]

Factors such as resource deficiencies, isolation, and dysfunctional organization severely crippled Japan's technological and scientific effort in the military sphere during World War II. In spite of these disabilities, the U.S. military in the Pacific Theater was continually surprised by the technological ingenuity of its opponent. Although the American naval historian Samuel Eliot Morison expressed disdain for the overall direction of the Japanese navy in World War II, he nevertheless praised the speed and maneuverability of their ships, the effectiveness of their aircraft, and the superiority of their torpedoes, binoculars, and flares.[8] Accounts of the Pearl Harbor attack rarely fail to mention the U.S. Navy's disbelief that the Japanese could have developed the shallow-running torpedo that was used with such devastating effect against warships in the harbor.[9]

The technological and scientific component in Japanese military power seems to have reached its peak of effectiveness in the late 1930s. Patrick has pointed out that not only was the scientific community in Japan alienated by the misuse of technology by the Japanese military in wartime, but also the Occupation authorities were intent upon destroying Japan's military potential

> first by destroying all armaments and halting all military production, then by physically taking control of the entire country, purging military, political, and business leaders, and punishing those found guilty as war criminals. This was meant, over the long run, to destroy the economic and political bases of military strength and to curtail Japan's willingness to use war as an instrument of national policy.[10]

Thus Japan entered the age of nuclear weapons and missile delivery systems, of supersonic fighter-bombers and airlifted strike forces, and of global communication networks for command and control practically disarmed and committed by Article IX of the new Japanese constitution to remain so. National security rested on Japan's relationship

---

7. Japan's objectives from a naval perspective are summarized by Louis Morton. "The Japanese Decision for War," *U.S. Naval Institute Proceedings* 80 (Washington, D.C., December 1954): 1325–35.

8. Samuel Eliot Morison, *History of United States Naval Operations in World War Two*, Vol. 3, *The Rising Sun in the Pacific, 1931–April 1942* (Boston, 1948), chapter 2, "The Two Navies, 1931–1941." He also stresses the apparent low regard for personal safety on board Japanese warships.

9. An example is John Toland, *The Rising Sun: The Decline and Fall of the Japanese Empire, 1936–1945* (New York, 1970).

10. Hugh T. Patrick, "The Phoenix Risen from the Ashes: Postwar Japan," in *Modern East Asia: Essays in Interpretation*, ed. James B. Crowley (New York, 1970), pp. 299–300.

as the junior partner with a technological and scientific superpower, the United States. It is not surprising that military technology and science in the immediate postwar period were of largely marginal and indirect interest. Yet as an industrial nation Japan could not ignore the impact on economic growth and competitiveness of the military-oriented research and development (R & D) of other nations.[11] This is the fundamental quandary of national security policy and the paradox of Japan's military technology: that a great economic power should remain an inferior military power.

The paradox is, however, less than total; military technology is extremely heterogeneous. Two distinct levels of capability are discernible—nuclear and missile capability and conventional capability—and at both levels the Japanese experience is unique. In the aggregate, Japanese military technology may have to be evaluated in other than standard terms.

Nuclear and Missile Technology

Military nuclear and missile technologies are each separable into actual and potential capabilities. For numerous reasons of domestic and foreign policy, Japan has not developed nuclear weapons or missiles and asserts its intention not to do so. Doubts of this intention, though resting on slim evidence and tenuous arguments and countervailed by a logical, persuasive, and richly documented case in support of expressed national policy, persist principally because of the tendency of statesmen and analysts to think only in terms of realpolitik and to equate power only with weaponry.

While lacking actual capability, Japan does indeed possess a potential capability in military nuclear and missile technologies. Differences of opinion in this regard cluster around the questions, How long would it take to convert potential into actual capability and how effective would such capability be once acquired? Potential military nuclear capability rests on the two premises that power reactor materials, or the industry that furnishes them, could be converted to military purposes and that the technology of managing a controlled thermonuclear reaction for producing heat is equivalent or applicable to the technology of producing an instantaneous reaction for destruction.[12]

11. Japan reports zero military R & D expenditure to the Organization for Economic Cooperation and Development, which prepared the most detailed and reliable international comparisons of national capabilities. My own estimate is that in the decade of the 1960s Japanese military research was 1 to 2 percent of government-financed R & D.

12. A lucid example of such arguments is in Shelton L. Williams, *Nuclear Nonproliferation in International Politics: The Japanese Case*, Social Science Foundation and Graduate School of International Studies, University of Denver, Monograph Series in World Affairs, 9 (Denver, 1972): 425–54.

Assuming that both premises are correct, what are some indications of Japan's potential capability?

Kahn and Wiener, speculating on Japanese nuclear power development and its military potential by the late 1970s, thought Japan would have enough plutonium byproducts for five hundred to a thousand small bombs a year.[13] The editors of the *Military Balance* thought Japan's research reactors alone would produce enough U-238 for more than a dozen bombs by 1963 and, with the commissioning of power reactors, nearly one hundred by 1968.[14]

These possibilities rest in turn upon Japanese ability to build and fuel a nuclear research establishment and a nuclear power industry. The research establishment, in comparison with those of the nuclear weapons powers, is small and poorly financed. The national effort in applied research is concentrated in the Japan Atomic Energy Research Institute at Tokai-mura. Japan's budget for government-sponsored nuclear research has increased substantially in the period for which there is reliable internationally comparable data but remains modest in comparison with that of the nuclear weapons powers (see table 5.1).[15] These comparisons do not take into account industrial nuclear research and development expenditures. It may be assumed, however, that the military capability implicit in existing or planned industrial capacity is highly dependent on a significant government R & D establishment and a level of effort capable of making it effective in the event it is used for military purposes.

Langdon correctly observes that "Japan depends completely upon foreign sources of fuel, technology, and, to some extent, even investment capital for its nuclear development program."[16] Enriched uranium for power and research reactors is provided through agreements with the United States and United Kingdom. Private Japanese firms have entered joint-venture agreements with U.S. firms to prospect for ore in third countries. An agreement between the Japanese and French governments has established the basis for cooperative development of a fuel-reprocessing facility. The technology for power plants now under construction and contemplated in the decade of the 1970s is of British

13.   Herman Kahn and Anthony J. Wiener, *The Year 2000: Framework for Speculation on the Next Thirty-three Years* (New York, 1967) pp. 244–45.

14.   International Institute for Strategic Studies, *The Military Balance, 1964–65* (London, 1965). Subsequent annual surveys do not update these estimates.

15.   Keith Pavitt, "Technology in Europe's Future," *Research Policy* 1 (1971–72): 268–69, reviews the efforts to compute a research exchange rate, arguing that R & D costs in Europe represent about 60 percent and in Japan about 55 percent of the U.S. level.

16.   Frank C. Langdon, "The Attitudes of the Business Community," in *Forecast for Japan: Security in the 1970s*, ed. James W. Morley (Princeton, 1972), pp. 126–27.

TABLE 5.1   Government Expenditures for Nuclear R & D

	1964			1967		
Country	Millions current $US	Millions current $US adjusted[a]	Percent	Millions current $US	Millions current $US adjusted[a]	Percent
United States	208	208	5.5	198	198	4.9
United Kingdom	145	241	27.0	149[b]	248	22.8
France	264	440	57.1	422	703	52.1
Germany	2	3.3	4.0	15	25	13.8
Japan	29	53	5.7[c]	42	76	8.5[d]

[a] Adjustment factors are taken from Keith Pavitt, "Technology in Europe's Future," *Research Policy* 1 (1971–72): 268–69, in which Pavitt, reviewing the efforts to compute a "research exchange rate," argues that R & D costs in Europe represent about 60 percent of the U.S. level, and in Japan about 55 percent.

[b] Figure is for 1966.

[c] Calculated from Japanese data.

[d] Calculations from Japanese data show this as 8.9 percent. The discrepancy is probably due to an OECD adjustment.

Sources: Data for all countries except Japan (1964) from Organization for Economic Cooperation and Development, *International Statistical Year for Research and Development, 2: Statistical Tables and Notes* (Paris, 1968), pp. 222–23, table G1; and OECD, *International Survey of the Resources Devoted to R and D in 1967 by the OECD Member Countries, Statistical Tables and Notes, 2: General Government Sector* (Paris, 1970), pp. 26–28, tables T.G.O. (G) and T.G.I. (B). Japanese data computed from Science and Technology Agency, *Summary White Paper on Science and Technology* (Tokyo, March 1970), pp. 72–73, figs. 11–12.

and American origin. Nuclear engineers, scientists, and technicians frequently spend training periods at one of the U.S. national laboratories.

While it is possible to argue technically and in the abstract that Japan could manufacture nuclear weapons, practically it would be very difficult for Japan to do so. Tentative steps in that direction, or even developments in research that were misinterpreted abroad (such as withholding government R & D expenditure data) could bring reactions from foreign governments and private firms. In this perspective, the industrial nuclear power program can be considered a potential military nuclear capability only in an extreme situation and under circumstances of international relations quite different from those of post–World War II nuclear deterrence. Certain questions do not really arise until a different situation exists. Can Japan make a bomb in three months or three years? Can Japan make many small, clean bombs or a few dirty ones? And can Japan conceal either the intention to acquire such weapons or determinations regarding the conditions of their use?

The distinction between actual and potential military capability can also be applied to Japanese space research activities. After fifteen

years of careful preparation, a group of academic engineers and
scientists under the aegis of the Tokyo University Space and Aero-
nautical Research Institute in 1970 launched a satellite into earth
orbit.[17] The military implications of this feat were minimal or nonexistent. The program from the beginning has been organized and
operated by scientists and engineers who shun the military and express-
ly dissociate their efforts from those of the Science and Technology
Agency, which has been supporting some rocket research in cooperation
with the Defense Agency. Furthermore, the academic program has
chosen to concentrate on solid-fueled rockets, whose technology is
fraught with problems of achieving adequate power and controlling
the rate at which the fuel burns. Guidance of these rockets is simply a
matter of determining the launch angle and the rate of ascent of each
stage. These facts, together with the overtly scientific character of the
academic space research program, make it clear that the program
itself cannot justly be interpreted as producing an actual missile
capability.

Japan's potential missile capability is hardly more convincing than
its actual capability. The situation is similar to that in the nuclear field
(see table 5.2). Government investment in R & D is small compared to
that of other industrial powers. This conclusion seems to be justified
even though comparative data is less completely reported for missile
than for nuclear R & D.

With initially minuscule expenditures (less than $1 million in 1960)
Japan began rapidly increasing R & D in this sector, signaling the
intention not to fall as far behind as was the case in the nuclear field
in the mid-50s. Even so, the unadjusted Japanese currency outlay by
the early 1970s was still far less than that of any other major industrial
nation. The question remains: can this basically civilian program be
translated into a potential military capability?

As in the case of nuclear weapons, the question can be put in terms
of the time required to achieve the capability and its effectiveness once
achieved. In late 1969 the Japanese government implicitly recognized
the failure of an effort of several years to establish cooperation between
the academic space research enterprise and government-sponsored
activities administered by the Science and Technology Agency. A new
organization, the National Space Development Agency, was established
in 1969 to coordinate space research and development other than that
taking place in the universities. Also in 1969 an agreement was reached

---

17.   The Japanese success was qualified by the fact that the "satellite" was only the third stage
of a launcher. In 1971 the same group orbited a 50-lb. satellite carrying scientific experiments and
communication equipment.

TABLE 5.2   Government Expenditures for Space R & D

Country	1964 Millions current $US	1964 Millions current $US adjusted[a]	1967 Millions current $US	1967 Millions current $US adjusted[a]
United States	1,298	1,298	5,320	5,320
United Kingdom	145	242	159	265
France	5.1	8.5	240	399
Germany	2	3.3	82.5	137.5
Japan	7.3	13.3	15.6	28.4

[a] Adjustment factors are taken from Keith Pavitt, "Technology in Europe's Future," *Research Policy* 1 (1971–72): 268–69. See table 5.1 above.

Note: It is not clear from the data whether expenditures are exclusively space or aerospace. Only in the United Kingdom data were they clearly identified as "aerospace."

Sources: Data on United States, France, and Germany for both years from the Organization for Economic Cooperation and Development, *International Statistical Year for Research and Development*, pp. 222–23, table G1; and OECD, *International Survey of Resources Devoted to R and D*, pp. 26–28, tables T.G.O. (G) and T.G.I. (B). Ibid. for data on United Kingdom for 1964; data for 1967 from Norman J. Vig, "Policies for Science and Technology in Great Britain," in *Science Policies of Industrial Nations*, ed. T. Dixon Long and Christopher Wright (New York, 1975). Data on Japan from Science and Technology Agency, *Space in Japan, 1968* (Tokyo, 1968), p. 27.

with the United States for the transfer to Japan of liquid-fueled rocket technology.[18] This was the necessary preliminary step to future agreements involving U.S. firms, such as the agreement in 1973 between McDonnell-Douglas and the Japanese government for the sale of a Thor-Delta system.

The intention of the Japanese is to acquire a commercial capability. Domestic solid-fueled rockets will be linked with U.S. first-stage liquid-fueled rockets for launching "applications" satellites. The first, planned for 1976, will transmit weather data and infrared photographic surveys and provide a navigational reference for ships. The longer-term objective is to launch a geostationary communications satellite.[19] These objectives require thrust and guidance capabilities appropriate for launching nuclear warheads. Ironically, the Japanese will probably soon be able to deliver a weapon that they do not have, do not want, and probably could not get within the present range of circumstances and intentions. Unlike nuclear technology and resources, missile technology and resources are not likely to involve continued reliance on foreign suppliers or partners.

18. Cecil Brownlow, ed., "Japanese Aerospace Nears Parity with the West," *Aviation Week and Space Technology* 95 (1 November 1971): 65, special report.

19. Ibid., p. 64.

CONVENTIONAL MILITARY TECHNOLOGY

Japan's air, sea, and land "self-defense" forces—so named because
of the constitutional prohibition (Article IX) against the maintenance
of military forces—are small by world or regional standards. The
all-volunteer forces total 226,000 men, and defense expenditure has
remained generally less than 1 percent of gross national product for
the past fifteen years.[20] Given the widely acclaimed fact of better than
10 percent annual growth in real GNP, this steady proportion has been
a growing absolute amount.

Reviewing the objectives of the Third Defense Build-up Plan, Morley
underscored some important qualitative indicators:

> By the end of 1971 it was hoped to provide a Ground Self-Defense
> Force of approximately 180,000 uniformed personnel, organized
> into thirteen divisions and equipped with medium tanks, artillery,
> and Hawk surface-to-air missiles; a Maritime Self-Defense Force
> of approximately 142,000 tons, its largest units being destroyers,
> submarines, and antisubmarine aircraft; and an Air Self-Defense
> Force of approximately 880 aircraft, centering on F-104J and F-4
> Phantom interceptors, Nike-Ajax surface-to-air missiles, and the
> Badge automatic radar (warning and control) system.[21]

It is interesting to view this conventional capability in the perspective
of Japan's experience in applying Western technology and science to
military objectives. The role of the navy, which loomed so large up to
World War II, has been drastically curtailed.[22] The air force, on the
other hand, is large, modern, and technologically advanced. In the
western Pacific, only India and North Korea have air forces of roughly
equal size and diversity.[23]

Military R & D on conventional weapons is probably small to the
point of being inconsequential. Furthermore, such research and

---

20.   Frank Langdon, *Japan's Foreign Policy* (Vancouver, 1973), p. 118, table 6·1.

21.   James W. Morley, "Economism and Balanced Defense," in Morley, *Forecast for Japan*,
p. 15.

22.   Stockholm International Peace Research Institute, *Yearbook of World Armaments and Dis-
armaments, 1969/70* (Stockholm, 1970), table 1E2, p. 311, shows Japanese naval stock as representing about 1 percent of the world stock in 1968. Its growth rate for the period 1960–68 was
3.6 percent, about half that of the NATO and Warsaw pact groups.

23.   With the 1968 agreement with the United States for the latter to make available F-4EJ
Phantom jet fighters, Japan's air force was potentially strengthened and enlarged. "The Phantom
will succeed the F-104J as the mainstay of the Japanese Air Force," *New York Times*, 2 November
1968. As of 1972, the agreement called for Japan to acquire 186 planes by 1977, of which 158 were
to be built in Japan under license; International Institute for Strategic Studies, *The Military
Balance, 1972–1973* (London, 1973) p. 79, table 6.

development as are conducted serve the purpose of testing or adapting weapons purchased abroad. The principal supplier, apparent from the types of weapons cited above, is the United States:

> Since the formation of the Japan Air Self-Defense Force, Mitsu-bishi has license-produced the F-86 Sabre and the F-104J Starfighter jet aircraft, and Fuji has produced a licensed version of the U.S. T-33 jet trainer and the Beech T-34 trainer. The third defense program for the years 1967 through 1971 stresses license production of U.S. Hawk and Nike-Hercules SAM's as well as a Japanese follow-on to the presently U.S.-Sidewinder air-to-air missile.[24]

This is not to imply that Japan undertakes no military-oriented research at all. Equipment manufactured under license is gradually being supplanted by Japanese versions, such as a naval patrol bomber with turbo-prop engines, derived from the U.S. Neptune, "new multi-barreled rocket-launchers for targets up to 10 miles, a SAM for low-flying aircraft to replace Hawk, 105 mm. howitzers, mine detectors and detonators, and an all-purpose machine gun for vehicle use."[25] There has been a developing international trade in Japanese-made rifles, ammunition, and small naval vessels following a reinterpretation of the law making possible the export of "defensive" weapons.

There was considerable furor in 1965 when a Japanese firm proposed to export meteorological sounding rockets to Indonesia. At the time, the government stated that the equipment had no military application. Later developments suggest that short- and medium-range missiles may become a significant item in Japan's military inventory, along with several other sophisticated weapons systems. In 1971 the Ground Self-Defense Force demonstrated a new type of tank that can change its silhouette. As reported by the *New York Times*, "The tank moved in a circle and zigzagged while keeping its 105 mm. gun pointing in one direction. The gun has a laser range finder and stabilizing device coupled to a computer that keeps it on target regardless of the tank's movements."[26]

To summarize: Japan's conventional capability in military R & D is narrow. It is limited by the security relationship with the United States as well as by such domestic factors as industry's lack of interest and the hostility of portions of the scientific community. There has been relatively little impetus to innovate in the period since the end of

24. Lewis A. Frank, *The Arms Trade and International Relations* (New York, 1969), pp. 127–28.
25. Ibid., p. 129.
26. *New York Times*, 3 November 1971.

the Occupation. Conversely, innovations made elsewhere have been readily produced by Japanese firms under license, with the effect of creating more slowly and indirectly an advanced and adaptive military technology.

INDUSTRIAL POWER

In 1972 Foreign Minister Fukuda Takeo commented to a foreign correspondent:

> With the development of nuclear weapons it became evident that if they are used mankind will be annihilated.... Consequently economic strength becomes much more important than military strength. [We wish] to employ our economic strength to gain an increasing voice in the international community.[27]

The situation so described summarizes Japan's broad foreign economic strategy since the end of World War II. National attention has been riveted on economic growth as it was on imperial expansion in the prewar era. Economic growth has been defined principally in terms of the growth of heavy industry. And industrial growth has been concentrated in technology-intensive sectors, to the degree that the products of iron and steel, shipbuilding, and the chemical and electronics industries have come to represent national prestige in a way formerly reserved for Buddhas and battleships.

Japan's industrial situation, allowing for a postwar decade of catching up, is basically similar to that of industrial nations in Western Europe and North America. Economists can no longer explain economic growth solely in terms of the classical inputs of land, labor, and capital. So-called residual factors, particularly in the form of education and technological innovation, appear to account for up to half or more of past and potential growth. This being the case, it behooves national governments to promote these factors in a more systematic fashion.

Different national goals and unique institutional structures dictate quite different approaches to strengthening the residual factors. In Japan there has been broad consensus on the goal of catching up with the leading Western industrial nations—the United States, the United Kingdom, France, and West Germany. Cultural and institutional differences are greater between Japan and these nations as a group than among members of the Western group. Thus it is not surprising that the Japanese approach should have little specific resemblance to European and North American approaches, while demonstrating the same fundamental character.

The most prominent feature of the application of technology to the

27. *New York Times*, 10 March 1972.

development of Japanese industrial power lies in the character of relations between the state and private enterprise. Historically, the state has been a leader and innovator in Japan. In the United States, by contrast, the state is broadly considered servant, not master, of the private sector. The Japanese pay deference to the state; public officials are respected and public directives have moral as well as legal force. In the realm of technology and science, where the state took every major decision regarding introduction and promotion during the early years of the Meiji period (1868–80), the difference between the two nations was explicit.[28]

While authority for major decisions was assumed by and remained with the national government, implementation was increasingly delegated to the private sector, most dramatically in the sale of publicly owned business during the early Meiji financial crisis. The state retained other important powers, in banking and finance as well as in public overhead sectors such as transportation and communication, leaving operations of a local or "feeder" type to private initiative. The government organized and operated the central institutions, setting overall policy and thereby maintaining control.

Several generations of state initiative in the industrial sector and state domination of the educational system—especially of the universities, which were designed in large part to produce civil servants—contributed to the national goal of increasing industrial power. The objective of "catching up" was inculcated, and the obedience of the private sector to state directives was nurtured. The techniques for selecting and adapting foreign technology were developed to the point of stimulating the outside view of a national psychology of imitation. This was a dangerous oversimplification of Japanese capabilities in industrial technology.

Industrial Research and Development

Output indicators vary enormously with changes in economic and political conditions. However, the level of R & D expenditure provides a fairly consistent measure of investment in the maintenance and improvement of industrial technology. Compared with that of other industrial nations, the private industrial research and development effort in Japan represents a remarkably large proportion of the total national effort. Data collected by the Organization for Economic Cooperation and Development (OECD) show that no large member nation both finances and performs as high a proportion of gross domestic R & D in the private enterprise sector (see table 5.3).

28. The role of the state in the Meiji period is elaborated in my "Science and Government in Japan," *Svensk Naturvetenskap 1967* (Stockholm, 1967), pp. 299–305.

154 T. DIXON LONG

TABLE 5.3   R & D in the Private Industrial Sector

Country	% Performed by private industry		% Financed by private industry	
	1964	1967	1964	1967
United States	66.4	66.6	32.0	32.8
United Kingdom	67.3	66.3	40.3	43.0
France	49.5	54.2	33.1	31.5
Germany	65.9	68.2	56.5	57.5
Japan	64.6	62.5	64.3	62.8

Sources: OECD, *International Statistical Year for Research and Development, 1: The Overall Level and Structure of R and D Efforts in the OECD Member Countries* (Paris, 1967), p. 57, table 1; and OECD, *International Survey of Resources Devoted to R and D, 1:* p. 10, table (A).

The difference between the R & D performed and R & D financed by the private sector shows how comparatively little is supplied by the Japanese government, unlike the substantial contribution of funds for industrial R & D supplied by government in other nations in the form of grants, contracts, or subsidies. Support in other nations may be linked to major national purposes such as defense; the stimulation provided elsewhere largely through defense is absent in Japan, which in this respect resembles the smaller Western European nations (Belgium, the Netherlands, and Italy)—though compared with Japan all three provide somewhat more government funds for research in industry.

The actual amount of private industrial R & D expenditure puts Japan toward the low end of the scale of larger European nations. These nations spend less than one-tenth of what the U.S. private industrial sector puts into R & D (see table 5.4).

The contribution from domestic government (together with a minor amount from foreign governments) to private industrial R & D confirms the situation established by the funding and performance figures. The smallest transfers in another major industrial country were those of West Germany: $133 million in 1964 and $222 million in 1967. In Japan, $2 million of government funds was directed to industry in 1963 and $5 million in 1967.[29]

Scientific and technical manpower in private industry is almost totally in the manufacturing sector—93 percent in France, 95 percent in Germany and Japan, and similar proportions elsewhere. Japan's total pool of R & D manpower in the private industrial sector is substantially smaller than that of the United States but larger than that

29. OECD, *International Statistical Year*, p. 42 table T1 (c); and OECD, *International Survey of Resources*, Paris, 1970, tables T.1.1. (A), T.1.2 (A).

TABLE 5.4   Research Performed by Private Industry

Country	1964 Millions $US	1967 Millions $US
United States	13,353	15,541
United Kingdom	1,369	1,742
Germany	883	1,420
France	725	1,370
Japan	677	1,053

Sources: OECD, International Statistical Year (1967), pp. 38–39, table T.1 (a); and OECD, International Survey of Resources (1970), vol. 5, table T.1.2 (A).

of other OECD member nations. In gross (and perhaps misleading) comparison with total population or total labor force, Japan is roughly on a par with France. It is sometimes useful to compare the most highly skilled category (qualified scientists and engineers) with technicians, since the ratio of the former to the latter gives some indication of effectiveness. The figures for 1967 (the most recent reliable international comparison) are: United States, 2.40; United Kingdom, 1.54; France, 0.89; Germany, 0.59; Japan, 1.21.[30]

The Japanese economic boom of the early 1960s was paralleled by a "research laboratory boom." Of sixty-one central research laboratories surveyed in 1963 by the Science and Technology Agency, 60 percent had been established since 1959, and fifty-four of the laboratories were in firms in the largest category of capitalization in the food processing, chemical, iron and steel, and electrical machinery industries.[31] Another development of the early 1960s was the establishment of research corporations by large-scale, high-technology firms, such as Honda Motors, Toyota Motors, and Matsushita Electric, as well as the atomic energy groups established with the urging of the Ministry of International Trade and Industry (MITI). A number of new research corporations came into existence, and several schemes to establish industrial think tanks were aired, but not until 1973 was a substantial commitment made by MITI to share the capitalization.

Japan has followed the pattern of the United States and Western Europe, where research-intensive and growth-oriented firms have expanded through aggressive marketing, acquisition, and merger. The process is illustrated by changes in the ranking of Japanese firms on the Fortune list of largest non-U.S. industrials. Especially in the technologically intensive industries, the number of firms has been reduced

30. OECD, International Survey of Resources, Paris, 1970, vol. 5, total tables, pp. 36, 38, table T.2.1 (A), T.2.2 (A).
31. OECD, Reviews of National Science Policy—Japan (Paris, 1967), p. 144.

through a combination of governmental persuasion and economic pressure during cyclical recessions. Those remaining in the mid-1960s had substantially achieved the financial and technological capabilities to sustain international competition.[32] The total of eleven Japanese firms in *Fortune's* top one hundred in 1960 grew to twelve in 1965 and to thirty-one in 1970. The industries represented were steel, motor vehicles, petrochemicals, food products, and electrical machinery— those that in Western Europe and North America are technologically most sophisticated.[33]

TRADE IN TECHNOLOGY

The introduction of foreign technology has had a great impact on postwar Japanese industrial power. Payments for imported technology are one measure. From 1950 through 1960 Japanese firms spent $255 million for know-how, with annual payments below $50 million through 1958 and below $100 million through 1960. Then the curve rose sharply to $482 million in 1970.[34]

Trade in technology is a two-way operation, but among the major industrial nations only the United States has been a significant net creditor throughout the postwar period. In the OECD's first international statistical year the ratio of receipts to payments on patents and licenses was 5.9 for the United States, 1.1 for the United Kingdom, 0.4 for France and Germany, and 0.2 for Italy.[35] A calculation for Japan based on similar (though not identical) data yields a ratio of 0.09. However, Japanese exports of technology have been growing: from a low of 0.05 in 1957, the ratio of receipts to payments grew to 0.13 in 1970. Put another way, exports of know-how in 1970 were $59 million, up from less than $1 million in 1958 and $17 million in 1965.[36]

In comparison with industrial nations other than the United States, Japan's technology trade has the same features of high imports and low exports. Sales of technology among six major OECD nations in

---

32. The process is described by Kozo Yamamura, *Economic Policy in Postwar Japan* (Berkeley, 1967), chapter 5 ("Toward the Pro-Monopoly Policy") and pp. 183–85.

33. *Fortune's* list, which appears annually in the September issue with rankings for the previous year, is based primarily on sales but also records assets, profits, and employment. The leading Japanese firms in 1970 were Nippon Steel (sixth) with sales of $3,992 million and Hitachi Electric (eighth) with sales of $2,835 million. U.S. firms with comparable sales were Union Carbide, Bethlehem Steel, and Boeing Aircraft. On the 1960 list, Yawata and Fuji, who later merged to form Nippon Steel, were twenty-sixth and forty-sixth respectively. Hitachi was seventeenth.

34. Science and Technology Agency, *Kagaku Gijutsu Hakushō—Showa 46 Nendo* [White paper on science and technology—fiscal 1971] (Tokyo, 1972), p. 348, table 2-19.

35. OECD, *Gaps in Technology: Analytical Report* (Paris, 1970), p. 203, table 10.

36. Science and Technology Agency, White paper, 1971, p. 348, table 2-19.

1964 were valued at $732 million, of which Japan's purchases totaled $130 million or about 18 percent. Italy stood a little higher, and Germany at over 20 percent. Japan took only 0.7 percent of the receipts from those exchanges compared to Italy's 4 percent and Germany's 7.5 percent.[37]

The fact that Japan runs a deficit in technology exchange should not overshadow the tremendous benefits the manufacturing sector has reaped from technological imports. A U.S. analyst estimated in 1970 that Japan had achieved a 22.5 percent growth rate between 1955 and 1965 in five major research-intensive industries: chemicals, electrical machinery, nonelectrical machinery, scientific instruments, and transportation. The comparative growth rates were 3.9 percent for the United States, 4.1 percent for the United Kingdom, 6.8 percent for France, and 8.4 percent for West Germany.[38] During a roughly comparable period, Japanese payments for imported technology in the chemical, electrical machinery, and nonelectrical machinery industries totaled about 75 percent of all such payments (and about 75 percent by number of contracts).[39]

The amount and concentration by industry of Japanese technology imports is centrally directed; it does not result simply from decisions of individual firms acting out of economic self-interest. Technology import policy is organized and controlled by the government in a framework of national policy and it serves the overriding national objective of catching up with the Western levels of industrial competitiveness through technological sophistication and the scale of the manufacturing units.

The key objective of national policy has been to retain control of Japanese industry in Japanese hands, a goal that has been achieved through the Foreign Exchange Control and Foreign Investment Laws of 1950 administered by the Ministry of Finance with the advice of a foreign investment council. Lockwood has summarized the effective policies:

> The government decides license applications case by case, requiring strong justification in terms of the technical benefits for Japanese industry. Equity participation of joint ventures has rarely been permitted to exceed 50 percent; more often it has been held to 35 percent or less. Foreign purchases of company

37. Ibid.
38. Philip M. Boffey, "Japan (III): Industrial Research Struggles to Close the 'Gap'," *Science* 167 (16 January 1970): 204, quoting Michael Boretsky of the U.S. Department of Commerce.
39. OECD, *Reviews of National Science Policy*, pp. 156–57, tables 43 and 44.

shares have likewise been limited to 10 to 15 percent of the stock outstanding.[40]

Only in exceptional cases has the desire to introduce particular technologies and to catch up more rapidly in key industries overridden this fundamental aim (two exceptions, computers and integrated circuits, are noted below).

A corollary objective of national policy has been the technological upgrading of industries vital to international competitive capability. Lockwood calls these "national policy" industries, giving as examples petroleum, steel, and electrical power and reciting the bureaucratic arguments for making these industries an "intermediate sector" that is neither wholly private nor wholly public.

Close observation and guidance in the introduction of technology prevent conflict with the established policies of cartelization and rationalization of the whole of modern industry. This entails a coordinated program of review and official approval for all forms of technological import: know-how agreements, cross-licensing, coproduction, and patent registration.

The "know-how agreement" was the most significant form of technology import from 1950 to 1970. Under the provisions of the Foreign Exchange Control and Foreign Investment Laws, MITI and the Bank of Japan may approve or deny know-how agreements. In practice denial is rare, but delay to the point that it achieves the same result is common.

Know-how agreements are divided into two types: those that involve the payment of foreign currency and whose term exceeds one year (Type A contracts) and those that involve only Japanese currency and whose term is one year or less (Type B contracts). The numbers in each category have run roughly parallel, though with considerable variation in the number of Type B contracts in the late 1960s. The amount paid for Type B technology agreements averages only 10 percent of the total.[41] The liberalization of trade undertaken in conformity with Japan's entry into the OECD in 1964 extended also to technology imports: the machinery was simplified, the monetary limits raised, and authorization given for automatic approval below these levels by the Bank of Japan in Type A cases and the Science and Technology Agency in Type B cases.[42]

40.   William W. Lockwood, "Japan's 'New Capitalism'," in *The State and Economic Enterprise in Japan*, ed. William W. Lockwood (Princeton, 1965), p.489.

41.   Science and Technology Agency, White paper, 1971, p. 348, table 2-19.

42.   Science and Technology Agency, *Kagaku gijutsu hakushō—showa 39 nendo* [White paper on science and technology—fiscal 1964] (Tokyo, 1965), p. 144.

The preferred means for importing foreign technology into Japan (principally from the United States) began by 1970 to change from know-how contracts to cross-license and coproduction arrangements, fostered in the liberalized trading system by the OECD and by the rules of General Agreement on Tariffs & Trade (GATT) and International Monetary Fund (IMF) membership, and to joint ventures and the establishment abroad of Japanese manufacturing facilities. As the means diversified, the drive to upgrade industrial technological capabilities continued. Some observers as early as 1962 had considered the Japanese as sophisticated in most fields as their major industrial competitors, particularly in processes to improve quality, raise yields, or reduce price.[43] On the other hand, Japanese government policies have long been based on the dual foundations of protection and pursuit. The continued evolution of industrial technology abroad, fed by sources of innovation that the Japanese do not possess, dictates the continuation of government initiative, guidance, and control.[44]

TECHNOLOGICAL INNOVATIONS

Many of the same factors that create a demand for imported technology determine, as well, domestic innovative capacity. Postwar Japanese technology policy has been consistently concerned with what was deemed a lack of creativity. The 1960 report of the Council for Science and Technology stressed four elements in the foundation of a national science and technology policy: the encouragement of basic science, the development of new fields, the promotion of technological innovations and productivity, and the improvement of international scientific and technical relations.[45] Each reflects a different facet of the same underlying assumption: that the creative impulse and its translation into practical results requires the support and guidance of the state. In other industrial nations, support has generally been accepted, but guidance has been and is the focus of profound disagreement.

Conventional measures of innovative capacity give Japan relatively low ratings. Two Nobel Prizes have been awarded to Japanese. Only two Japanese innovations appear in a tabulation of commercially significant discoveries, inventions, and innovations in four industries surveyed by the OECD: a pharmaceutical product and the tunnel diode (the latter invented by a Sony engineer but exploited commer-

---

43. Yamamura, *Economic Policy in Postwar Japan*, pp. 182–83.

44. Data supporting this alternative position are from Science and Technology Agency, White paper, 1964, p. 63, chart II-10.

45. U.S. National Science Foundation, trans., *Report of the Inquiry into the Promotion of Science and Technology for the Next Ten Years* (Tokyo: U.S. Embassy, 8 May 1961), pp. 9–13.

cially by RCA in the United States).[46] In a general survey of thirty-seven other sectors, the OECD study discerned three significant Japanese innovations: the low-cost transistorized tape recorder, the transistorized FM radio, and automated railroad train control. In a list of 110 significant inventions since 1945 Japan was responsible for 4—about the same as Sweden, Switzerland, and Italy but better than France, Austria, and Belgium.[47]

Efforts to close this "innovation gap" have taken the forms familiar to students of industrial development policy: tax incentives, grants and subsidies, loans, and stimulation of cooperative research. National and local tax laws give favorable treatment to R & D expenditure, whether for straight experimental costs, research-related capital investment, or philanthropic support of R & D in the educational sector.[48] Grants are awarded by government departments in very small numbers and amounts that total about 0.5 percent of government R & D expenditure. The largest portion of these funds has been concentrated in the program of MITI's Agency of Industrial Science and Technology (AIST). In 1965, AIST had approximately $2 million for "national research projects," and the figure grew to $15 million by 1970, over 40 percent of MITI's entire research and development budget. In theory these projects involve universities and private industry with the government as central funder and coordinator. In practice the choice of projects is made by government and the research is performed by industry. Table 5.5 shows the objectives of these projects as well as the government outlay for them.

The Japan Development Bank, with $51.4 million capital in fiscal 1971, is authorized to make loans totaling $1 to $3 million on five-to-ten-year terms for the industrialization of new technology. MITI also has some modest funds available for the support of cooperative research associations. These may be supplemented by tax-deductible contributions to cooperative research from individual firms. A loan fund was established in 1970 for commercialization of new technology in medium- and small-scale firms, and its capital was increased to $5.1 million in 1971.[49]

The net effect of these policy instruments varies with the degree of coordination within the government and with the capacity of government officials to elicit cooperation from private industry. As seen by outside observers, overall coordination is comparatively great. In

46. OECD, *Gaps in Technology*, pp. 189–96.
47. Ibid., p. 197, table 7; and p. 198, table 8.
48. Science and Technology Agency, White paper, 1964, p. 39.
49. Idem, White paper, 1971, pp. 273–75.

TABLE 5.5   National Research Projects

Project	Period	Budget in millions $US
Magneto-hydrodynamic generator	1966–1972	$14.8
Super-high performance electronic computer systems	1966–1971	$27.8
Desulfurization processes	1966–1971	$ 6.9
New process for olefin products	1967–1973	$10.8
Sea-water desalination and by-product recovery	1969–1975	$13.9
Remote-controlled undersea oil drilling rig—first phase	1970–1974	$14.2
Electric automobile	1971–1975	$13.9
Pattern information processing system	1971–1978	$97.2
Turbofan engine for aircraft—first phase	1971–1975	$18.6

Source: Japan, Science and Technology Agency, Kagaku gijutsu hakusho—showa 46 nendo [White paper on science and technology—fiscal 1971] (Tokyo, 1972), p. 265, tables 3–28.

Lockwood's words, "The metaphor that comes to mind is a typical Japanese web of influences and pressures interweaving through government and business, rather than a streamlined pyramid of authoritarian control."[50] Inside observers and participants call attention to areas of the economy where fragmentation and excessive competition continue to dominate the scene and to the minimal contribution of academic research activities to the innovation process. It is difficult to find evidence of a profound or diversified domestic innovation capacity, despite the application of various supportive policies and the continued insistence of leaders on the importance of stimulating domestic creativity.

OPPORTUNITIES AND CONSTRAINTS

Central to the national policy in postwar Japan of "catching up with the West" has been the development of industrial power. Perhaps the major dynamic of this emerging industrial capability is technological modernization. A less important (though not negligible) feature of Japanese strategy is military power, especially in its conventional forms.

Postwar policies for the introduction of foreign technology, and for promoting a more vigorous indigenous capability for technological innovations, are entirely consistent with this broad pattern. Indeed,

50.   Lockwood, "Japan's 'New Capitalism'," p. 503.

the strategy is but the aggregation of tactical moves. The flaws in the strategy result from too great reliance on traditional methods, which, despite past success, have created severe conflicts between Japan and other industrial nations. A significant example is the slow rate of progress toward liberalization of foreign trade and investment, especially in the high-technology sectors. Too little attention is given to unconventional, forward-looking strategies that would make use of Japan's growing reservoir of technology, both military and industrial, highly sophisticated and conventional.

In the sensitive matter of the potential conversion of peaceful industrial activities to military purposes, Japanese policy in the postwar period has been to steer between two theoretical choices. One is to develop and maintain a range of options by supporting industries that would, under some foreseeable circumstances of hostility, be available for quick conversion to military needs. The other is to concentrate limited resources on those industries that promote most directly the national wealth and welfare.

The first choice would have required, for example, developing the "nuclear option" that some analysts have perceived and would involve keeping abreast of civilian nuclear technology under the guise of an "atoms-for-peace" policy while systematically shortening the lead time to bomb production. The second choice, using the same example, would involve full commitment to a nuclear power generating program without regard to externally imposed limitations, created in the process of securing access to foreign technology, raw material, and capital.

Pure choices do not exist in the real world but they do illustrate the spectrum of options. Attention has already been given to nuclear and missile capabilities, showing that, somewhat ironically, a nuclear capability probably exists within the framework of the second of these theoretical choices. The situation is complicated, however, because steps to achieve a nuclear capability could not be taken without first freeing the nuclear power industry from its involvement with foreign partners and suppliers. Missile delivery capability, on the other hand, lies in the balance, if not closer to the first option, because it is relatively free of such foreign involvement.

The aircraft manufacturing field has also been touched upon. Here small annual production of domestic designs—the YS-11 short-haul passenger aircraft and the MU-2 executive model—indicate that a decision has been taken to support the airframe industry for other than purely economic purposes.[51] Grants-in-aid of the Ministry of Inter-

51. Mitsubishi announced in the spring of 1973 the decision to establish an MU-2 manufacturing facility in Texas.

tional Trade and Industry show concern also for development of an aeroengine industry. MITI expressed in 1967 hope of organizing a consortium to build an engine equivalent in thrust to Rolls-Royce's advanced design for the Lockheed Tri-Star.[52] Thus independence in airframes is balanced by dependence in engines—at least in the short run.

Electronics is the third in the triumvirate of industries with military implications. In fact, nuclear and aerospace capabilities in the military or civil spheres are unthinkable without computers and microminiaturized components. In this field, Japan's capability has been almost totally dependent, principally because of the dominant position of two U.S. firms—International Business Machines in the field of calculators and Texas Instruments in the field of integrated circuits. By permitting an exceptional degree of participation in the Japanese market in the form of an IBM subsidiary more than 50 percent owned by the parent and a Sony-Texas Instruments joint venture, Japanese policymakers arranged for the introduction of these technologies with the long-term object of reducing dependence.[53] While Japan stands third in the world in use of computers (after Germany, and far behind the United States), independence in manufacture and distribution exists only with respect to desk and pocket-sized models. Other forms of hardware—which are key in military terms—and software are accessible mainly by purchase, license, joint venture or other arrangement with a foreign partner.

The industries ranking just below the nuclear, aerospace, and electronic industries in military significance—shipbuilding, steel, petrochemicals, automobiles, pharmaceuticals, and aluminum—have been singled out as areas of notable technological achievement by Japan.[54] On the other hand, it is practically impossible to equate either export performance or domestic market performance (which are the conventional measures of peacetime capability) with a conversion capability. They are simply indicators, though good ones, of Japan's generally high level of technological and scientific capability. The point is surely not lost on the military planners of other nations.

Japan's power position in the world is profoundly—and perhaps irreversibly—ambivalent. Japanese leaders may recognize the subtle economy of a military potential that is not quite realized and of an industrial potential that is sharply limited by a web of trading and alliance relationships. As former prime minister Eisaku Sato put it, "It is entirely a new case that a country such as Japan, possessing great

52. *Nihon Keizai Shimbun* [Japan economic journal], 22 August 1967.
53. Nicolas Jequier, *Le Défi Industrial Japonais* (Lausanne, 1970), pp. 73–77.
54. Ibid., pp. 45–109 (which includes a discussion of the electronic and aerospace industries).

economic strength, has no significant military power and yet makes its presence felt throughout the world."[55]

His statement suggests that the Japanese might be satisfied to find a place in a bifurcated world, where one branch of power assessment follows the conventional military route and another, still tentative branch follows an industrial and technological route. If the super-powers are indeed trapped in the absurdities of overkill, then the future belongs to the nations that risk a different policy.

A new model of power and status requires small but technologically advanced defensive military capabilities. It requires a major national commitment—the moral equivalent of national security—to international industrial competition and ceaseless technological modernization. It involves a substantial degree of international interdependence with regard to raw materials, manufactured goods, and technology.

If this model seems too obviously and exclusively Japanese, it should be added that it can also be applied with a few adjustments to France, Germany, the United Kingdom, and Italy. With the exception of the raw material factor, it could describe the strategy of Canada and Australia. It comes very close to the long-term perspective of smaller nations such as Sweden and the Netherlands. There is much in such a model that would be attractive to the more advanced developing nations, such as Mexico, Argentina, and Brazil. To be acknowledged a leader in this company of nations would mark the achievement of Japan's long quest for a new place in the world.

55. *New York Times*, 9 April 1970, p. 10.

6

Changing Labor Force Characteristics
and Their Impact on Japanese Industrial Relations

ROBERT E. COLE

Patrick argues that the basic constraints on Japanese prosperity in the years to come will not be international but <u>domestic circumstances</u>. Robert Cole examines these constraints in greater detail as he focuses on the composition and attitudes of the labor force.

Cole suggests that the nature of the labor force will change in predictable ways. A less fertile population means relatively fewer young people and more aged. After 1970 the proportion of the population in the labor force declines continually, and the dependency ratio—the proportion of unemployed to employed—rises correspondingly. The spread of higher education, the shift of the work force out of agriculture, and the increasing adequacy of pensions will also tend to decrease the percentage of the population in the labor force. These changes will take place together with a slowing down of economic growth to a rate of 6 or 7 percent per annum (Cole's estimate is on the low side of Patrick's general range).

A number of consequences will follow. There will be a shortage of labor in certain sectors of the economy, especially if the shift to a welfare economy is pronounced, because production in these sectors is less capital-intensive than in others.

As the growth rate declines, the game of who gets what will become increasingly zero-sum, and the fight for a share of the pie will intensify.

Declines in productivity, together with labor shortages, which will increase pressure for higher wages, will squeeze corporate profits. Management will try to resist the pressure for wage increases, but as labor-saving equipment is installed productivity will rise and so will wages.

The traditional Japanese work ethic would counsel dedicated service to the employer even under adverse circumstances; but Cole sees a secular decline in traditional values and predicts that this transformation of attitudes will mean greater dissatisfaction and industrial strife.

In a stationary population, there will no longer be places of authority open to

This paper benefited from the critical comments of James Cramer, Rex Leghorn, Solomon Levine, Funahashi Naomichi, Hugh Patrick, Gary Saxonhouse, and Shimada Haruo.

the old simply because of the accumulation of experience. Consequently, the con-
ventional expectation of automatic advancement with increasing age will be
disappointed. The scramble for promotion will intensify and management will
increasingly insist on merit as the basic criterion.

Labor mobility will be affected by a number of factors. An aging labor force
is generally less likely to move. On the other hand, as the structure of the economy
changes, redundancies and shortages of labor will be frequent; management will
continue to push rationalization of operations; and the traditional paternalistic
ideology of lifetime hiring will be less and less attractive to business. Ironically,
the tradition will hang on longest in the largest, most "modern" firms, which
will be better able to insulate themselves from financial pressures than small and
medium companies.

An aging labor force, a declining rate of growth, increased rationalization,
and the disappointment of traditionally conditioned expectations of job security
will lead to increased conflict between old and young, management and labor,
right and left. Only one circumstance could invalidate this prediction, and that
would be the large-scale entry of women into the labor force. Under these condi-
tions labor shortage would disappear and its consequences would be drastically
modified. Thus Cole's forecast must be read with an eye to Pharr's analysis of
the future role of women. But if the key factor—sex-role stereotyping—does not
change, Cole predicts politicization, privatization, and alienation as the future
of the working population of Japan.—L.A.

To create a picture of what specific aspects of Japanese society and
economy will look like in 1980, I judge it advisable to begin with an
exposition of relatively firm data and then gradually move toward
more speculative observations. Such a cautious approach is not
designed to produce predictions of discontinuous events, but it does
have the virtue of being grounded in data in which we may place some
confidence.

Specifically, this chapter will begin with estimates of Japanese
population for the year 1980, then consider the somewhat more speculative estimates of labor force size and composition, and finally turn to
the difficult task of predicting the impact of these changing population
and labor force characteristics on the Japanese pattern of industrial
relations. The particular aspects of industrial relations to be considered
are: *nenkō joretsu* (age and length of service reward system), permanent
employment, and the oft-mentioned harmony of labor-management
relations. These practices are most fully institutionalized in the major
corporations and it is here that I will place the central emphasis. I will
not deal with the social determinants of Japanese economic growth
rates.

In 1973 most of the 1980 Japanese population were already born, and most of the expected 1980 labor force was already employed. These simple facts permit us to place a good deal of confidence in the following estimates and distinguish our efforts from a more spectacular if less valid futurology.

THE AGE OF THE POPULATION

The first subject to be considered is the age composition of the population, a subject that has drawn increasing attention from Japanese demographers. Their concern stems from drastic changes in population composition that are now occurring and will continue to occur for some time.[1] The changing age composition is primarily the result of a remarkable postwar decline in the gross reproduction rate—from 2.20 in 1946 to unity by 1956.

The magnitude of this shift in fertility behavior with its consequences for shifting age composition is already beginning to have an unprecedented impact on the Japanese economy, society, and polity. Data on the percentage distribution of population by three broad age groups for almost fifty years, with estimates until the year 2000, show that this distribution was quite constant over time until marked shifts began to occur in 1955 (see table 6.1). At this point, a rapid decline in the 0 to 14 age group started to take place that, when projected to 1980, reduces this age group to only 24.1 percent of the population. Meanwhile, the aged population (60 and above), which held steady at 7 to 8 percent of the population for some thirty years, began to show notable increases in 1955; it is expected to rise to 12.6 percent of the population by 1980. One indication of the importance of this shift for the polity can be found in the 1972 general election. For the first time, both the ruling and opposition parties made the improvement of old age pensions a prominent part of their campaigns.

The rapid falloff in youth population combined with the slower rise of the aged population produced the lowest dependency ratio in Japanese demographic history in the year 1970 (see table 6.1, column 4). That is, until 1947, for every 100 persons of working age, there were approximately 80 children and old people that had to be supported. In 1970 the number of dependents per 100 working-age persons declined to 53. From this low point in 1970 the dependency ratio is expected to rise gradually in the future as the aging of the Japanese population

1. Toshio Kuroda, "Jinkō kōzōron josetsu-nihon jinkō no nerei Kōzō Hendō o Chūshin to shite" [A study on population composition: Special reference to Japan], *Jinkō Mondai Kenkyu* (July 1971): 1–12; Yōichi Okazaki, *Rōdōryoku no chōki tenbō* [Long-range outlook for the labor force] (Tokyo, 1968).

TABLE 6.1   Age Composition of Japanese Population:
Past and Future

	Percentage of total population accounted for by age group			Dependency index	Aging index
	0–14	15–59	60 +	$[(1+3) \div 2] \times 100$	$(3 \div 1) \times 100$
	(1)	(2)	(3)	(4)	(5)
1920	36.5	55.3	8.2	81	23
1925	36.7	55.6	7.7	80	21
1930	36.6	56.0	7.4	79	20
1935	36.9	55.7	7.4	80	20
1940	36.0	56.2	7.8	78	22
1947	35.3	57.2	7.5	80	21
1950	35.4	56.9	7.7	76	22
1955	33.4	58.5	8.1	71	24
1960	30.0	61.1	8.9	64	30
1965	25.6	64.7	9.7	55	38
1970	23.9	65.4	10.7	53	45
1975	24.6	64.3	11.8	56	49
1980	24.1	63.3	12.6	58	52
1985	23.4	62.8	13.9	59	59
1990	22.1	62.2	15.7	61	71
1995	21.0	61.4	17.6	63	84
2000	20.9	60.2	18.9	66	90

Sources: Toshio Kuroda, "Jinkō kōzoron josetsu-nihon no nenrei kōzō hendō o chūshin to shite" [A study on population composition: special reference to Japan] *Jinkō Mondai Kenkyu* (July 1971): 1–12. Estimated in August 1969 by the Institute of Population Problems. Medium estimation. The medium projection is based on an average of the maximum and minimum age-specific fertility rate. In addition, it reflects life expectancy at birth of 72.5 years for males and 75.8 years for females in 1975; mortality rates prior to 1975 are based on a linear projection to the expected value in 1975; the mortality rates after 1975 are held to be constant at the 1975 level. For further discussion of assumptions see Jinkō Mondai Kenkyūjo [Institute of Population Problems], Research Series, no. 192 (September 1969), published by the Ministry of Health, Tokyo.

continues. The aging of the Japanese population is most notable when we construct an age index by dividing the number of those over age 60 by those age 0 to 14. This index (see table 6.1, column 5), which registered in the low twenties until 1955, jumps sharply by 1960 to 30 and continues to rise thereafter. Finally, it should be noted that the working-age population (see table 6.1, column 2), as a percentage of total population, experiences moderate increases reaching a high point in 1970 of 65.4 after which it gradually starts to decline in response to the aging of the population.

To put the preceding discussion in perspective, it is instructive to compare the Japanese experience to that of other industrial nations.

TABLE 6.2 International Comparisons of Population Composition,
Dependence Rates, and Average Age

Population composition
(in percentage)

	Less than 15 yrs. old	15–64 years old	65 yrs. old and more	Dependence ratio per person in gainful work
		1960		
United States	31.0	59.7	9.2	1.50
Britain	23.3	65.1	11.7	1.09
France	26.4	62.0	11.6	1.31
West Germany	21.3	67.8	10.8	1.09
Italy	23.4	67.6	9.0	1.31
Japan	30.1	63.9	6.1	1.10

	Less than 15 yrs. old	15–64 years old	65 yrs. old and more	Dependence ratio per person in gainful work	Average age of working pop. (years old)	Average age of total pop. (years old)
		1969				
United States	29.2	61.2	9.6	1.41	37.1	32.0
Britain	23.9	63.4	12.6	1.16	39.2	36.1
France	24.9	62.3	12.8	1.41	38.0	34.9
West Germany	23.2	63.9	12.9	1.25	39.2	36.0
Italy	23.2	66.4	10.3	1.68	38.0	34.1
Japan	24.0	69.1	6.9	1.03	35.5	31.4

Sources: Economic Planning Agency, Economic Survey of Japan (1970–1971) (Tokyo, 1971), p. 73. For the population composition and the dependence rate per person in gainful work see OECD, Labour Force Statistics (1958–1969). Average age was estimated from United Nations, Demographic Yearbook and PMO, Total Population Classified by Age Groups. For average age, that of 1968 was used for France, while West Germany and Italy's age was that in 1967. Average age of working population = 15–64 years old. Dependence rate/person in gainful work = Total population ÷ No. of persons in gainful work — 1.

Table 6.2 provides this comparison. In the period from 1960 to 1969, Japan alone experienced a sharp shift in the percentage of population under 15 years old and the percentage in the 15 to 64 group. In 1960 Japan along with the United States had the highest proportion of the population in the less-than-15-year-old category. By 1969, however, the proportion of less-than-15-year-olds had fallen in Japan from 30.1 to 24.0 so that the Japanese situation became quite comparable to the profiles of Western European nations. Similarly, the percentage of

TABLE 6.3   Observed and Estimated Trend in Population in
Productive Ages, 1955–2000

	15–29	30–44	45–59	Total (in thousands)
1955	24,633 (100)	16,177 (66)	11,422 (46)	52,232
1960	25,836 (100)	18,575 (72)	12,659 (49)	57,070
1965	28,285 (100)	21,717 (77)	13,582 (48)	63,584
1970	28,671 (100)	23,825 (83)	15,071 (53)	67,567
1975	27,635 (100)	25,324 (91)	17,644 (64)	70,653
1980	24,924 (100)	27,795 (112)	20,694 (83)	73,413
1985	24,493 (100)	28,520 (116)	22,813 (93)	75,826
1990	26,143 (100)	27,276 (104)	24,187 (93)	77,606
1995	27,696 (100)	24,563 (89)	26,588 (96)	78,847
2000	27,986 (100)	24,143 (86)	27,241 (97)	79,370

*Change
during
interval*[a]

	15–29	30–44	45–59	Total
1955–60	1,203	2,398	1,237	4,838
1960–65	2,449	3,142	923	6,514
1965–70	386	2,108	1,489	3,983
1970–75	− 986	1,499	2,573	3,086
1975–80	− 2,761	2,471	3,050	2,760
1980–85	− 431	725	2,119	2,413
1985–90	1,650	− 1,244	1,374	1,780
1990–95	1,553	− 2,713	2,401	1,241
1995–2000	290	− 420	653	523

[a] Recorded for each age group: $t_2 - t_1$ = recorded change.

Note: Ratio of each age group in parentheses, taking age group 15–29 as a base for a given year.
Source: Kuroda, "Jinkō josetsu-nihon no nenrei kōzō hendō."

Japanese population in the 15 to 64 age category moved from 63.9 in 1960 to 69.1 in 1969. Looking at the proportion of the population over 65, we see that Japan remained well below the Western nations with a rate of 6.9 in 1969. But the aging process had already begun (compared to 6.1 in 1960), and, as shown in table 6.1, it will accelerate in the coming years to reach the present levels of Western nations.

Compared with the six nations in table 6.2, Japan in 1969 still had the lowest dependency ratio (1.03), the lowest average age of working population (35.5), and the lowest average age of total population (31.4). Yet, when these data are compared with those from 1960, it is apparent that an aging trend has already been set in motion that will continue in the future to move the nation toward an age composition similar to that of the Western industrial nations. For example, the average age of employees in firms of more than ten employees went from a low of 30.9 in 1958 to 33.1 in 1970.[2]

The changing pattern of age composition of the Japanese population thus far discussed may be characterized as a process of population aging. The absolute and relative increase of old people in the total Japanese population is a pattern quite similar to that experienced in the West. The aging process also proceeds in terms of the increase of higher age groups in the productive age population. Kuroda Toshio, upon whose work this section is based, dramatically depicts this dual process of aging in table 6.3. In 1956, within the productive age population, the 15 to 29 age group was by far the largest category with the 30 to 44 age group being only 66 percent as big and the 45 to 59 group only 46 percent as big. The situation by 1980 will look quite different, as a consequence of the large increases expected for the 30 to 44 and 45 to 59 age groups coupled with decreases in the 15 to 29 age group. The 30 to 44 age group will actually exceed the 15 to 29 age group, while the 45 to 59 age group will have significantly closed the gap separating it from the other two age categories. Specifically, taking the total for the 15 to 29 age group as 100, the 30 to 44 age group will move from 66 in 1955 to 112 in 1980 while the 45 to 59 group will move from 46 to 83. In actual numbers, the 15 to 29 age group is expected to decline by about 3.8 million during the period from 1970 to 1980 while the 30 to 44 age group will increase by 3.9 million and the 45 to 59 age group will show an increase of 5.6 million. The trend toward convergence in size among the various age groups is expected to continue up through the year 2000.

THE STRUCTURE OF THE LABOR FORCE

The thesis presented in this paper is that these unprecedented changes in age composition will have a major impact on Japanese social and economic organization.[3] Before pursuing these relationships,

2. Japan Productivity Center, *Katsuyō rōdō tokei: 47* [Practical labor statistics: 1972] (Tokyo, 1972), p. 112.

3. It is not my intention to pursue the thorny relationship between age composition and economic growth. It can be argued that the youthfulness of Japan's population has been an asset in the rapid economic growth of the 1960s insofar as it allowed employers to pay low wages and insofar as young employees are more flexible in adjusting to shifting occupational demands occasioned by a rapidly expanding economy. On the other hand, the lack of accumulated specific education available to a youthful labor force can be counted as a liability. Moreover, as Japan moves toward a more capital intensive economy with a concomitant upgrading of skills, the specific and general skills accumulated by an aging labor force may be a major asset in the continued economic growth of Japan. In addition, maintenance of high savings rates among older Japanese as compared to other industrialized nations suggests that, in terms of capital formation, aging may have some positive impact on economic growth. Tuvia Blumenthal, *Savings in Post-War Japan* (Cambridge, Mass., 1970).

ROBERT E. COLE

TABLE 6.4   Total Population, Population in Productive Ages (15–60),
and Population in the Labor Force

	Population[a]	Population in productive ages[a]	Population in labor force[a]	Labor force participation rate[b]
	(1)	(2)	(3)	(4)
1955	8,931	5,955	4,230	71.0
1960	9,346	6,539	4,533	69.3
1965	9,828	7,324	4,816	65.3
1970	10,384	7,906	5,169	65.4
1975	10,993	8,358	5,392	64.5
1980	11,597	8,806	5,615	63.8
% *Increase:*				
1955–60	0.9	1.9	1.4	
1960–65	1.0	2.3	1.2	
1965–70	1.1	1.5	1.4	
1970–75	1.1	1.1	0.8	
1975–80	1.1	1.1	0.8	

[a] In ten thousands.
[b] In percentage.

Source: Economic Deliberation Committee, *Rōdōsha no nōryoku hakki no mondai* [Problems of
development of ability among employees] (Tokyo, 1972), p. 5.

an examination of labor force characteristics is in order. The total
Japanese population shows a fairly steady, though small, increase
throughout the five-year periods from 1955 to 1980 (see table 6.4).
When we turn to the productive age population (see table 6.4, column
2), however, we note that after a large increase in the 1960 to 1965
period of 2.3 percent, the rate of increase is expected to fall off significantly to 1.1 in the period from 1970 to 1980. An examination of those
actually in the labor force or expected to be in the labor force in the
future (see table 6.3, column 3) reveals an even lower increase rate
than in the productive age population. In the periods from 1970 to
1975 and 1975 to 1980, the increase of the labor force is expected to be
only 0.8 percent respectively. In actual numbers, the total labor force is
expected to grow only about four-and-one-half million from 51,690,000
in 1970 to 56,150,000 by 1980.

The lower increase rate in the labor force as compared to that for
the productive age population appears in the declining labor force
participation rates (see table 6.3, column 4). Labor force participation
fell from a high of 71 percent of the productive age population in 1955
to 65.4 percent in 1970 and is expected to fall further to 63.8 percent
by 1980. Despite a sustained labor force demand resulting from

TABLE 6.5   Age Composition of the Labor Force

Age categories	1960	1965	1970	1975	1980
15–24	23.4%	23.3%	21.6%	16.0%	13.1%
25–39	36.2	37.1	36.3	37.5	36.8
40–44	8.5	9.5	11.4	12.1	11.9
45–64	26.8	25.4	26.2	29.5	33.2
65+	5.1	4.8	4.4	4.8	5.1
Total	100.0%	100.0%	100.0%	100.0%	100.0%
Base population[a]	4,533	4,816	5,169	5,392	5,615

Note: The overall totals as well as totals for given age categories depend on the kinds of assumptions one makes about labor force participation rates for each age category. The overall totals here are based on the participation rates reported in table 6.4. The estimates in table 6.6 represent a middle ground between the higher and lower estimates that have been constructed. Due to rounding of figures, column totals in some cases do not equal 100 percent.

[a] In ten thousands.

Source: Economic Deliberation Committee, Rōdōsha no nōryoku hakki no mondai.

continued economic growth, the labor force supply will decline not only because of the declining rate of population growth but also because of a declining labor-force participation rate. Major reasons for this decline in labor-force participation are the extension of formal education and the raising of living standards (e.g., expansion of social security system, especially medical care, and in the future the expansion of old age pensions). Therefore, the decisions to work, particularly by family members and older individuals, are not made on the basis of economic need. The agricultural sector, for example, is one that has high participation rates based upon the need for all members of the family to engage in productive work and the relative ease with which family members can do so without disrupting child raising and other routine behavior. The continuing shift of the Japanese population out of agriculture contributes to the declining participation rate.

We can get a better picture of the consequences of the anticipated decline in labor force participation by examining the age composition of the labor force. In table 6.5 we see a falloff in both absolute and relative terms in the numbers of 15 to 24-year-olds in the labor force. The basic factors operating here are the decline of this age group as a proportion of the population along with the increasing extension of school age. The other notable change is the increased role in both relative and absolute terms that the 40 to 64 age groups will come to play in the economy. Here again, it is their increased proportion of the

TABLE 6.6   Observed and Estimated Trend for
Newly Graduated Employees by Level of Education

	Bases for percentages[a]	Composition in percentage		
		Middle school	High school	University
1960	1,282	53.4%	37.4%	9.3%
1965	1,407	44.4	44.8	10.7
1966	1,495	34.9	54.6	10.5
1967	1,464	30.5	57.4	12.2
1968	1,434	26.9	58.9	14.2
1969	1,340	24.2	58.5	17.3
1970	1,255	21.6	58.1	20.3
1971	1,186	18.6	57.4	23.9
1972	1,199	16.6	57.6	25.8
1973	1,188	14.3	58.3	27.4
1974	1,174	13.4	58.7	27.9
1975	1,142	11.8	59.1	29.1
1976	1,128	10.6	59.2	30.1
1977	1,194	9.2	61.8	29.0
1978	1,176	8.8	61.3	29.8
1979	1,171	8.8	60.7	30.5
1980	1,182	8.4	61.1	30.5

[a] In ten thousands.

Note: The category High school includes students in the comprehensive system. University students are daytime students, junior college students, students in advanced specialty schools, and those in the process of securing a master's degree.
Source: Economic Deliberation Committee, Rōdōsha no nōryoku hakki no mondai.

population combined with the rising labor force participation rate of females in this age category that accounts for this outcome.

Implicit in the preceding discussion is a rapidly expanding education structure that both delays entrance into the labor force and produces a labor force with a rapidly changing educational stock. In table 6.6 the Economic Deliberation Committee has compiled figures on the rapidly changing supply of new school graduates at different school levels with projections until 1980. In the Japan of 1980 there will be an estimated 21.4 million school graduates who have graduated from school since 1960 compared with an estimated 56 million in the labor force (see table 6.4). The total number of graduates in 1980 will be slightly over 1 million; this represents a falloff from the high of almost 1.5 million in 1966. The raw figures from 1960 to 1980 show a drastic falloff of middle school graduates from 684,000 to 99,000, a moderate growth of high school graduates from 477,000 to 722,000 and a marked increase of university graduates from 119,000 to 361,000. Middle

TABLE 6.7   Composition of Employed Industrial Sector

	Primary[a]	Secondary[b]	Tertiary[c]	Base for percentages[d]
1960	32.6	29.2	38.2	43,690
1965	24.7	31.9	43.4	47,638
1980[e]	9.0	40.0	51.2	55,445

[a] Includes: agriculture, forestry and hunting, fisheries, and aquiculture.

[b] Includes: mining, construction, manufacturing, electricity, gas, and water.

[c] Includes: wholesale and retail trade, finance, insurance and real estate, transportation and communication, services, and government.

[d] In thousands.

[e] The projection for the 1980 distribution is based on the assumption that economic activities will reflect a significant shift toward realization of a welfare economy with the real economic growth rate at 9.3 percent per annum. It is also based on the assumption that the wage differentials between "knowledge labor" and "nonknowledge labor" remain essentially similar to what currently exists. Were such differentials changed, the labor supply to given industrial sectors would be influenced, thus altering the 1980 distribution.

Source: Japan Economic Research Center, "Showa 55 no rōdōryoku juyō" [Demand for knowledge labor in 1980], Nihon Keizai Shimbun, December 1, 1972.

school graduates, as a percentage of total graduates, decline from 53.4 percent in 1960 to a low of 8.4 percent in 1980; high school graduates rise from 37.4 percent of the total to 61.1, and university graduates register over a threefold increase from 9.3 to 30.5 percent. It would be hard to exaggerate the importance of these changing educational statistics. In introducing new skills to the population, changing people's aspirations, and delaying entry into the labor force, the shift in educational stock has an important impact on social, economic, and political behavior.

The emergent industrial structure provides the framework within which the newly graduated individuals will be employed. Table 6.7, prepared by the Japan Economic Research Center, presents the ongoing transformations of the employed population by industrial sector from 1960 to 1965 with projections through 1980. Notable is the rapid decline of the agricultural sector, which accounted for 32.6 percent of the employed population in 1960 (14,236,000), but is anticipated to account for no more than 9.0 percent in 1980 (4,990,000).[4] As presented in table 6.7, the secondary sector is expected to account for 40.0 percent of all employment by 1980, up from 31.9 percent in 1965. The tertiary sector is also expected to gain, increasing from 43.4 percent in 1965 to 51.2 percent in 1980.

It is notable that the tertiary sector is expected to continue to

4. For purposes of comparison, the total for West Germany in 1967 is 10 percent and 5.0 percent for the United States.

maintain its proportionately higher share of employment relative to
the secondary sector up through 1980. Throughout Japanese industrialization the tertiary sector has exceeded the secondary sector in
employment. This is contrary to the stage model suggested by Colin
Clark in which the secondary sector is expected to exceed the tertiary
sector until a mature stage of industrialization is reached.[5] The situation in Japan results from a historic labor surplus economy with an
abundance of people forced to eke out an existence in the low productivity sectors of urban areas.

Even today, the weight of the wholesale-retail trade and other
miscellaneous services is quite high in the Japanese employment
structure when compared to that of the United States; interestingly
enough, the weight of government employees is quite low and has
shown no tendency to rise as has been the case in the United States.[6]

TABLE 6.8   Distribution of New School Graduates by Industrial Sector

Education	Bases for percentages[a]	Primary sector[b]	Secondary sector[c]	Tertiary sector[d]
Total				
1960	1,282	10.0%	50.4%	39.6%
1965	1,407	4.8	51.1	44.0
1970	1,255	3.4	46.5	50.2
Middle school				
1960	684	13.8	61.5	24.7
1965	625	7.4	66.3	26.3
1970	271	5.2	69.0	25.8
High school				
1960	479	6.8	38.2	54.9
1965	631	3.5	39.0	57.6
1970	729	3.6	40.2	56.2
College				
1960	119	0.9	35.5	63.5
1965	151	0.5	39.2	60.3
1970	255	0.7	40.3	59.0

[a] In thousands.
[b] Includes: agriculture, forestry, and fisheries.
[c] Includes: mining, construction, and manufacturing.
[d] Includes: wholesale and retail trade, finance, insurance, real estate, transportation and communication, public utilities, service, public employment, etc.

Source: Adapted from Economic Deliberation Committee, Rōdōsha no nōryoku hakki no mondai,
pp. 16, 18.

5.   Colin Clark, The Conditions of Economic Progress (London, 1951), pp. 395–96.
6.   Koichi Emi, "Employment Structure in the Service Industries," Developing Economies 7
(June 1969): 140.

In the past, employment in the tertiary sector served to maintain or increase employment in times of business slowdowns. The sharp increase of the service sector in the period from 1965 to 1968 suggests a new situation in which tertiary sector employment increases even in periods of rapid expansion. What seems to be emerging is what V. R. Fuchs in his analysis of employment trends in the postwar United States called the service economy, an economy in which more than half of the employed population is not involved in the production of food, clothing, houses, cars, or other tangible goods.[7] The Japanese often refer to these same trends as the growth of the information society or leisure industries.[8]

An indicator of future employment structure by industry is the shifting employment composition of new school graduates (see table 6.8 for the distribution during three successive five-year intervals beginning in 1960). As expected, the percentage of new school graduates entering the primary sector declines sharply from 1960 to 1970 at each educational level. In 1970, for the first time, the total number of new school graduates entering the tertiary sector (50.2 percent) exceeded the number entering the secondary sector (46.5 percent). It has been the middle school graduates that supplied the bulk of their numbers to manufacturing rather than the tertiary sector. Concomitant with the decline of middle school graduates and the increase in high school and university graduates, the majority of new school graduates are now entering the tertiary sector.[9]

Paralleling shifts in industrial structure is the redistribution of occupational skills required by a more advanced industrial economy. Because it is difficult to anticipate the nature of technological innovation, the precise character of the occupational structure in the 1980s cannot be made clear; however, some general characteristics are apparent.

Table 6.9 indicates that significant shifts in occupational structure took place in the period 1955 to 1970. Especially notable are the increases in the percentage of employment accounted for by the clerical category (8.4 to 14.0 percent) and production-process workers (22.1 to 31.7 percent) coupled with the sharp decline in agricultural occupations (47.7 to 19.2 percent). Also notable is the marked slowdown

7. Victor Fuchs, *The Service Economy* (New York, 1968).

8. Ken'ichi Tominaga, "Post-Industrial Society and Cultural Diversity," *Survey* 78 (Winter 1971).

9. This suggests lowered productivity gains for the Japanese economy in the future based on the assumption that rapid gains in productivity are more difficult to achieve in the tertiary sector; it is an extremely heterogeneous sector, but it is marked by a high proportion of labor intensive services.

TABLE 6.9   Transition of Employment by Major Occupational Categories

	1955	1960	1965	1970
Professional	4.4%	4.9%	5.6%	6.7%
Managerial	1.8	2.3	3.0	3.9
Clerical	8.4	10.4	13.0	14.0
Sales	8.4	10.6	11.7	12.0
Agriculture, forestry, and fishing	47.7	32.6	24.5	19.2
Mining	1.2	0.8	0.5	0.3
Transportation and communication	1.7	3.3	4.4	4.5
Craftsmen, production process and laborers	22.1	28.6	30.1	31.7
Protective service	4.3	1.1	1.2	1.3
Service		5.4	6.0	6.5
Total	100.0%	100.0%	100.0%	100.1%
Bases for percentages[a]	393,436[b]	436,793[b]	476,099[b]	520,263[b]

[a] In hundreds.
[b] Numbers are for both sexes combined.

Source: Data for 1960–70 adapted from Economic Deliberation Committee, Rōdōsha no nōryoku hakki no mondai, pp. 24–25. Data for 1955 computed from Sengo rōdō tokeishi [A statistical history of labor in the postwar period].

in the growth of the craftsmen, production process, and laborer category after 1960, as measured in percentage increases. However, if one takes the increases in size of the labor force into consideration, the rate of numerical increase for this category shows no sign of decline. The professional category does not show the marked increases that we might expect of a nation characterized as entering the threshold of an "information society." This may result from the narrower definition of the professional category in Japan as compared to other industrial nations as well as the lack of "professionalism" in Japan resulting from the strong commitment of employees to bureaucratic organizations.

The rapid growth of white-collar occupations even at the expense of blue-collar occupations can be seen most clearly in an analysis of the changing distribution of occupations of new school graduates. In 1960, 41 percent of new school graduates went into blue-collar occupations while only 26.8 percent went into white-collar occupations, but by 1970, 38.9 percent were entering white-collar occupations and only 35.9 percent entering blue-collar occupations.[10]

10. Economic Deliberation Committee, Rōdōsha no nōryoku hakki no mondai [Problems of development of ability among employees] (Tokyo, 1972), p. 19. The percentages do not add to 100 because totals include new school graduates entering sales and service occupations as well as agricultural occupations.

These trends in occupational structure can be expected to continue through the 1980s. For example, in 1972 there were some 50,000 computer experts in Japan. The Data Processing Education Council established by the Ministry of Education estimates that by 1980 Japan will need some 500,000 computer experts, ten times the present number. It is the growth of such occupational categories that will move Japan into the "information age."

Changing Industrial Relations

I now turn to the final and most difficult part of this paper, that of speculating about the impact of these changing demographic, employment, industrial, and occupational structures upon the Japanese form of industrial relations. This speculative leap brings two problems immediately to mind. First, industrial relations are played out at the level of the individual firm, yet changes in labor force characteristics are aggregate measures. Sometimes these aggregate measures are results of different and conflicting trends; therefore, these summary measures may have little or no relevance to behavior at the individual firm. For example, although there may be a persistent national labor shortage reaching into the 1980s, this is not incompatible with many individual firms experiencing labor redundancy, particularly in the context of the practice of employees serving the same employer until retirement age. Middle-aged and older employees are commonly singled out as the strata often made redundant by rapid technological change. Similarly, the extent of labor shortage will vary with industry, enterprise, occupation, and nature and scope of technological innovation.

In a different vein, although the aging of the labor force may occur over a wide range of individual firms, variance in age composition in different industries and different-sized firms makes clear the selectiveness of the aging process. Generally speaking, those industrial sectors that show the highest rate of employment growth are the ones that most successfully resist the aging process; productive units in these sectors are able to hire large numbers of young employees.[11] Differences in the aging process by industry become apparent when we compare sectors over time on an index of aging as measured by the percentage of total employed in a given sector accounted for by those from age 45 to 64.[12] Agriculture as an industry of low growth and productivity went from 32.7 on this index in 1960 to 41.7 in 1970. The aging process was more

11. More precisely, the brakes put on the aging process in rapidly growing industries refers to large firms in these industries. Smaller firms, if not growing rapidly, would presumably be less able to resist the aging process. I am indebted to Hugh Patrick for calling my attention to this distinction.

12. Economic Deliberation Committee, *Rōdōsha no nōryoku hakki no mondai*, pp. 8–9.

retarded in the secondary sector where manufacturing went from 16.9 in 1960 to 21.2 in 1970. The tertiary sector experienced the smallest increase on our aging index, going from 22.7 in 1960 to 23.7 in 1970.

The selective nature of the aging process is nowhere more evident than in an examination of age structure by size of firm. Table 6.10 provides dramatic evidence that although the aging trend is occurring in both large and small manufacturing firms, it is most pronounced in small firms. For example, those employees under age 20 declined from 18.9 percent in 1960 to 14.2 percent in 1970 in firms of over 100 employees, but the decline was much more marked in firms of 10 to 99 employees where those under 20 went from 23.8 to 8.5 percent. Similarly, those from ages 40 to 49 actually declined as a percentage of the labor force in large firms from 1960 to 1970 (from 15.6 to 15.4 percent), but in smaller firms the percentage increased from 12.3 to 19.5 percent. These differentials are even more pronounced in the case of females.[13] In short, although the dual economy may be breaking down with respect to such factors as wage differentials, the increasingly discrepant age structure will continue to have profound consequences on productivity, life styles, and political orientation.[14] Although large firms will not be able to avoid the aging of their employees in the future, their superior strength and higher employment growth rates will most likely result in the aging trend being felt more strongly in the smaller firms.[15] Further analysis of this question would involve consideration of the various institutional mechanisms that produce these outcomes. For example, a standard practice of large firms involves sending retired employees over age 55 down to work at reduced wages in small and medium subcontractors. Thus we are not dealing with the simple mechanical impact of differential growth rates in employment and replacement but with questions of power and resource allocation.

These differential changes point up the difficulty of inferring a uniform impact of aggregate level change such as age composition on individual firm and industry units. Although I will try to deal with

13.   Okazaki, *Rōdōryoku no chōki tenbō*, p. 88.

14.   It is interesting to note that, in the immediate postwar period, it was the larger firms that were saddled with a much older labor force.

15.   One must be mindful of tautology here since those small firms that hire large numbers of new employees and maintain low mean wages, by definition, become large firms, thereby confirming our proposition. More careful investigation of the proposition would involve examining the same firms over time without allowing a change in size classification. One further caution involves our concentration on growth in employment as the key factor allowing employers to hire large numbers of young employees and thereby maintain low mean wages for their total employment. Insofar as high separation rates obtained for older employees, this would theoretically allow for replacement by younger employees.

TABLE 6.10   Age Composition of Regular Employees in
Manufacturing by Firm Size

Firm size

Age	100 or more employees			10–99 employees		
	1960	*1965*	*1970*	*1960*	*1965*	*1970*
Below 20	18.9%	18.1%	14.2%	23.8%	15.4%	8.5%
20–29	37.1	41.0	40.9	36.5	33.8	29.6
30–39	23.2	21.3	23.0	18.1	22.6	25.5
40–49	15.6	14.0	15.4	12.3	15.2	19.5
50+	5.2	5.9	6.6	9.3	13.0	16.8
Total	100.0%	100.0%	100.0%	100.0%	100.0%	100.0%

Note: Column totals have been rounded to 100 percent in some cases.
Source: Economic Deliberation Committee, *Rōdōsha no nōryoku hakki no mondai,* p. 36.

data that take this factor into consideration, the reader must recognize the tentativeness of the following discussion precisely because of the relative lack of such data. In particular, we must be sensitized to the fact that large and growing organizations with greater resources and flexibility are better able to resist, insulate, and "buffer" themselves from changing environmental conditions as compared to smaller and weaker units;[16] moreover, because of the high dependency of many small firms upon larger firms, the effects of environmental pressures upon the large firms are transferred to small firms (via financial arrangements, technology transfers, and labor inputs) thereby intensifying already existing pressures upon the smaller firms.

There is a second problem in trying to speculate about the impact of these changing demographic and employment structures upon characteristic forms of Japanese industrial relations: we are not dealing with all the relevant variables that influence the shape of industrial relations. A comprehensive model of the industrial relations system would incorporate variables representing the distribution of power in the wider society as well as among the relevant actors: management, employees, government, and consumers. It would include the impact of technological innovation and a variety of economic variables. Consideration would also be given to value orientations of the respective parties as well as a variety of other sociological variables.[17]

Although I will touch upon some of these variables, this paper is not an attempt to measure the relative impact and relations of the variables

16.   James Thompson, *Organizations in Action* (New York, 1967), pp. 20–24.
17.   For a model of industrial relations systems, see John Dunlop, *Industrial Relations Systems* (New York, 1958).

discussed in the first section with the variety of other variables that will determine the actual direction of the Japanese industrial relations system. Rather, it is an attempt to delimit a particular subset of variables focusing around demographic and employment structure characteristics and to assess its likely impact upon specific industrial relations practices. This is done with full recognition that interaction with other variables will strengthen in some cases and counterbalance in other cases the effects that I suggest. Notwithstanding this caution, I do suggest that the particular subset of variables I have chosen to examine is a particularly important subset, because made up of conditioning variables. These conditioning variables close off certain options, minimize the probability of others occurring, and increase the probability of still others. The most that I can hope to accomplish, then, is to lay out these options and show how their probabilities are conditioned by demographic and employment structure characteristics.

The Growth Rate and Its Consequences

Rate of economic growth is one variable that lies outside our subset. It is clear that population composition and employment structure characteristics have a significant bearing upon rate of economic growth. Our concern here, however, lies in the critical importance of the rate of economic growth (as an independent variable) for determining industrial relations practices. The assumptions that one makes about the rate of future Japanese economic growth so affect one's conclusion about changing industrial relations practices that the subject must be dealt with directly.

Students of Japanese social conditions have often pointed out the large impact that a slowdown in Japan's high economic growth rate would have.[18] Throughout the 1960s the Japanese themselves became accustomed to looking at any growth rates in real GNP below 10 percent as recessions. Usually, discussions of a long-term slowdown in economic growth have been limited to such generalities as the prediction that it would produce an aggravation of social and political tensions. Recently, the possibility of such a slowdown has come to appear as a quite likely outcome; Japanese analysts themselves have begun to take a more serious look at the question.

My own judgment based on a sampling of the discussion leads me to conclude that a real growth rate of 6 to 7 percent seems a likely stabilizing point for Japan by 1980, though undoubtedly there will be fluctua-

18. Zbigniew Brzezinski, *The Fragile Blossom: Crisis and Change in Japan* (New York, 1972), p. 57.

tions throughout the 1970s.[19] This is not the place for an extended discussion of the economic growth potential of the Japanese economy, nor am I qualified to undertake the task; nevertheless, a few words on the subject are in order. The rapid expansion of the GNP in recent decades has been based on the priority given to private equipment investment focused on the heavy and chemical industries as well as the priority given to exports and acquisition of foreign exchange. The whole financial and administrative structure is arranged to give preferential treatment to equipment investment and exports.[20] These policy decisions have had serious negative domestic and international repercussions in recent years, arising to a great extent from their success in the past. On the domestic scene, the resource allocations implicit in these policies (i.e., low social capital investment) have become increasingly untenable in the face of environmental destruction and "livelihood destruction." Internationally, these policies have come under foreign criticism with strong hostility being directed toward Japan's export policies. Finally, the recent raw material shortages and the rapidly rising prices of raw materials, capped by the Arab oil cutbacks, have forced Japanese leaders to recognize their inability to maintain current increase rates of raw material imports and the difficulty of sustaining their current competitive position.

For now, it is important to emphasize the significance of the 6 to 7 percent prediction of future growth rates, however precarious such a prediction may be. For example, with a growth rate of 6 to 7 percent, labor shortage will remain a serious problem.[21] Should the Japanese growth rate drop well below this figure, the labor shortage would be

19. Henry Rosovsky in "Japan's Economic Future: An Overview," in Jerome Cohen, ed., *Pacific Partnership: United States Japan Trade* (New York, 1972) arrives at an estimate of 6.5 percent. Kenneth Kurihara, who seems to take a more optimistic position on Japan's growth potential, provides a summary of many of the relevant arguments in Kenneth Kurihara, *The Growth Potential of the Japanese Economy* (Baltimore, 1971). For a still more optimistic view see Hisao Kanamori, "The Economics of Growth Rate Acceleration," *The Japan Interpreter* 7 (Winter 1971): 26–35. My own estimate of a real growth rate of 6 to 7 percent was arrived at in the fall of 1972 when I wrote the first draft of this paper. Recent events suggest the increased probability of this conservative estimate being correct; indeed, it may prove to have been on the high side.

20. Kazuji Nagasu, "Japanese Economy in the Seventies," *Japan Quarterly*, (April–June 1972), p. 143.

21. In the past, one questioned the seriousness of this shortage knowing that a large proportion of the labor force continues to be employed in the low productivity sectors. Yet insofar as at a given point of time and demand labor inputs cannot be easily shifted from low productivity to high productivity sectors, then the shortage is very real for individual employers. Moreover, the rapid rise in the wages of young employees that I will discuss below testifies to the reality of the shortage for given employee categories.

a much more minor matter with far less impact than proposed in this paper.

The Ministry of Labor[22] has recently formulated estimates of the gap between labor supply and demand up through 1975. Based on a projection of a 1975 labor supply of about 54 million (see table 6.4), and under the different assumptions of real economic growth rates of 10 percent and 8.5 percent, the ministry estimates a labor shortage gap of about 4.5 million and 2 million respectively. This presumes a growth in labor demand from 1970 to 1975 of 2.4 percent annually (total 6.5 million) under the 10 percent growth rate assumption and 1.5 percent annually (total 3.5 million) under the 8.5 percent assumption.

These estimates further assume that the relatively heavy weight of the heavy and chemical industries in the growth from 1965 to 1970 will be maintained. These industries, serving the export market to a great extent and based on high levels of capital investment, have been able to sustain high rates of productivity increase without major inputs of labor (compared to the rest of the nonagricultural economy). If the shift to creating a welfare economy were realized in accord with the current rhetoric of government leaders and under the assumptions of the same growth rates of 10 and 8.5 percent, then the labor shortage would be more severe than envisioned in the above estimates. This is because the kinds of investment necessary to produce a welfare economy are more labor-intensive than the pattern characterizing Japanese economic growth of the late 1960s.

Some final cautions are in order. First, we cannot simply extrapolate the kinds of shortages discussed here to the 1980 period; they are not cumulative in any simple fashion. Employers have a need for labor in specific time periods and if the labor is not available, they may pass up certain opportunities, reorganize workplace operations to reallocate labor already employed, or they may invest in technology. Secondly, the estimates rest on some simple assumptions that project existing relationships between productivity and economic growth as well as levels of productivity increase. Were investment efficiency and labor efficiency ratios to rise, the kinds of labor shortages envisioned would be reduced. Moreover, there are alternative labor force estimates that show marked increases based on an increasing participation rate for older women.[23] Were such estimates correct, the labor shortage anticipated in the above estimate would be reduced. Finally, lurking

22. Ministry of Labor, *Rōdōryoku jukyū no chōki teki tenbō* [A long-range outlook on labor force supply and demand] (Tokyo, 1972), pp. 63–65, 274–83.

23. Ibid., pp. 276–77.

in the background is the possibility of large-scale recruitment of Korean and Southeast Asian labor. Were this path chosen, Japan would follow the West German model of alleviating the labor shortage. Although this policy position is still a minority one in Japan, there are now strong voices being heard from selected business and government circles in support of importation. In 1973 a major issue developed over a plan to import Korean labor to complete the International Ocean Exposition in Okinawa. The powerful Ministry of International Trade and Industry supported the plan, which was opposed by the Ministry of Labor. The plan was finally rejected, but not until it reached the highest levels of Liberal Democratic party (LDP) decision-making. Nevertheless, there are those who believe that the pressure for importation will prove irresistible by 1980. My own judgment is that the Japanese leaders will continue to resist this pressure, first because of the opposition of the unions, which see it as an attempt to dampen wage increases and lower the level of working conditions. Secondly, business and political leaders are aware that they have reaped many benefits from the homogeneity of the Japanese population and that importation of foreign labor would reopen many old wounds and create a whole host of new long-term problems.

The sociological axiom that underlies expectations that a slowdown from the 12 percent growth rates of the 1960s will have important social and political consequences is as follows. Under conditions of a rapidly increasing GNP pie, both the advantaged and disadvantaged sectors of the population can anticipate increased material prosperity. Looked at in terms of the distribution of material rewards in a society, constant expansion of the pie permits the relative gap between the advantaged and the disadvantaged groups in the population to be closed without causing a decline in absolute rewards for the advantaged. The consequence is that such a rapid expansion allows rapid social change with a minimum of social conflict.

The above description provides a fairly accurate picture of Japan in the postwar period. A remarkable transformation has been achieved in productive capacity and in the nature and degree of urbanization of the Japanese population. The dramatic reforms of the immediate postwar period combined with an annual rate of increase in real income of 6 to 7 percent, the highest in the world, have led to a significant narrowing of the income gaps between various social groups. This leveling of income distribution has involved the following consequences: closing of the gap in wage level between blue-collar and white-collar employees; increase in farmers' earnings and the wages of construction workers relative to the earnings of urban workers; reduction of the gap between younger and older workers; reduction of differentials in wages in large and small firms, especially among the younger age categories; decline of wage differentials by educational level; and the closing of the gap between earnings in the civil service and private sector, with a more rapid increase in the latter.[24] Significant here is that these gaps have been closed with a minimum of social conflict as a consequence of the advanced group in each case being able to increase its absolute share (as measured in standard of living) even while its relative share was declining.[25] One hypothesis would be that the more one narrows the differences between groups, the greater the dissatisfaction and tension felt by disadvantaged groups who now have their appetites whetted for still further equalization. Whatever the conditions that might lead to such an outcome, they do not seem to be present in contemporary Japan.

The significance of a marked decline in the Japanese economic growth rate would be that the distribution of social rewards would be transformed into operating more as a zero-sum game. That is, with more stabilized rewards, the gains for one social group would come at the expense of other social groups not only in a relative but in an absolute sense as well. It is this principle that is the basis for the heightening of social and political tensions that scholars associate with a declining rate of economic growth. This having been said, it should be clear that a growth rate of 6 to 7 percent, as we have assumed, by no means suggests a zero-sum game. It is still well above what most other industrial nations have been able to achieve in the last decade. Yet we are dealing here with expectations that are created by peoples' experiences within a given nation. Although we cannot

24. Overall conclusions are derived from Economic Planning Agency, *Economic Survey of Japan (1970–1971)* (Tokyo, 1971). Wages of employees in the age group 50 to 59 in major corporations were three times as much as wages for workers aged 20 to 24 in 1955. By 1970 they were earning only twice as much (Ibid., p. 105). In the period from 1964 to 1970, the average monthly contractual earnings (bonus not included) of male blue-collar middle school graduates in manufacturing went from 66 to 75 percent of the average monthly contractual earnings of male university graduates in manufacturing. Ministry of Labor, *Year Book of Labor Statistics: 1964* (Tokyo, 1965) p. 129; Ministry of Labor, *Year Book of Labor Statistics: 1970* (Tokyo, 1971) p. 137. A final caution: the leveling suggested by these figures would not be as pronounced if we included nonwage income. Indeed, the 1972 labor white paper reports that although the distribution of wage income is becoming more egalitarian, there has been a marked increase in recent years in the amount of nonwage income and this tends to be far less equally distributed. In particular, the possession of real estate has taken on new importance as a result of skyrocketing land prices. Generally speaking, the accelerating inflation of the early 1970s increases the gap between those on fixed income such as the elderly and those whose incomes keep pace with inflation.

25. Gerhard Lenski argues in *Power and Privilege* (New York, 1966) that this situation is characteristic of industrial societies, which, contrary to agricultural societies, reveal a growing equality in their distribution of rewards.

expect the dynamics of reward distribution in Japan to change into a zero-sum game, we can expect that an economic slowdown will reduce the growth in the amount of rewards available for distribution relative to citizen expectations. It may be that a couple of sharp recessions would be enough to realign employee expectations to better conform to reality. But it is my view that we can anticipate a heightening of social and political tensions as the growth rate declines.

The Struggle Over Wages

Assuming this decline in economic growth, there are some key questions we would like answered. Will the advantaged groups continue to allow a decline in their relative advantages when they can only anticipate modest absolute gains? In cases where market factors are operative in producing a leveling, how will previously advantaged groups respond? Similarly, will disadvantaged groups that have become accustomed to large annual improvements in their economic position tolerate reductions in their increase rate? If such reductions occur, how will they respond? Will there be a political response, a heightening of workshop tensions, and consequent loss of motivation to work, or will employees turn to a more privatized consumption of leisure time? These are some of the questions to be treated in the following sections. The significance of growing employee disaffection would lie in its impact on lowering employee motivation and commitment to work. It could also have the effect of creating a stronger union and a political movement that could better represent wage-earner interests. To the extent that this situation develops, a feedback loop is operative whereby the lowered rate of economic growth increases worker disaffection, which, in turn, operates to create a further drag upon rates of economic growth.

The lines are drawn on these issues most clearly in the case of wage increases. The relationships between wage increases and labor productivity are extremely complicated ones. On the surface, they might seem to be fairly straightforward if we look at recent Japanese economic indicators. In three recent five-year periods, nominal employee per capita income rose 6.8 percent between 1956 and 1960, 12.8 percent between 1961 and 1965, and 14.0 percent between 1966 and 1970. Adjusting for inflation, the real income increases work out to 5.0, 6.1, 8.0, respectively. These gradually rising percentage increases in income. were roughly matched by rising per capita increases in real productivity.[26] However, more careful examination of the past cyclical movements in the Japanese economy shows that there is a time lag

26. Japan Productivity Center, *Katsuyō rōdō tōkei*, pp. 27, 29.

between movements of business activity and wages. In economic downturns the strong upward pressure on wages lingers, while in upward swings the wage increases lag behind. At the same time, output per man-hour, the commonly used measure of "partial productivity," tends to weaken in the late stages of a business upswing as plants become overloaded and marginal workers are hired. In the early stages of an economic slowdown, this decline in labor productivity becomes sharper as plants cannot cut their payrolls fast enough to match falling output. In Japan's case, the high rate of economic growth experienced even in times of business downturns means that labor productivity seldom declines but that the rate of increase falls. Toward the bottom of an economic slowdown, productivity stabilizes and it begins to rise sharply as the business upturn begins.

Events in 1972 support this interpretation. Despite the uncertainty and confusion resulting from yen revaluation and the economy being in a marked downswing with an accompanying decline in the rate of increase in output per man-hour, the average monthly wage increase in the unions' "spring offensive" showed a surprisingly high increase rate of 14.8 to 15 percent over the previous year (about ¥9,800–9,900). These wage boosts exceeded those of 1971 in absolute terms and were only slightly lower in percentage terms. At the conclusion of the 1972 spring offensive, widespread concern was voiced in the business community to the effect that enterprises now appeared to be compelled to pay high wages independent of labor productivity.

It is interesting to examine directly the relationship between rate of real economic growth and rate of increase in monthly wages per employee (including seasonal bonus payments; see table 6.11). Since 1963, the rate of real economic growth has fallen below 10 percent only two times: in 1965 it was 4.5 percent and in 1971 it was 6.3 percent. These two years account for two out of the three years since 1963 when the rate of increase in monthly wage per employee suffered declines (see table 6.11). The decline of the rate of increase in monthly wages in 1971 to 14.5 percent came about primarily from a reduction of overtime and bonus payments.[27]

These observations do not, however, tell us what would be the response of wages to a marked decline in rate of economic growth stretching beyond one-year periods. Notwithstanding, assuming a downward movement in economic growth rates to about 6 to 7 percent by the early 1980s, we would expect that wage rates would follow this decline, though with considerable time lags and even then not completely.

27. Ministry of Labor, *Rōdō hakusho showa 47* [White paper on labor: 1972] (Tokyo, 1972) pp. 11–12.

TABLE 6.11   Rate of Real Economic Growth
and Rate of Increase in Monthly Wages (Per Employee)

	1963	1964	1965	1966	1967	1968	1969	1970	1971
Rate of real economic growth	10.6[a]	13.3	4.5	10.0	13.5	14.4	11.9	10.5	6.3
Rate of increase in monthly wages	10.7	9.9	9.6	10.9	11.7	13.7	15.7	17.0	14.5

[a] In percentage.

Note: Monthly wages per employee includes all industries and establishments with 30 or more employees.
Source: Japan Federation of Employers' Associations, "Conditions of Labor Economy in Japan," Nikkeiren News 49 (October, 1972).

The slower growth of the labor force combined with a continued strong demand for labor (resulting in an increase in the value of per capita labor), militant union demands spurred by rapidly rising consumer prices, and the significant impact of previously established expectations by both management and labor, all these forestall any management-labor convergence. The 1974 spring labor offensive settlement under which wages increased 32 percent in response to inflation running over 20 percent a year reflects the strength of these factors. It may be that the annual increases of 10,000 yen a month will be maintained for some time, though this will gradually produce smaller percentage increases, with annual wage increases becoming stabilized at around 10 percent. The Japan Economic Research Center estimates, incidentally, that by 1980 the average wage of Japanese employees will equal about 80 percent that of U.S. employees.

The maintenance of a high level of wage increases under conditions of declining economic performance can be expected to put pressure on corporate earning capacity—though not as much, as we shall see, as Japanese management would have people believe. Under such pressures, management will likely respond with strong efforts to resist labor's wage demands and with higher investment in labor-saving equipment in existing facilities to the extent that they are not successful. Even in the business decline of 1970, in which the rate of new business investment fell off drastically and wage increases held firm, labor-saving investment in existing facilities remained strong.[28] Insofar as we anticipate management to have added incentive to invest in capital-intensive technology to offset the labor shortage, the rate of increase in the marginal productivity of labor may remain strong, thus making it possible for management to maintain relatively high

28.   Economic Planning Agency, Economic Survey of Japan (1970–1971), p. 29.

levels of wage increases. The extent to which this will occur is hard to predict, but it requires that we moderate Japanese management's dire predictions about the "enormous" pressure that will be placed on their corporate earning capacity as a result of high wage increases.

Employees have not only become accustomed to high annual wage increases but to *rising* rates of increase. On balance, the above discussion suggests that although there will be time lags and the correspondence will not be complete, wage increases will gradually moderate as they come into line with national economic performance and respond to the continued strength of Japanese management and government. How will employees respond to resistance to their efforts to achieve wage increases consonant with past performance? If we assume that the Japanese have internalized a traditional work ethic and are totally unable to resist management authority for reasons of their need for dependency and the persistence of traditional values, then a slowdown in wage increases should bring no significant changes in work behavior; no marked increases in labor discontent should occur. Although this interpretation may appeal to those Western observers who are obsessed with notions of an unchanging Japan, almost no serious Japanese scholar in the industrial relations field takes this view seriously.

An alternative interpretation with a good deal of intuitive appeal is that significant worker frustration about work conditions and urban living conditions has increased over the period of rapid economic growth since 1955, but this frustration has been held in check by rapidly rising real income. In essence, large wage increases have served to mute overt expression of dissatisfaction. In this period, the moderate Dōmei union federation explicitly concurred with the new management policy of higher wages for increased productivity. Sōhyō, the largest union federation, resisted this formula at the national level with left-wing ideology and "antirationalization" movements, but at the enterprise level, its members agreed to the policy just as did the Dōmei unions.

The significance of this past history is that if an economic slowdown were to restrict the increase rate of wages, as seems likely over time, economic rewards would be less able in the future to compensate for the lack of noneconomic rewards, as has been the case over the last twenty years. To the extent that worker expectations are formed on the basis of nominal absolute increases (rather than real absolute increases or rates of increase), then the amount of dissatisfaction may be less. In all probability, expectations are formed on the basis of all of these, perhaps in the order mentioned.

It is of interest that 1971, a year of reduced corporate business performance, continued inflation, and a reduced rate of increase in monthly wages per employee, was also the year that the number of labor disputes registered its highest level. Presumably, worker efforts to maintain prior levels of wage increases accounted for this situation. The total number of disputes was up 51 percent over the prior year with the total number of workers participating in these disputes up by 19 percent. The level of dispute activity was considerably above the prior recession year of 1965.[29] It would be dangerous to project this kind of measure of dissatisfaction into the future since successive years of decline in corporate business performance might produce different responses. Nevertheless, the response to the 1971 slowdown is suggestive and hard to reconcile with the image of the subservient Japanese worker.

The Consequences of Worker Dissatisfaction

If we consider how dissatisfaction with a declining rate of wage increases might be expressed, a number of alternatives come to mind. Some, though not all, of these alternatives are compatible with one another. Of great interest is whether worker dissatisfaction manifests itself in greater involvement in political activity. The likelihood of workers achieving satisfaction from involvement in this area may be far greater than commonly thought. The continued reduction of LDP vote pluralities seems to be quite probable. The non-LDP parties are increasingly successful in focusing on the wave of social problems that has been created by the high economic growth policies of the LDP. Destruction of livelihood (seikatsu hakai), public nuisances (kōgai), and the housing problem (jūtaku mondai) are all increasingly effective slogans for the non-LDP parties. If the LDP really were to make a major shift in building a welfare state, it might be able to turn these issues to its own political advantage (though this would not necessarily reduce worker dissatisfaction in the shop). In the last decade, however, the LDP has used the slogans as rhetoric without making a major policy commitment to solve the problems. Barring such a commitment in the future and barring drastic shifts in the international situation that would permit the LDP to rally national support, a continued weakening of the party seems probable.

Notwithstanding this likelihood, the ability of the opposition parties to build a viable ruling coalition seems slight. Cooperation between the Socialist (JSP), Clean Government (CGP), Democratic Socialist (DSP), and Communist (JCP) parties seems possible on limited issues, such as has been the case with regard to changing Japan's

29. Ministry of Labor, White paper, 1972, pp. 38–40.

position toward China. The kind of united front necessary to build a lasting government majority, however, seems outside the grasp of the opposition parties, given their ideological differences. Electoral success by the Communists and Socialists in the lower-house election of 1972 led to a marked heightening of their antagonisms. Nevertheless, while a viable coalition seems unlikely, I do believe it is possible that an unstable opposition coalition will assume control of the government in the early 1980s if not before. This is contrary to the position taken by Thayer in this volume and the implicit assumptions of large numbers of Western policymakers and scholars. It is my judgment, however, that Western observers have become addicted to and comfortable with the continuous rule of the LDP. Consequently, they fail to recognize the potentially radical shifts in the political system that may occur as the system confronts for the first time since the initial postwar chaos a significant threat to continued one-party rule. The instability of such a coalition, based on interparty jockeying for power within the government, suggests that at best workers will receive the symbolic satisfaction of seeing their parties in power. Such instability seems to preclude legislative decisions that would effectively meet the needs of wage earners.

Although I seem to have less trouble envisioning a coalition of opposition parties than do other observers, a more likely alternative does seem to be a coalition between the LDP and one of the opposition parties, especially the DSP (if it survives) and possibly the CGP. Even here, the easy position to take is that such a coalition would leave the LDP in its dominant position. Yet for the DSP or the CGP to participate in a coalition government would open them up to charges from the Socialists and Communists that they had "sold out." To protect themselves against such charges and to maintain their constituency, they would have to adopt strong positions in the area of social legislation and more generally in the area of investment in social capital stock. On the other side, a once confident LDP forced into a coalition government and fearful of further losses that would make it a permanent minority could well be expected finally to take seriously its official commitment to the public interest. In short, such a coalition government would seem to promise more concrete satisfaction for wage earners than outright assumption of power by a coalition of opposition parties, at least in the short run. It would, however, provide less symbolic satisfaction than a worker-oriented government. The above discussed scenario depends on the LDP reacting to the growing strength of the opposition by moving to the left. One cannot dismiss the possibility, however, that the party will respond with a sharp shift to the right, with the potential for stalemating governmental action until it can exploit a national crisis to its benefit. The emergence of an organized group of young rightists (the *Seirankai*) within the LDP in 1972 suggests this possibility.

A second way for employees to express their dissatisfaction is to turn inward to leisure time consumption and/or a privatized "my home-ism." This individual solution may derive from increased alienation from work with consequent lowered commitment to work. It may well be that different segments of the labor force will opt for the political versus the individual solutions. Management spokesmen already see a lowered will to work as a major problem to be combatted in the coming decade. Such current slogans as "making every man a manager" and the spread of quality control circles reflect management's deep concern with this issue.

A third alternative for expressing worker dissatisfaction lies in increased opposition to management at the shop level. Without large wage increases to offset the expected stepped-up labor intensification (*rōdō kyōka*) policies of management, employees are likely to put more pressure on union leaders to defend their interests in the shop. Thus far, unions have largely given management a free hand in the shop as part of their cooperation to raise productivity in exchange for higher wages. An economic slowdown that led to lowered wage increases and increased efforts to raise productivity levels in existing facilities through labor intensification practices would make this bargain appear most one-sided.[30] Consequently, the unions, whatever their ideology, might well be forced to make greater efforts at protecting worker interest in the shop on such matters as job transfers, speedups, occupational health standards, environmental issues, leisure time consumption, and the like. There are signs that the unions are already moving to confront some of these issues, issues on which they have been notably silent in the past. For example, a 1973 decision by the Central Labor Commission reversed the dismissals of union leaders whose members had distributed circulars at a union rally supporting allegations of neighboring farmers that pollution of farmland was being caused by improper disposal of factory wastes. The decision was expected to strengthen union efforts in this field.[31] How effectively unions tackle workshop and environmental issues may well have a major impact on

30. With the slowdown in 1971, some observers were already suggesting that the Dōmei strategy was obsolete. In Dōmei's 1973 wage white paper, the federation for the first time demanded a pay raise "in excess of productivity growth." In the past, Dōmei had always endorsed management's position that high wage increases are only possible if they are linked with high productivity increases. For Dōmei leaders to reverse this policy suggests that they are under great pressure from the rank and file to offset serious inflationary pressures.

31. Asahi *Evening News*, 11 January 1973.

the future of unions in Japan. Nevertheless, the ability of management to prevent the unions from getting involved, except in roles directly supportive of management interests, should not be underestimated.

THE SENIORITY SYSTEM AND GENERATIONAL CONFLICT

The combination of a slowdown in the rise of total wage packages and a selective labor shortage, particularly of young employees, seems guaranteed to fuel the growing conflict between younger and older employees as older employees see their wage advantages eroded. In the late 1960s the greatest pressure-producing changes in the *nenkō* (seniority) wage system was the growing labor shortage, primarily of younger workers. This forced up the wages of young employees at a much more rapid rate than that for older employees, resulting in a de facto weakening of nenkō. Although an economic growth rate of 6 to 7 percent will reduce labor demands relative to the period of the 1960s with its higher growth rates, the supply of young employees, as discussed above, will decline still more drastically in the coming decade. As a consequence, there will be continued shortage with sustained pressure to raise the wages of young employees.

Because of predictable management efforts to hold down the size of their total wage bill under conditions of declining economic growth rates, older employees will be even more hard pressed to achieve wage hikes commensurate with those of younger employees. Moreover, management is faced with the prospect of a rapidly rising wage bill as a result of the aging labor force. This will put severe pressure on the nenkō wage system, with management attempting to hold down the wages of older workers. One appealing way to legitimate this holding the lid on wage increases for older employees is publicly to shift toward a wage system more exclusively based on merit. This is a shift that appears already underway in the larger firms. Indeed, the absence of a strict nenkō system in the smaller firms with their high proportions of older employees is quite explicable in these terms. In summary, significant modification of the nenkō wage system is already occurring and will be accelerated by a combination of an aging labor force, continuing labor shortage, and declining economic growth rates. This is not to say that age and length of service will disappear as wage determinants. I have discussed elsewhere the source of their persistence.[32] Briefly put, rewarding seniority represents the value of accumulated experience (specific training) at a given employer.[33] Moreover,

32. Robert Cole, *Japanese Blue Collar* (Berkeley, 1971).

33. In a recent study of the Chicago labor market, Albert Rees and George Shultz found that seniority was the best predictor (the highest value of all independent variables) of their dependent variable, wages per hour at work. Albert Rees and George Shultz, *Workers and Wages in an Urban Market* (Chicago, 1970), pp. 147–54.

Sōhyō continues to be a strong supporter of the egalitarian approach represented by nenkō.

The weakening of the nenkō wage system will not affect all occupational categories equally. Those categories of employees that are in the greatest need, such as blue-collar workers and technicians, seem likely to experience the most marked changes. Although some differential based on age seems likely to be retained, the substance will be quite different from that of the past. Among many white-collar employees and management personnel, nenkō will undoubtedly persist in a form quite comparable to present practices. The increased number of college graduates (an anticipated 361,000 in 1980 as compared with 309,000 in 1972) will result in the labor shortage being felt less strongly for management personnel; consequently, the pressure to raise the wages of young employees in this category will be less marked.

As a consequence of sharp modification of the nenkō wage system among large numbers of employees, generational conflict among employees and between older employees and management seems likely to grow. A good deal of the generational conflict will be fought out in employee struggles over union policy.[34] Young employees, although receiving higher wages than young workers in the recent past, are conscious of their limited means of experiencing the leisure life trumpeted in the mass media. They are also conscious that union policy is oriented toward the needs of older workers on the one hand and management on the other.[35] Young employees have become accustomed to the rising curve of wage increases; dissatisfaction will grow with management's strong efforts to cut back on these increases. The settled union leadership of the last fifteen years seems likely to become a thing of the past as young employees attack union leaders for being too cooperative with management policies.

From the other side, older employees are increasingly upset at seeing wage and other advantages disappear. The response of workers to the partial introduction of payment-by-ability wage systems in a number of industries is instructive. Such new wage payments systems made rapid inroads in the 1960s. Older workers, in particular, became increasingly upset that the payment-by-ability wage systems allowed for younger workers who achieved the top skill grades for their jobs to earn more than older workers who were in lower skill grades for their jobs. As a consequence, they have pressured the unions in certain

34. Ronald Dore, *British Factory–Japanese Factory* (Berkeley, 1973), p. 191.

35. For an extended discussion of the generation gap in labor unions, see Okamoto Hideaki, "Shakai hendō to rōdōsha ishiki: kumiai undō ni okeru sedai no mondai" [Social change and worker consciousness: Problems of generation in the labor movement], *Nihon rōdō kyokai zasshi* [Journal of the Japan Institute of Labor] (January 1971): 14–29.

industries (steel, electric, private railways, textiles) to demand a "guaranteed minimum wage" *(sangyō betsu saitei hoshō chingin)*. Management has in many cases agreed to these demands. The guaranteed minimum wage established minimum wages for specific points in the age cycle designated as critical (e.g., ages 15, 18, 22, 27, 35, 40) and consequently serves to hold erosion of the nenkō wage system in check. We see, in short, a shifting back and forth in wage payment principles in response to pressures from dissatisfied age groups. These dissatisfactions in both young and old seem sure to be intensified by the aging of the labor force, continued labor shortage, and declining economic growth rates.

It is not only the nenkō wage system that is under attack from these forces. The system of promotion according to age and length of service is also vulnerable. Ansley Coale, the noted demographer, expressed the issue in general terms:[36]

> The most conspicuous disadvantage (of zero population growth) is the age composition implied by a stationary population, especially at the low mortality that has been achieved in advanced countries. A stationary population with an expectation of life of 70 years has as many people over 60 as under 15. This distribution is essentially vertical up to the age of 50 or 55. The median age is about 37 years. . . . In a stationary population, as Myrdal pointed out years ago, there is no longer the consonance between the pyramid of responsibility and the age pyramid that there is in a growing population. When the population is stationary, there is no longer a reasonable expectation of advancement in authority with age, since the number of 50-year-olds is little different from the number of 20-year-olds.[37]

Although Japan is still far from the stationary population envisioned by Coale, it has moved rapidly in that direction. The aging index (those over 60 divided by those 14 and below) reported in table 6.1 moved from 24 in 1955 to 45 in 1970 and is estimated at 90 for the year 2000. Although Coale's statements on the implications of increasingly discrepant authority and age structures must be regarded as hypotheses, the available data on changes in the nenkō promotion structure provide some support for his conclusions.

36.   I am indebted to James Cramer in his working paper "Demographic Models of Bureaucracy" (mimeo., Ann Arbor, 1973) for pointing out this line of thinking by Coale. The Cramer paper was also useful in sensitizing me to the dangers of applying conclusions from aggregate data to the individual firm level.

37.   Ansley Coale, "Should the United States Start a Campaign for Fewer Births?" *Population Index* 34 (1968): 467–74.

In the late 1950s and 1960s rapidly expanding industrial facilities led to the creation of large numbers of new supervisory and managerial positions. It was just those industries that were rapidly expanding that also had labor forces marked by extreme youthfulness. Thus management was not faced with large numbers of middle-aged employees with expectations of promotion according to age and length of service. Instead, the relatively small number of older employees came to the promotion age at just the time that supervisory and managerial positions were undergoing rapid expansion. This meant that those employees over age 35 with "normal" abilities and qualifications had every reason to look forward to promotion at least to the first steps on the ladder.[38] Indeed, it is reported that rapid expansion in many companies led to a reduction of the promotion age from the early 40s to the early 30s as management sought to meet its supervisory needs.[39]

This situation is now beginning to change quite rapidly. On the supply side, with the aging of the labor force deemed a factor with significant dimensions, management is faced with the prospect of ever larger numbers of older employees with expectations of nenkō promotion. It is already clear that many will be disappointed. The squeeze on nenkō promotion becomes even tighter if we look at the demand side as compared to the 1960s. Demand (vacancies) arises from retirements, reorganization, and expansion; with the curtailment of the economic growth rate there will be a corresponding decline in the rate of increase of supervisory and managerial positions. The pressure to hold down the total wage bill discussed above will provide further incentives for management to scrutinize supervisory positions with an eye to cutting out those that are not economically justified. Moreover, those companies that experienced rapid growth in the 1960s and

38.   The above analysis is intended as a broad generalization with full recognition that there are significant variations in age structure and rate of expansion of different industries and firms. The discussion applies most fully to the new industries such as automobiles and electronics. Even here, promotion was hardly assured, although expectations might have been justifiably high. Rohlen's examination of cross-sectional data on male promotion in a fairly rapidly growing Japanese bank in the late 1960s provides unusually detailed data on promotion practices among white-collar employees. He reports that by age 32, 71 percent of all male ordinary employees achieved the first rank on the promotion ladder of regular employees. By age 38, some 80 percent of the regulars had reached the next step on the promotion ladder of deputy with the remaining 20 percent having much reduced chances of ever making the rank. By age 39, 30 percent were promoted further to deputy chief; declining percentages were promoted to chief and the still higher position of director. Generally speaking, the more talented members of each age cohort were promoted earlier to each step, an occurrence that marked them for still further promotion later in their career. Thomas Rohlen, "The Organization and Ideology of a Japanese Bank: An Ethnographic Study of a Modern Organization" (Ph.D. diss., University of Pennsylvania, 1971), chapter 6.

39.   Ibid.

responded with lowered promotion ages will be saddled longer with existing incumbents and consequently cannot rely on attrition through retirement to open up large numbers of vacancies in the decade of the 1970s.[40] Furthermore, whereas the promise of promotion could be effectively used to insure individual employee cooperation in intrafirm transfers in the rapid growth era of the 1960s, a lowered rate of economic growth toward 1980 will make it more difficult for firms to "sweeten" intrafirm transfers with promotion. As a consequence, we can anticipate more worker dissatisfaction around the issue of intrafirm transfers as well as greater employee reluctance to accept them.[41]

In summary, at many companies the coming decade will be characterized by an increasing number of aspirants eligible for nenkō promotion who will scramble for a more stabilized number of available vacancies. The scramble for promotion has, of course, always been present; the matter at hand is the effect that changing rates of economic growth, shifting age composition and labor supply, and contemporary organizational characteristics will have upon intensifying this scramble. Judging by its past pragmatism, Japanese management's course of action will be toward de-emphasizing nenkō promotion and instituting merit criteria as a basis for selection. This has the virtue not only of rewarding able employees but also of serving as ideology to legitimate the failure of many employees to be promoted.

A similar attempt to "cool out" those who would otherwise fail to be promoted is the growing managerial practice of providing some symbolic mark of promotion for older employees as exemplified by the status-ranking system (shikaku seido). This is a system that tries to provide recognition of long-term service with a ranking that has a small economic payoff; this is an alternative to giving employees line authority with a large economic payoff.[42] Both of these shifts are already underway.[43]

How employees will respond to this changing situation is unclear. A good deal may depend on how committed they are to nenkō promotion and whether they will be bought off by symbolic positions. It may be that the criteria for promotion are less important than the simple

40. The traditional retirement age of 55 in large companies is commonly legitimated in Japan in terms of the need to make a place for young employees. In the labor shortage of the 1960s many firms extended the age to 58 and 60.

41. Tsuneo Ono, "Intra-firm Labor Markets: Personnel Practices and Mechanisms for Adjustments," *Japan Labor Bulletin* 12 (April 1973): 4–16.

42. See Robert Cole, *Japanese Blue Collar*.

43. See M. Y. Yoshino, *Japan's Managerial System* (Cambridge, Mass., 1968); Arthur Whitehall, Jr., and Takezawa Shin'ichi, *The Other Worker* (Honolulu, 1968); Dore, *British Factory– Japanese Factory*.

fact that smaller proportions of those in the eligible age grades will experience promotion to line authority; this alone should give rise to considerable dissatisfaction. In terms of the impact of structural changes in the economy, the growth of the service sector may be relevant.[44] It is a sector with a large proportion of smaller firms relative to manufacturing and in general (excluding government) it would seem to be characterized by less bureaucratic forms of organization. These characteristics may allow for greater opportunities for self-realization and alternative modes of providing status to employees in terms of such things as more attractive work environments. A second structural change of importance is the occupational upgrading of the labor force. The increasing proportion of the labor force located in professional, managerial, and clerical occupational categories may permit more individuals to derive greater satisfaction from their work and even expand promotion opportunities. Although we can only speculate on some of these implications, it would seem important to examine the moderating impact of long-term structural changes in the economy upon the propositions suggested in this section.

A current situation that perhaps provides some clues to the future is one pertaining to the National Railways Corporation (*Kokutetsu*). The corporation represents an industrial sector that is already experiencing a rapidly aging labor force, a fact owing primarily to the industry's lack of economic growth. The average age of Kokutetsu employees has risen gradually from a low of 32.5 in 1954 to 36.2 in 1960 and 38.6 in 1971. Management has responded to the resultant rapid rise in labor and other costs with an intensive rationalization program using the slogan of *marusei* (full productivity).[45] In seeking the active cooperation of employees, management made behind-the-scenes efforts to sponsor a second union that would be more sympathetic to its productivity goals than the current *Kokurō* (National Railways Workers' Union) and *Dōryokusha* (National Railways Locomotive Engineers' Union). An important issue in the dispute has been the alleged discrimination by management against opposition union leaders who were allegedly not promoted to lower supervisory positions. The issue came before the Public Corporation and National Enterprise Labor Relations Commission in December 1971; that commission ordered the Kokutetsu management to refrain from intervening in union activities through their promotion policy. At the same time, the Locomotive Engineers' Union carried out a fairly successful

44. I am indebted to Robert Evans, Jr., for pointing out this line of analysis.

45. This rationalization program dates back to the first National Railway Modernization Plan in 1956, which included efforts to curtail personnel costs.

action to win control over the promotion system for engineers. In summary, the features of this situation are an aging labor force, low rate of economic growth, management advancement of cost-cutting rationalization programs, increased numbers of employees arriving at the age ranks that make them eligible for promotion to a stable or declining number of positions, increased tension between management and labor, and increased union activity in the area of promotion policy.

One must be careful in generalizing from the Kokutetsu situation to all Japanese industry in the future. The Kokutetsu unions are particularly militant, and the situation in the government sector is quite different from that in the private sector. Promotion policy seems to be more of an issue as a political strategy rather than as a response to changing age composition. Management, unable independently to set freight and passenger rates, is completely subject to government control. The government, in turn, is upset by the left-wing political activities of the railway unions. Nevertheless, it is instructive to examine the consequences of a rapidly aging labor force employed in a sector experiencing a minimum of economic growth. Although the nenkō promotion system will not disappear, it appears to be somewhat vulnerable to the forces I have described.

Attitudinal Change

There is another dimension to generational conflict that accentuates the competition between employees of different ages and between younger employees and both company and union officials. This dimension is the impact of the shifting age structure in conjunction with the dramatic value and behavioral changes generated by recent Japanese history.[46] Those of the postwar generation are gradually becoming a majority of the labor force with sufficient numbers both to make their values and behavior dominant as well as to challenge existing leadership in companies and unions. If we take somewhat arbitrarily those born after 1940 as representing the postwar generation, two characteristics are apparent. First, they do not have the "depression mentality" that has dominated the thinking of older employees who vividly experienced the immediate postwar chaos in Japan as members of the labor force. Instead, this postwar generation came to maturity in an era of rapid industrial expansion, an era in which ideas of consumption rather than production begin to dominate. They are the children of an emergent affluence, and as a consequence we would expect them to adopt quite different attitudes toward work and leisure.

46. For a parallel analysis focusing on management see Eiji Mizutani, "The Changing Picture of Lifetime Employment in Japan" *Japan House Newsletter* 19 (May 1, 1972).

A second characteristic of the postwar generation is that they have been exposed to a revamped educational curriculum in which ideas of civil rights and democracy have come to the fore. Moreover, as is apparent from table 6.5, the spreading educational revolution is unprecedented in the increasingly larger numbers of youths kept in school for longer periods of time. This process of youth segregation is not new to Japan but dates back to before the Meiji restoration; however, the rapid expansion of education in the postwar period in which graduating from high school has replaced middle school as the norm and a college education has become a realistic goal for large numbers of the population results in an unprecedented segregation of youths from their elders. Moreover, this segregation becomes associated with a geographic concentration of youths at high educational levels. In 1970 over 50 percent of all university students were located in either the Tokyo metropolitan area or in Osaka prefecture.[47] The significance of the accelerated process of youth segregation and concentration is that youths come to be influenced more by peer groups than the values and behavior of their elders; a common overarching set of symbols and attitudes comes to be formed that we characterize as youth culture. This contributes to a weakening of that continuity in behavior and values that has been so notable a feature of Japanese industrialization. The impact of these developments, like that of growing up in an emergent age of affluence, is that the postwar generation may think and act in ways quite different from their elders. I will turn to that subject shortly, but first it is important to get a sense of the scope of the challenge and its temporal location.

The postwar generation began entering the labor force from high school around 1958 and from the universities in 1962. At this time they still constituted a small minority of the labor force and could easily be influenced by the dominant majority to accept existing values and behavior. Indeed, observers often noted the strength of the Japanese social order by pointing with delight to the quick socialization of radical school youths to conformity with dominant values and behavior. The labor shortage had not yet made a major impact on worker behavior; jobs were still scarce and corresponding loyalty to one's firm high. In 1965 the oldest of the postwar generation were 25 and altogether they totaled over 10 million, constituting about 23 percent

47. Economic Planning Agency, *Economic Survey of Japan (1970–1971)*, p. 125. There are stereotypes of the average American college student living in dormitories and the average Japanese student living with family and relatives. In fact, the differences between the two societies are not that great. In the United States, census data indicate that in 1971 some 32 percent of all college students lived with friends and relatives while for Japan the corresponding figure for daytime students is about 50 percent.

TABLE 6.12   Attitudes Toward the Relationship Between Work and Leisure

Age	Total	Work is an obligation	Work is work; recreation is recreation	Work is a pleasure	Need rest in order to work	Other
Total	100.0%	14.5%	40.3%	10.2%	24.0%	11.1%
20–29	100.0	8.0	54.0	5.9	22.5	9.6
30–39	100.0	8.0	43.1	10.5	26.5	11.1
40–49	100.0	22.7	25.3	12.6	28.8	10.6
50–69	100.0	27.5	25.0	15.5	18.0	14.0

Note: Column totals have been rounded to 100 percent in some cases.
Source: Ministry of Labor, *Rōdō jikan, kyujitsu, kyuka, kankei tokei shiyo* [Statistical materials relating to working hours, holidays, and vacations] (Tokyo, 1971).

of the labor force (estimates based on table 6.5). By 1980, however, the oldest of the postwar generation will have reached the age of 40, will total some 28 million, and will make up about 50 percent of the labor force; they will also be arriving at the age at which Japanese generally begin to assume leadership positions. It is no exaggeration to say that until now the postwar leadership in Japan in almost all spheres has come from the prewar-educated age groups.

Many studies have illuminated the differing attitudes and behaviors with regard to work and leisure that characterize older and younger employees. For example, a 1968 survey by the Citizens Livelihood Research Center [48] sampled 1,097 employees living in Tokyo for their attitudes on the relation between work and leisure. The percentage distributions are reported by age in table 6.12. The gap separating older and younger employees seems especially pronounced above and below age 40 for the first two choices (i.e., "work is an obligation" and "work is work, recreation is recreation"). Although only 8.0 percent of the 20 to 29-year-old category and 8.9 percent of the 30 to 39-year-old category view work as an obligation, 22.7 percent of those between 40 and 49 do, while 27.5 percent of those between 50 and 69 do. A similar sharp break is apparent in the second choice of viewing work and recreation as two separate spheres. Young respondents strongly support this view while only a quarter of the older respondents do. The data do not support our hypotheses insofar as the major break seems to be between those born after 1929 (age 16 in 1945) and those born before this time rather than our designated year of 1940.

Studies such as these are deficient for purposes of predicting future behavior because we cannot be sure that young employees will not "see the light" and adopt the views of their elders as they themselves age. Nor can we be sure that contemporary older employees did not

48. Ministry of Labor, *Rōdō jikan kyujitsu, kyuka, kankei tokei shiryo* [Statistical materials related to working hours, holidays, and vacations] (Tokyo, 1971), p. 284.

TABLE 6.13   Life Orientation

Question: "There are all sorts of attitudes toward life. Of those listed here, which one would you say comes closest to your feeling?"

		1953	*1958*	*1963*	*1968*
A.	Work hard and get rich	15%	17%	17%	17%
B.	Study earnestly and make a name for yourself	6	3	4	3
C.	Don't think about money or fame; just live a life that suits your own tastes (Nontraditional)	21	27	30	32
D.	Live each day as it comes, cheerfully and without worrying	11	18	19	20
E.	Resist all evils in the world and live a pure and just life (Traditional)	29	23	18	17
F.	Never think of yourself, give everything in service of society	10	6	6	6
Other & Don't know		8	6	6	5
		100%	100%	100%	100%

Source: Suzuki, *A Study of the Japanese National Character*, p. 12.

feel the same as contemporary youths when they were younger. The data to be discussed permit greater confidence in the view that the contemporary workers' more casual attitude toward work and greater commitment toward leisure will have a lasting impact on future industrial relations as well as the renowned high work motivation of Japanese employees.

The Research Committee on the Study of Japanese National Character has carried out four nationwide surveys with 3,000 to 4,000 Japanese age 20 and over at five-year intervals starting in 1953. One of the question items that has appeared four times bears on the subject of general work attitudes.[49] Table 6.13 reports the question item and the percentage distribution of responses for the four surveys. The most notable changes over the fifteen-year period are the gradual increases in response C ("live a life that suits your taste") from 21 percent in 1953 to 32 percent in 1968 and the increase in response D ("live a life without worrying") from 11 percent in 1953 to 20 percent in 1968.[50] Almost all

49. The following discussion draws upon and reinterprets the analysis of Suzuki Tatsuzo, *A Study of the Japanese National Character*, part 4 (Tokyo, 1970).

50. The 32 percent who choose "live a life that suits your own taste" in 1968 is reported to be far in excess of this response in prewar surveys. Suzuki reports that in a 1931 Ministry of Education survey only 10 percent of the respondents chose this response. Similarly, in prewar days, some 30 to 40 percent of respondents chose the traditional response E ("resist all evils...") as compared to 17 percent in 1968, and 20 to 30 percent chose the self-sacrifice represented by response F ("never think of yourself") as compared to 6 percent in 1968.

Figure 6.1

Percentage Selecting "Live a life that suits one's own taste" (By Birth Cohort)

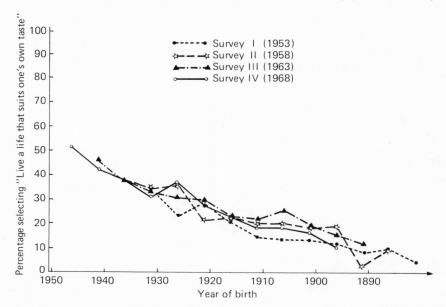

Source: Tatsuzo Suzuki, *A Study of the Japanese National Character—Part Four* (Tokyo, 1970), p. 31.

of these increases are accounted for by declines in the traditional choices E and F. By 1968 the rather easygoing approach to life symbolized by responses C and D garnered over half the respondents.

With the introduction to this question complete, we may now compare responses by age. Figure 6.1 plots the percentage selecting response C for each of the four surveys at five-year intervals by birth cohort. This permits us to compare youths over time as well as to make some observations about sources and consequences of differences and similarities.

The first thing to be noted is that there is a strong age effect in each survey. Younger members of the population consistently show higher support for the statement than do older people. An age effect can arise from one of two factors. It can result from individual life-cycle experiences whereby an individual becomes more "conservative." In the case of this question, for example, one might expect that as young people became committed to their work and developed family responsibilities they would lessen their support for response C and develop more serious work-oriented attitudes. A second source of an age effect is that the historical experiences of the birth cohorts are quite different. In this case, the argument would be that the more recent birth cohorts, especially the postwar generation (1940 + cohorts), have had unique historical experiences that led them to adopt more favorable views to response C. This is clearly the argument that has been set out in the preceding pages. Figure 6.1 permits us to discriminate between these two "hypotheses" at least for the question at hand.

Because the four curves more or less overlap each other, the influence of individual life-cycle effects were slight. Those born within a given time period have not appreciably changed their views during the fifteen years covered by the surveys. This also shows that the influence of current social circumstances at the time of the survey had little impact on responses. The overall increase in the percentage selecting response C shown in table 6.13 is caused almost entirely by the new entrants into the population. If individual life-cycle effects had been operative, there would be four parallel curves with successive surveys showing reduced support for the statement as already surveyed birth cohorts aged. In terms of our earlier discussion of the postwar generation, it is useful to emphasize that the 1950 + cohorts show the highest support for the statement, registering over 40 percent support in the 1963 survey and over 50 percent support in the 1968 survey. This compares, for example, to a little over 20 percent support for the 1915 cohort (48 years old in 1963) in all of the four surveys.

In summary, significant attitudinal change is taking place reflecting the unique historical experiences of different birth cohorts. This seems likely to have a lasting impact on Japanese industrial relations and work motivation. As older birth cohorts die off, the views of the newer cohorts become dominant.

One further piece of evidence is reported by Eiji Mizutani;[51] he notes the results of an annual attitude survey of 100,000 employees in more than 1,000 companies. The Morale Survey Center, which conducted the survey, reports that the most dramatic change in the fourteen attitudinal variables investigated over the last sixteen years has involved that of loyalty to one's employer. Specifically, there has been a drastic decline in this value over the last sixteen years. Here the uniqueness of the postwar generation is reinforced by the impact of a growing labor shortage of young workers that makes it more in the interests of those in the labor force roughly up to age 35 (born in 1937 for the year 1972) to consider alternatives to lifetime loyalty to one employer.

In summary, the generational conflict that has so fascinated the

51. Mizutani, "The Changing Picture of Lifetime Employment in Japan."

Japanese public and scholars is likely to grow in the coming decade. It will grow because the postwar generation are bearers of new values and experiences not as widely shared by the older generation. It will grow because the era of consumption is rapidly replacing the era of production that shaped the values and behavior of the older generation. The continuing rapid rate of technological innovation contributes to the persistent conflict between a younger generation more ready to grasp the new and an older generation more committed to the old. Furthermore, the continuing labor shortage and a growing material affluence combine to weaken just those values of loyalty, harmony, and high work motivation that constitute the human backbone of past rapid economic growth.

Yet there is nothing in the data to suggest drastic transformations. The changes represented in figure 6.1 are, after all, relatively moderate; moreover, they suggest a secular trend toward moderation of a strong work ethic beginning in the prewar period rather than supporting our hypothesis that those born after 1940 had totally unique experiences. In addition, we must not confuse changes in attitudinal measures with significant behavioral changes. Many other studies conducted by Japanese industrial relations scholars emphasize the great significance of generational differences; nevertheless, they often conclude that the pull of Japanese culture and the strength of socialization practices in industry are so strong that they significantly moderate youthful protest as individuals pass through the life cycle.[52] Finally, in discussing such variables as work motivation and commitment to work, we should be careful to distinguish them from the concepts of morale and work satisfaction.

It is quite possible that workers may have low morale and work satisfaction and still manifest high work motivation and commitment to work. For example, comparative data for Japan and the United States show that Japanese blue-collar workers generally register more dissatisfaction (controlling for industry) on such measures as "work pace too fast," "bored with job," and "job provides opportunity to display ability."[53] This may be because they have reason to hold higher expectations on these matters. In any case, although these differences serve as measures of morale and work satisfaction, they do not necessarily tell us that Japanese workers have lower work motivation or commitment to work. On a crucial measure of desire to change jobs, which taps the probability of individuals trying to take action to

---

52. Wakao Fujita, "Seinen kumiaiin to kambu" [Youthful union members and leaders], *Chūō Rōdō Jihō* [Central labor review], June 1971, pp. 2–13.

53. Yoshita Fujita and Ishida nideo, *Kigyō to rōshi kankei* [Enterprise and labor relations] (Tokyo, 1970), p. 199.

relieve dissatisfaction, Fujita reports that the Japanese respondents were markedly less likely to want to change jobs.

Labor Mobility and Labor Shortage

Much of the preceding discussion has implications for labor mobility. The kinds of shifts and transformations envisioned in the earlier discussion of industrial and occupational structures assume considerable labor mobility. The Japanese Ministry of Labor has long advocated policies that would increase labor mobility.

High rates of labor mobility conflict with the image of permanent employment in Japan held by Westerners.[54] Notwithstanding the distorted and exaggerated image of the immobile Japanese labor market held by many Westerners, the interfirm mobility of Japanese males has been quite low compared with that in countries such as the United States, West Germany, and Sweden. In the case of Italy, the low rate of voluntary job changing has increased noticeably in the decade of the 1960s as a response to rapid economic development and the reduction in labor surplus; the rate of voluntary job changing in Italy has now begun to approximate that of the more industrialized countries of West Germany and the United States.[55] The question is whether Japan will follow a similar route.

In the 1960s, an era of rapidly expanding industrial facilities, management could fairly easily absorb redundant labor. Thus the inflexibility that economists would expect to be associated with permanent employment was not a major problem for the Japanese. But in an era of declining growth rates in which new factories and expansion are no longer the order of the day, management in specific enterprises and industries may be faced with the problem of what to do with labor made redundant by technological advance. Furthermore, as discussed above, management will be under great pressure to cut costs via labor-saving equipment. The growing emphasis on rationalizing operations within existing facilities will further intensify the problem of redundancy in given firms.

Some clue to future developments may perhaps be found in the response of Japanese employers to the economic slowdown in 1971.[56] Personnel adjustments were considerably higher at this time than the

54. Permanent employment means that an employee enters a large firm after school graduation—whether it be middle school, high school, or university—receives in-company training, and remains an employee of that same firm until the retirement age of fifty-five. It is a pattern limited primarily to male employees.

55. International Labor Office, *International Differences in Factors Affecting Labor Mobility* (Geneva, 1966).

56. The following discussion derives from the labor section of the *Oriental Economist*, April 1972.

previous slump in 1965. A number of factors are relevant in accounting
for this difference. First, the Ministry of Labor noted that in 1965
Japan was in the middle of an extremely rapid business expansion
that management anticipated would resume after the slump; consequently, they were reluctant to give up any of their labor force that
they would soon need. In 1971, however, business circles were in
agreement that future economic growth in Japan would be more
moderate and, therefore, they were concerned about becoming saddled
with redundant labor. The Ministry of Labor conducted a survey of
700 major firms in 1971 to find out how they carried out their labor
adjustment programs. They found that management action included
five steps, with a given company taking the subsequent step when the
prior ones failed to solve the problem.[57] The steps were:

1. Reduction in overtime while maintaining existing labor force.
2. Cancellation of hiring of recent school graduates.
3. Reduction or cancellation in the number of employees hired
    with previous work experience (chutōsaiyōsha).
4. Sending members of existing labor force to different parts of
    company and related firms.
5. Temporary layoffs (at 60 to 90 percent of regular wage level).
6. Recruitment of "voluntary retirements" with special retire-
    ment incentives.
7. Outright discharge.

In the 1960s most companies were able to solve their overstaffing
problems by taking measures at the top of this list. What is significant
about the early 1970s is the tendency for firms to be forced down the
list toward more drastic measures. Although there is no reason to think
that the practice of outright discharges will become dominant by the
1980s, it does seem likely that pressures will intensify that force more
and more employers to move down the list toward severer measures.
Employer response to the 1974 economic slowdown conforms to this
prediction with employment cutbacks being still greater than those
taken in the 1971 to 1972 period.

   In the past, one major source of adaptation to shifting industrial
and occupational structures has been the key role played by new school
graduates. This is to be expected in the light of the low interfirm
mobility rates for males. The predominant role played by new school
graduates in adjustment of employment was by definition the essence
of the permanent employment practice. In the 1960s the bulk of the
new school graduates were hired in the expanding industrial sectors
of the economy. However, the rapid expansion of educational attain-

57. Whitehall and Takezawa, *The Other Worker*, pp. 149–50.

TABLE 6.14   Estimates of Labor Force Supply

Time period	Total employment beginning of each period	New labor force supply		
		Total	New school graduates	Others
1965–70	4,730ᵃ	1,248	701	547
1970–75	5,094	1,190	596	594
1975–80	5,306	1,248	585	663

ᵃ In tens of thousands.

Source: Adapted from Japan Productivity Center, Katsuyō Rōdō Tokei: 47 [Practical Labor Statistics: 1972] (Tokyo, 1972), p. 111.

ment and the impact of declining birth rates led the number of new school graduates to decline in absolute terms from a high of 1,495,000 in 1966 to 1,186,000 in 1971. This decline is expected to continue (with fluctuations) through 1980 at which time there will be a projected 1,182,000 new school graduates at all levels available for employment (see table 6.6). In particular, the supply of new school graduates suitable for blue-collar work will be reduced.

Table 6.14 presents a breakdown of new labor-force supply by five-year periods. Notable is not only the absolute decline but also the relative decline in the dominance of new school graduates as suppliers of employment replacements and pure employment increases. In the period from 1965 to 1970 new school graduates accounted for 56 percent of new labor force supply with the remainder coming from job changes and older nonlabor force recruits. In the period 1970 to 1975 the balance between the two types of labor is expected to be roughly equal, and in the period of 1975 to 1980 the balance is expected to clearly shift to non–new school graduates. Were a more detailed breakdown than table 6.14 to be provided, it would show that new school graduates have for some time been a minority in the supply of new labor to the tertiary sector. The shifts reported in table 6.14 represent a process by which new school graduates are becoming a minority in the supply of new labor in the primary and secondary sectors as well.[58]

In addition to the important role of new school graduates in adapting to the shifting industrial and occupational structure, the bulk of job changing and adaptation to new technology, in Japan as in other industrial societies, is carried out by young employees. The aging of the Japanese labor force, however, will make it less possible for youths to carry out this role of manpower reallocation in the future. Insofar as the mobility of the middle and older age stratum is not increased, an

58.   Economic Deliberation Committee, Rōdōryoku jukyū no tenbō to seisaku no hōkō [Prospects for labor force supply and demand and the direction of policy] (Tokyo, 1969) p. 25.

important restraint will be placed on Japanese economic growth. Judging by the voluminous literature that the Ministry of Labor produces on the subject, it expects considerable difficulty in raising the rates of mobility of older employees to compensate for the decline of younger more mobile workers.[59]

In summary, two different processes are operating and they pull in opposite directions. On the one hand, the aging of the Japanese labor force seems bound to hold down any major increases in the amount of interfirm job changing that might result from the forces of increasing labor shortage and the concentrated efforts of government officials to increase the mobility of older employees. This suggests that large firms will continue to use their own internal labor forces as major allocators of work adjustments. With this in mind, I suggest that we are not likely to see notable increases in the aggregate rates of job changing apart from cyclical movements.

Yet there is occurring a large-scale *compositional* shift that will be intensified in coming years and seems likely to have major consequences. This is the result of the declining role of new school graduates in both absolute and relative terms. Being forced to hire large numbers of occupationally experienced employees strikes at the heart of the permanent employment practice in large firms. Such employees do not provide the firm the young elite raw material that can be molded into strongly committed company employees. The rigorous entrance requirements designed for elite selection of new recruits are being increasingly discarded by large firms as they scramble to get their share of blue-collar employees. Occupationally experienced recruits can draw upon their past experience in ways that make them more resistant to company ideology. This leads to the establishment of new norms of behavior for both management and employees—norms that significantly undermine the meaning of continual employment in one firm (as well as shortening its length).[60] In short, I am suggesting that even without major increases in aggregate rates of job changing, the pattern of job changing and employment is undergoing a significant compositional shift that has far-reaching consequences for labor-management relations.

59. Minoru Tachi and Yōichi Okazaki, "Japan's Postwar Population and Labor Force," *The Developing Economies* 7 (June 1969): 178.

60. One may ask how it is possible to shorten the length of service of employees in large firms without increasing aggregate job changing rates. It is conceivable, in fact, for aggregate rates to fall. Employees in small firms experience higher inter-firm mobility than do large firms' employees. If employees in small firms, however, enter large firms, they often experience reduced interfirm mobility thereafter, thus bringing down aggregate rates of job changing at the same time that the length of service in large firms is reduced by virtue of using more occupationally experienced workers relative to new school graduates.

A comparison of the conditions surrounding labor shortage during and after World War I with conditions surrounding labor shortage in contemporary Japan is instructive as regards our entire discussion.[61] How is it that labor shortage could contribute to the initiation of the permanent employment practice in the World War I period and to its weakening in contemporary Japan? If both these assertions are correct, then we must presume that the content of the labor shortage, the conditions surrounding the labor shortages, or both the content and the conditions are different in the two periods.

The shortage that concerned management in the prewar period was primarily that of selected categories of skilled workers; the major problems were high turnover and how to systematize recruitment, training, and supervision. A ready ideology existed that could be manipulated to support the introduction of the permanent employment practice and cloak it in traditional values of familism, unity of the social group, and loyalty. By the introduction of the practice of nenkō wage at the same time, workers could be persuaded that it was in their interest to forego whatever benefits they derived from moving from one firm to another.

The content of labor shortage today is quite different. At the present time the major shortage is of young workers—commonly unskilled— who can be paid low wages. A separate though somewhat overlapping problem is the apparent unwillingness of large and growing firms to recruit in sufficient number and at advantageous wages those already employed in low productivity sectors of the economy or in other large firms (and perhaps the unwillingness of employees to move). The shortage of young workers is absolute in the sense that no more young workers than already exist in the labor force can be found quickly (except by increasing labor force participation rates, but this goes against the secular trend toward higher education). Management would indeed prefer to establish a long-term commitment to their young employees, but the demand for such employees is great and thus young workers have the highest propensity to move of all age groups (peak job-changing occurs at ages 19 to 20).

The level of general education is much higher in contemporary Japan than in World War I Japan, and large companies now have well-established training programs that allow them to produce the kinds of skills in a labor force that they desire. The significance of this

61. I am indebted to Shimada Haruo for suggesting that I pursue this line of analysis. For a historical description of the formation of the permanent employment practice see Robert Cole, "The Theory of Institutionalization: Permanent Employment and Tradition in Japan," *Economic Development and Cultural Change* 20 (October 1971): 47–70; and Mikio Sumiya, "The Development of Japanese Labour-Relations," *Developing Economies* 4 (December 1966): 499–515.

is that the cost of losing employees with established skills is far less today than it was in the past. One can recruit and train new employees —even job-changers—at a lower relative cost and at the same time have less fear that the loss of key skilled employees will have damaging effects on enterprise operations. In short, the incentive of employers to maintain permanent employment is reduced as a result of a different set of conditions surrounding the contemporary labor shortage. Finally, the traditional ideology that supported and legitimated permanent employment has increasingly been challenged in the post–World War II period. An emphasis on individual civil rights and the explicit models of foreign nations is manifest in the Ministry of Labor's outright support of increased labor mobility, in management's ambivalence toward lifetime employment, and in workers' increasing willingness to downgrade loyalty to a given firm.[62] More specifically, from the workers' point of view, the de facto reduction of wage differentials based on nenkō means that there are fewer advantages to be gained from staying with the same firm and fewer risks to be suffered in moving.

In considering this explication of the likely impact of specified demographic and labor force characteristics on selected Japanese industrial relations practices, the reader may reflect that a set of industrial relations practices quite different from that to which we are accustomed will be dominant by 1980. Yet the incomplete nature of the analysis hardly permits us to arrive at such conclusions. In omitting a consideration of all the relevant variables and their interactions, I have, in effect, chosen not to deal with the potential resiliency—the adaptive capacity—of Japanese society. Although there will be other changes in the political, economic, and social spheres that support the kinds of pressures on existing practices that I have outlined, there are resources in these institutional spheres that may be made available to modify and channel these pressures in such a way that their impact is minimized. In particular, large firms with their considerable resources drawn from the political, economic, and social spheres are in a better position to resist these pressures, should business leaders decide to do so. In the past, practices such as nenkō and permanent employment have been maintained in large firms at the expense of employees in small and medium firms. We will, in all likelihood, see some continuation of these differentials. It is a minor irony that scholars usually associate merit reward, high interfirm mobility, and growing worker discontent

62. Robert Marsh, "Lifetime Commitment in Japan: Roles, Norms and Values," *American Journal of Sociology* 76 (March 1971): 795–812.

with modernization. Yet it is the small and medium firms that will be under the greatest pressure to adopt more fully these practices. The large firms in the most modern economic sectors will be most able to resist such pressure and thus preserve a more Japanese-style industrial relations.

Japan exists, too, in an international environment in which the potential implications of the rising tide of nationalism are increasingly serious. One of the potential consequences of growing nationalism lies in a turn inward by Japanese management and a search for uniquely Japanese solutions based on strong employee commitment to management-defined goals. Although we cannot calculate the probabilities associated with this outcome, it is a sobering fact that some Japanese industrial relations experts foresee a move in these directions.

We can speculate with some degree of assurance on changing labor force characteristics and their likely impact on Japanese style industrial relations; however, we have a much more difficult time predicting the actual shape of these practices in 1980 because of the difficulty of accounting for the impact of a large number of other relevant variables. The most fruitful research strategy would seem to involve a thorough examination of a particular industry or set of firms undergoing the kinds of demographic and compositional changes in employment discussed in this paper. Such a tack would avoid many of the pitfalls inherent in the quite speculative approach adopted here.

7

Worker Sentiment in the Japanese Factory: Its Organizational Determinants

KOYA AZUMI AND CHARLES J. McMILLAN

Azumi and McMillan's data on workers' morale in the province of Tochigi tend to corroborate Cole's findings on alienation and discontent. Job satisfaction, in spite of the stereotypical image of the Japanese worker as selfless, untiring, and loyally dedicated, is no higher in Japan than elsewhere. A bare 51 percent of respondents, on the average, report positive sentiments about their jobs, and this is much lower than expected. Furthermore, Azumi and McMillan find that the young (as Cole suggests) and the women (as Pharr suggests) are the least happy.

Satisfaction is determined in part by "contextual" variables, i.e., the size of the enterprise, the sophistication of the technology employed, and the dependence or independence of the firm vis-à-vis other companies. Larger size raises morale; sophistication of technology, contrary to expectation, has no effect on it; and dependence lowers morale. The findings about size and dependence are of course two sides of the same coin because in Japan even more than elsewhere small firms are at the mercy of large ones and of the market. Another facet of this situation is the ability of the large firm, as Cole points out, to resist the pressure for alienating changes in traditional practices.

But more than contextual variables, one structural variable explains an even greater degree of the variance in the data. Hierarchy is strongly negatively associated with morale. The Japanese worker, like his counterpart abroad, is happier with more job autonomy, and more unhappy the more he feels at the mercy of superior levels of authority.

Ironically enough, it appears that increased plant size gives the Japanese worker the sense of relative freedom from authority, perhaps because authority in the large firm is more abstract and farther away than the patriarchal dominance still prevalent in the small firm.

The research project on which this paper is based has been supported by the East Asian Institute, Columbia University, and the Joint Committee on Japanese Studies of the Social Science Research Council and the American Council of Learned Societies. Financial assistance has also been provided by the Canada Council and the Management Center, University of Bradford in England. We are also indebted to David Hickson and Phelps Tracy for assistance at various stages of the project.

Azumi and McMillan conclude tentatively that as the percentage of Japanese workers employed in large firms continues to increase, morale will rise. And even if the relative freedom from authority felt in the large firm is recognized eventually as illusory or inadequate, the increasing shortage of labor will force management to acquiesce to increased worker participation in decision making as it seems to have forced acquiescence to higher wages. Against the darker observations made by Cole, Azumi and McMillan offer a note of cautious optimism.—L.A.

Japan's industrial workers are said to be a hardworking lot. UAW Vice President Douglas Fraser, after inspecting automobile assembly plants in Japan, is reported to have said to the union's executive board that "in some plants Japanese workers put together cars at speeds that would not be tolerated by American workers."[1] A newspaper report comparing workers in Japan, Germany, and the United States carried the headlines "On the Assembly Lines: In Japan . . . Dedication; In Germany . . . Thrift; and In the U.S. . . . Security."[2] As if to reinforce the Japanese reputation, visitors to an electric appliance plant encounter a workers' slogan on the wall: *Gyōsoku Shinkō* ("Work is religion"). The press fosters the image of the Japanese worker as selfless, untiring, dedicated, loyal, and efficient. Indeed, some academic literature lends support to this picture by claiming that Japanese values stress doing for one's collectivity[3] and group loyalty.[4] It has even been suggested that the Japanese system of worker compensation rewards loyalty toward the company, a system that is in harmony with Japan's traditional values.[5]

One would expect the morale of the Japanese worker to be high, and many have suggested that high morale must have been an important contributing factor in the nation's rapid economic growth. But if the Japanese worker is highly motivated and if this motivation has been a positive factor in economic growth, can the same positive sentiments be expected to continue into the future? To what degree are workers' sentiments identifiable, particularly with regard to the job, the plant, and the company? Are such sentiments changing, becoming more like those of other industrialized countries? Or do Japanese workers exhibit a pattern of their own as Dore, for example, has suggested?[6] Speculating on Japan's future, Brzezinski considered worker morale to

1. *New York Times*, 19 June 1972.
2. Ibid.
3. Robert N. Bellah, *Tokugawa Religion* (Glencoe, Ill., 1957).
4. Ezra Vogel, *Japan's New Middle Class* (Berkeley, 1963).
5. James C. Abegglen, *The Japanese Factory* (Glencoe, Ill., 1958).
6. Ronald Dore, *British Factory–Japanese Factory* (Berkeley, 1973).

be one of the unstable factors among the twenty that are thought to have contributed to Japan's economic success.[7]

Outside Japan there is a large body of literature suggesting that industrialization is necessarily bureaucratization and that as a result the worker tends to become alienated from his job. Bureaucratization makes for segmented and routine work, as exemplified by the assembly line, where working hours are spent in repetitive motions dictated by the conveyor belt. In the United States during the 1970s the theme of the blue-collar blues and white-collar woes has become increasingly familiar, as the HEW study *Work in America*[8] makes clear. One would expect that similar bureaucratization has occurred in Japan and that similar forces alienate the Japanese worker also.

In this paper we attempt to shed some light on these issues. Ideally we would use cross-national comparative data to assess Japanese worker morale, plus time series data as a base in attempting to forecast. Neither type of data is as yet available. We do have, however, a large body of systematic data that can answer some of the issues raised. We propose to outline results showing Japanese worker sentiment and their demographic and organizational referents. The data raise serious questions about the stereotypical notion of the Japanese worker and uncover general tendencies that help to estimate probable worker sentiment in the next decade.

Our strategy is as follows. We seek the best predictors of worker morale. The literature on morale suggests that we look for demographic factors (such as age, seniority, and education), structural factors in the organization in which the worker is employed (division of labor, formalization of rules and procedures, and hierarchy of authority), and factors contextual to the organization (size and technology). We draw from our data a set of propositions relating worker sentiment with other variables. We then speculate on the state of these determinants of morale in the coming decade.

THE DATA

The data were collected during the summer of 1972. In order to obtain as representative as possible a sample of manufacturing organizations in Japan, a standard prefecture was chosen: Tochigi. Tochigi prefecture ranks about midway among the forty-seven in the country in terms of a number of criteria including proportion of the labor force in agriculture (twenty-second), per capita income (twenty-second),

7. Zbigniew Brzezinski, *The Fragile Blossom: Crisis and Change in Japan* (New York, 1972).

8. Special Task Force to the Secretary of Health, Education and Welfare, *Work in America* (Cambridge, Mass., 1973).

diffusion of telephone services (twenty-fifth), and population density (twenty-second). Out of the *Directory of Establishments* published by the prefectural government (based on a survey in 1969), a stratified random sample of fifty establishments in the manufacturing industry with at least one hundred employees was selected. These fifty establishments represent nineteen of the twenty-one United Nations' standard industrial classifications; missing are oil, coal, and weapons.

Two modes of data collection were used. Information about the organization was obtained first through interviews with a few managers. The interview schedule was based mainly on that of the Aston group in England.[9] The other mode was the administration of a questionnaire to a stratified random sample of managers, foremen, and rank-and-file production workers in forty of the factories in order to obtain their individual views. Altogether 2,473 usable questionnaires were returned. The forty organizations for which we have both organizational and individual data range in size (number of employees) from 110 to 4,500, with a mean number of 935 persons. The sizes of the parent company—of which some of the forty factories are branches—range between 110 and 85,000, with a mean of 7,000 employees. Their products vary from quilts, synthetic yarns, ice cream, and ham to engines and aircraft.

MEASURES OF WORKER SENTIMENT

The question of immediate concern in this paper is a four-item scale of job satisfaction that taps worker sentiment with regard to work roles, job climate, managers, and the company in general. The respondent was given the four statements and was asked to judge how well each statement described his sentiment, namely, "very well," "well," "poorly," "very poorly," or "undecided." The four statements appear in table 7.1. The positive responses of "very well" and "well" are scored 5 and 4 respectively, the two negative responses of "poorly" and "very poorly" 2 and 1, and "undecided" 3. The respondent's "morale score" is the mean of his scores on the four items.

OVERALL EMPIRICAL RESULTS

Table 7.1 shows the percentage distribution of responses for each of the four statements. Between 25 and 33 percent of the respondents chose the neutral "undecided" response on the four items. The choice of response categories 5 and 4 showing positive sentiment was made by 42

---

9. D.S. Pugh, D.J. Hickson, C.R. Hinings, and C. Turner, "Dimensions of Organization Structure," *Administrative Science Quarterly* 13 (June 1968). 65–105; idem, "The Context of Organization Structure," *Administrative Science Quarterly* 14 (March 1969): 91–114.

TABLE 7.1   Positive and Negative Responses to Each
of Four Morale Items
(In Percentage)

Item	Response		
	Positive	Neutral	Negative
1. I feel the work I am doing in this company suits me well.	42	33	25
2. The atmosphere of this place is pretty good.	62	26	11
3. The managers here are generally trustworthy and dependable.	48	28	24
4. On the whole, this is a good company.	54	25	21

to 62 percent of the respondents. Negative sentiments were shown by 11 to 25 percent of the respondents.

The mean morale score on each item ranges between 3.1 and 3.5, indicating, as does table 7.1, overall positive morale among Japanese workers. We had suspected, however, that morale would be higher than we found.[10] Empirical studies of job satisfaction in the United States have consistently shown an overwhelming majority of workers to be satisfied rather than dissatisfied with their work.

Blauner,[11] having reviewed a large number of studies, states that "the majority of workers in all occupations respond positively when asked whether or not they are satisfied with their jobs." There is, of course, the question of the comparability of measures of job satisfaction, but the morale score of Japanese workers is much lower than might have been expected from their image as generally conveyed in the press.

There are certain patterns behind this finding in terms of worker characteristics. Positive sentiment rises along with age, seniority, rank, and educational attainment. Men as a whole have higher morale scores than women. Among the individual background characteristics, age differentiates the respondents more than others. This conforms to the general finding in other countries that the young are more dissatisfied than their elders.

Dissatisfaction is greatest with respect to work roles, the first item in

10. An international study commissioned by Japan's prime minister's office has shown Japanese youths to be far more dissatisfied with life in general than their counterparts in other nations, according to *Asahi Shimbun* 29 July 1973.

11. Robert Blauner, "Work Satisfaction and Industrial Trends," in Walter Galenson and Seymour Martin Lipset, eds., *Labor and Trade Unionism* (New York, 1960), pp. 339–60; reprinted in Amitai Etzioni, ed., *A Sociological Reader on Complex Organizations*, 2d ed. (New York, 1969), p.227–49.

the morale scale. Only 19 percent of the respondents age 20 or younger have positive sentiments toward their work roles. This percentage rises along with age and reaches a peak of 66 percent for the 41 to 45 age group, after which the percentage declines slightly. This finding may be partly explained by two patterns of employment found in Japan. The first is that new entrants into the labor force tend to choose their company before they choose their occupation. The second is that Japanese management practices intrafirm job training and assignment to jobs that are not necessarily related to the worker's background.[12]

The young workers' rather extreme dissatisfaction with their work roles is not reflected in attitudes toward their job climate, their managers, or their companies, although the pattern of lower satisfaction for youths and higher satisfaction for older people is maintained in these areas.

STRUCTURAL DETERMINANTS OF WORKER SENTIMENT

Worker sentiment is greatly influenced by the structure of the organization. While intraorganizational differences in individual morale scores are greater than interorganizational differences, it is eminently clear that morale is not a function of the worker's individual characteristics alone.

The work of Weber[13] has enabled the sociologist to isolate certain aspects of structure to make them both theoretically relevant and empirically measurable. There is considerable consensus that the most important properties of structure are specialization, centralization, formalization, and stratification. The terms used vary according to the researcher, e.g., "division of labor" and "complexity" for specialization, "hierarchy of authority" for centralization, "systems of rules" and "systems of procedures" for formalization, and "configuration" for stratification. The exact definitions of terms also vary, but specialization generally refers to the degree to which the organization is divided into specialized tasks; centralization to the extent to which decision-making powers are concentrated in upper positions of the organization; formalization to the extent to which rules of conduct and work procedures are written out and other aspects of organizational life documented; and stratification to the degree to which the organization is stratified in terms of power, prestige, and rewards.

The literature on the relationship between structure and worker

---

12. Koya Azumi, *Higher Education and Business Recruitment in Japan* (New York, 1969).
13. Max Weber, *The Theory of Social and Economic Organization*, trans. A. M. Henderson and T. Parsons (New York, 1947).

sentiment generally supports the view that, other factors being equal, the more specialized the organization, the higher is the worker morale, while the more centralized, formalized, and stratified, the lower.[14] The work conducted by Tannenbaum and his associates[15] on "control graph" has shown that more democratic structures are associated with positive worker sentiments. Aiken and Hage[16] have demonstrated that decentralization and deformalization increase the satisfaction of professionals in welfare organizations with their work and their fellow workers.

Let us now turn to our Japanese data and consider the relationship between structure and morale. For this purpose we shall use organizational, aggregate data. Our measures of structure are those used by Hall and Bonjean (see the Appendix, pp. 228–29).[17] In conformity with the manner in which organizational scores were computed for the structural variables, individual morale scores were averaged for each of the three levels of managers, foremen, and rank-and-file workers, and the organizational morale score is the mean of these three means.

Table 7.2 indicates the relationships between organizational morale and structural variables in zero order product moment correlation coefficients. Division of labor has no relationship with organizational morale $(r = .02)$. Hall-Bonjean's measure of division of labor taps mainly the routineness of tasks engaged in by the respondent and is different from the complexity measure by Hage and Aiken or the specialization measure by the Aston group. One may expect that the more routine and repetitive one's tasks, the lower one's morale, but inasmuch as our scale of worker sentiment includes aspects other than work roles the expected relationship is not observed.

It is hierarchy of authority that has the strongest correlation with

14. Jerald Hage, "An Axiomatic Theory of Organizations," *Administrative Science Quarterly* 10 (December 1965): 289–320.

15. Arnold Tannenbaum, *Control in Organizations*, (New York, 1968). See also Richard E. Walton, J.M. Dutton, and H.G. Fitch, "A Study of Conflict in the Process, Structure, and Attitudes of Lateral Relationships," in A. H. Rubenstein and C.J. Haberstroh, eds., *Some Theories of Organization* (Homewood, Ill., 1966); and Frank T. Paine, Stephen J. Carroll, Jr., and Burt A. Leete, "Need Satisfactions of Managerial Level Personnel in a Government Agency," *Journal of Applied Psychology* 50 (1966): 247–49.

16. Michael Aiken and Jerald Hage, "Organizational Alienation: A Comparative Analysis," *American Sociological Review* 31 (August 1966): 497–507.

17. Aston's measures of organizational structure are found to be little associated with morale and are not used in this paper. The problem of lack of congruence between "objective" and "subjective" measures of structure is discussed in Koya Azumi and Charles J. McMillan, "Subjective and Objective Measures of Organizational Structure," a paper presented at the annual meeting of the American Sociological Association, 1973.

TABLE 7.2   Product Moment Correlation Coefficients Between
Organizational Morale and Structural Variables

Structural variables	Pearson r with organizational morale
Division of labor	.02
Hierarchy of authority	−.60 (p ⩽ .001)
System of procedures	−.24 (p ⩽ .05)
System of rules	.19
Number of levels	−.20

morale ($r = -.60$); that is, the higher the degree of hierarchy of
authority in the organization, the lower is organizational morale.
This implies, as expected, that the further removed one is from the
decision-making process, the lower is one's morale. In partial support
of this finding, number of levels in the organization has a negative
correlation ($r = -.20$) with organizational morale. That is, tall
structures with a number of levels are associated with lower morale
scores. Unexpectedly, the two measures of formalization (system of
procedures and system of rules) are found to have conflicting influences
upon organizational morale. System of procedures is negatively correlated ($r = -.24$) with morale, indicating that the application of
standard operating procedures results in lowered morale. System of
rules, which is correlated .17 with system of procedures, is nevertheless
found to be positively correlated with morale ($r = .19$). These findings,
except the last one, were expected, and they support the thesis that
organizational morale for Japanese workers conforms to the general
pattern elsewhere.

CONTEXTUAL VARIABLES AND WORKER SENTIMENT

"Contextual variables" refers to the social resources that are brought
into the organization from the environment. They are the inputs of
an organization and include size, capital, knowledge (inclusive of
technology), and the degree of independence the organization can
claim from the environment. In the literature technology has been
claimed to have a great impact on morale.[18]

First we will consider size. Several indicators have been used as a
measure of size, including number of employees, assets, and sales.
All three of these are strongly associated with each other in our sample
(mean $r = .86$), so only one measure is used. We find number of

18.   Robert Blauner, *Alienation and Freedom* (Chicago, 1964); and Michael Fullan, "Industrial Technology and Worker Integration in the Organization," *American Sociological Review*
35 (December 1970): 1028–39.

employees to have a considerable and positive association with organizational morale $(r = .47)$. Why should large size promote organizational morale?

In Japan productivity, wages, other benefits, and prestige among companies differ considerably according to size.[19] Our field work took place approximately ten months after one of the series of events denoted as "Nixon shocks" in Japan. In August 1971 President Nixon devalued the American dollar, hitting hard those Japanese firms that were heavily dependent on export. This event was viewed with considerable foreboding by Japanese managers and workers alike. We found that the larger firms were less immune to the devaluation effect, but many smaller firms were severely constrained or expected great difficulties when existing contracts expired. Indeed, in one plant, listed in the 1969 directory as having at least 1,000 workers, the impact of the dollar devaluation was so great that the work force was reduced to only 300. Significantly, each of the displaced workers was compensated by severance pay and by relocation to another job in the area. So size as a predictor of morale is specially important in the Japanese economy. Large size means protection from market instability and international monetary instability; it helps assure job security and continuous wage and bonus compensation. Small size means dependence on the whims of the larger corporation for supply and marketing transactions, and threatens possible cutbacks in the work force and continuous and troublesome worries about survival.

Furthermore, size has a moderately strong and negative correlation $(r = -.43)$ with hierarchy of authority, which has been found to be the best predictor of organizational morale among the structural variables. Apparently, as the organization becomes larger the employees are less constrained by the sense of being subject to a hierarchy above.

The second contextual variable is technology. In recent years organizational sociology has placed a great deal of emphasis on technology as a major determinant not only of worker sentiments, but also of organizational structure. Blauner[20] studied worker sentiments within three industrial groups: craft (printing), mass production (automobile assembly), and continuous process (chemicals) industries. He found systematic variation by technological grouping, and his work foreshadowed Joan Woodward's highly influential work relating technology to organizational structure in England.[21] These

19. Azumi, *Higher Education and Business Recruitment*; and K. Okochi, B. Karsh, and S.B. Levine, eds., *Workers and Employers in Japan* (Princeton, 1974).

20. Blauner, *Alienation and Freedom*.

21. Joan Woodward, *Industrial Organization: Theory and Practice* (London, 1965).

TABLE 7.3   Product Moment Correlation Coefficients Between
Technology Variables and Organizational Morale

Technology variables	Pearson r with organizational morale
Automaticity mode	.05
Automaticity range	.12
Quality evaluation	−.17
Workflow integration	.18

books have had a strong impact on the technological school in organizational theory.[22] Fullan's study of worker sentiment in Canada is closely related to Blauner's and confirms our expectation that technology should have a similar impact on workers in Japan.[23]

Four measures of technology were used in our research. These include "automaticity mode," the level of automation of the bulk of equipment used in the organization; "automaticity range," the most highly automated piece of equipment the organization has; "quality evaluation," the degree to which products are inspected to maintain an acceptable standard; and "workflow integration," a measure similar to Woodward's scale from small batch, to mass, and to continuous process production. All these measures were carefully developed by the Aston group.[24] The product moment correlation coefficients between the technology scales and organizational morale are given in table 7.3.

Contrary to expectation, there is no strong correlation between technology and organizational morale. The automaticity level of equipment has only a low positive correlation with morale. There is a trend toward lower morale in conjunction with more strict demand for quality control of products as well as a trend toward higher morale in conjunction with greater continuity of production operations, but both relationships are weak. One might have expected that the relationship would be positive, given the strong relationship between size and morale, since size has been found associated with technology in its relationship to organizational structure,[25] but this is not the case here. Even when morale score is limited to rank-and-file workers alone, technology has only a small effect on morale.

22.   Charles Perrow, "A Framework for the Comparative Analysis of Organizations," *American Sociological Review* 32 (April 1967): 194–208; idem, *Complex Organizations*, (Glenview, Ill., 1972); David J. Hickson, D.S. Pugh, and Diana C. Pheysey, "Operations Technology and Formal Organizations: An Empirical Reappraisal," *Administrative Science Quarterly* 14 (September 1970): 387–97.

23.   Fullan, "Industrial Technology and Worker Integration."

24.   Hickson et al., "Operations Technology and Formal Operations."

25.   Ibid.

The third and last contextual variable considered is "dependence," which refers to the extent to which the organization is dependent on other organizations. The measure used was that of Aston, which consists of the four subscales of impersonality of origin, status of organization unit, public accountability, and size relative to owning group.[26] Dependence is found to have a negative correlation $(r = -.30)$ with organizational morale. That is, the more dependent the organization is on other organizations, the lower its morale.

The contextual variables of size, technology, and dependence together explain 31 percent of the variance in organizational morale, whereas 39 percent of the variance is explained by the two structural variables hierarchy of authority and division of labor. Among all the variables considered, hierarchy of authority is the best single predictor of organizational morale, explaining 36 percent of the variance.

FORECASTING JAPANESE WORKER SENTIMENT

We now have an empirical base upon which to speculate about the state of worker sentiment in Japan in the years to come. A clear message from our data is that a greater degree of worker autonomy and of participation in the decision-making process will enhance job satisfaction. It is illuminating to note that the current situation in the Japanese firm is not seen as completely desirable by the Japanese employee. Our individual questionnaire included several items on worker participation in decision making and on employee rights. Asked if the respondent agreed or disagreed with the statement "Employees in industry should participate more in the decisions taken by management," 65 percent agreed, only 6 percent disagreed, and 29 percent were neutral. The statement "Important decisions for the company ought to be made by the management and the employees should not criticize the decisions" elicited agreement from 19 percent, disagreement from 55 percent, and a neutral response from 25 percent of the respondents. Furthermore, employee rights and employee security received strong support in the responses to the two statements "A company may transfer its employees or send them on business trips, even if it means a great deal of inconvenience to the employees and their families"; and "A company should always consider raising its productivity, and it cannot be helped even if some people are fired as a result." Seventy percent disagreed with the first and 72 percent with the second statement.

A lessened degree of hierarchy of authority would be welcomed by workers, then, and morale would improve. This raises two questions.

26. J.H.K. Inkson, D.S. Pugh, and D.J. Hickson, "Organization Context and Structure: An Abbreviated Replication," *Administrative Science Quarterly* 15 (September 1970): 318–29.

One is whether or not Japanese manufacturing organizations will move toward lessening the degree of hierarchy of authority. The other is what implications a lesser degree of hierarchy of authority would have for other organizational variables.

Our speculation is that Japanese organizations will move toward a more participatory pattern of decision making. This study is incapable of showing the trend, but a long-time observer of Japanese industrial management claims that his data indicate a trend toward demo-cratization.[27] One factor is labor shortage. The supply of new middle and high school graduates has dwindled in the recent past and as a result wages for these two categories of workers have risen dispropor-tionately. To respond to workers' desire for greater participation in decision making may also be an organizational necessity.

Another approach to the first question is to consider the primary contextual determinant of hierarchy of authority. Our data show that size has the greatest correlation with $(r = -.43)$ hierarchy. Techno-logical variables are found to be little associated with hierarchy of authority. Government surveys show an increase of 69 percent in industrial labor force in Japan between 1957 and 1969, but the pro-portion of the work force in establishments with fewer than 100 workers decreased from 74 to 53 percent. During the same period the number of manufacturing organizations with 500 or more workers increased by 97 percent, claiming, by 1969, a quarter of the Japanese industrial labor force. The trend has been, then, toward larger organizations. While there is obviously a limit to organizational growth, we expect the trend to continue into the future. Thus, because size is negatively correlated with hierarchy of authority, and the latter negatively correlated with morale, the sentiment of Japan's industrial workers is likely to improve.

Our second question is raised from a systems perspective that holds that the parts of a system are interrelated and that a change in one necessarily affects the others. Table 7.4 shows the correlation coeffi-cients of hierarchy of authority with other structural variables. Hall[28] has shown hierarchy of authority to be positively associated with other structural variables as he measured them. Our data conform to Hall's findings except for the relationship between hierarchy of authority and system of rules, which is low but negative. Hierarchy of authority is associated with routine, repetitive tasks, an abundance of procedures, and impersonal social relations within the organization. That imper-

27.   Kunio Odaka, *Toward Industrial Democracy* (Cambridge, Mass., forthcoming).
28.   Richard H. Hall, "The Concept of Bureaucracy: An Empirical Assessment," *American Journal of Sociology* 69 (July 1963): 32–40.

TABLE 7.4   Product Moment Correlation Coefficients Between
Hierarchy of Authority and Other Structural Variables

Structural variables	Pearson r with hierarchy of authority
Division of labor	.23
System of procedures	.45 (p ≤ .01)
System of rules	−.10
Impersonality	.46 (p ≤ .01)

sonality has a relatively high and positive correlation $(r = .46)$ with hierarchy of authority was expected and adds to the credibility of the idea that hierarchy of authority is the major determinant of organizational morale.

High scores on these variables are associated with the type of organization that Burns and Stalker call mechanistic, in contrast to the opposite, which they call organic.[29] In the former, the emphasis lies on production; in the latter, on adaptiveness. Systems perspective would have it that an organization can only with difficulty have both high job satisfaction and high production.[30] Thus to meet demands for job satisfaction the organization must be prepared to curtail its goals of production and efficiency. We may conceive the great emphasis placed on production by Japan's industrial organizations in the past to have been at the cost of worker job satisfaction. Various organizational goals can be conflicting and pull the organization in different directions, and the characteristics shown by an organization at any given time may be thought of as a result of a precarious balance among various forces. It is our expectation that Japan will see no radical change in the order of priorities among organizational goals or in the structure of organizations, but what change takes place is likely to be in the direction of promoting welfare. Thus worker sentiment is likely either to improve or to remain stable.

The factors that we have considered here are of course not the only determinants of worker sentiment. Such factors as pay and job security, which we did not consider in our study, no doubt play a part in job satisfaction. The overall state of the economy in the country, its rate of change, and other social and political factors are likely to be associated with worker sentiment. International economic and political fluctuations are also likely to be associated, for the country cannot remain isolated from them.

We want to emphasize that any analysis predicated on a uniform

29.   Tom Burns and G. M. Stalker, *The Management of Innovation* (London, 1961).
30.   Hage, "An Axiomatic Theory of Organizations."

picture of the Japanese worker is highly questionable. This paper has analyzed worker sentiment data in the context of their demographic and organizational determinants and has found the stereotyped image of happy, hardworking loyalty to be misleading. In fact, the great variations in our data provide strong empirical support for the rejection of this image of the Japanese worker. The considerable individual and organizational variation in worker sentiment is not congruous with the stereotyped image portrayed by Western social scientists and journalists. Industrialization means social differentiation anywhere, and that means that there is an increasing probability of variation among Japanese industrial workers too.

APPENDIX

HALL'S BUREAUCRACY SCALE

On each statement the respondent is asked to indicate the degree to which the statement describes his organization. The response categories are: very well, well, poorly, very poorly, and undecided. Responses are scored between 1 and 5, where undecided is scored 3. Scores must be reversed on many items. For each variable, scores are added and then divided by the number of items. The organizational score is the mean of means for the three levels of managers, foremen, and rank-and-file workers. The items given below were selected by Charles Bonjean as an improvement over the ones previously used by Hall and were provided by Hall. The first and last items listed under "Impersonality" were not used in Japan.

Division of labor

1. There is something new and different to do almost every day.
2. Most jobs have something different happening from day to day.
3. Most jobs in this organization involve a variety of different kinds of activity.
4. Every employee has a specific function that he is to perform.
5. No two days are ever the same in this job.
6. We usually work under the same conditions from day to day.

System of rules

1. The employees are constantly being checked upon for rules violation.

2. Employees are expected to follow orders without questioning them.
3. People here make their own rules on the job.
4. The organization has a manual of rules and regulations to be followed.

System of procedures

1. Employees are often left to their own judgment as to how to handle most problems.
2. Most of us are encouraged to use our own judgment in handling everyday situations.
3. At times, going through the proper channels becomes more important than getting the work done.
4. Standard procedures are to be followed in almost all situations.
5. We are to follow strict operating procedures at all times.

Hierarchy of authority

1. Any decision I make has to have the bosses' approval.
2. I have to check with the boss before I can do almost anything.
3. Even small matters have to be referred to some higher-up for the final answer.
4. A person who likes to make his own decisions would be discouraged here.
5. I feel that I can act as my boss in most matters.
6. Only persons in executive positions can decide how a job is to be done.

Impersonality

1. No one here calls his superior by his first name.
2. We are expected to be courteous, but reserved at all times.
3. Management here sticks pretty much to itself.
4. People are to be treated within the rules, no matter how serious a problem they may have.
5. No matter how serious a person's problems are, he is to be treated the same as everyone else.

8

The Political Culture of Two Generations:
Evolution and Divergence in Japanese
and American Values

LEWIS AUSTIN

The political analyses of this volume have suggested a period of increasingly complex and delicate struggle between left and right, eventuating in cautious collaboration and coalition. The economic analyses have suggested that principal problems will be the conflict between traditional and modern attitudes held by workers, the conflict between traditional and modern practices undertaken by management, and the conflict between labor and management if and when the first two conflicts are not reconciled. Crucial factors in these prognoses are the goals, ideals, and values of the populace. What will the Japanese people expect and desire from their future?

Austin attempts to answer this question in part by comparing the values of two generations of Japanese and Americans. He creates data that provide evidence to answer the question of whether Japan and the West are growing more alike over time, whether "modernization" implies homogenization.

The answers suggested are ironic: Japan is indeed growing more like the West in terms of the political culture of everyday life, but "the West" is not a stationary benchmark. Western attitudes are shifting faster away from tradition than are Japanese, on balance. The net result of the process of change is a widening of the attitudinal gap. Japanese values are "modernizing" absolutely but not relatively.—L. A.

Any prediction about the future of Japanese politics and political attitudes rests on the acceptance of some theoretical generalization into which the case of Japan can be satisfactorily fitted. The literature of political development offers one such model that, however fragmentary and speculative, appears to have the character of orthodoxy or truism. That is the model of developmental convergence.

THE CONVERGENCE HYPOTHESIS

This model has the interesting characteristic of being defined more by its opponents than by its explicit defenders. Thus Brzezinski and Huntington attribute the model to all sorts of people but suggest that those people do not always state it clearly: "The argument that industrialization will produce increasing liberalization and therefore convergence is not always explicitly formulated."[1] Having formulated it, however, for its inarticulate defenders, they go on to claim its inapplicability to the case of the Soviet Union: "Evolution...but not...convergence, seems to be the undramatic pattern for the future."[2]

Similarly, Dahrendorf sees a prevailing orthodoxy of developmental convergence:

> The assertion of the convergence of all societies today unites scholars in East and West, indeed Eastern Marxists and re-visionists, Western liberals and socialists. The concept of the irresistible steamroller of industrialization is a basic dogma of the social self-interpretation of our time.[3]

Dahrendorf also denies that the hypothesized model has any usefulness or relevance in dealing with the facts of political modernization, at least for imperial Germany and its two successor states.

The model is generated by extrapolating from a relatively brief time period. It is a compound of images of progress in which liberal Anglo-Saxon democracy is the apex of development to which the history of all states tends. It is thus not only ethnocentric but also temporocentric. In addition, there lies at its base a metaphorical image drawn from biology and/or cybernetics; that is, growth consists in increasing complexity, differentiation, and capacity to handle or adapt to the vicissitudes of the environment. The model is not purely an intellectual construct but preserves at its core the aptness, the perhaps meretricious convincingness, of the poetic trope or the symbol. Finally, it sees "development" as inevitable, a vision that is by no means inarguable; why is not entropy inevitable, or decay? But where development is taken for granted, there is the assumption of progress, and of progress toward a goal. If goal, then inevitable convergence. The more developed the polities of the world, the more alike. So the Western value orientations toward change and universalism combine to construct a picture of the political world in which the developed nations are honorary Americans, and in which "development" consists in becoming more American.

1.   Zbigniew Brzezinski and Samuel P. Huntington, *Political Power: USA/USSR* (New York, 1965), p. 13.
2.   Ibid., p. 436.
3.   Ralf Dahrendorf, *Society and Democracy in Germany* (New York, 1969), p. 43.

In spite of the culture- and time-bound quality of this model, in spite of the suspicion of metaphor that attaches to it, in spite of the tinge of Judaeo-Christian historical teleology that is visible in its ancestry, and in spite of the reproach of ethnocentric self-satisfaction that can be made to those social scientists who predict that development will consist in the remaking of mankind at large in the image of their own polity, let us hypothesize that the model is applicable to Japan. Let us further hypothesize that Japan by the 1980s will be characterized by increasing industrialization, accumulation of capital, growth in GNP and standard of living, increasing social mobility, complexity, differentiation, and intensity of communication both within and without the society. Because of these economic and social structural developments, we suppose there will take place an increase in "modern" attitudes, beliefs, and values—a growth of pragmatism, rationality, secularity, liberalism, and freedom. The political consequences will be both increased democracy and increased governmental capacity; and we trust there will be no conflict between these two goals of the process we define as "political development."

This chapter examines some evidence bearing on the test of that hypothesis: to wit, that industrialization and social differentiation imply political-cultural convergence in the direction of liberal, secular, and progressive values. I will ask first what values and attitudes are predicted to change and in what direction; and second, whether Japanese values and attitudes are changing as predicted.

THE DATA

The data on which the test of the convergence hypothesis will be based were generated in Tokyo and New Haven in 1969 and 1972. In the first instance a sample of 192 middle- and upper-level Japanese administrators from government and private business completed a written set of projective and semiprojective questions tapping attitudinal dimensions theoretically relevant to political culture. Two-and-a-half years later an English-language version of the same questionnaire was completed by a sample of 42 Americans of comparable social status and age. The Japanese respondents were predominantly graduates of the imperial and the prestigious private universities, the Americans all Yale alumni.[4]

The total pool of respondents was divided into four categories on the basis of nationality and age. The older group in the Japanese case (age 46 to 70) comprised all those born during the Meiji and Taisho eras; the younger group (age 30 to 45) was born during Showa. The

---

4. The research is described more fully in Lewis Austin, *Saints and Samurai: The Political Culture of the Japanese and American Elites* (New Haven, 1975).

older Japanese completed their high school education and came of age before the catastrophic defeat of 1945; the younger thereafter. The older group of Americans was born before 1927 and completed high school before 1945; the younger were socialized more extensively in the postwar era.

All four groups, both Japanese and American, were members of a social and political elite. The older men in both nations are representative of that segment of society from which are now drawn the principal occupants of positions of authority. Their average age was 58; they were relatively wealthy; they commanded elevated posts in the large public and private organizations that dominate modern society; their political opinions were generally moderately conservative; they were at the height of their careers. The average age of the younger men was 38; they were groomed for elite status both at college (e.g., Yale or Tokyo University) and in their subsequent careers; they will be at the height of their influence on the policy making process of their respective nations in the 1980s. Neither group is representative of women, the poor, or ethnic minorities in either country; but in this my research follows reality.

We have, then, two nations and two generations. They are separated by twenty years, by twelve thousand miles, by two thousand years of history, and by their position on one side or the other of the historical and generational fault line represented by World War II. I will ask whether the younger generations have moved closer together, where the older generations were divided; whether the gap between generations has widened further among the Americans or the Japanese; whether the change of attitudes over twenty years has led both nations in the same or different directions. In short, I will seek to discover whether Japanese and American elites will be closer to each other in the future than they are at present: whether the process of political development hypothesized to be at work in both societies has led them toward an ultimate convergence of political culture, an eschatological harmonization and homogenization of the values that most directly affect political life.

Values most often proposed as central to the definition of political culture and to the measurement of political development can be classified along five dimensions: egalitarianism-authoritarianism, trust-mistrust, autonomy-dependence, conflict-harmony, and the Parsonian pattern-variable set equivalent to gemeinschaft-gesellschaft. I will seek indicators of value change along all these dimensions and will try to adduce evidence by which to determine the direction and the extent of Japanese developmental change. There are in this regard essentially three schools of thought, which may be denoted optimist-liberal, conservative-pessimist, and fence sitter. Their hypotheses are various, and some seem testable:

1. Conservative-pessimist Maruyama Masao: "In Japan, although we have modern specialization, premodern social relations are deeply ingrained. Democratic institutions such as the labor unions are walking along an almost impassable road through a swamp of premodern relationships."[5]

2. Conservative-pessimist Robert Bellah: "There is a real sense in which the Meiji period was a culmination and intensification of the central [traditional Japanese] values rather than a rejection of them, and they have remained strong throughout modern times."[6]

3. Conservative-pessimist Minami Hiroshi: "The reason for the psychological tendency of the Japanese to rely on familistic human relationships even in adulthood is the underdevelopment of the self. In other words there probably remains a spiritual childishness among Japanese adults."[7]

4. Conservative-pessimist Mishima Yukio: "I can even predict that from now on, to the extent that the action principles of Yang-Ming thought are imbedded in the Japanese spirit, perplexing political phenomena incomprehensible to foreigners will continue to crop up in Japan."[8]

5. Fence-sitter Ronald Dore: "There is better evidence of a trend toward greater equality resulting from the social changes of the last century than of an increase in self-sufficient individuation."[9]

6. Fence-sitter Robert Ward: "The long ascendancy among the bulk of the Japanese people of the official and authoritarian version of political culture has not in fact prevented the subsequent adoption by what seems to be a solid majority of the population of democratic values and attitudes. To be sure, the shift raises questions about the stability and reliability of these new orientations."[10]

7. Liberal-optimist Robert Cole: "If we assume that the Japanese have internalized a traditional work ethic and are totally unable to

5. Maruyama Masao, *Thought and Behavior in Modern Japanese Politics* (London, 1963), p. 264.
6. Robert N. Bellah, *Tokugawa Religion* (Glencoe, Ill., 1957), p. 19.
7. Minami Hiroshi, *Nihonjin no Shinri* [Japanese psychology] (Tokyo, 1953), p. 195.
8. Mishima Yukio, from *Kodogaku Nyumon* [An introduction to the study of action], excerpted in *Japan Interpreter* 1 (1971): 85. Mishima has in mind "[things] contrary to reason and intellect, unaccountable explosions, behavior resorted to with full knowledge of its ineffectiveness . . . nihilism . . . [the] demoniacal . . . fanaticism . . . intense and irrational awareness . . . escaping the yoke of reason."
9. Ronald Dore, "Mobility, Equality, and Individuation in Modern Japan," in R. P. Dore, ed., *Aspects of Social Change in Modern Japan* (Princeton, 1967), p. 150.
10. Robert E. Ward, "Japan: The Continuity of Modernization," in Lucian W. Pye and Sidney Verba, eds., *Political Culture and Political Development* (Princeton, 1965), p. 77.

resist management authority because of their need for dependency and the persistence of traditional values, then a slowdown in wage increases should bring no significant changes in work behavior.... Although this interpretation may appeal to those Western observers who are obsessed with notions of an unchanging Japan [and presumably to conservative-pessimist Japanese observers like those whose views are noted above] almost no serious Japanese scholar in the industrial relations field takes this view seriously."[11]

THE CORRELATES OF MODERNITY

Authoritarianism and Dogmatism

"Political development" is usually equated with the development of democracy. This statement of identity does not represent merely a surreptitious insertion of normative judgment into empirical analysis. Lipset has shown that economic development seems to be at least associated with democratic structures, and Almond and Verba have demonstrated that GNP correlates to a certain extent with democratic values.[12] Pye has stated the postulate concisely: "Traditional societies tended to emphasize and to provide moral justification for hierarchical relationships. Development demands effective leadership, but it also encompasses sentiments about equality."[13]

The convergence hypothesis predicts, then, that Japanese attitudes are becoming more democratic and egalitarian and that we can expect Japanese and American values on this dimension to be closer together for the younger elites than for the older. I have used as a principal measure of these hypothetical tendencies the Dogmatism scale (D-scale) developed by Milton Rokeach to measure closed-mindedness, stereotypy, antiintroception, hierarchical thinking, and authoritarianism. The D-scale measures essentially the same values and attitudes as the F-scale of "Authoritarian Personality" fame.[14]

The overall scores of the four groups—older Japanese, older Americans, younger Japanese, and younger Americans—are given in Figure 8.1. The answers are scored on an agree-disagree continuum that ranges from 6 to 1. In both the American and the Japanese groups

11. Robert Cole, in chapter 6 of this volume.

12. Seymour Lipset, "Economic Development and Democracy," in *Political Man: The Social Bases of Politics* (New York, 1960), pp. 27–63; Gabriel Almond and Sidney Verba, *The Civic Culture: Political Attitudes and Democracy in Five Nations* (Boston, 1965).

13. In Pye and Verba, *Political Culture*, p. 22.

14. Milton Rokeach, *The Open and the Closed Mind* (New York, 1960); Theodor Adorno et al., *The Authoritarian Personality* (New York, 1950). For confusing results when the F-scale is used in Japan, see Agnes Niyekawa, "Authoritarianism in an Authoritarian Culture: The Case of Japan," *International Journal of Social Psychiatry* 12 (1966): 283–88.

Figure 8.1
Mean Dogmatism Scores

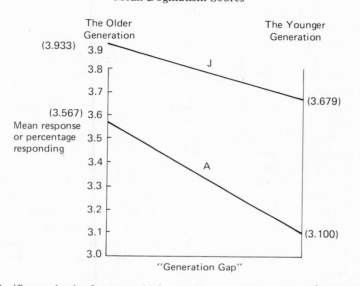

Note: Significance levels: Japanese old–Japanese young difference: $p \leqslant .027$; Japanese young–American young difference: $p \leqslant .001$; Japanese old–American old difference: p not significant; American old–American young difference: p not significant.

dogmatism is greater among the older men. The younger are less dogmatic or authoritarian than their seniors. And there is a greater gap between young Americans and young Japanese than between their elders, even though the Japanese respondents have moved in the predicted direction—that is, the younger are less authoritarian— with the passage of a generation.[15]

Trust and Suspicion

A second dimension of political cultural attitudes that is hypothesized

---

15.   Note that because the number of subjects in each generation-culture group is unequal (there are 69 older Japanese, 26 older Americans, 123 younger Japanese, and 16 younger Americans) a greater difference is required between American young and old to reach statistical significance than between younger and older Japanese. One consequence of this is that in some cases the cultural difference may appear to increase with the change in generation, as measured by scores or the slant of the lines connecting them; but the significance of the difference between the younger groups may be less than that of a smaller difference between the older. The principal consequence of this unfortunate artifact is that there is no easy standard by which to judge the relative impact of culture and generation in shaping attitudes (as is suggested in Kenneth Berrien, Abe Arkoff, and Shinkuro Iwahara, "Generation Difference in Values: Americans, Japanese-Americans, and Japanese," *Journal of Social Psychology* 71 (1967): 169–75.

to vary with political development and democracy is that of generalized trust and mistrust. Development is said by Verba to require trust: "The individual who believes that man is by nature trustworthy or cooperative is more likely to trust political leaders as well as political opponents, and more likely to be willing to cooperate with them."[16] Similarly, "The presence of diffuse distrust seems to impede seriously the creation of the kinds of public organizations essential for national development."[17]

To measure generalized trust and mistrust I used first the Faith in People scale developed by Rosenberg.[18] The results were disappointing. It appeared that the Rosenberg scale did not form a Guttman-type scale in Japanese and therefore could not be used for cross-cultural comparisons. The fifth item on the scale, "Human nature is fundamentally cooperative," was the problem. A shibboleth of traditional Japanese values, this assertion is a dubious and extreme proposition in the America where Guttman originated his attitude-measuring device.

Other data might clarify the picture. Some projective data were relevant. A TAT picture showed an old man and a young man regarding one another ambiguously.[19] When the percentage of respondents who described this picture in terms of plots, conspiracy, or collusion, is graphed we obtain a picture that runs counter to both the original hypotheses. While the older Americans and the younger Americans never produce such interpretations, and thus remain at a constant level of zero, the Japanese percentage rises over a generation from 1.4 for the older to 8.9 for the younger (p ≤.081). Not only do the two cultures grow farther apart, but the younger Japanese generation is less "trusting" (more prone to envisage the environment as threatening and ambiguous) than the old.

Further evidence can be drawn from two sentence-completion items. The first compares the percentages of individuals in the four groups who complete the sentence "He most often gets angry when..." with phrases like "he is betrayed," "he is tricked," or "he is made a fool of." In both the American and Japanese cases the percentage of such mistrustful responses declines. The older generation in Japan (46.4

16. Sidney Verba, in Pye and Verba, *Political Culture*, p. 522.

17. Lucian Pye, in ibid., p. 22.

18. Morris Rosenberg, "Misanthropy and Political Ideology," *American Sociological Review* 21 (1956): 690–95.

19. This TAT, like the others used, is adapted from Richard Solomon's modification of the instrument; see Solomon, "Mao's Effort to Reintegrate the Chinese Polity: Problems of Authority and Conflict in Chinese Social Processes," in A. Doak Barnett, ed., *Chinese Communist Politics in Action* (Seattle, 1969), pp. 271–364. The TAT pictures themselves are reproduced in Austin, *Saints and Samurai*.

percent) is much less trusting than the older generation in America (7.7 percent, p ≤ .002). The American level does not change much over a generation, with the American young scoring zero, which is not significantly different from the position of their seniors. The Japanese level, too, declines across the generations, from 46.4 percent to 27.6 percent (p ≤ .014). But the difference in trust between the two cultures remains significant (p ≤ .035).

The second sentence-completion item that is relevant is that beginning "He was most afraid of. . ." Among the men of the older generation responding "of being tricked or betrayed," there is a marked difference between Japanese (14.5 percent) and Americans (zero, p ≤ .094). The percentage of Japanese of the next generation responding in this way declines to 7.3, which is in accord with our hypothesis. But the percentage of younger Americans rises, which is not. No difference between groups, however, approaches significance, except that between the older Japanese and the older Americans, and that only barely.

In this case additional data raise more problems than they answer. The Faith in People scale was unsuitable as a measuring instrument because of the difference in the cultural estimation of "cooperativeness." The TAT picture showed younger Japanese more mistrustful, not less, than their seniors. The two sentence-completion items showed marked differences of the kind the hypothesis predicted in the older generation (the Japanese less trusting), and showed some convergence among the young. But this convergence left the two younger groups still significantly far apart in one case ("He most often gets angry when he is cheated, tricked, or betrayed"), and was due as much to an increase in American mistrust as to a decrease in Japanese in the other ("He is most afraid of being cheated").

Only much more extensive and carefully chosen data can approach an answer to the question of whether people become generally more trusting as they become more "modern."

Autonomy and Dependence, Group and Individual

One of the classic statements linking social and economic development to individuation and individuation to democracy and political development is found in Talcott Parsons's postwar meditations on Japan. If democracy is to be possible in that country, he suggests,

It is indispensable that conditions should favor the continual extension of "individualism" in the fundamental sense. . . a situation where the individual can become emancipated from the pressure of the particularistic group solidarities which have been so prominent in traditional Japanese society. By far the most favorable conditions are those of the Westernized type of urban society with occupational roles of the type best exemplified in urban industry.[20]

Political cultural progress is here equated with the "self-sufficient individuation" of Dore,[21] and traditional stagnation or reaction with the "undeveloped self" (*hattatsu shinai jiga*) of Minami.[22]

I can avoid here all discussion as to the efficacy of bureaucratization, rationalization, and the assembly line role structure in promoting "individuation"; and equally I may as well refrain from stressing the curious coincidence of the American ethic of individualism and a concept of political development that relies on the creation of individuals. Such purely ideological and rhetorical concerns will be of interest, if ever, only after we have been able to establish whether or not the values of individualism and independence are increasing in the younger generation of Japanese elites, and whether or not in fact this increase leads to a convergence of Japanese and American values along this dimension.

There are ten items measuring the autonomy-dependence continuum on which significant differences appear in our data. The sentence-completion test item "When he is worried, he usually..." may be completed by suggesting seeking help or advice from others. Japanese of the older generation (29 percent) are much more likely than their American peers (zero) to depend on others for counsel or assistance $(p \leqslant .006)$; and there is some indication that the younger Japanese (41.5 percent) are even more likely than the older to act in this way, but this relationship only approaches significance $(p \leqslant .118)$. Another response to trouble is to bear it in silence, to "grit one's teeth," to "keep a stiff upper lip," not to inflict one's problems on others. This attitude of self-chosen isolation divides Americans (older, 30.8 percent; younger, 31.3) from Japanese (older and younger, zero) in both generations at the .001 level.

Independence and dependence should produce characteristic reactions to rejection by others. The sentence completion test item "When he saw they didn't like him he..." tests such reactions. Older Japanese respondents (26.1 percent) are more likely than older Americans (7.7 percent) to express feelings of rejection: "He felt sad, lonely, unbearable" $(p \leqslant .094)$. Some convergence takes place: the

20. Talcott Parsons, "Population and Social Structure of Japan," in *Essays in Sociological Theory* (New York, 1954), p. 295.

21. Dore, *Aspects of Social Change*.

22. Minami, *Nihonjin no Shinri*.

difference between the younger Japanese and the younger Americans (22.8 percent and 12.5 percent respectively) is not significant.

The other attitude toward rejection by others is to deny its significance: "When he saw they didn't like him...he didn't care." The older Americans (34.6 percent) are much more likely than the older Japanese (10.1 percent) to give such tough-skinned, insouciant answers, and the difference is significant ($p \leqslant .012$). Not much change takes place over the generation. The younger Americans (31.3 percent) are still much less sensitive to rejection than the younger Japanese (8.9 percent), and the difference is still significant ($p \leqslant .027$).

American autonomy and individualism may be carried to such a point that they become dysfunctional for action. One projective device used to measure attitudes toward authority is suggestive in this regard:

A new department head is appointed who makes consistently unreasonable demands on the department members. What is the best course of action if you face this situation?

  a. Go in a body to the department head and inform him that this is not the way things are done here.
  b. Resist his demands by a program of covert noncompliance.
  c. Do the best you can under the circumstances.
  d. Complain over his head.
  e. View the problem as an individual, not a group matter, and adopt a wait-and-see policy.

The Americans in both generations (older, 15.4 percent and younger, 18.8 percent) are more likely than the Japanese (older, 5.8 percent and younger, 4.1 percent) to choose solution e: "View the problem as an individual, not a group matter." The difference between the younger generations approaches significance ($p \leqslant .072$). Here is a case of divergence: the culture gap grows wider.

The Japanese of both generations, for their part, are much more likely than the Americans, old and young, to choose solution a: "Go in a body to the department head and tell him this is not the way things are done here." The Japanese scores move over time from 62.6 percent to 58.0 percent; the American scores from 25 percent to 11.5 percent. The significance of the difference between the older generations is great ($p \leqslant .010$); but the significance of the difference between the younger generations is even greater ($p \leqslant .001$). The Japanese have grown perhaps a little less group-minded; but the Americans even more so. And the culture gap widens.

Four final self-focused or ego-centered responses can be seen as indicators of individualism. The first is "He was most afraid of . . . his own failure or inadequacy." The percentage of Americans giving this kind of response to the sentence-completion test ranged from 53.8 in the older group to 43.8 in the younger. The Japanese were much less likely to fear personal insufficiency, their responses ranging from 10.1 percent to 9.8 percent. One of the penalties of possessing a "well-developed" individualistic sense of self is that it must be defended constantly. The American respondents of both generations are paying that penalty. The differences between both the two older generations and the two younger generations are significant at the .001 level.

The second response is "In his relations with others, what he is most careful of is . . . his own image, creating a favorable impression". The older generation of Japanese is not preoccupied with projecting a persona or selling oneself; only 1.4 percent respond in this way. Nor does the tendency increase much over the years. Of the younger Japanese only 3.3 percent answer thus. But a sizable 19.2 percent of the older Americans and 18.8 percent of the younger ones care for nothing more intensely in personal relations than the image they are projecting of themselves. The difference between the older generations is significant (p ≤ .007) and that between the younger generations somewhat less so (p ≤ .040).

Another individualistic response is "He most often gets angry when . . . he makes a mistake or fails." This indicator, in a sense, is the corollary of "He was most afraid of his failure or inadequacy." Whether it produces fear or anger, personal individual adequacy is the focus of social and emotional life for those who respond in this way. In the older generation, a slightly higher percentage of Americans (11.5 percent) than Japanese (4.3 percent) fall into this category. In the younger generation the difference is much more marked. Both Japanese and Americans have become more likely to give such answers, but the increase in the percentage of Americans (to 25 percent) is much greater than the increase in the percentage of Japanese (to 5.7 percent). Here the culture gap has widened, and the difference is significant (p ≤ .023).

Finally another indicator of individualism or, in this case, perhaps of egotism, is "He most often gets angry . . . when he doesn't get his own way." Among older Americans 23.1 percent give this sort of answer, but none of the older Japanese do. Indeed, to them such an attitude would doubtless appear repellently uncouth and in bad taste. The percentage of younger Americans responding in this manner increases to 31.3, but the Japanese percentage, even among the young, remains zero. The differences between Japanese and Americans at both generational levels are highly significant (p ≤ .001). Individualism may be a hallmark of modernity, but it is not yet rampant in Japan—at least not this kind of individualism.

Figure 8.2 illustrates graphically the general pattern of generational change on these dimensions of group- and individual-mindedness in the Japanese and American samples. The Japanese and the Americans are fairly far apart in the older group; over time both groups shift in the same direction, but the Americans shift more.

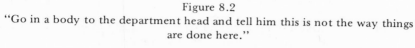

Figure 8.2
"Go in a body to the department head and tell him this is not the way things are done here."

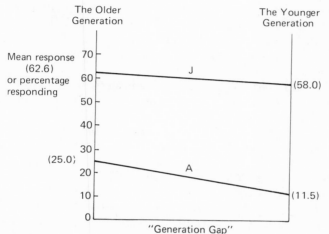

Note: Significance levels: Japanese old–Japanese young difference: p not significant; Japanese young–American young difference: $p \leqslant .001$; Japanese old–American old difference: $p \leqslant .010$; American old–American young difference: p not significant.

Conflict and Harmony

Attitudes toward harmony and conflict, division and cohesion, are hypothesized to be intimately related to political development and political democracy. For Eckstein, democracy is impossible without the willing acceptance of dispute and disagreement: "Democracy . . . is a form of polity that liberates conflict . . . [it] even presupposes the fact of political competition, for otherwise what sense would it make?"[23] Dahrendorf writes similarly, "Liberal democracy can become effective only in a society in which . . . conflicts are recognized and regulated rationally in all institutional orders."[24] It follows, as we might expect, that

23. Harry Eckstein, *Division and Cohesion in Democracy: A Study of Norway* (Princeton, 1966), p. 30.
24. Dahrendorf, *Society and Democracy in Germany.*

aversion to conflict is a basic trait of authoritarian political thought . . . the intellectual error underlying such aversion to conflict . . . consists of a dangerous confusion between social integration and social harmony. The confusion is dangerous because it suggests that creating harmony is the first task of politics; but this can never be accomplished except by repression.[25]

Traditional Japanese political culture, like that of China, is characterized by the overwhelming burden of value attached to the concept of harmony and by an equal aversion to conflict, competition, disagreement, or disharmony. That Dahrendorf and Eckstein are correct in supposing such a value orientation to be associated with authoritarian and repressive governmental structures Japanese history leaves us in no doubt.

The developmental convergence hypothesis predicts that harmony will appear less imperative and conflict less threatening and abhorrent to the younger generation of Japanese. It also predicts that American and Japanese values on this dimension will be closer together in the 1980s than they are at present. Let us examine some evidence bearing on this hypothesis.

Respondents were asked what traits were most important in a good subordinate. No Americans in either generation, but more younger Japanese (20.3 percent) than old (14.5 percent), answered that a harmonious character, team spirit, the ability to get along with people, were paramount requisites. These differences were not quite statistically significant (between the older groups, $p \leq .094$; between the younger, $p \leq .101$).

Responses to the TAT picture of the younger and the older man mentioned above were categorized according to whether the relationship between the two was marked by harmony, conflict, or neutrality. Figure 8.3 shows "harmony" responses and figure 8.4 shows "conflict" responses, by culture and generation. Three points seem significant: first, Americans perceive notably more conflict and less harmony than Japanese; second, generational change is marked in the American group but absent in the Japanese; and third, the result of this developmental process is to widen rather than to narrow the existing gap. These results (tentative, to be sure) tend to cast some doubt on the hypothesis that conflict is becoming generally more legitimate in Japanese society.

A sentence completion test item is relevant here: "When he was insulted . . . he fought." Both the United States and Japan have a

25. Ibid., pp. 184–85.

Figure 8.3
TAT, the Old Man and the Young, Perceived Harmony

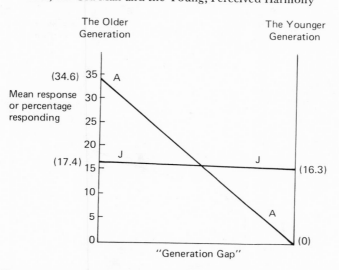

Note: Significance levels: Japanese old–Japanese young difference: p not significant; Japanese young–American young difference: $p \leqslant .173$ not significant; Japanese old–American old difference: $p \leqslant .123$ not significant; American old–American young difference: $p \leqslant .024$.

tradition of touchy masculine honor (frontier in the one case, feudal in the other) that enshrines and honors conflict under certain circumstances. Those who imagine themselves responding to an insult with violence are demonstrating that for them, here, conflict is legitimate. Twenty-five percent of the older Americans fall into this group, and 18.8 percent of the younger; of the older Japanese, zero, and of the younger, 1.6 percent. The difference between the representatives of these two cultures is significant at the .001 level in the older generation and at the .007 level in the young. Here the gap has narrowed somewhat, not, however, because the Japanese have become much more conflict-minded, but because the Americans have become more "harmonious."

Some final evidence may be adduced, again from responses to a TAT picture. This one shows two groups of three men each, huddled separately. The men in the foreground whisper among themselves, and eye the group behind them over their shoulders. The latter three stand close together, hands on hips, shoulders bent forward intently, staring fixedly at those in front—a problematic scene, but certainly designed to suggest conflict. Some respondents, more Japanese than

Figure 8.4
The Old Man and the Young: Perceived Conflict

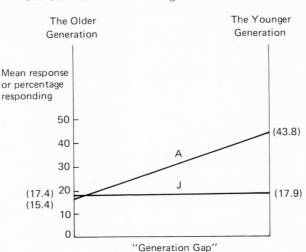

"Generation Gap"

Note: Significance levels: Japanese old–Japanese young difference: p not significant; Japanese young–American young difference: $p \leqslant .039$; Japanese old–American old difference: p not significant; American old–American young difference: $p \leqslant .096$.

American, fail to see conflict at all in the picture. But most interpret it in some way as a struggle between the two groups. Of interest, however, is not whether conflict is perceived, but, if it is perceived, whether it is perceived—and interpreted—as legitimate. Figure 8.5 presents the relationship of the two cultures and the two generations in graphic form. The younger in both cultures are more likely to perceive conflict as legitimate, their elders more likely to perceive it as "bad." But the shift in the Americans is much more marked, and the difference between the two cultures is more pronounced in the young, even though they have moved in the same general direction.

On this dimension, it appears that Japanese and American political-cultural values—and perhaps, we may hypothesize, political behavior—will be farther apart in the future than at present.

The Pattern Variables

Equality and hierarchy, trust and mistrust, autonomy and dependence, conflict and harmony: theories of political development and change can be elaborated ignoring these concepts or using them in different ways than does the orthodox theory we have taken as our hypothesis. But no sociology of development escapes the influence of

Figure 8.5

TAT, Opposing Groups: Conflict is Legitimate

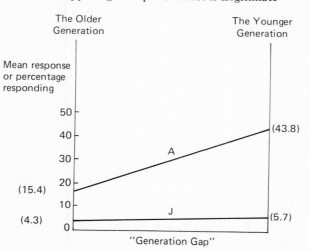

Note: Significance levels: Japanese old–Japanese young difference: p not significant; Japanese young–American young difference: $p \leqslant .001$; Japanese old–American old difference: p not significant; American old–American young difference: $p \leqslant .096$.

the sacred-secular, gemeinschaft-gesellschaft, progressive rationalization model. In dealing with this truism a few words suffice in most treatments. Thus Almond and Powell write, "The development of higher levels of system capabilities is dependent upon the development of greater structural differentiation and cultural secularization."[26] And for Ward, too, political development includes "an increasingly secular, impersonal, and rationalized system of governmental decision making."[27]

The classic definition of tradition and modernization in these terms is that set forth in Talcott Parsons's pattern variables.[28] If we want to examine the developmental convergence hypothesis as it relates to secularization and rationalization we must try to find indicators of particularism/universalism, affectivity/affective neutrality, diffuseness/specificity, ascription/achievement, and self-orientation collectivity orientation. The theory predicts that universalism, affective neutrality, specificity, achievement, and individualism are more

26. Gabriel Almond and G. Bingham Powell, *Comparative Politics: A Developmental Approach* (Boston, 1968), p. 323.

27. Robert E. Ward, ed., *Political Development in Modern Japan* (Princeton, 1968) p. 9.

28. Talcott Parsons and Edward A. Shils, eds., *Toward a General Theory of Action: Theoretical Foundations for the Social Sciences* (Cambridge, Mass., 1951).

marked in the younger Japanese generation and that the younger generations are closer together with regard to these values than the old.

The first of these pattern-variable dimensions is particularism/universalism. Universalistic values are essentially comprehended in the concept of "fairness": general rules applicable generally to everyone. Two sentence-completion test items measure this dimension. One is "The best way to treat a subordinate is . . . fairly." Here the percentage of Americans giving "universalistic" answers rises from 15.4 to 37.5 across the generations, while that of Japanese responding similarly drops from 10.1 to 3.3. The gap has widened, and the difference between younger Japanese and younger Americans is significant at the .001 level.

Another item is essentially a repetition: "The most essential trait of a good superior is . . . fairness." Here the American percentage shifts from 42.3 to 37.5 over the generation, while the Japanese percentage moves hardly at all from 1.4 to 1.6. The gap between cultures at both generational levels is significant at the .001 level.

A second pattern variable is the dimension of affectiveness/affective neutrality. Its implication is that traditional people tend to see the world and other people affectively, through a constant haze of emotion. "Modern" people, however, are able to divorce their relationships to things and people from emotion. They can treat them strictly as tools, or relate to them only insofar as the relationship is a useful means to an end. They can divorce their hearts from their heads, and give their heads the prerogative.

Two sentence-completion test items may be relevant to this dimension. The first is, "When he saw the others avoided him he . . . tried to find out why." This response avoids all the natural emotional responses to the uncomfortable situation of being left out, being isolated, and substitutes for them a purely rational and analytic task: not to feel, but to find out why. The percentage of Americans giving such responses rises from 30.8 in the older generation to 37.5 in the younger. The Japanese percentage goes from 15.9 to 16.3 This is suggestive, but none of the differences are significant except that between the younger generations, and it only approaches significance $(p \leqslant .088)$.

Another indicator of affectiveness/affective neutrality is the item "It is sometimes good to hide your true feelings about a person because . . . they might be mistaken." This question takes for granted that concealment of one's feelings is desirable on occasion. But the response defines the occasion as marked by a concern, not for the other person's sensitivities, not for social propriety, but for accuracy. This is affective neutrality indeed. Americans, as we may suspect, are much more likely to give such responses. The older generation does so 15.4 percent of the time, and the younger 18.8 percent. The Japanese percentage is 2.9 for the older and 4.1 for the younger. The differences between the cultures approach significance ($p \leqslant .079$ for the old and $p \leqslant .072$ for the young).

On this dimension of affective neutrality, imperfectly though we are able to measure it, it seems that both cultures are moving in the "modern" direction. But the Americans are moving faster, and the gap is widening.

The third pattern variable is diffuseness/specificity. This is related to affectiveness/affective neutrality, but it focuses more on the scope of personal relationships. Diffuse relationships are all-enveloping and multifaceted. Thus a wife in a traditional home may be coworker, coparent, cook, accountant, and lover. Similarly, the husband is many things to the wife. The "modern" pattern of specificity would make each relationship serve only one function, following the trend to specialization. So the modern husband in this case will work in a factory or an office, put his children in a day-care center, eat at a restaurant, take his finances to a specialist, and choose his sexual partners for sex only.

One of the sentence completion test items was hypothesized to tap this dimension: "The most essential trait of a good superior is . . . warmth and sincerity." The expected "modern" pattern would value in a superior chiefly fairness, perhaps, or efficiency. It is "traditional" to look for personal warmth in what is defined as a work relationship. And indeed we find that Japanese are much more likely to seek "warmth and sincerity" in their superiors than are Americans, 33.3 percent of the older generation and 26 percent of the younger answering thus. For the Americans the corresponding percentages are 7.7 and zero. The difference between the older generations is significant at the .03 level, between the younger at the .06 level.

Another test of affective neutrality is a TAT picture that shows a conference room, a table with papers on it in the middle, with four men sitting at it and talking. In the doorway, in the foreground of the scene, stands a fifth man, turned away from the group and facing us. On his face is an expression of intense thought or emotion, the nature of which is, however, unclear. A story told about this picture that described the scene as one of planning—totally rational, goal-directed activity, with no emotional overlay whatever—was considered to indicate affective neutrality. In both the Japanese and the American groups the percentage of respondents who perceive this scene as one of rational planning, affectively neutral, rises from the older generation to the younger. The increase for the Americans is from 11.5 to 31.3 percent, for the Japanese from 1.4 to 8.9 percent. The difference between the younger groups is significant at the .027 level.

The fourth pattern variable is ascription/achievement. An ascriptive orientation, characteristic of premodern societies, would see it as desirable that social status and privilege be ascribed and permanent, usually on the basis of birth. The Japanese neo-Confucian slogan "*taigi meibun*" ("the great righteousness is everyone in his place") expresses it perfectly. The achievement orientation expresses the belief that social status and privilege ought to be earned, usually by work or by ability. An ascriptive society would not encourage ambition; an achievement-oriented society would cherish it and strive to inculcate it. So we can measure ascription and achievement, it is reasonable to suppose, in part by the degree to which ambition for social advancement is expressed.

Two sentence-completion test items touch on this area. One is "He wishes he were...of higher rank." In this case the older Americans express ambition or need for achievement in 26.9 percent of the cases, and the younger in 6.3 percent. The older Japanese register 7.25 percent and the younger 16.3 Here is a dramatic convergence! The cultures not only converge, they move past each other. But the change is due not so much to an increase in Japanese ambition as to a decline in American ambition. The other item "Most of all he wants...to succeed," gives us a similar picture. The Americans drop from a high 53.8 percent to 25 percent, while the Japanese rise from 2.9 percent to 12.2 percent. In both these cases a significant difference between cultures in the older generation ($p \leqslant .026$ for "He wishes," and $p \leqslant .001$ for "Most of all he wants") disappears in the younger. But what we see is not an increase in achievement orientation as both nations "modernize" but a decrease for one nation and an increase in the other.

Finally, the self-orientation/collectivity orientation variable must be considered. The evidence in this case must be the same offered earlier for individualism and group-mindedness, autonomy and dependence. It should be remembered that a slight increase in Japanese scores was overbalanced by a larger increase in American. Here again the culture gap widened.

What is the situation, then, with regard to the Parsonian pattern-variable scheme for measuring modernity and tradition in the Japanese and American case? We find that part of the original hypothesis is correct: Americans are growing more universalistic, more affectively neutral, more specific, and more individualistic. They are not, however, growing more achievement-oriented. Changes between the Japanese generations are not so marked, and the level of the "modern"

Figure 8.6
TAT, The Conference Room: Rational Planning

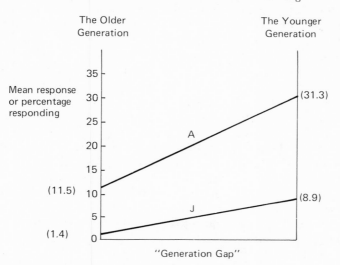

Note: Significance levels: Japanese old–Japanese young difference: $p \leqslant .081$; Japanese young–American young difference: $p \leqslant .027$; Japanese old–American old difference: $p \leqslant .103$ not significant; American old–American young difference: not significant.

attitudes—universalism, affective neutrality, specificity, individualism—is generally lower. But in the case of achievement orientation the picture is different. Here the Japanese younger generation evidences a sharp rise over their elders, but the presumably more "modern" Americans have declined. A peculiar kind of convergence this is.

The typical picture for four of the five pattern variables is shown in Figure 8.6.

We hypothesized that the Japanese and American political cultures are coming more and more to resemble each other, as a result of a process in which increasing industrialization, rationalization, and social differentiation are accompanied by a corresponding developmental or modernizing change in values and attitudes. To test this hypothesis the values of two "generations" of Japanese and American elites were measured on the dimensions open-mindedness/dogmatism, trust/mistrust, autonomy/dependence, harmony/conflict, and the Parsonian pattern variables.

The hypothesis of convergence was not verified, and the hypothesis of unidirectional developmental change was verified only in part. Dogmatic and hierarchical values have declined in Japan, but not enough to keep pace with an even greater decline in the United States.

The net result is divergence rather than convergence. The measurement of trust and mistrust produced no evidence of a cultural gap and no evidence of generational change, except for a few ambiguous and contradictory data. On the individual-group or autonomy-dependence dimension we find a marked increase in individualistic attitudes in the United States but little or no change in Japan; the net result is value divergence. The valuation of harmony and conflict presents a similar pattern: change in the predicted direction for the United States, little or no change in Japan, the result an increase in cultural distance. With the pattern variables universalism, affective neutrality, etc., the result is the same: change as predicted for the United States, relatively little or no change for Japan. The only variable on which convergence is unambiguously present is that of achievement-ascription; in this case the cultures grow closer together as younger Japanese show more and younger Americans less emphasis on success.

We can state cautiously that the developmental convergence or value modernization hypothesis is not borne out in the case of Japan. Japanese and American political values will probably not be closer together in the near future than they are at present. But this statement must be qualified.

It may be, first, that value convergence is indeed taking place, but either the twenty-year gap between our "generations" is not sufficient to allow it to reveal itself or a relatively short-lived eddy or turbulence in the stream of culture change has confused the picture. Perhaps the Showa-born appear no more "modern" than the Meiji- and Taisho-born because of a special historical trauma in the socialization process that counteracts the expected change rather than enhancing it.

Or it may be, again, that the pattern of our data is an artifact of chance. We have adduced "evidence" in some cases significant at the .05 level and above. It follows that if we have one hundred measurements, five of them are probably spurious. If those five are crucial then our interpretation will be in considerable error. This uncertainty is reduced in part by a careful concern for the overall tendency of the data. Replication of the measurements will reduce it even further.

A third possibility is that the data are entirely reliable and yet the conclusions I draw about the future are mistaken. The groups whose political-cultural attitudes I have examined are not representative of society at large. They are above average in income, status, and education, and their political views do not necessarily correspond with those of certain other larger segments of their societies. In short, they are elites. Any prediction of political behavior in the future based on their attitudes requires the assumption that these men or men like them will indeed inherit the authority for which they seem destined. A government drawn from different social strata in the Japan of the 1980s might or might not be characterized by attitudes similar to those I have examined.

This caution is more particularly relevant in the American case, for American society and culture are much more fragmented and American subcultures are much more abundant and vigorous than are Japanese. Yale graduates of this age represent predominantly a northeastern, moderately conservative, Anglo-Saxon, liberal-Protestant establishment, with little diversity. A shift in political power that lessens the influence of this minority will vitiate any predictions based on the assumption that its values will prevail.

Having stated these cautions I can discuss the results. I conclude most basically that value convergence does not take place. Furthermore, Japanese political culture does not move in the predicted direction except on a minority of indicators. Is such a conclusion simply a matter of demolishing a straw man or beating a dead horse? After all, the convergence hypothesis was formulated for us by men who rejected it: Dahrendorf for the modern Germanies and Brzezinski and Huntington for the Soviet Union. If nonconvergence were indeed accepted as legitimate for modern Japan, I would have demonstrated the obvious. Of course, if the obvious has not been demonstrated before, this is not a useless enterprise. For some reason (it may be a vested unconscious interest on the part of American scholars whose initial relation to Japan was established in the framework of the "reeducation" effort of the Occupation) it is easier to accept the idea that Russian political values remain Russian or that German political values remain German than that Japan has not changed and may not change in the American image.

Let us accept the results as they stand and explore their theoretical implications. There are essentially three possible interpretations. First, we could, if we like, hold fast to the convergence theory and argue that Japanese values are not changing because the Japanese polity is not developing. This alternative cannot be elaborated here and probably deserves no elaboration.

Or we might point to the contradiction in the idea of political development. On the one hand it implies the capacity, differentiation, and effectiveness of the state. On the other, I insist, it implies increasing quanta of democracy. The complex of attitudes and values examined in this paper is in part related theoretically to state efficiency (rationality, affective neutrality, achievement, etc.) and in part related to democracy (the acceptance of individualism, egalitarianism, and the legitimacy of conflict). It is unquestionable that the capacity and differentiation of the Japanese state apparatus has been increasing, not just since the Meiji restoration but since the Tokugawa settlement. But one could argue that the growth of authentic democracy has been much less marked, even in the postwar period (which, after all, has not yet seen the rise of a viable political opposition).

If this ambiguity in the theoretical construct of political development is seized upon, we can reconcile the results by modifying the theory. There is an aspect of political development that does not require democracy or the growth and spread of the values associated therewith. Hence, that individualism, the acceptance of the legitimacy of conflict, and nondogmatic egalitarian openness do not increase in Japan at the speed they do in the United States, or do not increase at all, does not mean that the Japanese polity is not developing. It means that it is developing in its own way and that state efficiency, capacity, and differentiation can be achieved by more than one route and with more than one set of value orientations.

Or, third, I could expand this interpretation to reject the theory of convergence in its entirety. To do so would be to move beyond the evidence onto the thin ice of intellectual-historical hypothesis. I can speculate that the American orthodoxy of political development and cultural change is haunted by the unacknowledged ghosts of Adam Smith and Voltaire and that the theory of the inevitability of rationalization and secularization is one of the guises taken by slogans from a revolution that was fought one and two centuries ago.

Rationality, affective neutrality, bureaucratization, individualism, competition—perhaps these values are not the image of an inevitable future but the demands of a particular political and economic style. Perhaps, indeed, they are economic values par excellence. It may well be that our entire concept of "modernity" needs revision.

Let us suppose that value structures are almost infinitely various, and let us entertain the possibility that development need not imply the rejection of being Japanese. To revere the group and shun individual selfishness, to condemn social conflict and to reject political and economic competition—such attitudes in the extreme are problematic, there is no doubt. But it is also increasingly apparent that an extreme rational-egalitarian-competitive-individual model may entail some problems. This conclusion will have at least three advantages. It will reconcile theory and evidence; it will take the assertion of value out of the study of values and leave it to the philosophers and theologians where it belongs; and it will make the political world more threatening and uncertain, it is true, but much more interesting, too.

9

The Future of a Tradition:
Japanese Spirit in the 1980s

ROBERT FRAGER AND THOMAS P. ROHLEN

Austin and Cole contrasted traditional to modern; Frager and Rohlen deal specifically with the content of "the traditional" in Japanese values. In the organizing concept of seishin ("spirit") they locate a key element in national mores. Seishin is antithetical to modernization as generally conceived. It is not democratic, not universalistic, not individualistic, not materialistic. It is rather the complex of loyalty, discipline, esprit de corps, and indomitable perseverance that is central to so many of the historical accomplishments of Japanese civilization, from art to economic growth.

Cole's chapter suggests that a secular process of rationalization is eroding traditional values, but Frager and Rohlen find the values of seishin flourishing and providing criteria for recruitment and training in all kinds of social groupings. The older and the more upper class the circles concerned, the more the seishin values are likely to prevail. Frager and Rohlen suggest that as the Japanese age they rediscover tradition and the values of the past. But Cole's figures on the secular modernization of values show for each of four age cohorts a tendency to liberalization and modernization with increasing age. How can these two opposing interpretations be reconciled? Perhaps the answer lies in the distinction between elite and mass, upper and lower class, left and right. Seishin thought may appeal to a particular segment or segments of the population only, or it may represent only a backwash in the tide of change.

But the segment, or the backwash, is significant: it encompasses military, police, business elites, youth groups, adherents of some new religions, and educational policymakers. And, as the authors suggest, the more difficult the problems of change, the more attractive becomes this traditional philosophy for confronting and conquering difficulties. The vitality of seishin is not least among the paradoxes of progress.—L. A.

Some things Japanese seem especially persistent amidst the skyscrapers, four-lane highways, trips to Europe, and all the rest of the

hustle and bustle so illustrative of modern change. One prominent
example of this persistence is the continuing Japanese interest in
matters pertaining to *seishin*, a term roughly translated as "spirit" that
we will discuss at length in this paper. At various times in recent history
this term has been a prominent rallying cry for those wishing to preserve
or reassert Japanese traditional ways, and during the 1930s and 40s
it was extensively utilized by military and right-wing leaders in their
efforts to inspire the nation. It is very important to note that, despite
its history as a panacea of nationalist and militaristic movements,
the Japanese orientation to seishin has a much broader and deeper
basis in the ongoing life of most Japanese, regardless of their political
persuasion. It is undoubtedly a crucial matter for every form of religion
in Japan; teaching it is a major goal of all traditional arts; parents and
schools worry about the spiritual development of today's youths; and,
in fact, virtually all aspects of life and behavior are grist for the seishin
perspective.

The question before us here is, What can be anticipated about the
prominence of this kind of emphasis in Japanese life as of the 1980s? Will
its associated traditional values and practices decline as some public
opinion polls would imply?[1] Will it perhaps experience a general
revival as has occurred several times in the last century? What, in fact,
is the situation regarding this sometimes quite volatile matter that is
sometimes indicative of national identity and the direction of political
life? Our answers to these questions require that we first clarify the
various implications of the term *seishin* and then enumerate the various
kinds of social groups that pay particular attention to seishin matters
today. To discuss seishin is to discuss one of the underlying streams of
essential meaning in Japanese life, and this requires a special flexibility
of approach, one that eschews the idea that tomorrow is best understood
in terms of the immediate trends of today (however true this is for some
matters). We prefer to underline the lasting appeal of the seishin outlook as part of a syndrome of alternative answers to the basic dilemmas
of Japanese life, and our schema for understanding the future of the
seishin perspective is therefore one that emphasizes the nature of its
ongoing appeal and the conditions that might cause it to become
prominent in national life again. In the post–World War II period the
seishin alternative has remained relatively inconspicuous in the public
realm, but that is a far different matter from saying that it has dis-
appeared from Japanese life altogether.[2]

1. See, for example, the special issue of *Gendai Esprit* on the subject "Changes in Japanese
Character" (1 April 1973).
2. See Kenneth B. Pyle, *The New Generation in Meiji Japan: Problems of Cultural Identity, 1885–
1895* (Stanford, 1969).

The Meaning of Seishin

To discuss the Japanese interest in seishin is to tackle a very general but rather unified complex of attitudes, interpretations, educational practices, and personal experiences found together by a common underlying perspective. This is analogous, perhaps, to such American concerns as freedom and responsibility. By an analysis of the seishin perspective we are not "explaining" actual behavior but rather attempting to understand an interpretive mode, or lens, by which behavior may be made meaningful to the observer and which may give behavior meaning for the actor. Clearly, most Japanese today utilize a variety of lenses, often contradictory ones, through which they attempt to view and understand the complexities of modern existence. The very multiplicity of understandings is a source of personal confusion at times, and this is a subject of considerable relevance to our subsequent discussion of the place of seishin thought in modern Japan.

Seishin versus materialism. Seishin is often used in contrast with *busshitsu*, the material world. *Seishin-shugi* and *busshitsu-shugi* literally mean "spiritualism" and "materialism," or reliance on things of the mind or spirit, and reliance on material objects. There is a tendency to view these two attitudes as mutually exclusive. Individuals who have strong materialistic interests and who are concerned with accumulating a great many possessions tend to be deemed shallow and lacking in spiritual concerns. Men of great power and influence who live simply and frugally are often held up as ideals to emulate.

Seishin and fortitude. Seishin is often associated with the capacity to endure suffering and anguish. Many of the most prominent words in the seishin vocabulary, such as *konjō*, *nintai*, and *gaman*, refer to endurance and fortitude. One frequent expression used in sports, the martial arts, and other strenuous activities is *gambatte*, literally "to hold out, to endure." Life has been metaphorically described as an ocean of waves and storms over which the person must ride to achieve his or her goal.

Seishin and single-mindedness. The seishin perspective is associated with terms related to good character and moral worth, such as *majime* ("serious" or "steady") and *makoto* and *seijitsu* ("sincere"). *Makoto* can also be translated as "faithful," "constant," or "single-hearted." Seishin points toward a state of mind that is without ambivalence or inner contradiction.

If something is worth doing, it is worth the dedication of one's total attention and energy. If a sense of dedication is lacking, extreme lassitude and alienation may set in, as noted by Wagatsuma and DeVos, for example, in their study of alienation in three Japanese intellectuals.[3] When present, this kind of dedication can provide a tremendous source of motivation and energy, not to mention a much simplified and unambivalent sense of the world. It is not surprising that the criticism of fanaticism has often been aimed at seishin enthusiasts.

Seishin strength. Seishin development is pursued for very practical aims in Japan. Men may meditate for long hours, endure physical hardships, and pursue other spiritual disciplines for rather mundane goals—to improve performance at work or at school, for example. This reflects a common belief that "man can do the unexpected and superhuman when his 'spiritual force' works upon a condition that seems to be beyond human wisdom and strength."[4]

In World War II Japanese were encouraged to demonstrate spiritual strength, "to match our training against their numbers and our flesh against their steel."[5] This attitude, which culminated in the Special Attack Corps (or *kamikaze* units), has lost its military objectives, but it can and is raised as a rallying cry in the more mundane worlds of scholastic achievement and business success.

Health and happiness. Material difficulties and privation need not affect the spirit. On the contrary, there is a great stress on positiveness and the notion that one's happiness depends on inner attitudes rather than on external conditions. To accept the external world as it is and to cope with it on its terms is commonly reiterated advice. A related belief is the notion that a positive mental set will ensure physical health and well-being.[6] Illness can be taken as an indication of spiritual weakness and upset, or a lack of sufficient will power.

Seishin in human creation. Because human life may be so deeply affected by seishin strength, the accomplishments of men can be interpreted as revealing their personal character; therefore, creations are valued as possessing seishin quality. The sword has been treated with special consideration throughout Japanese history. Reverence for it has exceeded that accorded a mere weapon; the sword became the

---

3. H. Wagatsuma and G. DeVos, "Alienation and the Author," in G. DeVos, ed., *Socialization and Advancement* (Berkeley, 1973).

4. Minami Hiroshi, *Psychology of the Japanese People* (Tokyo, 1971), p. 134.

5. Ruth Benedict, *The Chrysanthemum and the Sword* (Cambridge, Mass., 1946), p. 24.

6. Fukuzawa Yukichi mentions this attitude in his autobiography, *The Autobiography of Fukuzawa Yukichi* (Tokyo, 1960). During a period of illness, he followed his doctor's advice and dressed warmly, wore flannel underwear, stayed in well-heated rooms, and took plenty of medication. When this regime did not seem to help, Fukuzawa recalled the disciplines of his younger days. He took to wearing light clothing, minimized heating, and went out in all kinds of weather. He returned to chopping wood and rice pounding for exercise. His energy and vitality gradually returned and he threw off the lingering illness.

very symbol of the samurai spirit.[7] Similarly, works of art and scholarship are treasured in large measure as reflections of the creator's spirit.

Work thus reflects character. Japanese commonly feel that they can tell a great deal about a person from a very small sample of behavior, a bit of calligraphy, for example. The creative attempts of eminent men and women are prized, not because they evidence great artistic skill, but because they reflect their creators' highly developed seishin. This sense that a man and his work are one is not only applied to the great, it is a part of the daily world of endeavor.

Seishin training. Many different forms of activity can aid in the development of seishin. In general, the stricter and more painful the discipline, the better for character development. Like fine steel, character is forged and tempered by the heat of adversity. A smooth, easy life does not afford much opportunity for such strengthening. To paraphrase a common metaphor: like a Japanese sword, a man's character needs to be polished (*migaku*) constantly to avoid rust and dullness.

Training routines center on rather elaborately devised physical and mental disciplines.[8] The former aid the individual in overcoming his instincts for comfort, pleasure, and ease, while the latter help develop openness and flexibility of mind and the ability to accept what comes, including arbitrary authority and the demands of group existence.

Difficulties are not to be endured negatively, but rather accepted as something desirable for self-cultivation. A Japanese saying illustrates this: "There is nothing more beautiful in human character than a countenance that reflects great suffering."[9]

In many ascetic traditions the aim of spiritual discipline is to eliminate physical desires altogether. In Japan, however, the physical pleasures of life are perfectly acceptable, but in their own place. A serious, mature individual should be able to subordinate these desires to the demands of the spirit. The body needs to be overcome or ignored

7. Japanese officers in World War II were always encumbered by their swords. Despite the obvious ineffectiveness of these weapons in battle, the swords were carried for their qualities of spiritual inspiration.

8. One extreme form of discipline is known as *misogi*, literally "purification." Individuals are required to sit on their knees (*seiza*) and chant for over fifteen hours a day. There is little time for sleep; food and rest breaks are minimal. Monitors prowl constantly, on the alert for anyone who falls asleep or stops chanting vigorously. Offenders are struck on the back. Anyone who is not well-balanced and firmly seated is knocked over and then pummeled until he rises again. Sessions generally last three to four days. Trainees have said that after the second day they had thought dying would have been a preferable alternative to continuing. One man reported a feeling of numbness in his feet and toes for months after undergoing this training.

9. Robert Frager, "Traditionalism and Conformity," *Nenpō shakai-shinrigaku* [The Japanese annals of social psychology] 10 (1969): 233.

to accomplish anything truly important. One Japanese army officer kept his men on maneuvers for sixty hours with only ten-minute rest breaks, explaining, "They know how to sleep; they need training in how to stay awake."[10] In the West we tend to think of energy as a finite substance that we may deplete by overexertion. In Japan, the individual is trained to tap hidden resources in himself or in nature.

The proper attitude to take toward the discipline and rigor of training is not one of frustration or self-sacrifice. The goal is the great satisfaction that derives from self-mastery and self-development. Undergoing hardship and developing character are said to teach the individual to live and to savor life to the fullest.

Training in seishin tends to follow very simple patterns consisting of repetition of simple activities, often to the point of exhaustion. A particularly difficult or complex task is not as good as a simple one, for it tends to take one's mind off the goal of self-mastery. Whether the practice is fencing or the tea ceremony, repetition of basic movements continues for years before their mastery is recognized. In this process, the mind and body are unified in a natural and meaningful flow of action, and, of course, the extraordinary degree of patience required is finally rewarded.

In many sports, martial arts, schools of music, and the like, serious students sometimes go on weekend or week-long intensive training sessions, or *gasshuku*. Living together as a group they develop camaraderie and spirit. The aim of such gatherings is to dedicate as much time as possible to practicing one's discipline. It is interesting to note that these sessions are not limited to traditional Japanese disciplines. Baseball teams and even mandolin clubs also hold gasshuku. Once a fairly substantial level of technical proficiency is reached, training stresses refinement of technique and the development of a particular style. With refinement will also come greater attention to seishin factors in performance.

Seishin and performance. Seishin development is seen as essential for the true mastery of any art. One must first master one's self, it is said. Training first must develop seriousness and dedication, for mastery requires that all detail be learned thoroughly. Learning to concentrate completely is also considered a crucial aspect of mastery. One phrase for concentration, *seishin tōitsu*, literally means "seishin unification." Seishin strength enables the individual to overcome fear, hesitation, timidity, and other "psychological" obstacles to expert performance. It is thought to be particularly important as that quality of training that may be most easily generalized to the rest of one's life. Men and

10. Benedict, *Chrysanthemum*, p. 230.

women who have attained mastery in any seishin-related field are thought also to have achieved a certain general competence and self-discipline that will help them perform new and unrelated tasks. Thus all of human behavior can be viewed as an expression of seishin development, particularly if it is part of a clear course of skill development.

Relatively little stress is given to individual differences in innate ability. Perseverance and hard work in training are among the most important requisites for success. It is assumed that all beginners are more or less incompetent, and differences among them are not important. Similarly, all those who have undergone roughly the same degree of training are expected to be at the same general level of skill. The most important thing is to be teachable, that is, to comply with the teacher's wishes, to be able to take instruction.[11] Given a competent teacher, a pliable student, and sufficient time, the results are assured. Students who resist, who will not let themselves be molded properly by the discipline, cannot make the proper progress.

The self in seishin training. An important aim of seishin training is the containment of tendencies toward selfishness and egotism. Just as the individual works to overcome the demands of the body, he must learn to overcome the demands of ego (*ga*).

Seishin is developed in situations that require unconditional resignation and absolute submission to authority.[12] The whole ideology of seishin tends to support a hierarchical and absolute notion of authority. Good character makes one a good follower, loyal and unquestioning (and also, at the appropriate time, a good leader). The individual learns to overcome personal desires that impede group accomplishment. A classic phrase, *messhi hōkō*—"destroy ego and serve others"—is a startling expression of the relationship between seishin training and social involvement. In a position of subordination to authority, the individual may not be required to give up his life, as in the time-honored examples of samurai and modern soldiers, but he is often required to give up personal opinions, pleasures, or privileges if they interfere with the achievement of greater goals or duties.

11.   One important aspect of this pliability is the willingness to forget what one has learned already. The beginner has to be like a freshly washed blackboard, ready for the teacher to write whatever he wants. In one well-known Zen story, a university professor visits the Zen master Nan-in. Nan-in serves tea. When the visitors's cup is full, he keeps on pouring. The professor watches the tea overflow and finally is unable to contain himself. "It is too full. No more will go in."

"Like this cup," Nan-in says, "you are full of your own opinions and speculations. How can I show you Zen unless you first empty your cup?"

12.   Many people made to undergo seishin training experience great resistance and resentment. For this reason, many types of training will only accept those who indicate a strong desire to be trained.

Seishin in politics. As we have noted, the seishin perspective has been invoked by conservatives, nationalists, and militarists throughout the last century as the answer to all sorts of problems, from public immorality to national military preparedness. It is inevitably presented as contrary to Western materialism and individualism and therefore a unique possession and strength of Japan. The country's recent economic growth (in the face of tremendous material obstacles) is often explained as evidence of Japan's particular spirit or national character, which, if it declines (and it is generally seen as doing so), will greatly weaken the country.

The seishin perspective is patently contrary to the usual conceptualization of the proper education for democracy, and it is not easily reconciled with the universalist ideologies and theories, particularly those that emphasize the power of external social conditions. Consequently, even though in essence the seishin perspective is apolitical, public proponents of spiritualism (seishin-shugi) are usually ranged in opposition to proponents of a broad spectrum of political viewpoints associated with modern, Western thought, from liberal democracy to communism.

The influence of spiritualism can also be seen in the activities and personal style of rightists in Japan. Extreme devotion, a highly oversimplified understanding of events, a thirst for self-sacrificing action, and a preoccupation with the kind of training just discussed are all typical of rightists. At various times in recent history such men, small in number but terribly effective because of their sacrificial intent, have almost undermined normal political processes, and the fear of their action is never totally absent from the political scene.

Thus in public life today (i.e., the media, politics, and other national forums) the term *spiritualism* has a generally negative character. It is essential to remember, however, that there are almost an infinite number of contexts that lie below the level of public life and in most of them the insight, values, and training methods that make up the seishin perspective are positively regarded and in some of these they are actively encouraged. It is to some of the more prominent of this latter group that we turn next.

SEISHIN EMPHASES WITHIN CONTEMPORARY SOCIETY

Our discussion has not yet gone very far toward detailing the nature of variation within the seishin tradition. For warriors and soldiers and the whole nation in time of war, the emphasis has been on hardship, discipline, and authority. But at other times, especially in postwar Japan, the seishin perspective has been associated with practical daily affairs (e.g., success, health, happiness, and the pursuit of understanding), and training has been milder (more a matter of frugality, order, self-awareness, and emotional release). The exponents of resistance to authority and those who chose independence, as well as those who became obedient, have been appreciated by their Japanese countrymen, at least retrospectively, for their seishin strength, and all levels and occupations within Japanese society have found some reason to emphasize the seishin point of view. One illustration that is totally nonmilitary is the traditional stress on dedication and long, hard apprenticeship among artisans, shopkeepers, and merchants who have viewed craftsmanship and business as, among other things, expressions of spiritual accomplishment.

Work, training, and promotion in modern organization. Perhaps the sense of craft and vocation remain strongest in the narrowing realm of traditional enterprise. One of the least obvious yet notable areas of seishin orientation is the realm of everyday work. Company offices, government bureaus, and factories, are, of course, among the most prominent social environments. A recent study of a large bank by one of the authors[13] found the seishin point of view to be of considerable importance in such areas as the judgment of personal character, the intentions of the company training program, and the interpretations of career success.

To begin with company training programs, we note that during the sixties many large firms, including about one-third of those enrolled in the Industrial Training Association (*sangyo kunren kyōkai*) in 1969,[14] came to institute seishin-related activities as elements in their introductory training programs, particularly those for men. The variation in actual practices from company to company appeared to be large. The bank we studied in detail, for example, featured an extraordinary elaboration of seishin-oriented activities over a three-month training period, yet such intensity is not typical. It is more common to find one or two weeks given over to such activities as *zazen*, a marathon, other endurance tests, or brief training visits to Japan's Self-Defense Force camps.[15] Such programs emphasizing traditional values and methods of education continue to strike many Japanese as unusual and even anachronistic; indeed, there is reason to assume that a decline in such explicit and extensive programs will occur in conjunction with a decline in the general concern among adults with the

13. Thomas P. Rohlen, "Spiritual Education in a Japanese Bank," *American Anthropologist* 75, no. 5 (1973): 1542–62.

14. Private communication from the association.

15. See also Thomas P. Rohlen, "Sponsorship of Cultural Continuity in Japan: A Company Training Program," *Journal of Asian and African Studies* 5, no. 3 (1970): 184–92, for an account of spiritual training in an Osaka industrial firm.

question of whether the postwar education system is producing people who are unfit for adult responsibility (that is, according to the seishin perspective). The end of student unrest may initiate such a trend; therefore, while company spiritual training is noteworthy as an illustration of a persistent concern with traditional values in Japanese companies, it is not, in the final analysis, the crucial or even the central issue in the consideration of the relationship between the seishin perspective and Japanese work organizations.

Of greater significance is the manner in which personal ability is judged within the context of a company. The evaluation of people for the purposes of promotion necessarily involves, in addition to questions of technical and intellectual ability, judgments about personal character, and these are made in terms of a framework provided by the seishin orientation. Of note here is the fact that the difficulties accompanying work tend to be regarded as tests of strong character. The strains of working in a hierarchical system, the tedious repetition of daily tasks, and the anxieties that accompany new work situations are all regarded as problems that try a person's spirit. Those who prove most capable of perseverance in the face of such difficulties and who show themselves dedicated over the long haul to their work are the ones judged (according to the seishin perspective) to be most suited for future leadership.[16] In other words, the very nature of the promotion system serves to preserve a concern with seishin as a crucial framework of evaluation.

This preoccupation with seishin appears to be most true of white-collar workers who are moving toward future managerial positions. Promotion for them is less dependent on seniority, less easily measured by standards of technical skill, and more involved with the ultimate selection of an organization's top leadership. As a result, one will find greater attention given to seishin considerations the higher one goes in Japanese organizational life, particularly along those avenues to leadership positions commonly described as "the elite course." This has the further consequence of contributing a strong seishin component to what might be described as the organizational elite subculture, one that persists over time in part because the attitudes and emphases of a senior generation of leaders have a marked influence over the recruitment of their successors to high office. Today's leaders concerned with seishin strength are selecting people who are also motivated by seishin.

16. See Thomas P. Rohlen, "The Organization and Ideology of a Japanese Bank: An Ethnographic Study of a Modern Organization" (Ph.D. diss., University of Pennsylvania, 1971) for a more extended discussion of these considerations in the promotion system of a Japanese bank. It is quite true, of course, that much of the same kind of perspective is applied by American companies.

The fact that work difficulties are viewed as a form of spiritual test is of considerable significance to the conceptualization of learning within the work context. It is common to view the matter of personal development (both the acquisition of skills and the improvement of character) as a continuing process for which the attainment of a certain age or the completion of a particular course of study are but markers along an unending path of accomplishment. Among the difficulties that have positive educational value from the seishin orientation is the extended period of "apprenticeship" (i.e., low status and slow promotion for even those who are obviously very able). Character development is a long-term process that is enhanced by making the ambitious wait. One also finds in Japanese work situations a premium placed on the strict (*kibishii*) but devoted teacher, a man who insists his students push themselves to reach the highest standards of performance. Perhaps this is not uniquely Japanese, yet in Japan the application of a seishin point of view to matters of modern work and career is remarkably thorough and consistent. A well-developed seishin point of view is thus represented in organizational training through the application of an already widely appreciated vocabulary of terms and interpretations that are well known in Japan.

One final consideration that further serves to tie promotion, company education, and the seishin perspective together is the interpretation given to successful careers. The autobiographies of famous business leaders, like those of politicians and others, are filled with comments to the effect that the hardships (*kurō*) along the way provided the crucial educational experiences in the formation of their robust determination and their successful philosophy (inevitably characterized by a positive attitude, a sense of mission, and a grateful humility). Such autobiographies recognize the heartbreak and frustrations of working one's way up and yet hold out the promise of attaining a level of seishin strength at which the hardships of work are experienced with joy. Perseverance plus a positive attitude is the inevitable prescription.[17]

Even a cursory review of popular autobiographies by prominent business figures is enough to reveal the fact that this is a recurrent theme in all such writing. The American interpretation of success à la Horatio Alger requires material poverty as a starting point; by the progressive surmounting of difficulties the individual attains great prosperity and dignity. This sequence is also familiar to many Japanese readers. The Japanese version, however, seldom wanders from a primary focus on the growth of personal character. Horatio Alger's

17. See the writing of a semiautobiographical nature by Matsushita Konnosuke as an example.

heroes seem to be born honest and true and strong, whereas personal strength and wisdom develop over time in Japanese success stories. It is not at all surprising to hear admired business leaders referred to as "men who have suffered," and even in the gossip-filled columns of white collar workers' magazines the personal strengths and weaknesses of character of business leaders is a popular theme in the analysis of the rise and fall of company fortunes.

The military and the police. While work organizations continue to be our major focus, we should note the place of spiritual education in two large public organizations that before the war assumed leadership in the exemplification of seishin values. These are, of course, the military and the police. They both share a tradition of "spiritualism" that requires very little explicit educational enhancement. After almost three decades of careful avoidance of any extremes in educational technique or doctrine that might be reminiscent of the prewar days, it would be highly improper to imply that present conditions in these organizations are similar to the conditions during the thirties. Yet it would seem that a seishin emphasis is an inherent quality of military and quasimilitary organization and, furthermore, that awareness of the military and police traditions, the practice of traditional sports, and the general nature of training in both organizations greatly enhance the general but rather subsurface continuity of a seishin orientation.

Unfortunately, there have been no direct studies of either the military or the police in these terms. It has been said on occasion that the police and the military have a particular appeal for young men oriented to the traditional martial arts, and this would coincide with the general interest in the seishin perspective of the institutions. Police *dōjōs* (martial arts training schools) provide some of the best judo and kendo training in Japan; furthermore, much the same promotion process as that just discussed for business no doubt operates in these organizations as well. It could be argued that in the case of the Japanese military, promotion to high office must de-emphasize seishin qualities in order to preserve the more moderate postwar look. Certainly, the initial selection process creates a strong weighting in favor of the seishin-oriented individual, and the military must be careful not to allow overly fanatical seishin enthusiasts to achieve high office. In 1971 there were slightly over 288,000 people in the Self-Defense Agency and Forces and approximately 180,000 connected with the police force.[18] These figures are not likely to decline in the future.

The age order. The question of seishin orientation as it relates to

18. Ministry of Finance, *Nihon no Tōkei, 1971* [Statistics of Japan for 1971] (Tokyo, 1972).

relative age is one of the most important and most difficult to untangle. Attitude surveys almost inevitably reveal what is characterized as an "age gap" in opinions on most subjects. It is fair to generalize that attitudes closer to the seishin perspective are characteristic of older people and that there is a progressive increase in such attitudes that parallels increasing age.[19]

There are two obvious extreme interpretations that may be made of this "age gap" phenomenon. One is that the older generation has received a greater amount of traditional education and has been less influenced by the growing postwar orientation (in the schools, mass media, etc.) to modern, Western values than the younger. From this point of view, the attitudes characteristic of young people would be expected to extend gradually upward in the age bracket until what today is representative of the younger generation ultimately becomes representative of Japanese society as a whole. The focus here, of course, is on historical change and the necessary assumption is that people do not change in their fundamental ideas and basic outlook as they increase in age. An alternative interpretation assumes a perennial age gap distinction for any modern society and views the experience of life as the source of a gradual change in attitudes and orientation that accompanies the aging process. From this point of view the age gap phenomenon is of little relevance in the prediction of future change.

Rather than debating either the general relevance of attitude survey data or the alternative interpretations of the data collected,[20] we

19. This is common in the United States, too, where one finds age bringing new interest in religion, hobbies, and the like, but the trend seems much stronger among Japanese as they re-orient toward their own heritage.

20. One of the more striking aspects of doing field work or simply living in Japan is the fact that the data collected by the public opinion survey or questionnaire method concerning the attitudes of Japanese on various subjects seem so shallow and even misleading in the light of what one learns about the Japanese in the course of daily life. The separation between "scientific" reality and daily reality stems, it seems, from the fact that answering questionnaires and maneuvering through the intricacies of actual social life are two quite distinct (one is tempted to say almost unrelated) matters. Surveys of general attitudes may under certain circumstances be of particular value, such as in the case of an approaching election. But when more general issues involving what is referred to as values are the focus, the distance between the response to the questionnaire and subsequent thought and behavior can be enormous. The whole atmosphere created by attitude surveys is likely to elicit modern and "progressive" values. The highly educated poll taker, dressed in Western clothing, is clearly representative of a modern orientation, as are the usual questions that require a single, direct, and clear-cut answer. Our approach to the question of the persistence of "the Japanese spirit" has purposely taken a tack contrary to that adopted by those engaged in attitude research. And while there may be less initial hard "science" to our interpretation, we feel that in the examination of change in basic psychological orientations, that which can be quickly and simply converted to numerical schemes is hardly likely to provide a close approximation of reality.

wish to emphasize the readily observed fact that one finds Japanese, especially educated ones, rediscovering an appreciation for various aesthetic and spiritual traditions as they move out of the experiences associated with youth (the educational system, single marital status, and the initial adjustments to work). It is striking, for example, how many men and women return to or take up anew some form of traditional art or hobby in their middle and later years. Also, among middle-aged and older Japanese one often finds a subtle shift of vocabulary and of discussion topics toward the seishin point of view.

The assertion being made here—that the experience of Japanese life correlates the aging process with increasing concern for, and interest in, a traditional outlook—is more than common sense and yet less than documented fact. Virtually anywhere one may expect to find a comparable process, and yet in Japan this process is notably institutionalized, expected, and in agreement with the general sense of personal growth and change in the life cycle. Refinement and wisdom, two important goals of adult personal development, are pursued in Japan along avenues related to or at least parallel with those of seishin development. The result is considerable mutual reinforcement among the entire panoply of traditional pursuits and perspectives as they grow in prominence for the individual over time.

Volunteer movements with a seishin philosophy. Another interesting aspect of the "traditionalism" of older age is the number of clubs and public movements created (mostly by older people) for the purpose of improving society. These tend to be aimed at creating a simple, bright spirit of kindness and good will. Tokyoites know of the famous *chiisa na shinsetsu* ("small kindness") movement led by Shibata Takeshi, and one of the authors recently followed the growth of several similar efforts in Kyushu, one being *wa no kai* ("harmony society") founded by a former company president. Kawabata Yasunari's extensive devotion to the PEN Club also comes immediately to mind as an example of this general type. How might we succinctly characterize these efforts? They are public-service oriented; they have a faith in the goodness of people; they have a belief that "spiritual" improvement will bring general social betterment; and finally, they view the social world as an interdependent whole. The impression given to a cynical outsider is at best one of saccharine naiveté, yet many of the country's great men participate in and frequently lead such efforts with a degree of personal devotion and energy that is amazing.

Not only old people are involved in these activities. Some movements such as OISCA (Organization for International Spiritual and Cultural Advancement), which sends out its own peace corps, and MRA

(Moral Re-Armament)[21] with its efforts to establish a universal morality, are clearly youth oriented. Unfortunately, it is impossible to gauge the number of people involved in voluntary movements of this sort.[22]

Religions: old and new. We do have estimates of the enrollments of Japanese religious groups. While there has quite clearly been a revival of interest in Zen training, it is fair to describe most older religious groups as having to struggle to maintain themselves as institutions. Large numbers of temples are on the brink of bankruptcy and new town developments seldom include a new shrine or temple to serve the needs of the residents.

This is not true of the "new religions", however, and it is to their activities that we must turn for indications of doctrines and teaching practices of dynamic consequence for contemporary Japan. A rough estimate would give the "new religions" between ten and fifteen million members.[23] The number and variety of recently emerged religious groups is certainly great, but all these groups seem to have some qualities in common that relate to our general argument about the continuity of the seishin perspective. They are all characterized by the promise of greater well-being for the individual and society based on a positive attitude and a forgetting of the self, both of which are often facilitated by faith in the teachings of the specific religion. They resemble the movements created by older people in their emphasis on "spiritual" betterment that comes not so much through endurance tests and hardships as through a basic change from a selfish, pessimistic, and constrained attitude to one that is other-centered, optimistic, and expressive.

Each new religion has its own rather elaborate means for encouraging such change. *Seicho no Ie* has training centers in various locations around the country where members may go for ten-day sessions. *PL Kyōdan* uses spiritual training as part of its therapy at its hospitals, and it encourages all its members to participate in its artistic activities (including sports). *Soka Gakkai, Risshō Kōsei Kai* and most others emphasize small group discussion sessions (often led by a

---

21. Moral Re-Armament in Japan is said to have extensive backing from some large companies.

22. OISCA does not have more than a few hundred members, but MRA seems to be much larger with centers in several regions in Japan. How many other similar groups exist is unknown.

23. The "official" figures reported to the government are reported in Agency for Cultural Affairs, *Japanese Religion* (Tokyo, 1972), yet it is generally agreed that these figures are overestimates. Also see Edward Norbeck, *Religion and Society in Modern Japan: Continuity and Change*, Rice University Studies 56, no. 1 (1970).

teacher), and *Ittoen* promotes activities centering on service to others as well as a fundamental lifestyle (one of communal simplicity) designed to teach the proper spiritual outlook.[24] The fact that these efforts undertaken by the new religions are part of a very basic and widespread form of seishin training designed to use attitude change as therapy for illness, lethargy, neurotic states, lack of confidence, and much more can be realized if one compares them with the disparate but yet similar techniques described for Morita therapy, company training for mid-career failures, the teachings of aikido, and prisoner reform in the national penal system.[25]

At this point it would be of value to notice certain underlying differences between the generalized seishin-oriented interpretation of proper attitudes and that assumed to be characteristic of modern popular culture (as presented particularly in the mass media). The seishin outlook does not see the world as inherently divided into class or other interest groups; it chooses to view individuals less in terms of age, wealth, and the like, and more in terms of "spiritual" strength or weakness; it urges a sense of gratitude to others and to society rather than criticism or cynical detachment; it de-emphasizes the possibilities for doctrinal discussion or dispute in favor of psychological change and awakened personal experience; it considers order, individual sacrifice, dedication, hierarchy, thorough organization, a disregard for material disadvantages, and group activity to be expressions of proper attitudes and spirit; and it views traditional teachings and practices as consistent with modern science and industrial society, in effect saying that there is much that is of timeless value in the tradition. On all of these counts, the attitudes taught by the "new religions" are similar to other seishin-oriented teachings and are in rather strong conflict with the "modern" view of the world.

The older religious sects, though they lack institutional dynamics, contribute much the same message in various ways. Inspirational books by Buddhist priests are on best-seller lists,[26] priests appear on

24. Much greater documentation of these and other educational activities can be found in H. Neil MacFarland, *The Rush Hour of the Gods* (New York, 1967); Norbeck, *Religion and Society in Modern Japan*; Harry Thomsen, *The New Religions of Japan* (Tokyo, 1963); and Howard Wimberley, "Self-realization and the Ancestors: An Analysis of Two Japanese Ritual Procedures for Achieving Domestic Harmony," *Anthropology Quarterly* 42, no. 1 (1969): 37–51.

25. For Morita therapy see Richard K. Reynolds, "Directed Behavior Change: Japanese Psychotherapy in a Private Hospital" (Ph.D. diss., University of California at Los Angeles, 1969); for company training see Thomas P. Rohlen, "The Organization and Ideology of a Japanese Bank"; for aikido see Koichi Tohei, *Aikido in Daily Life* (Tokyo, 1966); for prisoner reform see J.I. Kituse, "A Method of Reform in Japanese Prisons," *Orient-West* 7, no. 1 (1962): 17–22.

26. In 1970, for example, the books *Kokoro* and *Michi* by Takada Koin were on the best-seller lists, along with the ever popular writings of *Soka Gakkai* leader Ikeda Daisetsu and those of the *Seichō no Ie* leader Taniguchi Masaharu.

television and at public forums to expresss their understandings, and
in more indirect ways the older religions retain a deep, but not very
dramatic influence in Japanese life. Again, opinion polls, membership
lists, and other quantitative measures cannot fathom the lingering
appeal of Buddhist insight to the average Japanese.

Certain types of youth groups. Readers of the monthly magazine *Jinsei
Techō* (Handbook for living) are treated to a series of articles from
other readers on how they overcame handicaps of one kind or another,
along with practical information on matters of health, career advancement, and the like. The contributors and readers are young people
who, according to their own accounts, lack the educational and social
advantages of the Japanese mainstream. Most are employees of small
firms, from rural backgrounds, and it appears they are typically
members of one general type of youth group (*seinendan* [young men's
association], *bunka sākuru* [culture circle], etc.) that is different from
the youth group activities of both the new religions and the political
parties. Most issues of the magazine run a dozen or so pictures of such
local groups; from the pictures they appear to be much the same type
of people that one will find visiting the national youth training centers.

How many young people are involved in this general framework is
difficult to calculate, but it is clear from the magazine that the basic
teaching involved is of the seishin-oriented kind. Hard work, persistence, and optimism are inevitably crucial ingredients in the solution of
personal problems. Lonely youths, underconfident and disadvantaged,
are attracted to these clubs, so quite naturally a basic theme, along
with club fellowship, is getting ahead by one's own efforts. In this
there are parallels with the membership and teachings of many of
the new religions. The points of overlap include the focus on developing
a sense of *ikigai*, roughly translated as a meaningful, purposeful and
vital sense of life. The stress is, again, on acceptance of problems with
a belief that they can be overcome if met with a sense of challenge and
serious determination. Ultimate success or failure, therefore, rests with
the individual and hinges on his or her strength of character. The
inequalities of the social system recede into insignificance with the
adoption of this perspective.

It is worth noting how similar are the messages in these magazines
to those implicit in the inspirational remarks of successful men as
related in their autobiographies. The readers in many cases are likely
to be the same kind of people. Matsushita's *PHP* (Peace, Happiness,
Prosperity) is, of course, another illustration of such magazines. In
this case, the journal is created by the modern master of the inspirational autobiography, and it, too, uses the personal anecdote as the
valued source of insight. It is as if the parent, teacher, and paternal
leader are not available to offer advice and encouragement for the

young people who typically join these groups and read the magazines and autobiographies. These writings are the descendants of Samuel Smile's *Self-Help*, a book that was a nineteenth-century best-seller in Japan and is still much in evidence today.

The search for value in Japanese tradition. The most recent best-seller on the subject of Japanese character, *The Japanese and the Jews*, is but one of dozens and dozens of other books on this subject (by such authors as Aida Yuji, Ishida Eiichiro, Doi Takeo, and Nakane Chie, to name the most outstanding) attaining general prominence. Many of the largest bookstores have a special table for books detailing the special qualities of everything Japanese from thought and prehistory to etiquette and psychological disorders. This, we think, is indicative of a trend. More and more one expects to find Japanese authors ready to acknowledge the vitality and even the virtue of the Japanese and their traditional legacy, and this no doubt reflects a readiness on the part of their readers to agree. What explains this growing interest in Japaneseness? It appears to represent but the second phase in the recurring pattern of enthusiastic embrace of foreign culture followed by disillusion and rejection in favor of "Japanese" traditions.

The unrivaled success of the country's economy is one factor often mentioned in explanation of this phase. Perhaps Japanese companies and Japan's social system are better than Western ones, a proposition that surprises and appeals to many. Success has brought unrivaled pollution and congestion, too, which raises serious doubts about the desirability of modern technological society—something learned from the West. In both cases what is particularly Japanese about Japan assumes a new importance. To these factors must be added such additional considerations as the crisis in Japanese education, student demonstrations, and the unhappy spectacle of American society over the past decade. This last item contributes to a growing sense that America (and perhaps Europe) has little left to teach Japan that is of value, thus the renewed exploration for value and meaning in what is essentially Japanese. This resurgence of interest is not a movement, nor will it, in and of itself, come to dominate the mass media, but as part of the wider field of seishin-oriented activities and change it is worth recognizing. The search for value within the Japanese tradition appears to be attaining a permanent place among the general topics of public concern in this decade, a situation very different indeed from the almost exclusive public emphasis since 1945 on all that was "democratic," modern, and Western.

One unexpected tangent here is that activist students are showing great interest in the studies of Yanagida Kunio and in Japanese folklore studies in general. Their emphasis on the simple, communal, festive aspects of premodern Japanese villages (a very different view from that of Ariga, Fukutake, and others who emphasized the "feudal hierarchy" aspect of village life) demonstrates a hope that at heart the Japanese folk tradition contains what the students of today desire and what foreign social experiments and ideology seem unable to achieve. This appears as one more variant of an emergent more nativistic frame of mind.

The search for the "true" Japan, it must be noted, is not an overwhelming trend by any means. What is increasingly certain is that individuals, institutions, and the government will not or cannot continue to rely as heavily on the Western shibboleths of economic growth and democratized society. The first goal has been attained and the second has much less promise today as a rallying cry. New goals— welfare society, the effective utilization of leisure time, a return to a clean environment, a better life for the aged—are readily tied up with traditional wisdom and pursuits, and in general the premodern past appears more rosy as these new perspectives and problems move toward center stage.

Traditional arts. One effect of more leisure time and more personal income has been a rapid growth in the number of people taking up some form of traditional art on what we would term a hobby basis.[27] The pursuit of any of these, from flower arranging to judo, involves the student in a serious program of spiritual education, for the growth of skill in these pursuits is closely, if not inextricably, tied to personal spiritual development. In many cases there is an explicit tie with Zen practice and philosophy,[28] making the matter of repetitious but concentrated practice an essential instructional tool designed ultimately to permit an effortless performance in which the self (ga) is forgotten or overcome. Most students, of course, never attain this level of accomplishment, and many are motivated to pursue the traditional arts for a wide variety of other reasons; nevertheless, all are deeply exposed to a seishin-oriented education, and through the experience of actual practice many become convinced of its credibility. People find it difficult to convey their experiences to others (the effects of proper posture and the sense of calm strength, for example), yet this fact itself

27. Precise figures on the number of people studying any particular traditional art have proved impossible to obtain for several reasons. Because of tax calculations, schools (*ryūha*) of art instruction refuse to release figures on the number of their students, and in the martial arts there is no close relationship between the various associations and the actual number of practitioners. Inquiries indicate that schools of tea and flower arranging are thriving, in large measure because of the growth of middle-class families wishing this for their daughters. Most other schools of traditional instruction are also thriving for reasons of general prosperity and greater free time.

28. D. T. Suzuki, *Zen and Japanese Culture* (New York, 1959).

seems to give the seishin perspective greater significance in Japan. What we would label vague and mystical is often appreciated in Japan as real and concrete.

Perhaps all of this is best analyzed as part of the leisure boom in general, but we should not ignore its effects on the manner of thinking of those who engage in such study. We should also notice the place of traditional arts in other social contexts already discussed. Companies, for example, support a variety of such activities for employees, the martial arts are an important aspect of police training, and PL Kyōdan (one of the new religions) makes the study of art a central focus of its doctrine and activities. Even, as in the last case, when there is no distinction between traditional and modern or Japanese and Western in the choice of pursuit, the serious involvement and sense of discipline Japanese bring to such studies is recognizably part of the seishin outlook.

Government educational activities. It is well known that until the end of World War II the national school system was the leading institution in the effort to strengthen the character of youth, teach the Japanese viewpoint, and create dependable and willing adults. To teach the "Japanese spirit" (*yamato damashii* and *nippon no seishin*) was a high priority goal for all levels of the nation's schools. The Occupation successfully opposed this as a proper goal of education on the grounds that it had been a cornerstone of Japanese militarism; but in doing so it created what many still regard as a moral and spiritual vacuum in the life of postwar youth. Older leaders, including those sponsoring company seishin training, point to this vacuum as justification for their efforts. A parallel trend is that sponsored by the Liberal Democratic party, which has been moving slowly toward the reconstitution of moral education (*dōtoku kyōiku*) as part of the national public school curriculum. The situation at present, however, hardly satisfies the older generation.[29]

The Ministry of Education conducts a few programs directed to the general purpose of teaching morality and developing in the young a seishin-oriented perspective. Norbeck offers a useful discussion of the official moral education textbooks offered to all secondary schools since 1958 (for use on a voluntary basis).[30] These emphasize upright-ness, public service, a bright, positive attitude, and efforts for self-improvement within a framework of interpretation that includes the seishin emphasis on endurance and proper attitude as crucial to a

29.   See John Singleton, *Nichū: A Japanese School* (New York, 1970) for an account of parental demands for greater moral education in one semiurban area.

30.   Norbeck, *Religion and Society in Modern Japan*, pp. 126–32.

strong character. The stories in the textbooks, like so much of the seishin form of education, are of a strongly sentimental nature, derived from the presentation of good and bad behavior in one of a variety of intimate social contexts such as family, friendship, and classroom. By showing how the strong in spirit can significantly aid others and preserve the valuable qualities of personal relations, stories in the moral textbooks tie the seishin perspective to personal emotion on the one hand and social well-being on the other. It is notable in this connection that, as Norbeck writes, "Kindness and thoughtfulness should flow from one naturally,"[31] much as in traditional arts a skilled performance should flow naturally or in work, joy and pleasure should come naturally.

The ministry has a few other notable ongoing training efforts that appear designed to support the moral education program. The encouragement of traditional sports, particularly judo and kendo in high schools, is one of the most prominent of these. The other with which the authors have some familiarity is the establishment of a number of national youth training centers[32] (*kokuritsu seinen no ie*) where groups of young people (mostly *seinendan* but also company and governmental and even university groups) may come ostensibly to pursue their own programs for self-development. These centers, all of which are new, are typically located in national parks, and their facilities (dormitories, gyms, cafeterias, playing fields, etc.) are comparable to the best in Japan. The resident staff are often former military men and the daily routine at the centers includes a flag-raising ceremony and group exercise period.

The government's efforts to sponsor morality and the Japanese spirit are obviously greatly diminished compared with the prewar effort, and there is no longer much emphasis on patriotic themes and military forms of self-sacrifice. In fact, the present school system is commonly interpreted as a factor contributing to the decline of traditional values. This assessment could only be challenged on empirical grounds that are presently lacking, but it is worth underlining the fact that the trend of official policy is not toward further "Americanization," but rather leads in the direction of a modest return of Japanese emphases and a general intensification of the socialization for good citizenship. The proper place for such efforts, most older people feel, is the schools, not assorted companies, religions, and other entities, and in the coming decade the schools are worth careful scrutiny in this regard.

Our emphasis on the persistence of the seishin perspective in an

31. Ibid., p. 127.
32. There are presently six of these.

assortment of contemporary social contexts has depended on a definition of the seishin outlook that is sufficiently broad as to include quite
different practices, interpretations, attitudes, goals, and social realms.
It is unlikely that the average Japanese would find our attempts to
lump so much together totally convincing at first glance. (How many
Americans will agree about similar general value concepts?) And yet
in the context of a comparison with the general stereotype of what is
Westernized and modern in the realm of popular attitudes, our discussion of a seishin world view delineates a fairly clear alternative
position. Also, the large overlap of basic vocabulary among the various
teachings discussed provides another, more empirical, indication that
we have not gone beyond the bounds of reasonable interpretation.

There are, however, some comments to be made about subcategory
variation that are also of interest. We should note that the higher one
goes in the modern social system and the older one grows, the more one
finds an emphasis on hard (kibishii) training, on Zen-influenced
perspectives and on the unity of art and seishin education. Company
white-collar training, the emphasis on expression in PL Kyōdan, the
study of traditional arts, and the interest in Zen among university
students are, in essence, all developments involving the urbanized
middle class already adjusted to the modern socioeconomic situation.
In comparison, the majority of new religions and the kinds of youth
groups we have discussed have tended to enroll people who are disadvantaged in various ways and who have not yet found a satisfactory
place in the modern social system.[33] In this latter group, the emphasis
tends to be on attaining or keeping good health, on overcoming disadvantages, and on achieving economic success. While these differences
are very important to note, it is perhaps more important to view them
as transformations of the basic seishin perspective. Each variation,
that is, depends greatly on the particular social context, especially the
needs, interests, and established understandings of the specific group
of people involved.

As regards the future import of the seishin perspective in Japanese
life, the following points would seem crucial:

1. Virtually all Japanese today are familiar with its tenets and most experience
    some form of seishin education. There is every indication that this will
    continue to be true in the 1980s.
2. The subgroups that focus on spiritualism are many and varied, some may
    go and others may arise, but the attitudes they represent are a permanent
    part of the scene.

33. The leveling off of the growth of the new religions probably reflects just such sociological
boundaries.

3. Extreme subgroups of a political nature such as Mishima's *Tate no kai* (Shield Society) are only a minute part of the general picture. They show no signs of growth into popular movements, but their particular brand of influence (forceful confrontation and assassination) requires few followers.

4. When social problems of any kind arise, it is likely that spiritualism will be one suggested solution. More moral education, stricter discipline, and harder training will continue to be advocated by some as reasonable answers to student unrest, business slumps, political turmoil, juvenile crime, and the like. The greater the problems, the more important seishin education will appear, and the larger the number of people who will, temporarily at least, stress its importance.

5. Yet only problems of cataclysmic proportions could lead to anything remotely resembling the prewar days. War and economic depression have in the past caused a massive shift toward the seishin perspective, but, needless to say, neither of these is likely prospect for Japan in the 1980s.

6. The trend toward a new interest in and appreciation of the Japanese heritage will provide some redress for the excessive preoccupation with the American model during the last twenty-five years, but such a trend hardly has the impetus even to begin to dominate Japanese life. Here again, only extraordinary events could bring it into prominence.

When the future development of popular thought and value in Japan is considered, the broad base of seishin education outside the school system and the family must be acknowledged and its influence within the much more general course of popular culture somehow calculated. The point here is not only that modern Japan will continue to be characterized by tremendous variation, especially as it is viewed along such dimensions as Japanese-Western and modern-traditional, but that most Japanese will continue to be informed by a number of very different ideological, aesthetic, and psychological perspectives. Because there is such variation among the institutions sponsoring seishin-oriented education, the perspective has remarkable resilience over time and broad currency over the entire society. For reasons of this kind, one can predict the continuity of the present collection of polarities of thought, the persistence of generational differences, and the continuity of cyclical shifts in fashion from one emphasis to another, revolving within an already established framework. Although a new appreciation of Japaneseness among the book-reading public is now fashionable, the new religions are slowing down in growth and influence, and in our general framework this represents a countertrend.

We predict that the seishin perspective will be a constant aspect of Japanese life in future years, in part because other changes in Japanese society will encourage a thirst for what it offers and will underline the continuing need for attention to the individual as something more than a worker, consumer, or pleasure seeker. As a counterpoint to the complexity, impersonal technology, and change of modern life, a seishin orientation will continue to hold out the promise of a different set of rewards and a different kind of ultimate meaning.

The *Danchi Zoku* and the Evolution
of Metropolitan Mind

CHRISTIE W. KIEFER

Christie Kiefer presents the struggle for a new synthesis of tradition and modernity in the Japanese mind in broader and more sweeping terms than Austin or Frager and Rohlen. He poses the problem in this way: Japanese culture is relatively particularistic, situational, sociocentric, and feeling-oriented. But urbanization, one of the most striking aspects of the development of Japanese society, makes people secular, rational, blasé, individualistic, and alienated. The conflict between the two worlds of past and present, moreover, is not a simple conflict; for "gesellschaft doesn't usually just replace gemeinschaft; it is added on." The extrarational in the most modern cultures of urbanization is still vital.

What then will be the psychological effects of accelerated urbanism in Japan? Kiefer suggests we look at the danchi (suburban high-rise apartment) lifestyle for clues to the future. Danchi life is a life of tiny spaces, physically cut off from the larger community and lacking collective facilities. The population is homogeneous, with no established social structure, and social control is minimal. Most danchi-dwellers hope to move out but have less and less chance of doing so because of the congested housing market. Informal relations among the population are cool and tentative; males are absent most of the time; the worst psychological problems are borne by women with young children and take the characteristic form of danchi noiroze ("danchi neurosis") or ikuji noiroze ("child-rearing neurosis"). The suffering of danchi women that derives from boredom and isolation is accompanied by freedom, the opportunity for greater voluntary social and organizational activity, and relatively high status.

The likely social outcomes of this unprecedented lifestyle are interesting. Kiefer suggests that leisure time will expand, work will be more cut off from life, and the mobility of people and ideas will increase. The extended family will die out, individual anonymity will increase, and community cohesion will decline. Women will be more independent and the nuclear family will make greater demands on all its members.

The psychological implications of the lifestyle are rather mixed. Kiefer predicts that diffuse gregariousness and "individuality" will increase with increased mobility. Similarly, mobility and privatization will mean that control over sexual behavior will be shifted to the individual from the group, through guilt rather than shame, autonomy rather than heteronomy. There will be greater awareness, and less repression, of aggression. But there will be less tolerance of dependency needs that were formerly socially accepted. The individual will suffer from a sense of loss of control, standardization, and regimentation because, while personal freedom will indeed increase, political power will be increasingly aggregated and centralized by big government and big industry. There will exist on the one hand a tendency toward self-differentiation and individualization, on the other a tendency toward merging into the large group; between them the traditional Japanese small-group lifestyle will disappear.

The danchi-ization of Japanese society will provoke individualism and autonomy but will offer at the same time fewer outlets for them. This view of the synthesis of tradition and modernity is one that predicts increasing unhappiness and frustration. These phenomena may take the private form of depression and neurosis or the public form of radical and millenarian political activism.—L. A.

Traditional Japanese society has valiantly survived—through many metamorphoses—a century of urbanization and industrialization. But the pace of change seems to be accelerating so rapidly that it now threatens to level the last seeding grounds of tradition and sow there an entirely new cultural strain: a rootless and thoroughly rational-industrial way of life. Although it is unlikely that any great changes in Japanese habits of thinking and feeling will take place in the next five years, there may be some indicators of the shape of things to come in the psychological effects of specific changes in family, community, work, housing, and leisure that have already been at work among the most visibly progressive elements for some twenty years.

My intention, then, is to examine the more significant behavioral changes that have accompanied the development of mass apartment housing in Japan and to forecast the future direction of such changes on the basis of these data. In order to make clear my reasons for choosing mass apartment housing, or *danchi*, as the barometer of psychological change, I must first discuss the psychology of urbanization in a broader context. Thus a sketch of the main characteristics of Japanese personality that seem to distinguish the average Japanese from his mainstream urban American counterpart will be considered against the idea of a universal metropolitan character.[1]

Compared with Western urbanites, Japanese tend to be particularis-

1.   In referring to "mainstream urban" America, I exclude certain culturally distinct ghettos in American cities. See Herbert Gans, *The Urban Villagers* (New York, 1962), and Ulf Hannerz, *Soul Side: Inquiries into Ghetto Culture and Community* (New York, 1969).

tic and situational, sociocentric, and feeling-oriented. Particularism and situationality refer to the tendency of Japanese to alter their perceptions and values according to the immediate social demands of the situation. In contrast to the "universalistic" Westerner, a Japanese is not likely to see any contradiction in being a Buddhist at a funeral and a Shintoist at a wedding on the same day. A wife who scolds her husband in the bath for some shortcoming will show him absolute respect in the presence of their children, with little sense of irony. Truth and morality are socially constituted; they are specific to the inter-action at hand. A correlate of this trait-complex is a nondualistic approach to logic. The Japanese tend to accept apparent contradictions as complementary facets of the same truth. They rarely insist on consistency and are inclined to refer to narrowly logical people as *rikutsuppoi*, that is, "reason-freaks."

Sociocentrism is another facet of personality in a society that tends to prefer relationships that are binding, stable, and all-encompassing to those that are contracted and dissolved on the basis of specific utility. Although kinship (and fictive kinship) is no longer the basis of nearly all important social relations as it was in ancient times, roles and attitudes characteristic of the family continue to provide archetypes for much of social life. The durability and functional diffuseness of groups are complementary features. Since one cannot be highly com-mitted to many relationships without experiencing severe role conflicts, the more functions served by each enduring relationship the better. Conversely, the willingness of partners in a relationship to look after a wide range of reciprocal needs helps to assure mutual loyalty and the stability of the relationship.

Thus the sense of the self is less separate from membership in specific groups than is the case in urban America. Although Japanese are often acutely aware of discrepancies, for instance, between inner feelings and outward role demands, they think of the latter, not the former, as the really important center of the self. Regarding feelings as highly idio-syncratic and hard to control, and therefore less reliable as sources of self-respect than statuses and roles, the Japanese tends to include within the boundaries of his concept of self much of the quality of the intimate social groups of which the individual is a member. In contrast, the urban American self-concept is apt to stop at the skin. The psy-chological cost of such Japanese personality organization is a certain rigidity and vulnerability of the ego in the absence of familiar social supports. Friendship is difficult to enter into, as well as difficult to lose.

Feeling-orientedness is also a correlate of particularism and socio-centricity. Because the spontaneous expression of strong emotion can disrupt long-term relationships, Japanese are in the habit of avoiding heated emotional confrontation. On the other hand, people who, like the Japanese, spend large periods of their lives in close contact develop great sensitivity to each other's subtle emotional messages, and Japanese are unusually sensitive to their own and others' feelings. This feeling-orientedness is seen in the rich introspections of Japanese literature as well as in the cultivation of sensory pleasures, both aesthetic and erotic. The reliance on feelings is borne out by self-concept data. Twenty-eight Japanese adolescents responding to the McPartland-Kuhn Twenty Statements Test turned out to be much more inclined to describe themselves by means of private feelings than to list social roles.[2] This contrasts sharply with American norms[3] and is substantiated by other studies in Japan.[4]

PSYCHOLOGICAL URBANIZATION

Certain parallels seem to exist between the Japanese character and the characteristic personality traits of nonurban peoples elsewhere, and this apparent similarity, together with the popular idea that urbanization has had a homogenizing influence on Western personality, tempts us to view Japan as a latecomer to a general process of urbanization, following at some distance in the psychological footsteps of the West. Students of urbanization in the West tend to focus on the decline of intimate, lifelong, face-to-face relations and the psychological effects of this process. Preindustrial society is seen as relatively homogeneous, slow-changing, and religious with a greater integration of the various levels of psychological functioning—emotional and intellectual—and an individual sense of participation in all areas of culture—religious, economic, political, and artistic. The urban person is seen in contrast as more secular and rational, more blasé, more individualistic, and more alienated from others as well as from the nonrational, emotional, "primitive" levels of his own psyche. The enormous increase in the size and complexity of the cultural environment is said to lead the city dweller to a perception of self and others as mere cogs in a machine that is ultimately beyond understanding and control.[5]

2.   Christie W. Kiefer, "Personality and Social Change in a Japanese Danchi" (Ph. D. diss., University of California, Berkeley, 1968), pp. 171–72.

3.   Manfred Kuhn and Thomas McPartland, "An Empirical Investigation of Self-Attitudes," *American Sociological Review* 19, no. 1 (1954):68–76.

4.   Akira Hoshino and R. Atsumi, "The Relationships between Self-Attitudes of Children and the Adjustment Level as Rated by Peer Group," *Japan Psychological Research* 4, no. 3 (1960): 135–38.

5.   Robert Redfield, *Peasant Society and Culture* (Chicago, 1956); George Simmel, "The Metropolis and Mental Life," in *The Sociology of George Simmel*, ed. Kurt Wolff (Glencoe, Ill., 1950), pp. 409–24.

Before we apply the above model of psychological urbanization to the future of Japan, I think we can improve it some by looking at the findings of urban ethnology in the last two decades. While there is little doubt that the scale and complexity of urban life is very different from that of nonurban life, it appears that most modern urbanites participate in something like a community that insulates them from mass society and its alienation. They develop skills for dealing with the fast-paced, rational, impersonal milieu of "downtown" but exercise this skill only periodically, between periods of retrenchment in more familiar company. In the course of their lives, urbanites typically pass through phases of both high and low participation in the free-flowing society of the cabaret and the market. Gans's "action seekers"[6] and Hannerz's "swingers"[7] represent developmental stages of high participation. Gesellschaft does not replace gemeinschaft; it is merely added on.

It is also my impression that the atrophy of the religious, extra-rational, emotional side of the personality that is supposed to come with urbanization is not a linear process. Schooler found, for instance, that in the United States a kind of self-conscious subjectivism was positively related to urban residence, religious nonfundamentalism, and father's education.[8] Individuality as an ethos can as easily promote a sense of the legitimacy of personal feelings and fantasies as alienation, hyperrationality, and mechanical thinking. The popularity of exotic belief systems and therapy modes in the modern American city gives some indication of the vitality of the extrarational among the most educated classes.

Even with these qualifications, the theory of psychological urbanization seems applicable to Japan, where, however, the process may not have gone as far as in the West. Such structural features of Japanese society as fictive kinship and the seniority system keep the urban individual in close, stable networks of association. The emphasis on formal interaction rituals between casual acquaintances produces an additional buffer between the typical urbanite and the anonymous macrocosm of his society. Japanese give the impression of being less comfortable than Americans in social situations where mutual familiarity is low, suggesting that the specific interaction skills associated with successful urbanism in the West have yet to reach a high level of development in Japan.

6.   Gans, *Urban Villagers*, pp. 28–31.
7.   Hannerz, *Soul Side*, pp. 42–46.
8.   Carmi Schooler, "Social Antecedents of Adult Psychological Functioning," *American Journal of Sociology* 78, no. 2 (1972):299–322.

It also appears to me that emotional life is less privatized in the Japanese city than in the Western. There are many occasions in Japanese social life that are set aside, as it were, for the expression and release of pent-up emotions that ordinarily must be suppressed. At parties, on holidays, and when drunk or ill, the urban Japanese can express these normally taboo feelings openly in the company of others. On such occasions, the normal distinctions of status and role are held somewhat in suspension, in a way that reminds one of the rites of intensification often described by students of folk and primitive societies.[9] Whereas one finds some parallels to these rituals in American society (such as the office Christmas party), my impression is that they are much less frequent and generally less giddy.[10]

THE DANCHI ZOKU

In order to forecast the psychological effects of accelerated urbanization in Japan in the coming years, I have chosen to apply this model of psychological change to a fast-growing and socially progressive sector of Japanese society—namely, the danchi zoku. The term *danchi* refers both to a type of living environment and to a social class. Any very large building or group of buildings full of small, low-cost modern apartments might qualify for the term, if it is available for occupancy by anyone who can afford the rent and its rental rates attract mainly young salaried men and their families. Although the native definition seems to exclude relief housing open only to low-income families, *shataku* operated by large firms for their employees, small private rental operations, and any kind of old fashioned housing, there remains a very wide variety of dwellings within the definition, such as large privately or cooperatively owned apartment developments, those developments owned and operated for general occupancy by municipalities (*shigaichi jutaku*), and developments built and operated by the nationally sponsored Japan Housing Corporation (JHC). Since the latter is the largest and best studied category of danchi, I will be using it as the standard and source of my remarks about the danchi zoku in general, unless otherwise noted.

My use of the danchi zoku as a kind of barometer of psychological change is not meant to imply either that they represent a qualitative departure from the norms of the wider society or that their specific lifestyle will ever become the predominant one in Japanese life.

9. See, for example, Victor Turner, *The Ritual Process: Structure and Anti-Structure* (Chicago, 1969).

10. Americans seem to prefer dyads when it comes to intimate emotional relations, in contrast to the Japanese preference for larger groups, though some recent American experiments in group living might indicate a reversal of this tendency.

Rather, I see them as a large and growing example of progressive trends in the culture. They are viewed by their countrymen and by themselves as "modernistic" (*kindaiteki*), "progressive" (*shimpōteki*), and slightly above average in living standard.[11] Their income is slightly higher than the average urban wage earner, they are better educated than average, they have smaller families, and a larger proportion work in large industries.[12] Most important of all, however, is their overall physical and social lifestyle, which is just about the most "rationalized," massified and standardized in Japan. Before discussing that lifestyle and its psychological consequences, I will outline briefly its origins.

At the end of World War II, one-fifth of the Japanese population had been without housing of any kind, and in the mid-1950s the Japanese government was still struggling with an urban housing crisis of disastrous proportions. A program of low-interest loans for new construction, and makeshift housing for the destitute, had taken some of the pressure of the crisis off the upper and lower strata of Japanese society, but there remained the problem of the growing young urban white-collar class. These people, by virtue of education and occupation, were a kind of elite, and yet they could not afford adequate housing anywhere near the major cities in which they worked. The Japan Housing Corporation (*Nihon Jūtaku Kōdan*), created in 1955 in emulation of the model of the public building corporations founded in postwar Britain under the New Towns Act, was authorized to deal with the problem in two ways. First, inexpensive mass rental housing was to be constructed for middle-income families, that is, families whose income totalled at least five-and-one-half times the rental rates of the housing units. The second approach was to develop tracts of unused land near urban centers and settle these tracts densely in an effort to deflate the cost of surrounding residential land, thereby bringing real estate ownership within the means of middle-income families in the cities.

By 1971, sixteen years after its creation, the Japan Housing Corporation had built 639,000 dwellings on 51,900 acres of land, providing housing for about two million people. Indeed, about 5 percent of the nation's total new construction in the last five years has involved JHC projects. Most of these dwellings are built either for rental or for sale in large housing complexes built on unused or redeveloped land near large metropolitan centers; that is, danchi in the true sense of the word. Some of these complexes house upward of 100,000—for example, the

11. Nihon Jūtaku Kōdan, '*Sumai' ni kan-suru shufu no ishiki chosa—danchi, apaato* [A survey of housewives' dwelling consciousness—danchi, apartments], May 1972, pp. 90–91.

12. Kasamatsu Kelichi, *Danchi no subete* [All about danchi] (Tokyo, 1963).

colossal Tama New Town in Tokyo has a target population of 410,000. A 1973 JHC survey revealed that only one out of four Japanese expects to own a single-family house when he gets married, and only one in eight expects to reach this goal in his first residential move after marriage. One-fourth expected to live in public apartment housing and another fourth in some form of private or company apartment housing after marriage.[13]

Physically, the white-collar danchi resembles a giant apiary. It is an orderly cluster of very large buildings, usually four or five stories tall and containing from sixteen to thirty identical apartments each. The apartments are tiny, even by Japanese standards, averaging about one-third the size of those of Whyte's "Park Foresters."[14] This tiny space is laid out for "rational" use, much as in a trailer or a boat, with a minimum of wasted space. Each apartment is self-sufficient, having its own tub, toilet, kitchen, living room or rooms, and balcony for drying clothes and airing bedding. With the exception of tatami flooring and sliding paper interior doors, materials are durable and require little maintenance. The tiny size and "rationalized" layout reduce the housekeeping task to a minimum, and, with the help of their electrical and gas appliances, women can run the home with a fraction of the time and effort necessary even in present-day "traditional" type housing. There are no collective facilities within the buildings where people live—no laundry rooms, storage rooms, lobbies, or game rooms. Community activities are concentrated in centralized service areas where the resident finds shops, schools, meeting halls, and other public facilities. The danchi stands out from the surrounding environment, its high concrete walls rising in well-disciplined ranks over the jumble of tile roofs, shops, and paddy fields of its surroundings. The residents of one danchi near Osaka proudly named their new neighborhood association the *Hakuakai*, "White Wall Association."

The physical distinctness of the danchi community is underscored by the unusual aspects of its social organization. Overwhelmingly populated by the new middle class, it is unlike most other Japanese communities in that its families are relatively homogeneous in age, occupation, education, and income. Since the danchi has not grown organically and has no history, it has no social structure on moving-in day. There is no elite class from which leaders might be chosen, despite the definite need for leadership. The creation of the danchi typically raises unforeseen problems in the local community, among them in-

13. Economic Planning Agency, *Kokumin seikatsu hakusho: Nihonjin no kurashi to sono shitsu* [White paper on national living standards: The life of the Japanese and its quality] (Tokyo, 1973).
14. William H. Whyte, *The Organization Man* (Garden City, N.Y., 1956).

adequate schools and transportation facilities, rising prices, and voting and tax problems. Responsibility for these ills is not always clearly defined, and often both the JHC and local community have to be pressured if the problems at the danchi are to be solved. The early years of the danchi-as-community are open season on leadership. Strong personalities tend to emerge as advocates of this or that reform, and these "self-government peddlers," as one Japanese journalist calls them,[15] vie for stable power positions in the community. In the absence of game rules, the contest sometimes gets pretty hot.

Related to the problem of finding leadership is the phenomenon of general apathy toward community government and cooperation. Whereas members of the middle class often play active leadership roles in ordinary Japanese communities, the efforts of would-be danchi leaders to build "community consciousness" among their neighbors are largely fruitless, for the great majority of the danchi residents are simply not joiners. The explanation of this situation is complex. It appears reasonable to assume that the noncommunality of the typical danchi resident stems from a lack of any stake in the future of the community. Since he hopes to move out of the danchi either to a danchi in some other city or to his own home some day, and since he has no equity in his danchi apartment, any enthusiasm for community organizations is hard to sustain. While transient status undoubtedly accounts for part of the situation, it does not explain the difference between the danchi dweller and other highly mobile middle-class populations. Whyte's "Park Foresters," for example, or Dobriner's "Levittowners"[16] were in much the same state of temporariness, yet, by comparison, they were veritable gluttons for organization.

If we stay with this comparison, we can see another obstacle to community-mindedness specific to the Japanese white-collar class. As Vogel noted, the salaried man works in a highly structured social environment remote from the community in both space and values.[17] Because the Japanese bureaucracy to some extent retains the quasi-kinship ethos of its archetype, the medieval clan, the work environment makes much heavier demands on the employee's time and loyalty than are made on his American counterpart. A cursory look at a lower-class housing project indicated to me that a lack of strong involvement in groups outside the community was partly responsible for a greater involvement on the part of the lower-class husband in the affairs of the community. By contrast, the absence of the middle-class danchi

15. Nozewa Hiroshi, *Danchi* (Tokyo, 1964).
16. William Dobriner, *Class in Suburbia* (Englewood Cliffs, N.J., 1963).
17. Ezra Vogel, *Japan's New Middle Class* (Berkeley, 1963).

male from his community is so conspicuous that it has earned him the title *geshukunin papa* ("lodger papa"), and his community itself *Beddo Taun* ("Bed Town").

Yet another reason for the absence of general cooperative activity within the danchi has been the lack of a real and present common enemy. When such an enemy did appear, in the form of threatened rent hikes in 1970, the national organization of Kodan Jutaku Jichikai set up a National Liaison Council to Oppose Rent Hikes. By mobilizing large numbers of residents to protest publicly the proposed rent hikes, the council succeeded in forestalling hikes at already occupied JHC dwellings in 1970 and 1971. Whether such activities will lead to a stable political organization centering on JHC tenants will be a question worth pursuing in the coming decade.

Aside from the matter of community spirit and formal organization, informal neighborhood relations in the danchi tend to be cool and tentative. This pertains primarily to women, because most of the men are absent for about twelve hours a day, six days a week, and tend to have few contacts with their neighbors. The self-sufficiency of a white-collar danchi family all but removes the necessity of the associations based on economic sharing commonly found in lower-class projects and in socioeconomically heterogeneous urban neighborhoods.[18] In fact, economic self-sufficiency is a point of honor with most danchi residents, as exemplified in another social pattern more conspicuous in the danchi than anywhere else in Japan—namely, keeping up with the Suzukis.

Viewing Japan at the end of World War II, novelist Osaragi Jiro wrote that the Japanese had always made a virtue of poverty but that the war and defeat had glutted their taste for it, and the new generation would value nothing that did not glitter.[19] Perhaps he was right, and perhaps Simmel was also right in ascribing an economic-materialistic view of the world to all thoroughly urban people. At any rate, given the value of material means and the need to acquire the respect of one's neighbors, two aspects of the danchi environment seem to fan the flames of conspicuous consumption. One is what Dobriner has called the "visibility principle."[20] In contrast to the traditional Japanese home, which was cloistered within its wall and its garden, the danchi apartment exposes its tenants and their possessions to the community. Looking up at the columns and rows of balconies on a typical danchi building, each festooned with the daily wash, one finds it temptingly easy to compare the qualities of socks and underwear.

18. Ronald Dore, *City Life in Japan* (Berkeley, 1958).
19. Osaragi Jiro, *Homecoming* (New York, 1954).
20. Dobriner, *Class in Suburbia*, p. 75.

There are, additionally, relatively few criteria other than material ones by which to evaluate one's status in the community. Young and Willmott[21] noticed a sudden thirst for material possessions on the part of East Londoners who moved from the slums to a New Town in the suburbs, a thirst occasioned by the draining away of their nonmaterial statuses as the son of so-and-so, the fellow with the best jokes, or the one who had had a small moment of glory on such-and-such a memorable day. To most of its neighbors, the danchi family is known largely by its appearances. These factors would lack meaning, of course, if it were not for the relative status deprivation of the upwardly mobile surrounded by upwardly mobiles.

The lack of formal structure and status hierarchy in the danchi community results in a great deal of latitude for individual self-expression in interpersonal relations. Since there is little effective means for enforcing community norms—in fact, little knowledge of what those norms are, if any—social control is minimal, and community ideals and goals are less obvious than personal ones. Given this state of affairs, danchi women must find their own guidelines for interaction in order to carry out their roles as mothers and wives, as well as to satisfy their needs for sociability.

Morioka Kiyomi, in an intricate study of the social relationships of a group of women in a Tokyo danchi in 1961,[22] discovered certain interesting patterns. For one thing, he found that informal sociability was particularly difficult for women with small children. Over half of the women interviewed who had children under three years of age reported having no intimate friends or neighborhood relations whatsoever. There are probably several reasons for this. Obviously, women with small children have less free time and less freedom of movement than those with no children or older children. Also, middle-class Japanese norms regarding ideal motherly and wifely behavior tend to condemn recreation and the pursuit of personal enjoyment for young mothers. I suspect that yet another factor is the association between having young children and having a tight family budget. Mothers with very young children (babies) are probably more often than not married to relatively younger men with lower salaries than are the mothers of older children; at the same time, they are burdened with expenses the nonmothers do not have. The now legendary isolation of the young mother in the danchi, coupled with a value system that puts tremendous emphasis on the grooming of children (from the

21. Michael Young and Peter Willmott, *Family and Kinship in East London* (London, 1957).
22. Morioka Kiyomi, "Life History and Social Participation of Families in Danchi Public Housing Project in a Suburb of Tokyo," *Japan Institute of International Affairs Annual Review*, n.d., pp. 92–158.

cradle on) for success in the highly competitive education and job markets of the metropolis, has given rise to the term *ikuji noiroze* ("child-rearing neurosis") to describe her cramped, anxious life.

Regarding the strain of living in close quarters with a minimum of human contact, a 1972 JHC survey reported that 24 percent of danchi wives interviewed said they themselves had at one time or another suffered from another new folk disease of similar etiology—*danchi noiroze*.[23] Although the physical environment was listed as a frequent cause of this epidemic difficulty, by far the largest cause listed (by 59 percent) was "human relations." The same percentage specifically mentioned human contacts outside the home as the way of overcoming danchi noiroze.[24]

Further analysis of Morioka's findings reveals an important pattern in *type* of informal social interaction: the higher the education and income of the woman, the more likely she is to associate with people in voluntary "circle activities" centering on educational and handicraft pursuits, friends living outside her neighborhood within the danchi and friends living outside the danchi. Conversely, the lower a woman's education and family income, the more likely she is to have her intimate relationships restricted to her neighborhood. It would appear that better education and higher income broaden the range of possible choice in informal relations.

The cultivation of purely voluntary relationships based on mutual interest may be a new pattern for young middle-class wives. The relative absence of an ethic of voluntary sociability can be gathered from a study of feelings of isolation conducted in three large danchi in the early 1960s:[25]

	Percent men	Percent women
Living in a danchi is desirable, because you can get away from people if you want to.	70.2	60.1
Living in a danchi is lonely, because people withdraw from each other.	8.2	15.3
Living in a danchi is annoying, because you can't get away from people.	6.2	10.5
Living in a danchi is desirable, because people can't withdraw from each other.	14.5	11.2

23. Nihon Jūtaku Kōdan, '*Sumai*' *ni kan-suru shufu no ishiki chosa*, p. 94.
24. Ibid., p. 95.
25. Adapted from Tsutomu Takenaka, *Danchi nanatsu no daizai* [The seven deadly sins of the danchi] (Tokyo, 1964).

According to the same study, over 70 percent of both sexes preferred living in circumstances where it is possible to withdraw from neighbors, and almost that many preferred the anonymity of the danchi to more traditional communities for that reason. My own observations in a danchi confirm this trend, although Morioka concludes from his data that informal socializing between women is on the increase.

If voluntary sociability is in fact growing among the most progressive elements in Japanese society, this trend could, in the long run, greatly affect the mental habits of the nation as a whole. I will return to this point below, but here I must say a word about some possible causes of greater voluntary sociability. I have already mentioned boredom as a motive. The confining space and the great reduction in housework characteristic of danchi living leave women with a good deal of free time and very limited ways of spending it within their own homes. Many are literally driven out of their solitude this way. Another very important factor is the relatively high status of women in the danchi. As I said, the vast majority of danchi husbands commute to work outside the neighborhood; therefore, during the day the danchi is a community of women. Much of the business of running the community, as well as the home, thus falls on the wives' shoulders. Furthermore, the danchi husband's status is typically anchored in his office group, and he tends to leave his status in his community to his wife. As long as she stays out of trouble, she is more or less free to associate with whom she pleases. Neither is she likely to be under the watchful eye of a parent or parent-in-law, since most danchi households are nuclear family in structure.[26]

Finally, the relative age and class homogeneity of the danchi has a complex effect on patterns of association. It leads to status competition among neighbors, but it also multiplies the possibilities of forming relationships on the basis of common interest, discouraging patron-client types of relationship of the sort familiar in traditional rural communities and urban neighborhoods.[27] Furthermore, the physical environment itself provides some impetus for the cultivation of mutual-interest relationships since there are few common facilities at the neighborhood level other than stairwells, dust chutes, and playgrounds for small children. Neighbors must seek each other out in order to form close ties.

THE DANCHI FAMILY

Current folk sociology in Japan seems to hold that the nuclear

26. In the danchi I studied in 1965–66, 10.3 percent of the households contained kin of the husband or wife, and 83.4 percent were nuclear families; "Personality and Social Change in Japanese Danchi," p. 53.

27. Compare Dore, *City Life in Japan*, pp. 191–210.

family is gaining ground against other institutions as the locus of values. One frequently hears such terms as "my-home-ism" and "leisure boom." Unfortunately, I have no solid historical data to document this trend among danchi dwellers. I did ask my danchi informants questions about the relative importance of family and job, family and community, family and authority (*ie*), and family and friends, but the responses were highly idiosyncratic and I have no time depth by which to plot trends. Comparison of my danchi responses with data gathered from a lower class "control" sample indicates no clear-cut differences, except that danchi tenants depict themselves as slightly more self-assertive in the face of authority or community pressure.

If "my-home-ism" is on the rise in the danchi, as folklore would have it, the twin reasons would appear to be the decline of community and ie authority, and the relative power of wives whose main loyalty is to the nuclear family. It is interesting that, in the danchi studied, many wives had begun to take active roles in such organizations as the Women's Association and the PTA and, through these organizations, to challenge traditionally male-dominated institutions such as schools and city government. Typically, women justified this sort of "questionable" behavior in terms of their duties to their husbands and children. I think it is safe to say, at any rate, that the status of the nuclear family in the danchi, vis-à-vis both personal-individual goals and those of other institutions, is in a state of flux. "My-home-ism" may be a transitional stage between the premetropolitan pattern and an ethic of stark individuality. Indeed, we are even beginning to hear about *ūman ribbu* (women's lib).

Upward Mobility

We now come to one of the most critical problems faced by the danchi zoku, the question of their status in the wider Japanese society. Salaried men are quite sensitive to such status indicators as income and consumption habits, and the press keeps them supplied with a steady stream of national statistics against which to measure themselves. Since so many danchi household heads are between 25 and 40 years old, it is not too difficult for a salaried man to accept danchi status during the early years of his marriage and career if he can continually reassure himself that he will have graduated to home ownership by the time he has reached the age at which staying in the danchi might be a sign of failure. For most, the desire to escape the danchi environment is strong, for the danchi is a kind of status limbo—a symbol of halfway success that serves to whet the appetite for the payoff of the middle-class dream. Thus a 1963 report on the Japanese housing situation reported a negative correlation between adequacy of housing, as determined by objective standards of space and sanitation, and satisfaction felt with housing.[28] A 1972 survey showed that only 22 percent of a sample of 500 danchi wives wanted to stay in the danchi a long time, and that more than half the sample actively disliked the term *danchi zoku*.[29]

Aside from the status implications of living in the danchi, there are other unpleasantnesses. The tenant feels helpless when facilities break down. Little attention is paid to upkeep on the buildings, either by tenants or management, and the danchi begins to take on a ragged look after a few years of use. With the standard of living rising, upwardly mobile families move out, and their places are often taken by people of humbler occupation and education. In order to escape this process of "slummation," some families give up their hopes for a real home and move to newer, larger, more expensive danchi.

The real difficulty is that the main raison d'être of the Japan Housing Corporation—to enable young middle-class families to plan toward home ownership—seems to be rapidly diminishing. Land prices continue to spiral around the major cities. Tanaka's archipelago plan, instead of reversing the trend, seems to be spreading it to outlying areas.[30] Building costs have risen sharply in recent years, too. The 1972 report of the JHC indicates that 80 percent of those who want to move have no immediate hopes of doing so.[31]

THE FUTURE OF THE DANCHI LIFESTYLE

In 1972 the construction schedule of the Japan Housing Corporation ran aground when, ironically, a combination of three factors made even danchi housing economically impractical: (1) the success of tenants in opposing rent hikes, (2) the marshalling by local governments of strenuous opposition to new construction with the argument that they have to bear an unfair share of the expense for schools and public utilities to support the influx of danchi populations, and (3) soaring land and construction costs. Meanwhile, waiting lists for new danchi vacancies continue to be long, for the alternatives for many appear to be either unfeasible or even less desirable. Public danchi housing, as apparently the most economical way to house the most people, appears to be a necessary evil and will likely become even more so in the next decade. The social and psychological habits peculiar to danchi life,

---

28. Kasamatsu, *Danchi no subete*, p. 54.
29. Nihon Jūtaku Kodan, '*Sumai*' *ni kan-suru shufu no ishiki chosa.*
30. *Japan Times*, "Public Housing Rents may Rise," 15 November 1972.
31. Nihon Jūtaku Kodan, '*Sumai*' *ni kan-suru shufu no ishiki chosa.*

then, will probably continue to spread along with the environmental phenomenon itself.

What about the propagation of the danchi lifestyle *outside* the beehive? There is little doubt that many of the upper-level managers and bureaucrats of tomorrow, and their wives and children, are living in danchi today. If and when they graduate from danchi zoku status, will they carry their high-rise culture with them and communicate it to others? I think the answer to this question depends largely on the effectiveness of the danchi lifestyle as an adaptation to the increasingly affluent and increasingly urban human environment of Japan as a whole. Realizing that I am on very shaky ground here, I will hazard a few predictions about this for the next decade:

1.   With shortened working hours, more home labor-saving devices, and few children per family, leisure for both men and women will continue to expand.

2.   With the increasing role of large industry in the economy,[32] the separation of work from other areas of life will continue to grow for most people.

3.   With improvements in mass public transportation and tele-communications, the mobility of both people and ideas will increase.

4.   As a result of (2) and (3), commutership, changes of post, and consequent anonymity and conspicuous consumption will increase, community cohesion and cooperation will decline.

5.   The extended family as a residence unit will continue to lose ground for several reasons: (a) with a higher standard of living, elders can be supported in separate quarters—a situation that many elders themselves prefer; (b) with increased reliance on the skilled wage earner as the economic basis of the family, the presence of retired people in the home becomes less economical; and (c) with increased mobility, retired people can stay in one place (which they tend to prefer), while their offspring move about, and visiting from a distance will be facilitated.

6.   Government and big industry will acquire increasingly greater roles in the provision of services formerly handled at the family and community levels. As a result of this, local and national political consciousness is likely to make headway. Political movements might continue to take the place of job-, home-, and community-based sources of identity. The extent to which this happens might depend on how far politics can be decentralized to capture the sense of intimacy and personal recognition now found in other face-to-face groups.

32.   Ministry of Labor, White Paper, 1971.

Another obvious condition for this process will be a reasonable level of success for political effort.

7. Women will become increasingly independent because of the decline in preindustrial institutions, the increase in leisure time, and the absence of the husband from the home, and their key importance as supervisors of children's education.

8. As a result of increased anonymity, increased leisure, and the increased power of women, the needs of the nuclear family will make greater demands on its members' time and energy.

This list is certainly not exhaustive, and may not even include the most important changes relevant to our question, but it will have to suffice as the raw material for my next exercise—the comparison of our model of the metropolitan mind and the picture I have sketched of the imminent Japanese society.

THE PSYCHOLOGY OF THE 1980s

The human psyche is probably a good deal more flexible than anthropologists have been willing to grant in the past. People change profoundly as they age and as the social circumstances of their lives evolve. Still, research on the subject indicates that people make an effort to preserve, in the face of rapid social change, those small habits and relationships that have given them the greatest satisfaction in the past. The massive changes in the macrostructure of society generally outpace changes in the fundamental personality characteristics of its members. People adjust. Often this means that they preserve a sense of continuity by equating, psychologically, new patterns with old ones. It is not so curious that Japanese boys now receive their "priest's haircut" (*boshi sampatsu*) and their military-looking uniforms with the first long pants when they enter middle school; in ancient times the young samurai received his tonsure and his swords at precisely the same age. There is continuity in the deep, symbolic meanings surrounding the initiation into manhood.

My prediction for Japan by the 1980s, then, is that the conditions that favor a metropolitan personality type will have increased substantially but that there will not be much fundamental personality change on a mass scale. I believe that existing patterns of socialization and interaction will be adapted to the macrosocial changes I have described. We can posit, at least roughly, the results of such adaptation.

Japanese will continue to feel most confortable in long-term associations with small groups.

The sociocentric sense of self, and feeling-orientedness, have their roots in early life experiences, that is, in a mother-child relationship that involves a great deal of physical contact and comparatively little verbal stimulation or autonomy training.[33] The small child identifies intensely with those around him. Later, this is reinforced by moral admonitions that his behavior in public reflects on the character of his family as a whole and by his recruitment into other close, familylike groups.[34] In the short run, then, we can expect little change in this characteristic. To the extent that leisure activities groups and political groups gain ground as sources of community, Japanese will probably be organized on a "cellular" basis, giving maximum chance for long-term face-to-face interaction between members. For the time being, the organization of work will follow this same pattern as much as economics permit.

Increased geographic and social mobility will place pressures on this pattern, as we have seen in the case of the danchi. Where the alternatives available are diffuse gregariousness versus social isolation, many will find the former more satisfying.[35] The long-range effects of social change on personality are much harder to forecast, but also more important. Increased parental leisure and increased importance of the nuclear family are factors that will contribute to the identification of the child with his parents—and so maintain one of the foundations of the sociocentric self. At the same time, mobility will lead to increased individuality, and mothers are bound to convey their growing sense of individuation to their children—an overall pattern that begins to resemble American middle-class norms quite closely.

An important corollary of the mobility/individuality issue involves sexuality. Control over the sexual behavior of the sexually mature—especially women—is an important function of the group in a sociocentric society; it serves to reinforce group power and identity and is for that reason a very grave matter for all concerned, even when pregnancy is out of the question. If, as seems likely in Japan, mobility and privatization increase the difficulty of group control in this area, control of sexual behavior will necessarily shift to the individual (I

33. William Caudill and Helen Weinstein, "Maternal Care and Infant Behaviour in Japan and America," *Psychiatry* 32, no. 1 (1969):12–43.

34. Christie W. Kiefer, "The Psychological Interdependence of Family, School, and Bureaucracy in Japan," *American Anthropologist* 72, no. 1 (February 1970): 66–75.

35. It is my belief that diffuse gregariousness and an individualistic or "egocentric" sense of self are closely related. The perception of oneself, and not circumstances, as the main architect of one's own social environment is bound up with the ability to engage that environment in a purposeful way. The skills appropriate to voluntary sociability in a heterogeneous urban society include the ability to objectify one's relationships—to see each actor in a social encounter as a discrete personality with an unique background and point of view and to systematically assume various points of view toward one's own behavior. This amounts to the objectification of the self, a large component of the individualized self-image.

doubt that anyone would argue for a society without any controls here). Such a shift was, in fact, noticeable in the urban middle class in America after the advent of the automobile. Internal control of the impulse life through guilt is qualitatively different from external control through shame. If and when it comes, such a change will set off a vast complex of personality changes in Japanese society.

A related set of changes may be predicated on intellectualism, secularism, and the splitting-off of the impulse life. Here it might be useful to carry the guilt/shame distinction further and distinguish between suppression and repression. The former refers to the more or less conscious holding-in of thoughts or emotions in stoic fashion, the latter to the forgetting or banishing from consciousness of thoughts or emotions such that they cannot be recognized for what they are. All societies teach their members to do both, but cross-cultural comparisons show variations in the content of what is repressed or suppressed. As I have described elsewhere,[36] my impression is that the Japanese emphasis on continuous harmonious group relations leads to the early and severe repression of aggression. Others maintain that feelings of dependency are relatively acceptable to the Japanese,[37] as are erotic feelings under some circumstances.[38] I have already alluded to the many rituals in Japanese society that provide outlets for the periodic public expression of such feelings. When such feelings are socially inappropriate, they tend to be handled by suppression.

Again, important changes in this area are not likely to occur in the next several years, but in the long run we may see a shift toward a more American pattern. Americans tend to be much more aware of aggressive impulses than Japanese because of the relative flexibility of group membership; but they tend to be more repressed in the areas of sexuality and dependency. Individuality and diffuse gregariousness require the person to keep others at a distance in order to maintain his autonomy. An American is in constant danger of being overwhelmed either by his own needs or by someone else's. To the extent that privation, mobility, and diffuse gregariousness make headway in Japan—to the extent that the small, stable, functionally complex group pattern is eroded—we might eventually see a shift toward the American urban pattern in the areas of suppression and repression.

Perhaps the largest and most elusive factor in the psychological urbanization of Japan is the change in the scale of institutions. There

36. Kiefer, "Psychological Interdependence."
37. See especially Takeo Doi, *The Anatomy of Dependence* (Tokyo, 1973).
38. William Caudill, "Patterns of Emotion in Modern Japan," in *Japanese Culture: Its Development and Characteristics*, ed. Robert J. Smith and Richard Beardsley (Chicago, 1962), pp. 115–31.

is little doubt that the individual will find himself a less and less conspicuous and unique part of larger and larger social units, and this is bound to result in a certain sense of anxiety. Each victim of this process will feel some loss of control over his own fate as well as some loss of personal worth as standardization and regimentation progress. This is already well documented as a feature of danchi life, and might be the principal cause of danchi noiroze and ikuji noiroze.

It is very hard to predict popular patterns of response to this kind of stress. Out of the wide range of responses that are possible, two general tendencies prominent in other times and societies have captured the attention of social scientists. I will call these tendencies "self-differentiation" and "merging."

Simmel, who treats the subject of self-differentiation in some detail, asserts that people in cities are forced to turn their attentions inward—to seek the source of their identity not in terms of their contribution to culture but in the stream of their private experience. He cites Nietzsche's railing against the metropolis as the enemy of spirit and Nietzsche's great popularity among urban readers. Such a protest is by no means foreign to Japan. The great novelists of the first half of this century—Natsume, Tanizaki, Nagai, Akutagawa, Kawabata, Dazai—were prophetically preoccupied with inner experience, too. A beautiful example of the exact process we are discussing can be found in Yamakawa Masao's short story "The Talisman."[39] Here, a young danchi dweller, so depersonalized that he begins to doubt his own independent existence, carries a stick of dynamite around in his briefcase in order to convince himself of the possibility of his having some impact on his surroundings. He is driven to this desperation by the absolute sameness of the dwellings in his danchi, by the sameness of the lifestyles of its residents even down to the interchangeability of wives. There is little doubt that such regimentation and massification will continue to grow in proportions, and along with it the type of response Yamakawa is talking about.

The second process, merging, has been dealt with by Freud, Fromm, and Riesman, among others.[40] This is the process whereby the draining away of personal power in the historical march of massification leads the individual to identify with an all-powerful group, surrendering his right to a private identity in order to take on an infinitely more powerful mass identity. Revolutions, totalitarian governments, and messianic and nativistic movements depend to a fair extent on this tendency.

39. *Life*, 11 September 1964, pp. 94–97.

40. Sigmund Freud, "The Future of an Illusion," in *The Standard Edition of the Complete Psychological Works of Sigmund Freud*, vol. 21 (London, 1959), pp. 5–58; Erich Fromm, *Escape from Freedom* (New York, 1941); David Riesman, *The Lonely Crowd: A Study of the Changing American Character* (New Haven, 1958).

Perhaps the diffuseness of the Japanese sense of self, which I have said much about already, both helps and hinders the tendency to merge identities on a mass scale. It helps in the sense that the investment of the group with authority is a psychologically familiar stance, and an easy one for most Japanese to take; a witness to modern mass demonstrations in Japan will need little convincing on this point. Yet it would be a mistake to assume that the Japanese are more given to mass conformity in general than other cultural groups. The tightknit, face-to-face groups (ie, batsu, etc.) in which most Japanese hold at least one membership do tend to be jealous of their autonomy and authority, and most are not easily merged into strong "faceless" organizations of a larger scale. When I questioned a group of white-collar salaried men about their loyalty to their company, they considered the idea of loyalty *to company* ludicrous. They would not change jobs, if the opportunity arose, because they felt intense loyalty to the "office gang" with whom they worked and relaxed during the largest percentage of their waking lives. Such groups not only act as a barrier to wider mergings that might occur but also stand as a buffer between the individual and the anonymous herd. Through participation in such groups, the individual is able to see himself not only as a cog in a giant clockwork but as one of several cogs in a wheel, which is part of a system of wheels and springs, without which the machinery will not keep good time. The real question concerns the extent to which this kind of group identification will atrophy as massification goes forward.

Cultural massification and urbanization will undoubtedly continue to spread at an accelerated rate in Japan during the next several years. Like the danchi zoku, the population of the future will be more materially comfortable, more mobile and rootless, more dependent on big government and big business, more nuclear-family centered, more feminist, more culturally homogeneous, and possessed of more free time than the present average. The institutions of ie, community, and to some extent work group will continue to slacken their hold on the individual's loyalty. Life will be less "organic" in the sense of an orderly patterning of relationships and activities into a well-rounded cultural life.

As a consequence of these changes, the Japanese of the future will be more interested in personal qualities and possessions as markers of social status, less interested in land and lineage. More subject to feelings of loneliness and the meaninglessness of his own life, he may be more inclined to join millenarian movements and political action groups. We might see an increase in clinical depression of the danchi noiroze and ikuji noiroze varieties in the population as a whole. Casual voluntary friendship will develop—and along with it possibly a certain amount of Western-style individuality and even American-style glad-hand superficial affability. These changes may come almost imperceptibly in the immediate future because of the historical lag between institutional and psychological processes.

The Japanese Woman:
Evolving Views of Life and Role

SUSAN J. PHARR

The problem of prediction, as we have seen, is tied organically to the problem of change in personal values and social roles. Cole suggests that a key to the likelihood of alienation in the work force, and thus to the prospect for economic prosperity and political harmony, is the future role of women. Kiefer points out that women will suffer most in the transition from traditional to modern lifestyles and will therefore be exposed 'to the greatest pressures for radical change and adjustment. It is Kiefer, too, who makes the point that the traditional Japanese ethos depends in part on the style of early childhood training; accordingly, as long as women do the child training any changes in their consciousness will have a consequent multiplier effect throughout the newest generation.

Susan Pharr writes of where women are now and where they appear to be going, and thus poses for us some of the biggest questions about the direction of change in Japan.

Pharr divides Japanese women into three groups: the "Neotraditionalists," who accept the one-role ideology of woman's basic inferiority and natural domesticity; the "New Women," who claim the right to participate in life in more than one role and on a basis of equality; and the "Radical Egalitarians," who reject traditional sex roles and traditional marriages altogether. The first group she sees as presently dominant, the second variant, and the third marginal.

The pressure for change is felt, however, in all three groups. Neotraditional aspirations to hearth and home become less realistic as houses grow more cramped, families smaller, and housework less meaningful. Not only is the content of women's education changing away from the traditional jukyogaku *(domestic studies), but a higher percentage of girls than of boys now goes on to high school from middle school. And even the Neotraditionalists accept entering the work force before marriage as a matter of course.*

This paper, originally prepared for the Advanced Research Seminar Series of the East Asian Council at Yale, has gone through several major revisions. Part of an earlier version was presented in April 1974 at the annual meeting of the Association for Asian Studies in Boston. I am grateful to Herbert Passin, David Plath, Lewis Austin, Marsha Hurst Hiller, Carol Berkin, and Stephen Butts for their valuable comments on the paper at various stages of preparation.

The New Woman would like both to marry and to work, and to do these simultaneously without upsetting a society that has not in the past facilitated the arrangement. She does not know exactly what institutional arrangements she wants, but she knows emphatically what she does not want.

The Radical Egalitarian has thought things through to a thoroughgoing Marxist and/or feminist position. She demands equality in social roles, in education, and in work; she condemns the government, the work ethic, the educational system, the family, and all customary patterns of social relations. But these attitudes cut her off from society at large and confine her to isolated subcultures.

Pharr sees the central tension at present to be between the Neotraditionalists and the New Women, with victory going unambiguously to the New Women. The decline of the extended family and nuclear privatization (Kiefer), a full-employment economy in which labor is short (Cole), a period of relatively secure prosperity (Patrick), the spread of Western attitudes (Austin), and the increased impact of higher education (Cummings) will combine to make the Japanese woman of the coming years overwhelmingly a "New Woman."

What will happen to these New Women and what will be their impact on Japanese society? They will be disappointed. The present generation of leaders does not understand the goals of the New Women; the labor market is still at its most rigid with regard to women; and the routine of clerical and factory work will not satisfy women who rejected the traditional domestic role for its lack of meaning. Thus the Radical Egalitarians will be presented an opportunity and an audience. If radical thought can come out of its isolated social enclaves in the coming decades and make common cause with the increasing mass of modern people who are frustrated by modernity, a new cycle of change will be at hand.

Pharr's analysis of the role of women encapsulates the central motif of this symposium. Modernity is victorious in the struggle with tradition only at the cost of creating its own discontents; and the primary paradox of progress is that it continually outmodes itself.—L.A.

A young editor of a woman's magazine was recalling her senior year several years before in a private coed university in Tokyo. "A strange thing happened once," she remarked. "One day I was sitting in the dorm talking with several of my classmates about the future. I mentioned that I would soon start looking for a serious job in publishing to begin after graduation. As I talked, gradually I realized that they were all staring at me. As it turned out, they were girls who were planning to marry as soon as possible after college. But the funny thing was, I had never realized . . . I had always assumed that we all felt the same way about things. . . ."

In today's Japan, and especially among younger generations of postwar women, there is much disagreement on the question of how women should conduct their lives. Even among young women of the same socioeconomic and geographical background there may be highly divergent attitudes toward education, marriage, and work. Women, as in the case of the editor, are sometimes astonished to find that their perspectives may be quite at odds with those of their friends and contemporaries.

This paper, based on interviews with one hundred young Japanese women, explores these differences in views of woman's role and suggests how they may change over the coming decade. The term "woman's role" specifically refers to the wife-mother role traditionally allocated to women in most societies of the world today. At issue in most contemporary analyses, and in the lives of my respondents, is the question of how the domestic role should be combined with other roles (worker, student, citizen, and so on) that a woman may play in her lifetime and, indeed, whether the homemaker role itself should continue to be assigned to women on the basis of sex. Three views of woman's role to be described here represent distinct answers to this question in terms of the life experiences and attitudes of one hundred women.

The interviews for the study were conducted in 1971–72 in Tokyo and the Kyoto-Osaka area from a sample of women in the age range from 18 to 33 who had grown up and attended school entirely under the new order instituted since the end of World War II. In keeping with the purpose of a larger study for which the data were originally gathered, all women chosen to be interviewed were participating in political activities ranging from political parties to the citizen's movement.[1] The informants represented many political interests and ideologies. At one end of the spectrum were women who stuffed envelopes and poured tea at the headquarters of the Liberal Democratic party (LDP), the conservative party in power, only because a father or husband was running for office on the LDP ticket. At the other end were a few student radicals in hiding from the police. Most of the informants, in their ideological convictions and in the amount of time they gave to politics, fell somewhere between the two extremes.

The three general viewpoints on the role of women in Japan that emerged from interviews will be described more fully later in this paper, but briefly they are as follows. First there was a *Neotraditional* perspective. Proponents of this view hold that the wife-mother role is primary in a woman's life and that, in general, all other life activities should be subordinated to it. Aspects of the view, as expressed by young women today, distinguish it from a still more traditional ideology of the woman's role current before the war, but its links to the past are strong.

Those whom I will call *New Women* maintained a second point of

1. See Susan J. Pharr, "Sex and Politics: Women in Social and Political Movements in Japan" (Ph.D. diss., Columbia University, 1975).

view that represents a subtle but fundamental change from the Neotraditional perspective. New Women accept the traditional assumption that the domestic role should be central to their lives as women, but, in what is a major change in attitude, hold at the same time that women should be able to engage in numerous other activities not relating to the homemaker role. Finally, there was the *Radical Egalitarian* view. Radical Egalitarians not only believe that adult women should feel free to play many roles simultaneously, but they also challenge the very basis of contemporary social arrangements by rejecting traditional patterns of sex role allocation that have made it woman's duty to maintain the home.

The above ideologies came to light in interviews with young Japanese women, but it is clear that the three views are in competition in a number of countries today.[2] Nations differ, however, according to how the three ideologies rank in relation to one another. In a society at any moment in history, one view generally prevails over the others in the degree of acceptance accorded it.[3] Among the sample for this particular study, the New Woman's view predominated. Sixty percent of the sample were New Women, with the remaining 40 percent divided equally between Neotraditionalists and Radical Egalitarians. But it is clear that a sample made up of women active in political causes is to some extent a special group. In society at large, the degree of support for each view is obviously quite different.

Drawing upon data from background interviews with women who were not active in politics and upon the findings of numerous authors, it can be suggested that the Neotraditionalists hold the view that has widest acceptance among young Japanese women today. The New Woman's view is a variant pattern in the population at large, tolerated, but denied full social approbation by a great many people. Finally, the Radical Egalitarian view is highly marginal, going far beyond what most Japanese men and women can even understand, much less accept. It might be pointed out that the views of virtually all young women to some extent reflect the high degree of social change characteristic of the postwar period. Certain beliefs of even Neotraditional women today were seen as either variant or deviant throughout much of Japanese history prior to 1945.

2.   For a discussion of sex role ideologies operating in other societies today, see Edmund Dahlström, *The Changing Roles of Men and Women* (Boston, 1971), and Jesse Bernard, *Women and the Public Interest* (Chicago, 1971).

3.   See Florence Kluckhohn's discussion of cultural ranking among value orientations in "Some Reflections on the Nature of Cultural Integration and Change," in *Sociological Theory, Values, and Sociocultural Change*, ed. Edward A. Tiryakian (New York, 1963).

THE TRADITIONAL VIEW OF WOMAN'S ROLE

All three of the views uncovered in interviews with young postwar women grew out of definitions of woman's role from earlier periods of Japanese history. In prewar society, certainly for all of recorded history, the great majority of people held that women were intended for one major role in life, that of wife and mother. Behind this belief were certain interrelated assumptions. Men and women were seen as essentially different beings. Though each was acknowledged to have special talents and abilities, it was man who was considered superior in most areas of endeavor. Men were therefore entitled to many rights not granted to women, and by the same token had certain duties and responsibilities women were thought incapable of assuming.

Men led, made decisions, and provided for the basic unit of society, the family. Women often contributed their labors on behalf of the family, but it was widely understood that a married woman's work plans were subject to her husband's approval and were secondary to his own plans as the main provider. Man answered to society for a household that bore his name. It was an orderly chain of authority. Woman answered to man, and man, to society.

These assumptions, taken together, constituted the traditional view of woman's role. They defined woman's goals and rewards and set her priorities. Largely cutting across the lines set by class and regional differences, they provided a comprehensive framework within which most women ordered their lives. In a woman's youth, she ideally prepared for the day when she would become a wife and, subsequently, a mother. In adult life, the homemaker role came first, and activities not relating to home and children were by definition secondary.

Society did offer a range of alternative role options to women. To become part of the *mizu shōbai*, the demimonde of geisha, entertainers, and prostitutes who provided leisure activities for a virtually all-male clientele, to eschew normal family arrangements in favor of a solitary life as a nun, scholar, writer, or the like—these were also possibilities, open throughout history to certain of the very beautiful, the very talented, and the unconventional among women, or, in the case of many who made their way into the demimonde, to the poor and the fallen. But to elect or even consider these routes was hardly the normal course for the great majority of Japanese women who instead sought the security of a permanent marriage arrangement.

The traditional view was in virtually no respect unique to Japan. The assumptions just described have operated in most societies evolving from patriarchal traditions. What was unusual in Japan, perhaps, was the persistence of the view, with only minor challenges, well into the twentieth century. After Japan emerged from centuries of feudalism and national isolation in the 1860s, most of these assumptions passed intact into the modern period and were reaffirmed by legal code and custom until the end of World War II.

Three features of the traditional viewpoint had particular impact on the lives of women before the war and to some extent influence attitudes today. The first was the degree to which status differences between men and women were thought natural and legitimate. Whereas in Europe romantic and chivalrous traditions had developed in the feudal era to soften the very real lines of status difference between men and women, in Japan with different feudal traditions the lines were very stark indeed. In the prewar period women showed deference to men of their own as well as higher classes through the use of polite language and honorific forms of address, bowing more deeply than men, walking behind their husbands in public, and in numerous other ways deferring to men. In the extended family arrangement common before the war, a new bride coming into the house was ideally expected to acknowledge her status inferiority in a number of ritualized ways: getting up first in the morning, going to bed last at night, taking her bath only after all other family members had bathed, eating after other family members, and taking the least choice servings of food.

Another feature of the traditional view supported not only in custom but also in legal codes in the modern period was the husband's authority over the wife. In the prewar family system, the head of household as-sumed full legal responsibility for all family members. Upon marriage, a woman could act in legal matters only with the approval of her husband's family. The Civil Code consistently favored the husband in provisions relating to divorce, marriage, property rights, and other questions coming under family law.[4] Adultery constituted legal grounds for divorce only if committed by the wife. When there was a dispute over the custody of a child, the wishes of the husband controlled the outcome. It was regarded as proper, if painful to the wife, for a husband to divorce her and keep the children in his own family to bear his family name. Similarly, if a man fathered children by women other than his wife he was legally entitled to adopt them into his family. If her husband died, a wife came under the authority of her eldest son as soon as he came of age. Most women in prewar Japan spent their entire lifetimes before and after marriage as legal dependents of male family heads.

4. For a valuable summary of provisions in the Civil Code, see B. James George, Jr., "Law in Modern Japan," in *Twelve Doors to Japan*, ed. John Hall and Richard Beardsley (New York, 1965).

A final feature of the traditional view that has endured well into the twentieth century is the notion that husband and wife belong in separate spheres of activity. As many writers note, industrialization has supported sex-role specialization by taking husbands out of the family productive unit (the farm or shop) and into the office or factory.[5] But the prevalence of attitudes supporting sex-role segregation today is also traced to the strength of this aspect of the traditional view in prewar society, especially among the upper classes. Upper-class married women in prewar Japan played few roles in affairs outside the home circle and neighborhood. In contrast to Europe and the United States, where upper-class leisure patterns brought husbands and wives together in many social contexts, Japanese society provided few such opportunities. Wives hardly ever ventured into the demimonde where many well-to-do men spent their leisure hours.

Sex-role divisions were less rigid among the working classes where work roles were often shared and where husbands had limited means for leisure activities; but the traditional view of woman's role among the upper classes has enjoyed greater support than their numbers might suggest. For as prosperity has spread, those ascending the social ladder have aspired to the style of life of those above them. Sex-role division stressed in the upper-class version of the traditional view of woman's role has thus survived the twentieth century and spread to other levels of society, accelerated by the impact of industrialization.

The traditional view of woman's role, reinforced by certain changes in the modern period, has been challenged by other views, especially in the postwar period. Japan's surrender in 1945 set off a series of changes that have affected women at almost every level of Japanese life. The Constitution of 1947 explicitly forbade discrimination on the basis of sex. Through reform of the Civil Code, the American occupying forces attacked the basis of women's status inferiority in the family by guaranteeing women free choice of a spouse, equal recourse to divorce, equal property rights, and so on. Meanwhile, democratization and legal reform have been supported by other postwar forces in their impact on women's status. Urbanization has sped the demise of the extended family system. Within the urban nuclear family, even where status differences are acknowledged they are far less ritualized than before. Prosperity, another force for change in postwar Japan, has made higher education available to daughters as well as sons. Improvements in home facilities resulting from a higher standard of living have lightened the burden of housework, freeing women for other pursuits.

These recent forces for change impinge on the traditional view of

5. See, for example, Ronald Dore, *City Life in Japan* (Berkeley, 1958), p. 116.

woman's role described above. Multiple currents, often pulling in opposite directions, conjoin to shape definitions of woman's role in present-day society. For the individual woman, meshing legal norms with social reality may be a major challenge. The result is the three views of woman's role in postwar Japan.

NEOTRADITIONALISTS

In a coffeeshop in Osaka, I sat with a young activist by the name of Honda Akiko, a woman of nineteen who eagerly awaited the day she would be twenty and could become an official member of the Clean Government party.[6] At the time of the interview she was participating in party activities unofficially by helping her older sisters, already party members, count out campaign pamphlets at home.

Akiko is the youngest of four girls, the daughter of an iron parts maker who has worked hard all his life and a mother who has spent most her married life doing double duty as a housewife and part-time factory worker. Together the parents have struggled to make a living for the six of them, and if they have a single ambition for a family with four daughters it is to see them all marry into a life of greater ease than they have known.

The year before I interviewed her, Akiko had graduated from senior high school and had immediately taken a job in a large company. There she performs the duties that thousands of young Japanese women today undertake for a few years before marriage. She is called an "O.L." in Japan, an "office lady" hired to do routine office work, to pour tea for company members several times a day, and to create a pleasant working environment for the men who do the serious work in the office. To suggest to Akiko that she apply for the kind of job done by the men would be like suggesting that she try for the position of prime minister. In the business world men and women are almost always hired for different kinds of work and there is little way in present-day society that she would cross those lines. More important, in her own mind she really does not see herself as able to do the work that men do. As she explained to me, in words echoing centuries of Japanese history, "Men are superior to women in every field. Women have a narrower mind, a more limited view." Finally, not only would the man's kind of work be beyond her abilities, as she sees things, but it would interfere with the main life plan of Neotraditionalists like Akiko: to become a full-time housewife and mother to the exclusion of most other pursuits.

---

6. To protect their identities, the informants' names have been changed, along with minor biographical details.

As we sat there, I asked her a number of questions about the future, her long-term goals and plans. Like many of the young activists I interviewed in Japan she first turned the question around and asked me about my own plans. I told her I aspired to be a college professor, but that I hoped to marry someday, too. With great tact, she asked me how old I was, and when I said I was twenty-eight, she looked worried and concerned for me. Then she said in a soft, but firm voice resounding with the hopes of a great many young women all over Japan today:

> As for me, I have no special person in mind, but I have a dream of marriage. It is stronger now than when I was graduating from high school. My dream is to create a warm atmosphere in a home even if it turns out to be a humble home. To find someone, first I must polish myself. That is what I am doing now. I am improving myself so that I can find an ideal husband.

For Akiko's plans her job now is perfectly suited to her needs. Her salary is low and she must live with her family, but she has funds to pay them for her upkeep so that she does not feel herself a burden on them. Beyond that, she has pocket money for clothes, makeup, magazines, and an occasional trip to a coffeehouse with former high school friends and girlfriends from the office. At work, she has a chance to gain the kind of practical experience in life that most young women today feel is an important credential for marriage. She is "polishing herself," and in the back of her mind is the hope that she may be able to meet an eligible young *sarariman*, one of the middle-class workers who are symbols of postwar prosperity, in the company.

Once she finds someone suitable, Akiko will quit her job. It is her earnest hope, shared by a great many young women today whose mothers in their early married years struggled to combine housework and child rearing with a tiring industrial job or hard work in a home productive unit in prewar Japan, that she will be able to give full time to the life task of making a home. But Akiko is realistic. If she does not meet a sarariman and instead marries someone of her own class, she will probably have to work, for it is not yet possible for most young working-class couples in Japan to live on the husband's salary alone. When I asked her if she would work after marriage, I was obviously touching on a subject that occupied many of her thoughts:

> If there is no way around it, of course I will. I'm hoping, though, that I won't have to. I would rather stay at home and keep a perfect house. I'd prefer that life—waiting for my husband to come home.

Many young women like Akiko are finding married life somewhat different from the way in which they had envisioned it. With the inflation that has been endemic for much of the postwar period, young middle-class husbands have a hard time providing for two people, even when their wives are frugal. Furthermore, the dreams of a great many young women today grew out of the aspiration of their mothers who started out in a different Japan when housing was more spacious, housework more demanding, and family size much larger. Today in the highly urban society Japan has become, many young housewives in big cities find themselves living in an apartment smaller than an average American living room. "Keeping a perfect house" —Akiko's dream—is a matter of a good two hours' work, and after that is done, until women have children, they may find themselves with a great deal of time on their hands. The problem is often especially acute if their husbands are "salary men," for frequently these men must work overtime, and in the typical pattern of Japanese business life, they may go drinking with coworkers after office hours several nights a week. The sarariman's wife, eager to serve and please her husband according to traditional formulas, may find herself waiting alone many nights in front of the television set in a tiny apartment, not sure when he will come home. The husband, to meet his job responsibilities as they are construed in Japan, may not be able to return in time for dinner, and because of long-established social custom would be averse to the idea of telephoning to inform his wife. While her children are young, the full-time urban housewife may feel that she has her hands full. But family size is small today, and soon the several children are in school. The housewife then may find her hours very empty indeed.

Today it is common to hear men joke about the modern wife. Shaking their heads, they say that unlike the industrious, hardworking mothers they remember, she spends much of her time sleeping late or sitting in front of the television. This kind of joking may be one reflection of an increasingly serious problem in Japan—the growing dysfunctionality of woman's major social role as it has been defined traditionally. What many Japanese men describe as a life of leisure enjoyed by the modern wife can, from another point of view, be seen as a life of boredom, personal inertia, and considerable loneliness. Women's magazines today reveal the other side of the picture in articles dealing with how a wife can make herself more sexually attractive as a way of luring her husband home from the office on time, how to prepare meals such as stews that can simmer for hours and be ready whenever a husband happens to return, and hobbies to fill the housewife's long hours at home; other articles describe how to put idle time to good use by helping children with homework. Some of these articles reflect considerable frustration—sexual, emotional, and otherwise—as well as many women's concern today for finding traditionally acceptable ways to adapt to a role the terms of which have changed profoundly in recent years.

The views attributed to Akiko so far appear to put her in the category with prewar traditional women. In what sense, then, is Akiko "neo"-traditional? What distinguishes her attitudes from those of prewar women? Certainly one area of change is in her attitudes toward a political role. Most Neotraditional women do not aspire to become active members of a political party, but there is no question that attitudes toward women's political participation have changed. Today, defying trends in other countries, the overall voting rate is slightly higher for women than men in Japan, and among young people in the 20 to 29 age group it is substantially higher.[7]

Another area of change is in attitudes toward education. In the prewar period girls were educated in a separate girls' track with a program explicitly designed to prepare them to become "good wives and wise mothers." Today, however, there is little doubt that most people regard the serious study of basic subjects as necessary for youths of both sexes. Ministry of Education figures show that when choosing among several curriculum options in senior high school, only 11 percent of the girl students elected the home economics concentration that almost surely would have been the natural preference of a great many prewar girls had they been confronted with study options.[8] The level of women's educational aspirations has also been rising. Whereas relatively few girls continued their formal schooling beyond the six years of compulsory education in prewar Japan, it is now within the ordinary hopes and expectations of most young Japanese women like Akiko to go to senior high school. In fact, by a slight margin, the rate of advancement to senior high school is higher for girls than boys and now stands at 82.7 percent.[9]

Even more significant are changing attitudes toward higher education. Akiko herself did not seek education beyond the high school level.

7.   The voting rate for women has exceeded that for men in every national election since the upper house election of July 1968. See table in Pharr, "Sex and Politics," p. 15. For the 20 to 29 age group, one election study reported a voting rate of 74.7 percent for women and 66.5 percent for men, the widest gap recorded for any age group. See Ministry of Labor, Women and Minors' Bureau (WMB), *Me de miru fujin no ayumi* [A look at women's progress] (Tokyo, 1971), p. 18.

8.   Results of a study cited in Tomoda Yasumasu, "Educational and Occupational Aspirations of Female Senior High School Students," *Bulletin of the Hiroshima Agricultural College* 4, no. 3 (December 1972): 248.

9.   The figure is for 1970, and compares with 81.6 percent for males. WMB, *Fujin no genjō* [The condition of women] (Tokyo, 1971), p. 6.

But her older sister, another Neotraditional woman, managed to finish junior college by working part time. In the prewar years, the percentage of women advancing to higher education generally was around 1 percent.[10] By 1972, it stood at 28.4 percent.[11] Many of these women, like Akiko's sister, attend junior colleges, where they make up 84 percent of the enrollment, rather than four-year colleges and universities, where they represent only 19 percent of the total; but compared to the prewar situation these developments are quite remarkable.[12] Following from their attitudes toward woman's role, many Neotraditionalists want a college degree as a new kind of marriage credential that many people now see as necessary for a young woman of the middle class or upper middle class who wants to attract a suitable husband. Because Neotraditional women want to marry a man who is superior to them intellectually, they are careful not to become more educated than the kind of men they hope to marry. Junior college is a particularly safe choice because it makes them eligible to marry almost any college-educated male. On the other hand, Neotraditionalists of upper-middle-class backgrounds, feeling fairly assured that they can marry a graduate of one of the top universities of Japan, may attend a middle-ranking university or a four-year woman's college.

Views of marriage have also changed, as evidenced by present-day attitudes toward mate selection. As many writers note, the arranged marriage system itself has changed remarkably in the postwar years, while overall the percentage of "love" marriages (*renai kekkon*) has outpaced that for arranged marriages (*miai kekkon*). A recent report of the Economic Planning Agency showed that in large- and medium-sized cities, around 60 percent of all marriages were "love" matches.[13] Akiko's desire to find her own mate, then, is quite usual in postwar Japan. In a recent study 82.7 percent of those under twenty who were questioned said they would prefer to have a "love" marriage.[14] The actual figures as cited above lag behind these expressed desires, but still the change in attitudes is a major one.

10.   In 1920 the enrollment rate for women was .4 percent (for males 3 percent); in 1930 it was 1.1 percent (for males 6.4 percent); in 1940 it was 1.2 percent (for males 8.1 percent). See Tomoda, "Educational and Occupational Aspirations," p. 247.

11.   WMB, *The Status of Women in Japan* (Tokyo, 1973), p. 6.

12.   Ibid., p. 7.

13.   Economic Planning Agency, *Kokumin seiatsu hakusho* [Report on national life], (Tokyo, 1971), p. 20. Data are from a 1966 study.

14.   Sankei Shimbun, *Iken to ishiki no hyakkajiten: Sankei Shimbun 1000-nin chōsa kara* [Encyclopedia of thought and opinion: From Sankei newspaper's survey of 1000 persons] (Tokyo, 1972), p. 85.

Finally, Neotraditionalists' feelings toward work reflect major signs of change. In the prewar period, many young girls took jobs for wages because of severe family hardship. Many would have preferred to stay home to prepare for marriage by studying cooking, flower arranging, and the like. Today, however, most young women like Akiko accept it as a matter of course to take a job for a few years before they marry. Of women in the 20 to 24 age group, 70.5 percent are now in the labor force.[15] As indicated by figures cited above, most of the others are in college. Obviously, few girls stay home any more preparing for marriage, and for most—whether for pocket money, personal enrichment, to find a husband, or, recently, to save money for a trip abroad—taking a job has come to be accepted as a natural and necessary stage of growing up.

For Neotraditionalists, basic goals and views of their role and place as women in Japan have not changed. But compared to the women of the prewar world, Neotraditional women are undoubtedly moving in the direction of more civic participation, fuller involvement with national life through work, an increasing quest for higher education, and, in all activities, a search for greater personal independence.

NEW WOMEN

One woman who typified many of the New Women I interviewed was Takai Setsuko, a quietly dressed young woman of twenty-three who at the time of the interview was a Japanese equivalent of a Nader's Raider. As a specialist in the chemical composition of fabrics, she was a persuasive and committed advocate of consumer protection, working full time at the headquarters of the Housewives' Association (*Shufuren*) in Tokyo.

In Setsuko's early experience there is little that readily meets the eye to set her apart from the Neotraditional woman. She grew up far from a major urban center in a small village in southern Shikoku, and she told me forthrightly that when she graduated from high school she had no particular thoughts except about someday getting married like her girlfriends. But over the summer after graduation she talked to former high school classmates back from their freshman year in various colleges in Tokyo. She had said to herself, "I've been thinking in my own limited world. I ought to go to college." Her father, a local official, was not enthusiastic, expressing fears that in their rural locale a college education would hurt her marriage chances. But he agreed finally to pay for her schooling. Thus in 1967, five years before I interviewed her, Setsuko had come to Tokyo to attend a woman's

15. WMB, *Status of Women in Japan*, p. 47. Figure is for 1970.

college, where she majored in home economics. So far she was on the Neotraditional course.

But at some point in her senior year in college something appears to have changed in Setsuko. She was then doing her graduation essay, a requirement of all seniors, and she became increasingly interested in her topic, which dealt with the safety of commercial fabrics used for clothes. She began interviewing manufacturers and consumer groups, including the Housewives' Association, and she was shocked to find that many widely-used fabrics were flammable and dangerous. Late in her senior year she decided that she would have to do something with the knowledge she had acquired from her research. Her family back home, worried about a daughter alone in distant Tokyo, wanted her home after graduation. In their letters to her they began to mention likely candidates for an arranged marriage. But Setsuko pressed to be allowed to follow her own course, and in the end her parents reconciled themselves. She accepted a job that she had been offered at the Housewives' Association and set out to find an apartment in Tokyo. Because she had heard that many Tokyo landlords might be reluctant to rent to a young single woman, she began looking for a place long before her job began. Most young women from distant parts of Japan who work in Tokyo live with relatives or girlfriends, partly for financial reasons, but also because many are afraid that if they live alone they will endanger their reputations and thereby hurt their marriage chances. Setsuko, however, went ahead with her plan because, she said, she wanted a taste of the independent life. At the time of the interview she was living by herself in a tiny apartment and spent most of her time in activities related to her job at the Housewives' Association.

When Setsuko was asked about the future, she immediately talked about her plans to improve her competence at her job. When I asked her about marriage, she obviously felt great discomfort. She wants to marry but she also wants to continue her job after she marries. She wonders if she can find a husband in Japan who will understand how she feels. Although Neotraditionalists, even when they become deeply absorbed in a job or other activity, are apt to see it as only a passing phase of youth before they take on their main life role, many New Women like Setsuko do not want to give up their outside interests. They want to marry, and they accept the sex role division in marriage that allocates to them the role of homemaker and child tender. But they want to play other roles as well.

What New Women want in terms of the actual content of the marriage relationship varies with the individual. Some, while handling their jobs or other activities, want to assume all the traditional obligations that go along with the homemaker role. They talk of taking on full child care responsibility, paying for it themselves, and say that they would expect no help from their husbands with housework. Others (though they, too, do not question that the homemaker role is really their responsibility) express the view that their husbands should lend an occasional helping hand. In their criteria for a husband, some New Women still openly hold certain traditional views and say candidly that they want someone more intelligent than themselves. Others say they would prefer someone closer to their own age (but, generally, slightly older), and of similar educational attainment. All express the hope that in the marriage they ultimately enter there will be somewhat greater companionship and more opportunity for sharing thoughts and feelings than tend to go along with the Neotraditionalist's model of marriage. Most New Women, however, are engaged in an experiment with their newly forged role in which neither their ideology nor the behavioral requirements for implementing it are clearly formulated in their own minds. Those who are unmarried have no clear model of what they actually want in the marriage relationship, and those who are know only what they do not like. If Freud were to talk to the New Women of Japan today, he might well be led to repeat his famous query, "What do women want?" New Women do not yet know in precise terms. They are searching for answers themselves.

Many New Women who are not yet married have difficulty finding men who share their view of woman's role and place in Japan today. The problem of finding a husband is complicated by the fact that the arranged marriage system, which even the most independent-minded Neotraditionalists consider a reasonably acceptable fallback, is largely unsuited to their needs. Even with all the recent changes in the system, it still functions to bring two people together in a traditional marriage relationship in which the wife is expected to follow a course set by the husband. As one New Woman, a freshman economics major at Tokyo University, explained:

> There are two kinds of arranged marriages in Japan. One is the old feudalistic kind where parents and relatives put a lot of pressure on the parties concerned. The other is the modern kind, which is basically an introduction method. I don't like either kind. I don't want to have to agree with a man's opinions about everything.

Even when New Women find a marriage prospect on their own, they may encounter problems. Many men who want to assert their independence by having a "love" match still have traditional expectations concerning woman's role. The number of New Women is growing rapidly today, however, and increasingly they are able to find men sympathetic to their views at work, in school, or, in the case of many New Women I interviewed, in their political group.

For already married women who come to the New Woman's view within a traditional marriage relationship there are other kinds of problems. The experience of Tanaka Keiko provides an example. At thirty-two she is a member of a Tokyo women's group made up of upper-middle-class Tokyo suburban housewives, all of whom want part-time or full-time jobs. At age twenty-five, Keiko, a graduate of a woman's college, had an arranged marriage to a young engineer whom she dated only eight times before the wedding ceremony. Following the accepted pattern—which she herself thought quite natural at the time—she quit her job at an electric company near her home in the Kansai when she married and moved to Tokyo to make a new life with her husband. Now, seven years and two children later, she wants a part-time job as soon as the children are both in school. Her reasons are those heard with increasing frequency in Japanese upper-middle-class suburbia: housework is monotonous, she has too much free time, and she is lonely in a community where she still knows very few people after seven years.

Her husband is frankly astonished at her attitude. From his stand-point he has gone above and beyond the traditional responsibilities to a wife by providing her with a more-than-adequate home, a car that she is able to use during the day, and ample spending money. Since he provides so well, it makes no sense to him that his wife would want to work. He also maintains the view, widely shared in Japanese society, that children require a mother's full-time physical presence and fairly constant attention, not only in the early years, but also well into the school years and even late adolescence, and that giving herself over to these tasks should give a woman her greatest satisfaction and be her main life purpose. Thus he can only see her plan, which calls for placing the children in a day care center or in the care of outside help for a few hours several afternoons a week, as serious neglect of her responsibilities and a failure of moral purpose as well. To heighten the tension, his own mother vehemently agrees with him and sides with him in disputes. This is a traditional marriage undergoing considerable strain as the discussion continues. Some women who came to the New Women viewpoint after marriage have achieved more success in gaining their husband's cooperation, particularly where the activity they want to take on is a job that will supply needed extra income to the family. But where family income is adequate, husbands generally are much harder to convince. The work available to even highly educated women without special skills generally pays very little—in many cases it is barely enough to pay for day care or a housekeeper to mind the children.[16]

A wide variety of environmental influences direct women toward a New Woman's view today. The experience of higher education is often a major factor. It is true that more than half of the women in higher education attend junior colleges and women's colleges, many of them following the typical Neotraditionalist path. But the number attending four-year coed universities is increasing rapidly. In 1950 women made up only 2 percent of the university enrollment, but by 1972 the figure had risen to 19 percent, a spectacular rate of increase far outpacing that for male students.[17] Even at prestigious Tokyo University the percentage of women almost tripled between 1960 and 1970. By the latter year, 10 percent of Todai's students were women.[18] Not all women attending universities are New Women, nor is the reverse always true. But there is much evidence of an important correlation between educational level and views of woman's role. A study by Blood conducted in a middle-class suburb shows that 69 percent of the college-graduate wives in the sample worked, whereas only 24 percent of the high school graduates were working.[19]

In my study I found that far more New Women came to their ideologies of woman's role as a result of educational experiences than as a result of working. Cases like that of Takai Setsuko, who found an interesting job with a consumer group, were rare. Japanese employers showed great reluctance to hire women for challenging jobs at good pay. Women's average wage in 1971 was still less than half that received by male workers.[20] Women held less than 4 percent of the jobs in the category of managers and officials, and the figure in 1970 was slightly less than the one ten years before.[21] As one New Woman, a Tokyo

16. Both public and private day care facilities are available in Japan, but demand for placement far exceeds available space. As of April 1973 there were 16,140 centers accomodating 1,449,019 children. Government of Japan, *Seminar in* [*sic*] *Public Administration Officers on Women's Problems 1973 Fiscal Year* (Tokyo, 1973), p. 65. But for the working wife of all but low-income families it is still difficult to make inexpensive day care arrangements. Fees at public day care centers are set on a scale based on ability to pay, with the fee determined by the income of the head of household. Thus for married women whose husbands provide an adequate income, the fee is likely to take a major portion of any income they can earn.

17. WMB, *Status of Women in Japan*, p. 7.

18. Figures based on data provided in Ministry of Education, *Zenkoku gakkō sōran* [National school report] (Tokyo, 1961), p. 2, and (1971), p. 2.

19. Robert O. Blood, Jr., *Love Match and Arranged Marriage: A Tokyo-Detroit Comparison* (New York, 1967), p. 149.

20. WMB, *Fujin rōdō no jitsujō* [The status of women workers] (Tokyo, 1971), p. 38.

21. WMB, *Fujin no genjō*, p. 52.

University graduate, remarked bitterly after she was turned down for low-paying editorial jobs at two big publishing houses, "Japan is an escalator society, and women just never get on the escalator."

For a number of women interviewed for this study, the situation in the job market was a major contributing factor in leading them to work in political and civic groups. Eager to develop new interests outside marriage, they had first sought interesting work. But failing to find it they had turned to political activities.

RADICAL EGALITARIANS

After a long series of introductions, I was at last able to meet Suzuki Fumiko, an eighteen-year-old member of the Red Army (*Sekigun*).[22] Fumiko's manner conveyed a sense of confidence and strong determination. Her eyes seldom left my face as we sat talking in the coffee shop. When she laughed, it was with great zest and feeling. Many of the women with whom I talked accepted the terms I had set for the interview and left me the initiative. Fumiko, however, took a much more active role in the exchange. She would answer no questions until she had asked me about my ideology, family background, my own relations with men, my plans, how I would use my research findings, and what I had found out so far about Japanese women. Only then, and after she had made clear what she would and would not discuss, was she willing to proceed.

Fumiko's feelings about woman's role came out rather early in the interview when I asked her how she felt about men and marriage. Thinking a moment, she made a strong statement of the Radical Egalitarian view and then described the course she had chosen:

> The war destroyed the [traditional] family system in Japan, but the basic problems remain. Marriage in this society involves a relationship between possessor and possessed, not between two individuals who think of each other as equals. My own relationship with a man is not that kind of relationship. It is a face-to-face relationship where we look directly into each other's eyes. We live together in the course of developing our ideas and thoughts.

At the time of the interview, Fumiko was living with a man, also a Red Army member, in a tiny apartment they had found together. Both

---

22.   For a study dealing with Japan's factionalized student movement, see Stuart Dowsey, ed., *Zengakuren: Japan's Revolutionary Students* (Berkeley, 1970). Formed out of previous groups in 1969, the Red Army is Trotskyist in its view and is thus committed to world revolution. Together with another militant group, the Red Army formed an organization known as the United Red Army (*Rengō sekigun*), which has engaged in a variety of terrorist activities inside and outside Japan. The informant referred to in the text was active in the Red Army before the merger.

were agreed, she told me, that the duties of daily life in the apartment should be shared, and that each should have large areas of personal freedom to do what he or she wished.

How each of the Radical Egalitarians I met had come to their view is a highly complex matter that does not lend itself to easy generalization. I have dealt with it at length elsewhere.[23] Briefly, however, many did appear to have at least one parent, most often a mother, who had given strong support, whether tacit or expressive, for their daughter's personal explorations. In Fumiko's case, her mother, left a widow early in her forties by the sudden death of her sararīman husband, had suffered severe financial hardship in trying to make her way alone as a woman in Japan. It was this experience, in part, that appeared to have made her supportive of a daughter's search for autonomy. Piecing together a marginal income from her deceased husband's pension and from making kimono, she had given her tacit consent, while outwardly voicing disapproval, when her daughter became involved in radical political activities during junior high school days. While her mother sewed upstairs in their large, rambling house in Kamakura outside Tokyo, Fumiko had turned the downstairs into a commune for the Red Army. The year before I interviewed her, Fumiko had dropped out of senior high school and had begun to live with her present lover, again with her mother's full knowledge.

Though the Radical Egalitarians I talked with had come to their views by somewhat distinctive routes and differed widely in personal qualities and such factors as class and educational background, there were certain characteristics they shared. One was a distinct personal style. While virtually all Neotraditionalists and most New Women tended to express themselves somewhat indirectly, uniformly using the polite forms of speech and expression considered appropriate for women, Radical Egalitarians spoke with great frankness and directness. In many cases they used plain forms of speech and numerous expressions that are commonly regarded as "men's language" in Japan.

Another characteristic was that most had given considerable thought to where they stood on many issues, both political and personal. Whereas Neotraditionalists and especially New Women often discovered inconsistencies in their behavior and feeling over the course of the interview, Radical Egalitarians, even the younger ones like Fumiko, had gone through fairly extensive self-examination. They were quick, in most cases, to admit shortcomings and failures to live up to their ideals. But, in a way that was quite striking, they had thought things through.

23. See Pharr, "Sex and Politics," chapter 5.

Unlike the New Women, who differed from one another about what they wanted in a relationship with a man, Radical Egalitarians were fairly agreed. Uniformly they expressed a strong dislike for the widely accepted criteria for choosing a mate in Japan, such as family background, socioeconomic status, and educational attainment. Many were ideologically opposed to the institution of marriage for the kinds of reasons cited by Fumiko. Almost all were struggling to achieve their personal aims in radical subcultures where they were surrounded by those who gave them strong, personal validation. Although a number of them maintained close ties with their families, most lived apart from relatives, generally with members of their group or with a man who shared their views. Almost all the Radical Egalitarians interviewed for this particular study were engaged in political activities in the context of which they were pressing for equality as women. Most were in one of two main types of groups. Half, like Fumiko, were in radical political organizations that are part of the New Left in Japan. These women were opposed not only to current notions of woman's role, but to the general pattern of social and family relations in Japan and other capitalist societies, to the work ethic as personified by the sararīman, to the present government, to all the existing political parties in Japan (including the parties of the left), and to an educational system in their country that they see as overcompetitive and dehumanizing. Within their group, many were pressing for their right to participate on an equal basis in all group activities, ranging from assuming leadership roles to engaging in physical combat in pursuit of the group's objectives. Most said that there were major barriers to achieving equality in their political activities. Disputes between male and female activists had broken out in numerous groups over such seemingly simple but extremely significant matters as who should pour tea at meetings.

The other half were members of radical women's liberation groups.[24] Many of these women had deserted the New Left because they felt that men in the movement failed to understand the seriousness of their

24. Japan has a number of organizations and groups committed to the goal of improving the status of women in society and the family; thus they could be considered a part of a "women's liberation movement" in the broad sense in which that term is used in the United States. However, "women's lib" ("ūman ribu") as used in Japan has a much narrower meaning. Specifically it refers to a small number of groups that appeared in the early 1970s and that make sexual liberation a primary objective. A major political goal of these groups is to end the ban on birth control pills in Japan and to counter government efforts to tighten restrictions on abortions. See Nagano Yoshiko, "Women Fight for Control: Abortion Struggle in Japan," *AMPO* 17 (Summer 1973): 14–20. The actual membership figures for these groups are fairly low, probably numbering in the several hundreds. But interest in their aims and activities is somewhat higher than this estimate would indicate. In May 1972, for example, a conference in Tokyo on "women's lib" drew about 3,000 participants.

struggle for equality and recognition. Joined by many women who were not from the New Left, they had formed numerous women's groups and collectives. Those associated with *Tatakau Onna* ("Fighting Women") generally held that before women can have equal relations with men they must first learn to express themselves among women and develop their self-confidence. This group operated several collectives where women lived and studied together, and most supported themselves by taking part-time jobs in coffeeshops or wherever they can find work. While living in the collective many have sexual relations with men outside it. Here they argue that Japanese women, long sexually repressed in a country with a strong tradition of a double standard, should overcome their timidity and sexual dependence on men by learning to have sex as many men do: with a variety of partners and on their own terms.[25] Radical Egalitarians in several women's groups not associated with Tatakau Onna had different objectives. Individual members were living with men and met occasionally in groups that functioned much like consciousness-raising groups in the United States. These young women felt that a woman must struggle for equality and recognition, not in a separatist movement, but in a joint struggle waged with a man who shared her view of woman's role and who was willing to create a new style of relationship between man and woman in present-day Japanese society.

THE FUTURE OF JAPANESE WOMEN

Amidst the Neotraditionalists, New Women, and Radical Egalitarians were, of course, many young women trying to find themselves, moving back and forth between the various views at different stages of their life experience. In Japanese society, particularly among the older generations above the age range of my informants, there are many women still struggling between the prewar traditional view of woman's role, which imposed still greater restrictions on women's right to participate in the affairs of society, and the Neotraditional view that is widely accepted in Japanese society today. Social values, including those bearing on woman's role and place, are in great flux today and it is only natural that a great many women find themselves vacillating between views, unsure what they want, undecided as to whether they are willing to undergo the great personal and psychological risk that comes when human beings try to move in new directions.

In present-day Japan the central tension is between the view of

---

25. Interview with Tanaka Mitsu, age 28, leader of Tatakau onna, Tokyo, 1972. Her views on women's liberation are set out in her autobiography: Tanaka Mitsu, *Inochi no onna tachi e* [That women might live] (Tokyo, 1972).

Neotraditionalists, who continue to have their strong one-role ideology that calls on them to subordinate all other major life activities to the role of wife and mother, and the view of the New Women of Japan, who still want to be wives and mothers but want to develop other personal interests as well. The Radical Egalitarians are far outside the mainstream of life in Japan. In society as it is today, their experiment is only possible within the subcultures they have created.

Over the next decade there will be growing tension between the views of Neotraditionalists and New Women. By the middle of the next decade, especially in the major urban centers, the view of the New Women will vie for prominence in the culture. The steps by which the New Woman's view gradually will come to dominance are deeply rooted in the nature of postwar change, particularly in developments among the urban middle class.

In the wake of a devastating war, Japan's leadership guided the nation into a program of major rebuilding that required most Japanese to make a great many personal sacrifices. Husbands worked long hours, stayed overtime at the factory or office, often took little or no vacation, and came home exhausted on weekends, in many cases with only one day of rest in which to collect themselves for the week ahead. Because of the heavy work demands on men, husbands and wives saw remarkably little of each other. Husbands came home too tired to talk and develop serious communication with their wives, and there was little money or time for joint activities. The home itself was for most urban Japanese a very modest place indeed. With housing shortages, living quarters were cramped, and families living on extremely limited budgets had little money to improve the quality of their home environment. This was certainly a major factor supporting the traditional segregated leisure pattern of Japan. Men exhausted from their labors looked forward to the male leisure environment outside the home—the bars and cabarets where they could stop off on the way home from work for much-needed moments of relaxation. To take a wife out and relax together not only ran against the grain of custom but also required money for two people's leisure activities that simply was not available. The pattern of postwar life through the present has certainly supported the traditional sex-role divisions of married life.

At the same time these developments were taking place among adult Japanese, a great many young people who had grown up entirely in the world of postwar Japan felt a growing desire for new styles of social relationships in keeping with the democratic values supported within the school environment. For many young Japanese, the university world was a testing ground for trying to develop new styles of relationships with the opposite sex. Looking ahead to their future lives in the big cities of Japan, they felt that the traditional marriage relationship, characterized by great social distance between husband and wife in the extended family, did not seem quite appropriate to the needs of two people making their way together in the urban setting.

Young men and women's hopes for new kinds of relationships are mirrored in statistics cited above showing the strong desire of a high proportion of young people to choose their own mates. But in a society struggling to regain its position in the world, these hopes, in a great many cases, were not realizable. Many young men left the university for a job and were soon caught up in a system that brought their era of personal exploration to a close. Many who at one point had wanted to find their own marriage partner turned to parents or others to find a mate for them. They had not had enough time or opportunity, either at school or while working in a country where easy friendship relations between the sexes are still difficult to achieve, to meet someone on their own. Nor was there much time for communication after marriage. Work demands left a man with little time to spend with his wife or to build a family life. Many young Japanese, in anticipation of entering a world of nonstop work, described feeling a certain emptiness in the 1950s and 1960s, and they dreaded leaving the university world.[26]

For growing numbers of young Japanese fast becoming adults, some of these problems will gradually ease, and there will be subtle, gradual changes in the nature of relationships between men and women. The five-day week and increased prosperity will have major impact in support of a change. Men will have more time to spend at home. There will be more money in the family for taking family trips and for an occasional night out together. Vogel, in a report a few years back, noted signs of all these trends in urban middle class life.[27]

As a response to these developments, young Japanese women will be strongly attracted to the Neotraditionalists' view for at least the next several years. They will set about creating a pleasant home environment with family funds that are now available for that purpose, and they will look forward to spending time with their husbands. For both the married and the unmarried, getting to know the opposite sex in a country where long-established traditions have kept men and women in separate spheres of activity will itself be a great adventure. In Tokyo offices younger men who are eager to get back home after work to be with their young wives face much joking and teasing from

26. Many writers dealing with the causes of student activism in Japan in the 1960s describe this feeling among Japanese youths. See Robert Jay Lifton, "Youth and History: Individual Change in Postwar Japan," in *The Challenge of Youth*, ed. Erik H. Erikson (New York, 1963).

27. Ezra Vogel, "Beyond Salary: Mamachi Revisited," *Japan Interpreter* 6 (Summer 1970): 105–13.

their coworkers. Many young workers in my English classes in Tokyo sheepishly admitted their pleasure in occasionally preparing breakfast for their wives on a leisurely Sunday morning, or enthusiastically described a Saturday afternoon they had spent in some activity with their son or daughter. This does not mean, of course, that there will be major changes in the basic sex-role divisions in marriage. Most Japanese men and women, for a very long time to come, will continue to feel that homemaking and child care responsibilities are primarily a woman's responsibility. For men, the segregated leisure pattern itself will continue to exist for some time to come. It is deeply a part of business and social life. Newer patterns of leisure activities in which couples can take part will grow up alongside the traditional pattern but will not replace it. What will change is the emotional content of married life— the growth of mutuality and common understanding between people who are building their lives together in modern urban society.

Why, then, will the Neotraditionalist ideology gradually lose ground to the New Woman's view? My own feeling is that a major impetus for change will come from factors beyond the immediate control of today's Neotraditionalists. As I have noted, a great many young women, eager to devote themselves to their husbands and children, even today are finding it difficult to occupy their full energies in this way. The average Japanese couple, according to a study issued in 1972, now wants two children.[28] The average wife has the first child when she is 25.3 years old, and the second at 27.9.[29] By the time a woman reaches age 40, both children will be in high school and long past need of her full-time care. Because average life expectancy for women even now is over 75, this means that at age 40 she is likely to face at least 35 years in which the wife-mother role cannot conceivably take up all her time. For a Japanese woman, long brought up to believe that serving and caring for husband and children was her exclusive and all-consuming life purpose, the increasing obsolescence of her role as it has been conceived traditionally is going to require major adjustments. In recent years there has been much discussion in Japan of *ikigai* ("the purpose of life"). Japanese women who have been involved in this discussion in growing numbers see the problem very much as I have described it: what is a mother to do with herself after her children are grown in a world where parents can no longer expect to live with their grown children? Where is she to find meaning in what will soon be the entire second half of her life?

28.   Results of a 1972 study conducted by the Ministry of Health and Welfare. Cited in *Japan Labor Bulletin* (1 July 1973), p. 2.
29.   Ibid.

A great many young Neotraditionalists face a major struggle in coming to terms with cold facts that will force them to begin developing new interests outside the home. Some will be helped through their difficulties by the changing nature of the labor market. If current trends continue there will be an increasing bid on the part of business and industry for the services of women workers over 40. Gradually the Neotraditionalist's work pattern is likely to change from what Ginzberg has called the "terminated" pattern, now the ideal, whereby young women quit the labor market to marry after a few years of work never to return again, to "periodic" or "intermittent" patterns whereby growing numbers of Neotraditionalists will move out of the labor market when they marry and back into it again after their children are well along in school.[30]

The spread of the New Women's ideology as it gains acceptance in Japan will cause many women to give thought to their work prospects after their children are grown, and it will lead others to consider the possibility of taking part in civic and political activities. Kiefer, elsewhere in their volume, notes the rising interest in civic participation among wives dwelling in Tokyo danchi today. It seems likely that as husbands are freed somewhat from work responsibilities over the next decade, there will be a tendency for young married people to join in civic affairs as couples, though this development will be fairly slow in coming, particularly outside urban areas. For the years immediately ahead, the most common pattern will be one in which women develop civic and other outside interests on their own while their husbands continue to invest much of their energy in their work. Recently, in Tokyo, Osaka, and other large cities, growing numbers of housewives are participating in some of the newer civic movements in Japan, such as the citizens' and the consumer protection movements.

Of the great dynamos operating behind the many changes that will occur in the lives of Neotraditionalists over the coming decade, one must be singled out for special note. This is the impact of higher education in changing women's notions of their role. Within the decade of the 1960s, the number of women enrolled in junior colleges increased 400 percent and the enrollment of women in universities increased 300 percent.[31] Barring the unforeseen, it is very likely that these trends will continue in a prosperous society in which parents can educate daughters as well as sons. For a great many women now preparing to go on to higher education, their initial motivations will be traditional ones—to find a suitable mate or, at any rate, to collect important cre-

30. For a discussion of women's work patterns see Eli Ginzberg, *Lifestyles of Educated Women* (New York, 1966), p. 78.

31. Ministry of Education, *Educational Standards in Japan 1970* (Tokyo, 1971), p. 30.

dentials for a good match. It is, however, important to point out the unintended consequences of higher education, which is now sought ostensibly as marriage preparation. Here is a remarkable case where a highly traditional attitude—a cultural stress on developing "credentials" for marriage, which grew out of a long tradition of arranged marriage in Japan—now is highly supportive of role change for women. Whatever the initial and conscious motivations for seeking higher education, there is little doubt that its long-range effects on the lives of growing numbers of Japanese women will be those already noted by many writers: to lead them toward new expectations as they become increasingly involved in the subjects they study, and to make them less able to accept traditional marriage arrangements that restrict the outside interests of a wife.[32]

By the mid-1980s, if present trends continue and if all these predictions are borne out, Japan will be well on its way to becoming a nation of New Women. Those women will still manage the house and assume responsibility for their children, but they will gradually take on a wide variety of other life activities including part-time or full-time work at various stages of their lives before and after marriage, civic and political work, and a great number of personal pursuits unrelated to homemaking.

If this is to be the future for the Neotraditionalists of today, what does the future hold for women who, in the mid-1970s, already hold the New Woman's view? Many will experience considerable frustration trying to find life satisfaction over the coming decade. Some will look for fulfillment in hobbies and other activities. But many will be searching for part-time or full-time employment. It is here, as indicated earlier, that they will encounter major barriers. The present generation of business and political leadership has very little sympathy for the work goals of many New Women today. The labor market is almost exclusively geared to the needs of Neotraditionalist single women wanting to work for a few years as marriage preparation, or Neotraditionalist wives forced to work for family economic reasons. Today in Japan there are extraordinarily few job opportunities for young educated women. Unless the system changes radically over the coming decade, the New Women of today and the years immediately ahead are going to feel increasing disappointment with their life prospects as their employment needs are not met. The kind of clerical and factory work that industry will hold out to eager takers among Neotraditionalists will not be relevant to the needs, interests, and, in many cases, educational attainment of many of today's New Women.

---

32. See Blood, *Love Match and Arranged Marriage*, p. 149, and Herbert Passin, *Society and Education in Japan* (New York, 1965), p. 111.

Will the New Women of tomorrow turn in great numbers to the Radical Egalitarian view by the mid-1980s? No, a role change of such magnitude for large numbers of women seems highly unlikely in such a short span of time in a society with such long traditions of male dominance in social and family life. By the 1980s, however, the Radical Egalitarian view will no longer seem quite so avant-garde, partly because it is already on its way to gaining currency in the United States and other Western societies that, through the media, have major impact on Japanese life and thought. Today many Radical Egalitarians combine their desire for equality as women with political aims and specific policy objectives that the majority of women in Japan cannot begin to accept. Many, it is true, have found their own answers. Many of today's Radical Egalitarians find satisfaction in living for and, in some cases, fighting for ideals they share with those around them. But their personal answers, developed in subcultures far from the mainstream of life, have very little relevance to the needs of most young Japanese women who must struggle for their own answers in Japanese society as it is and will become.

About the Contributors

The chapters in this volume evolved from papers delivered at the Seminar on the Future of Japan, which met at Yale University in 1973 under the chairmanship of Lewis Austin and Hugh Patrick.

LEWIS AUSTIN studied history, international relations, and political science at Harvard, Columbia, and M.I.T., receiving his Ph.D. from the last. He spent six years in Japan, three of them with a multinational firm and two doing research under the auspices respectively of the Foreign Area Fellowship Program and the Social Science Research Council. He is assistant professor in the Department of Political Science at Yale University and is currently engaged in a cross-cultural study of psychopolitical symbolism. He is the author of *Saints and Samurai: The Political Culture of the Japanese and American Elites* (1975).

KOYA AZUMI is associate professor of sociology at Rutgers University. A graduate of Haverford College, he received his Ph.D. in sociology from Columbia University and has taught at N.Y.U., Wisconsin, and Columbia. His publications include *Higher Education and Business Recruitment in Japan* (1969), *Organizational Systems: A Text-Reader in the Sociology of Organizations* (with Jerald Hage, 1972), and a number of papers. He is currently engaged in a cross-national comparative study of organizations.

ROBERT E. COLE received a Ph.D. in sociology at the University of Illinois, as well as a master's degree in industrial and labor relations. He is currently associate professor in the Department of Sociology at the University of Michigan, where he has taught since 1967. He is also director of the Center for Japanese Studies. Professor Cole's research is in the area of the sociology of the labor market and the work behavior of employees. He has published *Japanese Blue Collar*, a study of Japanese blue-collar employees in two firms, and is now writing a book based on a comparative study of work history patterns in Detroit and Yokohama, a case study of job systems and motivation in an auto factory, and an analysis of the meaning of the Japanese work ethic.

WILLIAM K. CUMMINGS (Ph.D., Harvard University, 1972) has lectured at Wesleyan and Tsuda Colleges and the University of Maryland Far East Division. He is now assistant professor of sociology at the University of Chicago. He has been a Fulbright Fellow in Japan studying social mobility and educational egalitarianism. He is the author of

Nihon no Daigaku Kyoju [*The Japanese University Professor*], as well as several articles on Japanese education.

ROBERT FRAGER (Ph.D., Harvard University) spent three years in Japan as a student and research scholar and has published numerous articles on conformity, Japanese psychology, and aikido. He is co-author of *Personality and Personal Growth* (1976). He has taught psychology and religious studies at the University of California, Santa Cruz, and has led workshops and seminars in aikido, body awareness, and body therapy. He holds a fourth degree black belt in aikido. He recently founded the California Institute of Transpersonal Psychology to provide graduate training in transpersonal psychology; he is currently director of the institute.

CHRISTIE W. KIEFER is assistant professor of anthropology in the Department of Psychiatry, University of California, San Francisco. He spent 1965–66 in Japan writing his thesis on apartment living and personality change and received his Ph.D. from the University of California, Berkeley, in 1968. Since 1967 he has served as specialist on adult personality at the Langley Porter Neuropsychiatric Institute and Department of Psychiatry. He is past editor of the *Medical Anthropology Newsletter* and author of *Changing Cultures, Changing Lives*, a study of Japanese-American personality and aging. Since 1975 he has been associate director of the Human Development Program at the University of California, San Francisco.

T. DIXON LONG is associate professor of political science at Case Western Reserve University in Cleveland. He has been a staff member of the Directorate for Scientific Affairs of the OECD in Paris, and in 1973–74 he was a resident fellow in the Office of the Foreign Secretary of the National Academy of Sciences. He was the rapporteur for the OECD's *Review of National Science Policy—Japan* and is the editor, with Christopher Wright, of *Science Policies of Industrial Nations*, to which he also contributed a chapter on Japan. He is the author as well of a number of papers. Dr. Long holds a B.A. from Amherst, an M.A. from the Fletcher School of Law and Diplomacy, a certificate from the East Asian Institute, and a Ph.D. from Columbia.

TERRY EDWARD MACDOUGALL, assistant professor of government at the University of Virginia, received his Ph.D. from Yale University. He has taught at Doshisha High School in Kyoto, Japan. He is the author of *Political Opposition and Local Government in Japan* and is presently working on a biography of Asukata Ichio, the Japanese socialist leader.

CHARLES MCMILLAN teaches in the Faculty of Administrative Studies,

York University, Toronto. A Canadian, he was educated at St. Dun-
stain's University, the University of Alberta, and the University of
Bradford in England, where he has held teaching and research posts.
His current research interests are organization theory, cross-cultural
management, and multinational enterprise. He has contributed several
papers to anthologies and journals, including *Sociology*, the *Academy
of Management Journal*, and the *McGill Law Review*.

HUGH PATRICK is professor of Far Eastern economics at Yale University. He has held ACLS, Guggenheim, Fulbright, and Fulbright-Hayes
fellowships, mainly for research in and on Japan, where he has been
affiliated with Hitotsubashi and Tokyo Universities. His publications
include *Monetary Policy and Central Banking in Contemporary Japan,
Japanese Industrialization and its Social Consequences* (editor), *Asia's New
Giant—How the Japanese Economy Works* (editor, with Henry Rosovsky),
and numerous articles.

SUSAN J. PHARR is a political scientist at the Social Science Research
Council in New York. A recent Columbia Ph.D., she is currently
revising her dissertation, "Sex and Politics: Women in Social and
Political Movements in Japan," for publication. While doing research
for her dissertation, she was a Visiting Foreign Research Scholar at
Sophia University in Tokyo. She has served as a consultant for the
Ford Foundation Task Force on Women and has published a number
of articles dealing with the status of women in Japan.

THOMAS P. ROHLEN is associate professor of anthropology at the
University of California, Santa Cruz. Before taking a Ph.D. at the
University of Pennsylvania in 1971, he spent two years as a foreign
service officer in Japan. He has done field work in villages, a large
bank, a factory, and most recently on urban high schools. He is the
author of *Harmony and Strength: Japanese White-Collar Organization in
Anthropological Perspective*.

NATHANIEL B. THAYER, currently a visiting professor at Harvard
University, is the director of Asian studies at the School of Advanced
International Studies in Washington, D.C. He is the author of *How
the Conservatives Rule Japan*. His latest study is *Do We Need a New Security
Treaty with Japan?*

The following persons also participated in the Seminar on the Future
of Japan. The ideas and suggestions that they generated in discussion proved especially valuable in the formulation of the chapters in
this volume.

Rodney Armstrong, The Japan Society; Burton Clark, Department

ABOUT THE CONTRIBUTORS

of Sociology, Yale University; James Crowley, Department of History, Yale University; Shigeko Fukai, University of Tennessee; Harry Gelber, Department of Political Science, Monash University; Takehiko Kamo, Department of Political Science, Waseda University; Kenneth Kodama, Department of Political Science, Colby College; Edward Lincoln, Department of Economics, Yale University; Roy Lockheimer, The Japan Society; Robert Marsh, Department of Sociology, Brown University; Joseph Massey, Department of Government, Dartmouth College; Larry Meissner, Department of Economics, Yale University; Ryoichi Mikitani, Department of Economics, Kobe University; James Morley, Department of Government, Columbia University; Sharon Nolte, Department of History, Yale University; Konosuke Odaka, Department of Economics, Hitotsubashi University; Merton J. Peck, Department of Economics, Yale University; Mary Mikami Rouse, Department of Anthropology, Yale University; Robert Runitz, The Japan Society; Yukio Sato, the Embassy of Japan; Gary Saxonhouse, Department of Economics, University of Michigan; George Silver, Department of History, Yale University; Richard Staubitz, Department of History, Yale University; Martin Weinstein, Department of Political Science, University of Illinois; Michael Yoshino, School of Business Administration, University of California at Los Angeles.

Index